Macmillan Law Masters

Land Law

Company Law   Janet Dine and Marios Koutsias
Constitutional and Administrative Law   John Alder and Keith Syrett
Contract Law   Ewan McKendrick
Criminal Law   Jonathan Herring
Employment Law   Deborah J. Lockton
Evidence   Raymond Emson
Family Law   Paula Davies and Paven Basuita
Intellectual Property Law   Tina Hart, Linda Fazzani and Simon Clark
Land Law   Mark Davys
Landlord and Tenant Law   Margaret Wilkie, Peter Luxton, Jill Morgan and Godfrey Cole
Legal Method   Ian McLeod
Legal Theory   Ian McLeod
Medical Law   Jo Samanta and Ash Samanta
Sports Law   Mark James
Torts   Alastair Mullis and Ken Oliphant
Trusts Law   Charlie Webb and Tim Akkouh

Macmillan Law Masters

Land Law

Mark Davys

Senior Teaching Fellow, Keele University

Eleventh edition

Eleventh edition published 2019 by
RED GLOBE PRESS

Previous editions published by
PALGRAVE

Red Globe Press in the UK is an imprint of Springer Nature Limited,
registered in England, company number 785998, of 4 Crinan Street,
London N1 9XW.

Red Globe Press® is a registered trademark in the United States,
the United Kingdom, Europe and other countries.

ISBN 978–1–352–00519–6 paperback

This book is printed on paper suitable for recycling and made from fully
managed and sustained forest sources. Logging, pulping and manufacturing
processes are expected to conform to the environmental regulations of the
country of origin.

A catalogue record for this book is available from the British Library.

A catalog record for this book is available from the Library of Congress.

For Annabelle

Contents

Part II   Title

Part III   The estates and interests

Preface

> This book is intended to be a clear and straightforward explanation of basic land law rules, a text which both introduces the subject and will be referred to during a land law course. A further aim is that the book should remove the unwarranted reputation of land law as a difficult and abstract subject. I hope to encourage students to consider the role of land law in their own world; I wish all who read it a lasting interest in land law and its concerns.

The world has moved on since Kate Green wrote these words in the preface to the first edition of this book, published in 1989. However, although the law and the teaching of law have changed, land law's reputation as a challenging subject seems to remain undented. The aim of this edition, like that of its predecessors, is to introduce its readers to the sometimes 'long and winding roads' that comprise land law; to help them grow in confidence in their own ability to navigate them; and to recognise the relevance of what they encounter to themselves and to the society of which they are part. Sometimes this book gives directions. Sometimes it invites the reader to stop, stare and (hopefully) consider. Sometimes it identifies paths by which the journey may be extended. Sometimes, as with the maps of old, the territory will be marked, figuratively at least, '*Hic sunt dracones*' ('Here be dragons').

I wish to express my gratitude to Kate Green and Joe Cursley for entrusting me with the ongoing realisation of their vision for this text. This 11th (and, incidentally, 30th anniversary) edition takes account of recent developments, including the Law Commission's recommendations in *Updating the Land Registration Act 2002* (Law Com No 380, 2018) and the Supreme Court judgment in *Regency Villas Title Ltd* v *Diamond Resorts (Europe) Ltd*. I have also sought to improve the text in response to the helpful suggestions from students and the anonymous reviewers, to whom I offer my thanks. The most obvious, but not the only, result is that proprietary estoppel now has its own chapter, with Chapter 17 being renamed to better reflect its main focus.

I am also grateful to those who have shared with me their enthusiasm for the study and practice of land law, and most of all to Ian Lennox, alongside whom, in the closing years of the twentieth century, at least one articled clerk (what is now called a trainee solicitor) discovered a love of land law and its practice. So far as this edition is concerned, I particularly wish to thank my colleagues Michael Haley, Lara McMurtry, Ray Cocks and Sally Whelan, who have each contributed to it in their own way. I am indebted to Mark Shelton for passing on the now somewhat old joke included in Chapter 4.

My final thanks are reserved for Helen Bugler and Aléta Bezuidenhout of Red Globe Press for their encouragement, support and patience, and to the production team who generously allowed me to make significant changes to Chapter 10 at proof stage following the handing down of the Supreme Court's judgment in *Regency Villas* on 14th November 2018. I was also able to add a brief account of the Court of Appeal's decision in *Rashid* v *Nasrullah* to Section 16.3.3. Otherwise, the law is stated as at 31st August 2018.

Mark Davys
The Feast of St Andrew the Apostle, 2018

Table of cases

Table of legislation

UK secondary legislation

European documents

The companion website to accompany this book can be found at:
www.macmillanihe.com/davys-land-law-11e

Resources posted on this site include:

- updates on the law and comments on recent cases;
- advice on how to approach law essay and problem questions;
- suggested answers/approaches to the problem and essay questions included in the end of chapter exercises;
- quizzes for each chapter;
- annotated bibliography; and
- additional diagrams and 'mind maps'.

The following symbol occurring in the text indicates where particularly relevant material can be found on the companion website: .

References

A complete citation for a case comprises:

1. the name of the case;
2. the neutral citation (when available); and
3. the citation for the most authoritative of the law reports in which it appears.

In this book the complete citation is provided in the Table of Cases. However, for convenience the neutral citation is not repeated in the text where an authoritative law report was available by the end of November 2018.

For an accessible introduction to the 'story' of land law, see Gardner and MacKenzie, *An Introduction to Land Law* (4th edn, Hart Publishing 2015). To begin exploring land law in its wider, socio-economic context, see Cowan, Fox O'Mahony and Cobb, *Land Law* (Great Debates in Law, 2nd edn, Red Globe Press 2016).

Unless stated otherwise, all web pages cited were accessed on 19th October 2018.

Glossary

*Numbers in brackets, such as (8.6) refer to the section in this book where the term is introduced or explained. References to terms explained elsewhere in the Glossary appear in **bold**.*

A

abatement:
A self-help remedy allowing a **dominant tenement** owner to enforce an easement (10.8).

absolute, of a fee or estate:
An interest that is neither **conditional** nor **determinable** (6.2). Note that this is not the same as **absolute title**.

absolute title:
The best class of **title** available to a registered proprietor of an **estate** in land (4.4.1).

adverse possession:
The acquisition of title by dispossessing the original owner for the requisite period (see Chapter 16).

alienation:
The act of transferring property to another.

animus possidendi:
'Intention to possess'; a requirement for title to be acquired by **adverse possession** (16.3.2).

assignment:
The transfer of an interest in land, usually the interest of a **landlord** or **tenant** (7.3 and 8.3–8.5), but also of the benefit or burden of a covenant (12.4 and 12.5).

authorised guarantee agreement (AGA):
A form of guarantee falling within section 16 of the Landlord and Tenant (Covenants) Act 1995 (8.5.2).

B

beneficial interest:
The interest of a **beneficiary**; the **equitable** right to the benefits of the land (for example, occupation or **rent**) as distinct from the legal ownership vested in a **trustee** (2.2.3(a)).

beneficiary:
The person entitled in equity to land or other property held on **trust** (2.2.3(a)); also used to describe persons entitled to benefit under a will.

C

charge:
An interest securing the payment of money (Chapter 11). Although often used synonymously with **mortgage**, a charge does not automatically give the lender an estate in the land. Charges by way of legal mortgage do transfer an estate by virtue of section 87 of the LPA 1925. Alternatively, (i) an abbreviation for **land charge** (see the LCA 1972), or (ii) any burden upon an **estate**, especially one that is registered.

chattel:
Physical property other than land (3.5). For historical reasons, leasehold estates are *chattels real*, not real property, but this is rarely significant today.

commonhold:	A form of registered **freehold** that can be used to divide the ownership of a building or **estate** with shared common parts (6.5).
common intention constructive trust:	A **trust** arising out of an express or implied agreement to share the ownership of property (17.3).
conditional, of a fee or estate:	An interest that gives the grantor the right to re-enter the property (and terminate the interest) if a specified event occurs or fails to occur; compare **absolute interest**, and **determinable interest** (6.2).
constructive trust:	One of a number of types of **trust** that arise by operation of law rather than express words (17.3; see also **resulting trust**).
conveyance:	(i) the transfer of **title**; (ii) a **deed** of grant which brings the transfer of **title** about. Note that the term is not limited to dealings with freehold land, but includes the granting of mortgages and leases: LPA 1925, s 205(1)(ii).
co-ownership:	A form of ownership where **title** is shared between two or more people (concurrent co-ownership is considered in Chapter 13).
covenant:	A promise made in a **deed**.
covenantee:	The person to whom the promise in a **covenant** is made.
covenantor:	The person making the promise in a **covenant**.

D

deed:	A formal legal document satisfying the requirements of section 1 of the Law of Property (Miscellaneous Provisions) Act 1989 (15.5.1).
demesne **land:**	Land which the Crown owns for itself as feudal overlord (4.11).
demise:	A **lease**; the land is 'demised' to the **tenant** (7.3).
determinable, of a fee or estate:	An interest that lasts only until a specified event occurs or does not occur; compare **absolute interest** and **conditional interest** (6.2).
disposition:	The creation or transfer of an interest (15.4.2(b)).
distraint:	See **distress**.
distress:	An ancient remedy for the non-payment of **rent**, entitling the landlord to seize goods belonging to the **tenant**, replaced by the provisions of Part 3 of the Tribunals, Courts and Enforcement Act 2007 from 6th April 2014 (8.6.1(b)).
dominant tenement:	The land to which the benefit of a right, such as an **easement**, is attached (10.3).

E

easement: A right enjoyed over a **servient tenement** for the benefit of a **dominant tenement** (Chapter 10).

entail, also **fee tail:** An interest in land that can only be inherited by the issue of the original grantor (6.2).

equitable: A right or remedy operating only in equity; that is, originally derived from the jurisdiction of the Court of Chancery (1.3.2 and 2.2.3).

equity of redemption: The rights of the **mortgagor** in the land subject to the **mortgage**; in particular, the right to recover the mortgaged land upon payment of the moneys due (11.2.2 and 11.4.1).

Equity's Darling: A *bona fide* purchaser of a legal **estate** for value without notice (5.2.2).

estate: An interest in land that allows its owner **exclusive possession** of the land for a prescribed period (2.2.1). Alternatively, (i) the property of a deceased person, or (ii) an area of land.

estate contract: A contract for the creation or sale of an interest in land (15.3; see also 5.4.2(c)).

estoppel: An equitable doctrine preventing a person from denying facts stated by them or which they have led or allowed another to believe are true. There are various forms of estoppel, each with its own rules. **Proprietary estoppel** is the most common type of estoppel encountered when studying land law (Chapter 18).

exclusive possession: The rights of an owner of land, in particular the right to exclude other people, including a landlord, from the land (7.5.1).

F

fee simple: The short form of fee simple absolute in possession, the larger of the two legal **estates** and the basic unit of ownership in English land law (Chapter 6). Usually synonymous with **freehold** in modern usage.

fee tail: An interest in land that can only be inherited by the issue of the original grantor (6.2).

fixture: An object that is part of the land (that is, not a **chattel**). There are rules as to who may remove fixtures, depending on who brought them on to the land (3.5).

foreclosure: The transfer of legal and equitable title in mortgaged land to the **mortgagee** (lender), free from all the rights of the **mortgagor** (11.5.4).

forfeiture, also **right of entry:** The right of a **landlord** to re-enter the land subject to a **lease** following a breach of **covenant** by the **tenant** (8.6.1(c) and 8.6.2(a)).

freehold:	An **estate** of uncertain duration; now usually used to refer to the only such estate capable of existing at law, the **fee simple** (Chapter 6).
Freehold reversion:	A freeholder's right to repossess the land at the end of a tenancy.

H

headlease:	The **lease** out of which a lesser leasehold **estate** has been granted (7.3).
hereditaments:	Rights in property that survive the death of the owner; they can be inherited.
human rights:	Rights that protect an individual from unfair treatment or discrimination by the State and public bodies (1.5).

I

implied trust:	A **trust** that is created by operation of law rather than by express words or statutory provision (14.2).
in gross:	A right that exists without benefiting a **dominant tenement**.
indefeasible, indefeasibility	Immune from all claims (usually in the context of **registered title**, see 4.2.2).
injunction:	A court order requiring a person to do or refrain from doing a specified act.
interests capable of overriding, also overriding interests:	Interests in a **registered title** capable of binding third parties even though they do not appear in the **Register of Title** (4.6).
inter vivos:	'Among the living'; taking effect during the lifetime of the transferor (compare a gift in a will, which will only take effect upon the death of the person making the gift).
ius accrescendi:	The right of survivorship (13.3.1).

J

joint tenancy:	A form of concurrent **co-ownership** in which all the co-owners own the whole legal or beneficial **title** to the land (13.3.1); compare **tenancy in common**.

L

land charge:	An interest in **unregistered land** capable of protection through registration in the Land Charges Register under the Land Charges Act 1972 (5.4).
landlord:	The grantor of a **lease**; the lessor.
lease:	A **term of years absolute** in possession, the lesser of the two legal **estates** in land (Chapter 7).
leasehold:	See **lease**.
legal charge:	A **mortgage** created pursuant to section 87 of the LPA 1925 (11.3.1).
lessee:	The **tenant** of a **lease**.

lessor:	The immediate **landlord**.
licence:	Permission to enter on land (Chapter 9).
M	
mesne:	'Middle' (as in '*mesne* landlord' at 7.3). Pronounced 'mean'.
minor:	A person under 18 years of age.
minor interest:	An interest in **registered land** requiring protection by registration. The term is found in the LRA 1925, but is not used in the LRA 2002.
mortgage:	The transfer of property as security for a loan or other obligation; see also **charge** (Chapter 11).
mortgagee:	The person to whom the interest in mortgaged land is granted, the lender (11.2.1).
mortgagor:	The person creating a **mortgage**, the borrower (11.2.1).
N	
new tenancy:	A **lease** granted on or after 1st January 1996: section 1(3) of the Landlord and Tenant (Covenants) Act 1995 (8.3.1).
notice, doctrine of:	The rule, now of limited application, which governed whether a purchaser of an unregistered legal **estate** for value took the **title** subject to any equitable interests in the land. There are three types of notice: actual, constructive and imputed (see 5.2.2). Proper registration of a **land charge** in the Land Charges Register is deemed to be notice of the charge (5.4).
notice, registered title:	An entry in the **Register of Title** protecting the priority of the interest to which it refers (4.5.1).
notice to quit:	The method by which a landlord or a **tenant** terminates a **periodic tenancy**.
O	
overreaching:	A statutory procedure whereby a **beneficial interest** is detached from the land and transferred to the proceeds of sale (14.6.1).
overriding interests, also **interests capable of overriding:**	Interests in a **registered title** that are capable of binding third parties even though they do not appear in the **Register of Title** (4.6).
overriding lease:	A **lease** granted under section 19 of the Landlord and Tenant (Covenants) Act 1995 (8.4.3(c)).
P	
periodic tenancy:	A **tenancy** for a specific period (monthly, yearly, etc.), which continues to run until one of the parties serves **notice to quit** (7.4.2).
personal rights:	Rights that regulate a particular relationship and which are usually only binding upon the parties to that relationship (1.4). These rights are also referred to as 'obligations' and typically arise out of a contract and the commission of a tort.

premium:	An upfront capital sum paid by the **tenant** to the **lessor**.
prescription:	Acquisition of an **easement** by long user (10.7.6).
privity of contract:	The relationship between the original landlord and the original **tenant**; this contractual relationship continues even if one or both of them has assigned the **lease** (8.4).
privity of estate:	The relationship between the **landlord** for the time being and the **tenant** for the time being (8.4).
profit à prendre:	The right to take something from somebody else's land (10.10).
property rights:	Rights that are capable of binding third parties (1.4).
proprietary estoppel:	An **equitable** doctrine enabling a claimant to enforce an informal representation or assurance relating to land that the claimant has relied upon to their detriment because it would be unconscionable for the person who made the representation or assurance to be allowed to enforce their strict legal rights (Chapter 18).
puisne **mortgage:**	A legal **mortgage** of unregistered land not protected by the deposit of title deeds and which must be protected by registering a Class C(i) land charge under the Land Charges Act 1927 (5.4.2(a)).
Q	
quasi-easement:	An interest in land that would amount to an **easement**, but for the fact that the **dominant** and **servient tenements** are owned by the same person (10.5.3, 10.7.4 and 10.7.5).
R	
real property:	Usually used to refer to land, although **leases** are actually *chattels real*.
rectification:	(1) The correction of a mistake in the **Register of Title** that prejudicially affects the title of the registered proprietor (4.9.2). (2) An **equitable** remedy allowing the court to correct errors in a document such as a contract (15.4.3(d)).
Register of Title, also **Title Register:**	The record of the extent and ownership of an **estate** in land that has been registered at the Land Registry, together with the registered interests to which it is subject (Chapter 4).
registered title, or **registered land:**	A system in which **title** to land is based on or proved by entries in a State-controlled register of title; in England and Wales, a reference to land that falls within the scheme contained in the LRA 2002 (2.3.3, Chapter 4).
remainder:	An interest in land that will not take effect until a prior interest has expired (for example, to A for life, remainder to B in fee simple).
rent, also **rent service:**	Usually shorthand for 'rent service', the payments made to the landlord by the **tenant** under the terms of a **lease**.

rentcharge:	A periodic sum charged on **freehold** land (2.2.2). Not to be confused with **rent service**, payable under the terms of a **lease**.
restriction:	An entry in the **Register of Title** imposing conditions that must be met before any dealings with the title can be registered (4.4.2).
resulting trust:	A trust arising by operation of law in which the **beneficial interest** is vested in the person who financed the acquisition of that property or in the person who transferred the property to the legal owner without also transferring the entire beneficial interest (17.2).
reversion:	The right remaining to the grantor of an interest after that interest has been granted. For example, a landlord's right to repossess the land at the end of the lease is the 'landlord's reversion'.
reversionary leases:	A **lease** with a term that will begin at a date in the future (not the same as a 'lease of the reversion': see 7.4.7).
right of entry, also **forfeiture:**	(1) The right of a landlord to re-enter the land subject to a lease following a breach of **covenant** by the **tenant** (8.6.1(c) and 8.6.2(a)). (2) A right of re-entry arising on the breach of the conditions imposed by a **rentcharge**.

S

seisin:	Historically, the right to possess a particular piece of land. Unity of seisin of the **dominant tenement** and **servient tenement** extinguishes an **easement** (1.2 and 10.5.3).
servient tenement:	The land which is subject to a right, such as an **easement**.
settlement, also **settled land:**	A disposition of property granting a series of successive interests in land. Previously used to keep land 'in the family' and regulated under the Settled Land Act 1925, this method of land ownership is now almost obsolete.
severance:	The conversion of a **joint tenancy** into a **tenancy in common** (13.5).
subject to contract:	An express arrangement that the parties do not wish to have legally binding consequences until further steps, usually the completion of certain formalities, have been taken (15.1 and 15.4.2).
sublease, also **subtenancy:**	A **lease** granted out of a leasehold estate (the **headlease**). The sublease must be for a term that is shorter than that of the **headlease** (7.3).

T

tacking:	The use of an existing **mortgage** or **charge** to secure a further loan from the same lender (11.7.1).
tenancy:	Another word for **lease**. The two words can be used interchangeably, although tenancy tends to be used for

	shorter or informal leases. Not to be confused with **joint tenancy** or **tenancy in common**.
tenancy in common:	A form of concurrent **co-ownership** in which the beneficial title is divided between the co-owners in separate interests (13.3.2); compare **joint tenancy** (13.3.1).
tenant:	(1) A lessee, the person to whom a tenancy or lease is granted. (2) Historically, a person with an interest in land, preserved in the terms **joint tenancy** and **tenancy in common**.
tenure:	Almost all land in England is ultimately held from a lord, usually the Crown. Tenure describes the conditions upon which the land is held (2.2). The doctrine of tenure is almost obsolete, although its terminology is used to describe the relationship between **landlords** and **tenants** (historically not tenure at all) and co-owners.
term of years absolute:	A **lease** (2.2.1).
title:	The right to hold an **estate** in land; proof of such a right (2.3.1).
trust:	An equitable device allowing ownership to be divided between the legal owner (the **trustees**) and beneficiaries who have an **equitable** right to enjoy the land (2.2.3(a)).
trustee:	The owner of the legal **title** to land that is subject to a trust (2.2.3(a)).
trustee in bankruptcy:	The person appointed to manage the estate of a person who is bankrupt.
trust for sale:	A **trust** where the property is held subject to an immediate and binding duty to sell it (although the sale may be postponed). The LPA 1925 provided that almost all land held concurrently by co-owners was held on a statutory trust for sale, but this was repealed by the Trusts of Land and Appointment of Trustees Act 1996 with effect from 1st January 1997 (14.1).
trust of land:	See section 1(1)(a) of the Trusts of Land and Appointment of Trustees Act 1996 (14.1).
U	
unregistered, of title, or land:	In England and Wales, land that does not yet fall within the scheme of **registered title** contained in the LRA 2002 (2.3.2, and Chapter 5).
W	
words of severance:	The words in the grant or transfer of land indicating that it is to be held by the new owners as **tenants in common** (13.4.2).
waiver:	The abandonment of a legal right.

Part I

Introduction

Chapter 1

Introduction to land law

Key concepts

▶ **Human rights** – rights that protect an individual from unfair treatment or discrimination by the State and public bodies.
▶ **Personal rights** – rights that regulate a specific relationship and which are usually only binding upon the parties to that relationship.
▶ **Property rights** – rights that are capable of binding third parties.

1.1 Approaching the study of land law

Land law is an interesting and challenging subject, which engages with profound questions about the way we choose to live our lives and the values of the society in which we live them. For humans to function together as a society, even a technological, high-speed society where transactions are as likely to be virtual as material, they need to share the physical environment around them. The law of England and Wales calls this environment *land*. Frequently, and especially where the supply of land is limited, as in England and Wales, different people will want to put the same land to different purposes. Sometimes these purposes are reconcilable, sometimes they are not. Consequently, the task of the land lawyer is to discern what people want to do with the land available to them, before deploying the legal rules to enable those people to achieve their goals. It is important when studying land law, and especially at the beginning of those studies, not to allow its sometimes dry and legalistic façade, created by its artificial language and its technical concepts, to conceal this fundamental issue: the land law of England and Wales is ultimately about sharing out the enjoyment of part of a small island on the north-west edge of Europe.

Land law has been developing ever since people got ideas about having rights over certain places, probably beginning with the cultivation of crops. In England (and Wales), the long process of its development has included periods of gradual change, and more dramatic transitions such as those heralded by the Norman conquest of 1066, the property legislation of 1925 and, most recently, the Land Registration Act 2002. Even when the changes have been sudden, lawyers have continued to use and adapt the words and ideas of their predecessors. Consequently, while English land law is a thoroughly contemporary subject concerned with realities of daily life and existence, it retains much of its feudal roots and language. Perhaps this is why this branch of law can seem obscure. It does mean that the student of land law needs to be something of a historian. Sometimes, understanding the contexts within which a particular doctrine has developed can be a valuable step towards understanding how that doctrine works (often more effectively than one might think) to meet the needs of twenty-first century landowners and land users. It also means that it can be helpful, especially at the start, to treat the study of land law like learning a new language. With a good knowledge of the vocabulary and a growing grasp of the grammatical principles, land law need not be as daunting as it at first seems.

The more you read, especially cases, but also articles and textbooks, the more familiar the vocabulary becomes; and, contrary to how it might appear at the outset, a coherent structural framework to much of the subject will begin to emerge.

The vocabulary of land law

One of the factors that seems to deter many students approaching land law for the first time is its language: the sheer number of unfamiliar technical terms alone can seem overwhelming. They need not, however, be so great a problem if faced up to from the outset. When encountering a technical term, especially for the first time:

▶ pause; consider the word, in its context; decide if you are confident that you have at least a provisional understanding of what it means;
▶ if not, look the word up (in the Glossary at pages xxxiii to xi of this book, for example, or in a printed or online legal dictionary);
▶ record the word and your provisional understanding of its meaning in a notebook or an easily accessible electronic form;
▶ then continue to read, ready to let what you read modify, deepen or revise your understanding of the term.

It is important to realise from the beginning of one's studies that English land lawyers tend to be principally, but not exclusively, concerned with various rights to land, called 'interests in land', rather than with the physical land itself. They might talk about someone 'owning land' or 'owning property', but really they mean someone owning *an interest in* the land, or, more technically, *having property in* the land. These interests (the 'property') are not the land itself (the earth and the buildings), but abstract concepts, such as the **freehold** and the **lease**. So, as Stanley Burnton J explains (*R (on the application of the Lord Chancellor) v Chief Land Registrar* [2006] QB 795 (QB), [25], when ownership of a building is transferred from one person to another:

> The building has not moved. What is transferred by a transfer of property is the bundle of rights and obligations relating to that building.

The different types of abstract interest in land recognised by English law are introduced in Chapter 2 and the most important are considered in more detail in Part III of this book.

The first thing to do when studying a particular interest in land (or any aspect of land law) is to grasp the definition thoroughly. That means asking:

▶ what does it mean; and
▶ how do I recognise it?

This helps to avoid two of the most depressing things that can happen to land law students. The first is staring at a tutorial or assessment question without having any idea of what it is about. The second (possibly worse) is recognising what the question is about, but feeling incapable of writing anything down. If in doubt, start by identifying the interests in the land.

Handling the interests in land can be compared to playing a game like chess: there are various 'pieces' (corresponding to the various interests in land) which can be moved about according to strict rules. Unfortunately for the new student, English land law is often played to not one but two sets of rules simultaneously. The relationship between the two sets of rules, those of law and those of equity, is introduced in Section 1.3.2. Alternatively, the rules which govern the various interests in land can be compared to a complicated machine: moving one lever, or adjusting one valve, will have a significant effect on what is produced. The owner of an interest in land has limited freedom of action, but one small change in their position can affect the relative value of other interests in the same land. In practical terms, the complicated connections within the machine mean that one part of the subject cannot be fully grasped until all the others have been understood. In other words, there is no single starting place when it comes to beginning the study of land law. Instead, it is necessary to watch the machine, trying to discern how it works, how one piece relates to the other pieces, until the connections become clear. It is useful, from the beginning, to ask, 'What do I think would happen if … ?'; 'If one lever is moved, what interests do I think will be affected, and why?' Do not expect there to be a single right answer, and do not expect to get it right every time. Indeed, being prepared to make mistakes is an essential step towards being able to grasp the way the rules relate to one another. It *will* eventually come together, with hard work and faith and hope; the charity, with any luck, will be provided by the teacher.

It is important to realise, however, that interests in land, and the relationship between them, are the means, not the end, of land law. The language used by land lawyers expresses the way in which they think they see the world. This is a world in which people's relationships to land can only occur within the legal structure of interests in land, so lawyers squeeze the facts of ordinary life into the pre-existing moulds of 'the interests'. A land law student's job is to learn the shapes of the moulds and how to imitate this squeeze so that they can:

▶ use the law to analyse and solve problems concerning land; and
▶ analyse and evaluate the law itself in the light of the various objectives (personal, social, political or economic) that society wishes land law to achieve.

1.2　Land and society

Different societies tend to treat land in different ways. These attitudes are coloured by the wider values of the particular society, although these might, in themselves, be influenced by the location in which that society finds itself. The type of land available (for example, good farmland, desert or jungle) tends to determine the uses to which it can be put. The relative scarcity or availability of land may also influence how land is regarded. In places where land was plentiful, it was not normally 'owned'. For example, when European colonists arrived in America, the indigenous people believed that (according to McLuhan, *Touch the Earth* (Abacus 1972), 54):

> the earth was created by the assistance of the sun, and it should be left as it was … The one who has the right to dispose of it is the one who created it.

Similarly, native Australians regarded the land with special awe. As concluded in one of the cases about Aboriginal land claims, it was not so much that they owned the land, but that the land owned them (*Milirrpum v Nabalco Pty Ltd* (1971) 17 FLR 141). Native **title** was subsequently recognised as part of Australian land law in the landmark case of *Mabo v Queensland (No 2)* [1992] HCA 23. A traditional African view was that the land was not capable of being owned by one person but belonged to the whole tribe. In the words of a tribal chief to the West African Lands Committee in 1912 (TNA CO 879/118/1, 183):

> land belongs to a vast family of which many are dead, few are living and countless numbers still unborn.

In England, however, as in much of Western Europe, land has long been treated as a type of wealth, something that can be 'owned' and controlled by an individual. In early English land law, the fundamental concept was **seisin**. The person who was seised of land was entitled to recover it in the courts if they were disseised. Originally, 'the person seised of land was simply the person in obvious occupation, the person "sitting" on the land' (Simpson, 1986, 40). Seisin thus described the close relationship between a person and the land they worked and lived on. This simplicity was refined and developed over centuries, and the concepts of ownership and possession took over. Nevertheless, actual possession can still be of great importance in land law, for example in claims of adverse possession (see Chapter 16).

Over the past three or four hundred years, the land law of England and Wales has been developing alongside the growth of capitalism and city living, and a huge increase in the population. People's attitudes to, and expectations of, land have also changed. For example, during the second part of the twentieth century, there was an enormous increase in the number of ordinary people who owned land, reaching a peak of nearly 70 per cent of households by the time of the Census in 2001. Since then, rising house prices and other economic circumstances have made it more difficult for people (especially young people) to buy their own home. For most owner-occupiers, the land they own is subject to a huge debt in the form of a **mortgage**. Despite this, they will probably regard the land as their retreat from the world, a status symbol and, they hope, an inflation-proofed savings bank that they can leave to their children (or use to finance health care at the end of their lives). For other people (for example, those who **rent** their home on a weekly or monthly **tenancy**), home ownership, with its apparent psychological and financial advantages, may be only a hope for the future. In the meantime, their relationship with their land is less secure, subject to the authority of a landlord, and, in the case of most residential tenancies, capable of being terminated whenever the landlord decides. However, in a lawyer's view, **tenants** are also 'landowners', albeit for a limited period of time and subject to certain restrictions (see Chapters 7 and 8).

It can be seen from this brief survey of land use in England and Wales that the same piece of land may be subject to a number of levels of ownership. For example, a flat may be 'owned' by a landlord and by their tenant, both of whom may be subject to the rights of the financial institution which provided money (secured by a mortgage) to help the landlord finance their acquisition of the land. What is more, different people will have different expectations of the property they 'own': the main three motives for owning land are set out in Table 1.1, with examples of how they have influenced English land law. One of the tasks of the land lawyer is to try to reconcile these various expectations when they come into conflict.

In order to maximise the value of land, ownership must be capable of being freely and safely traded, while people who have lesser interests in the land must also feel secure. The market certainly seems to have influenced the development of the law.

Table 1.1   Three underlying motives for land ownership

Motive	Consequence	Examples
Land as the location of human existence (for example, shelter and work)	The law must reflect the reality of land use and give value to the interests of those in actual occupation. Parliament may need to intervene to protect the vulnerable from the unscrupulous.	Seisin (see Section 1.2). Protecting the interest of people in occupation: paragraph 2 of Schedule 3 to the LRA 2002 (see Section 4.6.2). Parliamentary protection for residential tenants and residential mortgagors. (see Chapters 7, 8 and 11).
Land as an investment	Interests in land are treated as investment assets: they need to be freely marketable and realisable, free from the risk of undisclosed interests. It is more convenient to think of interests in land as abstract concepts than as physical land.	*National Provincial Bank Ltd v Ainsworth* [1965] AC 1175 (HL) (see Section 1.4.2). The doctrine of overreaching (which transfers beneficial interests from the land to the proceeds of sale of the land; see Section 14.6.1).
Land as a community resource	Land needs to be managed and protected for the wider good of society rather than the profit of the individual owner.	State intervention, such as planning regulations (planning law lies beyond the scope of this book). Private rights, such as covenants (see Chapter 12) may also be used to try to maintain the character of an area. The conservation of nature and natural resources (see Rodgers, 2009).

When there was a slump at the end of the nineteenth century, judges tried to ensure that liabilities attached to land (that is, the lesser, third-party interests) were minimised so that the land would be attractive to buyers. Conversely, periods of booming prices, such as the 1970s, 1980s and the early 2000s, tended to stimulate a greater interest in the security of such lesser, third-party interests. Falling markets, such as during the early 1990s and that of the end of the first decade of the twenty-first century, produce their own response, significantly influenced by the interests of lenders such as building societies and banks (see Chapter 11).

1.3   The sources of land law

Land law is made up of rules in statutes and cases; case law rules are further divided into legal and **equitable** rules. That is, the rules are created:

- by an Act of Parliament; or
- by either
  - a court of 'common law'; or
  - a court of 'equity'.

1.3.1   Statutes

A significant proportion of the rules that make up modern land law is found in statutes, and in the cases interpreting them. For many students, land law will be the first subject that they have studied that is so statute-dependent and it is worth taking the time to ensure that you are familiar with the structure of statutes and the basic rules of statutory interpretation before proceeding further.

Most of the statutory rules used by today's land lawyers are found in the following statutes:

- the **Law of Property Act 1925** (usually abbreviated to 'LPA 1925');
- the **Land Registration Act 2002** (usually 'LRA 2002') which replaced the LRA 1925: see, especially, Chapter 4; and
- the **Trusts of Land and Appointment of Trustees Act 1996** ('TOLATA' in this book) which replaced the Settled Land Act 1925 and amended the LPA 1925: see, especially, Chapter 14.

Care should be taken when citing or referring to a particular statute, as there are often Acts of Parliament with similar (or even identical) names from different years.

1.3.2 Law and Equity

Although all English courts have been courts of law and equity for over a century, the distinction between the two sets of rules is still important, especially in land law. Consequently, it is necessary to know a little legal history if the principles of modern land law are to be fully understood. The detailed story is well told by others (see, for example, Part II of Burn and Cartwright, *Cheshire and Burn's Modern Law of Real Property* (18th edn, Oxford University Press 2011) and Simpson, *History of the Land Law* (2nd edn, Clarendon Press 1986)).

1.3.2(a) The story of law and equity

In the years following William of Normandy's conquest of England in 1066, there were three main groups of courts:

- *Local courts.*
  The new administration largely preserved the Saxons' shires and their hundreds (the name given to the administrative parts into which the shires were subdivided). Each shire and hundred (and some boroughs) had its own court for dealing with local matters, including serious crimes.
- *Feudal courts.*
  William distributed most of his new territory among his main supporters in return for them providing certain services, including fighting men. Because they held their land directly from the king, these nobles were his tenants in chief. They, in turn, distributed the land among their family and supporters, who did the same, so that there was a hierarchy of great and lesser landholders. Each of these lords held a court which resolved the disputes between the lord's tenants, especially disputes relating to land.
- *Royal courts.*
  The royal courts emerged from the most senior of the feudal courts, held by the king for his tenants in chief.

By the end of the thirteenth century the royal courts had extended their jurisdiction to cover many of the matters previously confined to the other types of court, especially in relation to land. It was this extension of a single set of rules to the whole of the country, regardless of shire or feudal lord, that ultimately led to a *common law* shared by the whole of England and Wales.

As the common law developed, a number of factors contributed to it becoming increasingly rigid. The circumstances in which a person could seek a remedy from the court were strictly limited, and the judges followed the strict letter of the law in reaching their decisions. Aggrieved citizens who found themselves without an effective remedy for the wrongs they suffered (unable to mount a social media campaign) wrote to the king, who was regarded as the fount of justice for his kingdom. Initially such petitions were heard by the whole of the king's council, but ultimately they went direct to his 'secretary', the Chancellor, who employed the king's power to override those decisions of the king's judges which he believed to be unjust. Appealing to the Chancellor's conscience (or to 'equity') grew in popularity, and from about 1535 the Chancellor's court (Chancery) was regularly making decisions overriding the law in the royal courts. However, the Chancellor did not seek to replace the rules of common law; rather, he merely intervened when conscience required it. To quote from the judgment in *Dudley and Ward* v *Dudley* (1705) 24 ER 118, 120, equity:

> qualifies, moderates, and reforms the rigour, hardness, and edge of the law, and is an universal truth ... this is the office of equity, to support and protect the common law from shifts and crafty contrivances against the justice of the law. Equity therefore does not destroy the law, nor create it, but assist it.

Until the mid-sixteenth century it was considered that a bishop and other senior members of clergy were the persons best qualified to be the Chancellor and to exercise the king's conscience in such matters. After that, it became usual (until the role was changed at the beginning of the twenty-first century) to appoint a lawyer, trained in common law, to the post. One consequence of this was that the doctrine of precedent began to have an impact upon decisions in the Court of Chancery. What had once been a question for the conscience of an individual Chancellor became subject to rules that would, ultimately, become as fixed and complex as those of the courts of common law.

The courts of common law and the Court of Chancery existed separately, each with distinct procedures and remedies, and to the great profit of the legal profession, until the final quarter of the nineteenth century. By then, things had become intolerably inefficient (see, for example, the seemingly perpetual case of *Jarndyce* v *Jarndyce* in Charles Dickens' novel, *Bleak House*, 1852–3), and the two courts were merged by the Judicature Acts 1873 and 1875. Despite this merger, lawyers continued to keep the legal and equitable rules and remedies separate.

1.3.2(b) The significance of the distinction

There are two main reasons why it is important to know whether an interest is 'legal' or 'equitable'. The first is that equitable interests depend on equitable remedies which, in turn, are more to do with trying to prevent the harm than putting a price tag on the loss that occurs. Equitable remedies are also at the discretion of the court. The court of equity, being 'a court of conscience', only grants a remedy if the claimant has behaved fairly. However, legal remedies, such as damages, are available 'as of right'. A claimant is entitled to damages if their strict legal rights have been infringed, whether or not this is fair. Thus, in *Tse Kwong Lam* v *Wong Chit Sen* [1983] 1 WLR 1349 (PC) (see Section 11.5.2(b)), the Privy Council refused to set aside an improper sale of mortgaged land by a lender because the borrower had been 'guilty of inexcusable delay' in bringing the action. The borrower was, however, entitled to monetary damages (a legal remedy). The principles used by the courts in determining whether it is equitable to grant a remedy are summed up in the so-called maxims of equity (an explanation of which can be found in any standard text on equity and trusts).

The second reason to distinguish between legal and equitable interests is much less significant than it used to be. Historically, the courts could not bring themselves to enforce equitable rights against a completely innocent and honest legal purchaser. Prior to 1925, the rule was that the owner of an equitable interest in land would lose it if someone paid for the legal **estate**, in good faith and without notice of the interest ('**Equity's Darling**': see Section 5.2.2). This rule, known as the 'equitable doctrine of notice', has no application where, as in the vast majority of cases, the **title** to the land is **registered** under the scheme in the LRA 2002 (see Chapter 4). Even in **unregistered land**, the doctrine now only applies in a highly modified form (see Chapter 5).

1.3.3　1925 and all that

The year 1925 is an emotive date for land lawyers because it saw a major revision of the rules of property law in England and Wales. The law was actually changed by a very long Law of Property Act in 1922, but instead of bringing that Act into force it was divided into a number of shorter statutes all dated 1925. One of the aims of the 1925 legislation was to make conveyancing (buying, selling, mortgaging and other transactions concerning land) simpler in order to revive the depressed market in land and to make it easier to deal with commercially. Although the statutes contained many radical reforms which simplified land law in many ways, Parliament not only preserved the distinction between those rules derived from the common law and those derived from equity but also deployed them in new ways. The 1925 statutes also contained 'word saving' provisions, some of which had appeared in earlier statutes. At one time, lawyers were 'paid by the yard', so the more words they used, the better for their bank balances. In the 1925 Acts, Parliament ensured that many common promises in land transactions no longer needed to be spelled out in full because they would be implied by statute. In effect, the customs of conveyancers (lawyers who manage the transfer of land) became enshrined in statute. Significant examples of such provisions that will be encountered when studying land law are set out in Table 1.2.

Table 1.2　Significant examples of 'word saving' in the Law of Property Act 1925

	Provision	Referred to in this book
Section 62	Buildings, fixtures (see Section 3.5), and other interests automatically included in a conveyance of land	Section 10.7.5 (easements and profits) and 15.5.1(d) (the effect of a deed of transfer)
Sections 78 and 79	The benefit and burden of freehold covenants (promises about the use of the land) automatically run with the land	Sections 12.4.2(b), 12.5.1(c) and 12.5.2(a) (freehold covenants)
Sections 101 and 103	The power of a mortgagee (the lender) to sell the mortgaged land under certain circumstances	Section 11.5.2 (mortgages)

It is impossible to say whether the 1925 legislation had its desired effect. It seems unlikely that the great increase in home ownership in the twentieth century was the direct result of the reforms, some of which were unsuited to the modern world of owner-occupation. More recent statutes have introduced further reforms to better reflect modern attitudes to land ownership and to equip land law for the electronic age (including the Trusts of Land and Appointment of Trustees Act 1996 and the Land Registration Act 2002, respectively).

1.4 Property rights

Land law is one branch of the wider discipline of property law. Traditionally, property law was divided into the rules that applied to land (the law of **'real property'**) and the rules that applied to every other type of property (the law of 'personal property'). Over time, further branches have been added, including the law of 'intellectual property', which is concerned with the ownership of ideas (including patents, trade marks and copyright). Some of the reasons for treating land differently from other types of property are considered in Section 3.2. The task of this section is to explain what land lawyers mean when they talk about 'property rights' or 'interests in property'.

1.4.1 The characteristics of property rights

English law recognises a distinction between rights that are 'personal' and rights that are 'property' rights (or interests in property). Most other legal systems recognise a similar distinction, although the terminology differs.

- **Personal rights** are rights that regulate a specific relationship between a limited number of people, usually because:
  - they have each entered the relationship voluntarily (the law of contract) or
  - one person has acted in breach of their legal obligations to the others (the law of torts).
- **Property rights** are much more powerful because they are capable of binding people who were not parties to the transaction that created the right in question. Such people are usually referred to as 'third parties'.

Consequently, when the law recognises a person as having 'property' in an object, it is recognising that they have a significant degree of control over that object: a degree of control that necessarily limits the rights exercisable by others in respect of the same object. The result is the kind of triangle shown in Figure 1.1.

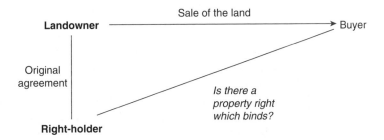

Figure 1.1 The property triangle

▶ *Landowner* agrees to allow another person to use their land in return for payment. For example, they might allow the person to occupy the land for a limited time, or to lay service cables or pipes beneath it.

▶ *Right-holder* now has contractual rights that they can enforce against *Landowner*. In most cases, such personal rights will be sufficient to deal with any dispute between them to *Right-holder's* satisfaction.

▶ *Landowner* sells their land to *Buyer*. There is no contractual relationship between *Right-holder* and *Buyer*, so *Right-holder* cannot use contract law to enforce their right to use the land directly against *Buyer*.

▶ If, however, the original transaction created a recognised property right, that right will survive the transfer of the land to *Buyer* and *Right-holder* will be able to enforce it against *Buyer*, even though *Buyer* was not a party to the original agreement.

One way of describing property rights is to say that they are attached to the land; they bind the land itself, not just its owner for the time being.

Land lawyers use the term 'interest in land' when referring to property rights. Reference to an interest in land is significant, therefore, because it shows that the rights and duties of the people concerned are not merely personal or contractual. Interests in land:

▶ are attached to the land itself (and will automatically pass to anyone who buys or inherits the land);

▶ can bind third parties; and

▶ can be transferred to other people (for example, a tenant may assign their **lease** to someone else, or a lender may decide to sell its portfolio of **mortgages** to another financial institution).

In lawyers' vocabulary, interests in land are 'property'.

1.4.2 The closed list

The advantage of a property right is its persistence: the right-holder can be confident that their right will be valid, regardless of whose hands the land passes into. However, the persistence of such rights also means that these rights can do harm. For example, the buyer of the land might be bound by a property right that they did not know about, even if they could not have easily discovered it when they acquired the land. Property rights are essential to a buoyant market in land, but the possibility of too many such rights may undermine that market (this seems to be one of the reasons why the courts stepped back from recognising positive freehold **covenants** as property rights; see Section 12.2). One of the ways in which land lawyers have sought to balance these tensions is by strictly limiting the number of rights that are capable of being enforced as property rights. The list of property rights is referred to as *numerus clausus*, which means 'closed number'. The current form of the *numerus clausus* is considered in outline in Section 2.2, and its most important members are examined in detail in Part III of this book. One of the most important questions to ask when approaching a problem in land law is which of the possible interests in the *numerus clausus* may be present on the facts. However, when it comes to analysing and evaluating the law, the *numerus clausus* only lists the proprietary interests presently recognised by English law; it does not provide any tools for deciding when and whether new rights should be added to the list; or, indeed, whether some rights should be removed.

The *numerus clausus* may be a closed list, but it is not a fixed one. Not all the interests now recognised as having proprietary status have always been treated as such. Both **leases** and **restrictive covenants** are relatively late additions, and the twentieth century saw a determined effort by some judges to raise certain types of **licence** to proprietary status (see Chapter 9). As Gray and Gray have pointed out (*Elements of Land Law* (5th edn, Oxford University Press 2009), para 1.5.1):

> Few concepts are quite so fragile, so elusive and so frequently missed as the notion of property … Our daily references to property therefore tend to comprise a mutual conspiracy of unsophisticated semantic allusions and confusions which we tolerate – frequently, indeed, do not notice …

However, while new rights can be, and have been, added to the *numerus clausus*, the authority to do so lies with Parliament and the courts. As Brougham LC observed in *Keppell v Bailey* (1834) 39 ER 1042, 1049:

> it must not … be supposed that incidents of a novel kind can be devised and attached to property at the fancy or caprice of any owner. It is clearly inconvenient both to the science of the law and to the public weal that such a latitude should be given.

What is it that makes a right a property right? This was a question that Lord Wilberforce considered in the case of *National Provincial Bank Ltd v Ainsworth* [1965] AC 1175 (HL). Mr Ainsworth had left his wife, who continued to live in the former matrimonial home. The house was originally owned by Mr Ainsworth (Mrs Ainsworth having made no contribution to the purchase price), but when he incorporated his business he transferred the house to his new company and used it to secure the company's debts by granting a **mortgage** in favour of National Provincial Bank. When Mr Ainsworth's company failed to repay its debts, the bank sought possession of the house from Mrs Ainsworth. The House of Lords had to decide whether Mrs Ainsworth's occupation of the house amounted to a property interest in it; in other words, was her right to occupy the house as Mr Ainsworth's wife binding on the bank? This kind of problem, in which a transaction between buyer and seller or a borrower and a lender involves a third person's interest in land (in this case, Mrs Ainsworth's spousal right to occupy the house), is a typical example of the triangle illustrated in Figure 1.1. In this case, Mr Ainsworth was the equivalent of *Landowner* and the bank was in the position of *Buyer* (granting a mortgage is equivalent to a sale for these purposes). Mrs Ainsworth claimed that her right to occupy the house as Mr Ainsworth's wife was an interest capable of binding the bank. Although their Lordships were sympathetic to Mrs Ainsworth's plight, they felt unable to give her interest proprietary status. Lord Wilberforce said at 1247–8:

> Before a right or an interest can be admitted into the category of property, or of a right affecting property, it must be definable, identifiable by third parties, capable in its nature of assumption by third parties, and have some degree of permanence or stability.

There is, as Gray and Gray and others have observed, a certain circularity in this approach. What rights bind third parties? Proprietary ones. What rights are proprietary? Those capable of binding third parties. In fact, the question 'What rights should be recognised as having the power of property?' is one that must be answered by the society of which the law is part. Different societies will answer the question in different ways, and the same society may answer the question differently at different times.

1.5 Human rights

Since the relevant provisions of the Human Rights Act 1998 came into force in October 2000, the rules and practices of land law have been open to challenge in the English courts if they offend against rights contained in the European Convention on Human Rights and Fundamental Freedoms (usually referred to as the European Convention on Human Rights or ECHR). The Human Rights Act requires the courts to interpret legislation 'in a way which is compatible with the Convention rights' (s 3). It is directly applicable against public authorities (s 6), which include courts and tribunals, central and local government and anybody exercising functions of a public nature.

In the context of land law, the most important Convention rights are:

▶ Article 1, Protocol 1 – the right to peaceful enjoyment and protection of possessions;
▶ Article 8 – the right to respect for a person's private and family life and home;
▶ Article 6 – the right to a fair and public hearing; and
▶ Article 14 – the right to enjoy Convention rights without discrimination.

Article 1, Protocol 1 guarantees a person's right to enjoy their property free from interference from the State except where such interference is in the public interest and in accordance with the law. This might well allow the compulsory purchase of a person's land by a local authority, for example. It certainly permits long leaseholders of houses to buy the **freehold** of their land under the Leasehold Reform Act 1967 because it is in the interests of social justice that they should be able to do so (*James* v *UK* (1986) 8 EHRR 123 and Section 7.6).

Under Article 8, no public authority may interfere with the exercise of the right to respect for a person's private and family life and home, except in accordance with the law and to the extent that it is necessary in a democratic society. In *Harrow LBC* v *Qazi* [2004] 1 AC 983, the House of Lords held that the Article concerned rights of privacy rather than property. Consequently, it could not be used to defeat contractual and proprietary rights to possession, including the powers of a local authority to recover possession from a former tenant. However, in *Connors* v *UK* (66746/01) (2005) 40 EHRR 9, the European Court of Human Rights at Strasbourg decided that there were circumstances in which the exercise by a public authority of an unqualified proprietary right under domestic law to repossess its land would constitute an interference with the occupier's right to respect for his home. For repossession in these circumstances to be lawful, it must be shown that the authority had sufficient procedural safeguards in place to ensure that so serious an interference with the occupier's rights was justified and proportionate in the circumstances of the case.

For several years after *Connors*, the House of Lords continued to hold that the relevant question in Article 8 cases was not whether repossession was a proportionate remedy in the particular case, but whether the statutory scheme under which possession was being sought was Article 8 compliant. Finally, in *Manchester City Council* v

Pinnock [2011] 2 AC 104 (SC), the Supreme Court accepted that English courts must consider the question of the proportionality of a local authority's action within the circumstances of the individual case, provided that the issue was raised by the claimant. This is unlikely to give rise to a flood of successful challenges to eviction. First, the reasoning in *Pinnock* is expressly confined to cases concerning local authorities ([50]). Second, the proportionality of a local authority's action is only one of a number of factors that the court must take into account. In most cases, it is likely to be outweighed by others, including the local authority's proprietary interest in the land and especially its duty to properly manage and allocate its housing stock. This proved to be the case in both *Pinnock* and the slightly later case of *Hounslow LBC v Powell* [2011] 2 AC 186, also heard by the Supreme Court.

Section 6 of the Human Rights Act 1998 makes it unlawful for any 'a public authority to act in a way which is incompatible with a Convention right' unless the act is 'private' (s 6(5)). In *R (on the application of Weaver) v London & Quadrant Housing Trust* [2010] 1 WLR 363 (CA) the Court of Appeal had to decide whether evicting a social tenant for non-payment of **rent** was a public act or a private act within section 6. The majority concluded that the housing association was acting publicly: the status of an act depends upon the context in which it occurs (in this case, the provision of social housing) not the nature of the right being exercised (in this case, contractual).

The extent to which the Act is applicable in a dispute between two private individuals (what is known as its 'horizontal' effect) was addressed by the Supreme Court in *McDonald v McDonald* [2017] AC 273 (SC). In this case, a couple had purchased a house with the help of a **mortgage**. The house was occupied by their daughter (who suffered from a mental disorder) under the terms of an assured shorthold **periodic tenancy**. The rules for terminating this type of tenancy are set out in the Housing Act 1988. When the McDonalds were no longer able to keep up the instalments on the mortgage, the lender sought possession of the house by serving the appropriate form of notice on the daughter to terminate her tenancy. It was argued on behalf of the daughter that the grant of a possession order would amount to a disproportionate interference with her right to respect for her home under Article 8 of the Convention. Lord Neuberger and Baroness Hale, with whom the other judges agreed, observed at [46] that:

> there are many cases where the court can be required to balance conflicting Convention rights of two parties, eg where a person is seeking to rely on her article 8 rights to restrain a newspaper from publishing an article which breaches her privacy, and where the newspaper relies on article 10. But such disputes ... [are] in sharp contrast to the present type of case where the parties are in a contractual relationship in respect of which the legislature has prescribed how their respective Convention rights are to be respected.

Consequently, Miss McDonald could not rely on Article 8 to defeat the **notice to quit** served by the lender. The focus on the contractual nature of the transaction seems somewhat at odds with the reasoning in *London & Quadrant Housing Trust*. It seems that Article 8 does apply where a housing association terminates a tenancy under the Housing Act 1988, but not where a private landlord terminates a tenancy relying on the same statutory provisions. Perhaps, as Susan Pascoe (2017) suggests, it reflects implicit judicial reluctance to impose the cost of dealing with Article 8 cases on private landlords. The outcome in *McDonald* means that the Human Rights Act, and the Convention rights it incorporates, is unlikely, for the present at least, to be of any use to claimants in property disputes between private parties.

Summary

1.1 In your approach to land law, it is essential to grasp the language and definitions of interests in land as well as the rules about them.

1.2 Land law is the product of, and servant to, a particular society. The status of specific rights in land will depend upon the values and priorities of the society concerned. There are a number of reasons why a person might wish to 'own' rights over land. Where land is shared, land law must resolve any disputes that arise where the motivations of different 'owners' conflict.

1.3 Historically, the rules of land law developed in the royal courts (the rules of common law) and in the separate court of Chancery (the rules of equity). Although these two sets of rules are still the foundation of land law, many of the rules have been significantly modified by Parliament, and land law is increasingly concerned with statutory interpretation. The most important statutes are:

- Law of Property Act (LPA) 1925;
- Land Registration Act (LRA) 2002; and
- Trusts of Land and Appointment of Trustees Act (TOLATA) 1996.

1.4 There are three types of right:

- personal rights;
- property rights (or 'interests');
- and human rights.

Land lawyers engage with all three types of right, but are especially concerned with property rights, which, unlike personal rights, are capable of binding third parties. Human rights protect individuals from unfair treatment by public authorities, but are unlikely to be applicable where all the parties to a dispute are private individuals or private corporations.

Exercises

 1.1 Complete the online quiz on the topics covered in this chapter on the companion website.

1.2 What is the purpose of land law? What does contemporary society require from its legal rules relating to land?

 You can find a suggested answer plan to exercise 1.2 on the companion website.

Further reading

Burn and Cartwright, *Cheshire and Burn's Modern Law of Real Property* (18th edn, Oxford University Press 2011) Parts I and II

Gray and Gray, *Elements of Land Law* (5th edn, Oxford University Press 2009) Part 1.5

Pascoe, 'The End of the Road for Human Rights in Private Landowners' Disputes?' (2017) 81 Conv 269

Rodgers, 'Nature's Place? Property Rights, Property Rules and Environmental Stewardship' (2009) 68 CLJ 550

Simpson, *History of the Land Law* (2nd edn, Clarendon Press 1986)

Chapter 2

The foundations of land law

Key concepts

- **Equitable interests** – the interests recognised by the courts exercising their equitable jurisdiction; historically binding only on persons who had notice of them.
- **Legal estates** – the two types of interest listed in section 1(1) of the LPA 1925 and the basis of land ownership in England and Wales.
- **Legal interests** – the interests listed in section 1(2) of the LPA 1925.
- **Personal rights** – rights that regulate a specific relationship and which are usually only binding upon the parties to that relationship.
- **Property rights** – rights that are capable of binding third parties.
- **Title** – the right to hold an estate in land; proof of such a right.
- **Trust** – an equitable device dividing the legal ownership from the beneficial ownership.

2.1 The case of the occupying wife

It is now normal, when a couple purchase a home together, for them to do so in joint names. Indeed, it will often be the only way that they can do so as both their salaries will be needed to pay the instalments on the **mortgage** that they almost certainly need to finance their purchase. It has not always been so. In the third quarter of the twentieth century, when a husband and wife purchased a home it was more usual for the land to be conveyed into the name of the husband alone, even if the wife was able to make some contribution towards its purchase in her own right. However, when Mr and Mrs Boland purchased their first matrimonial home in 1961 they did so in joint names; they were both in work and both contributed to the cost. Eight years later they sold this house and used the proceeds to finance the purchase of 11 Ridge Park, Purley. Although there was no doubt that Mrs Boland contributed significantly to the cost of the new house, it was (apparently without her realising it) conveyed into the sole name of Mr Boland. Mr Boland was a builder and he borrowed large sums from Williams & Glyn's Bank to help finance his business. The bank, unknown to Mrs Boland, insisted that the loans be secured on the house (that is, the bank took a mortgage over the matrimonial home). Sadly, Mr Boland's once-thriving business failed, and the bank sought to enforce its **charge**. Mrs Boland claimed that she had an interest in the land by virtue of her contribution to the purchase price, and that this interest took priority over the bank's mortgage. The potential consequences for Williams & Glyn's Bank (and other lenders) meant that the case was ultimately heard by the House of Lords, whose decision is reported in *Williams & Glyn's Bank Ltd* v *Boland* [1981] AC 487 (HL).

To succeed against the bank, Mrs Boland had to demonstrate that:

- she had a property right (see Section 1.4) over the land; and
- her property right took priority over the bank's interest.

How she did so is explained at Sections 2.2.4 and 2.3.4, respectively.

2.2 Property rights recognised by English law

Land lawyers tend to view a piece of land as a number of abstract **property rights** or interests (the basic characteristics of property rights are considered at Section 1.4). For historical reasons, they see people as owning interests in land, rather than owning the physical land itself. Only a limited number of property interests are recognised by English law (see Section 1.4.2); they are divided into three main categories:

- legal **estates**;
- legal interests; and
- **equitable** interests.

The main estates and interests are shown in Figure 2.1.

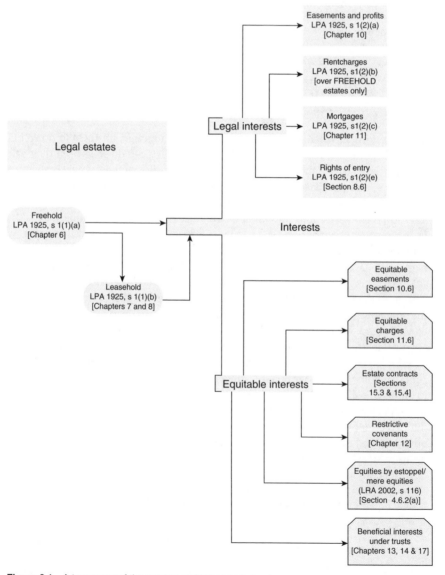

Figure 2.1 A taxonomy of the estates and interests in land

Tenures and estates

One of the characteristics of English law is that it does not recognise ownership of land in the absolute sense, at least not for the ordinary citizen. Instead, 'landowners' own an estate in land; that is, the right to enjoy the land for a particular slice of time. This approach is by no means essential to a sound system of land law (most of Europe has survived quite happily without the doctrine of estates), but is, like the story of law and equity (see Section 1.3.2), a consequence of English history.

When William I claimed the whole of England by right of conquest in 1066, he adopted the continental system of feudalism, in which everyone except the king was bound by promises and duties to the lord above them in a sort of feudal pyramid, with the king at the top. What was unusual in the case of England, however, was that the hierarchy was applied to the ownership of land in a fairly pure form. The king held (owned) all the land as feudal overlord and granted land to his **tenants** in chief in return for the performance of specified obligations and duties. These tenants in chief then granted some of their land to tenants of their own, also in return for specified duties, and so on down the pyramid. This gave rise to two important doctrines of English land law:

 ▶ tenure (the terms upon which the land was held); and
 ▶ estates (the duration for which the land was held).

There were a variety of free tenures, including military duties (*knights service*) and the provision of grain and other produce (*socage*) as well as labour-intensive unfree tenures, such as *villeinage* (unfree, because there was no limit to the actual service that could be demanded). Today, the doctrine of tenure is almost completely obsolete. The number of tenures was reduced to two in 1660, and one in 1922 (*socage*, although no one is expected to send food to the Queen as a condition of keeping their land). Tenure survives in the doctrine of *escheat*, whereby **freehold** land reverts to the Crown if there is no one to inherit it under a will or through the rules of intestacy, and in the language of the very different doctrine of the modern **lease**.

Estates can conveniently be divided into freehold estates and estates less than freehold (leases). Until 1925, there were a number of freehold estates that could be held in land, as illustrated by the following passage from *Walsingham's Case* (1573) 55 ER 805 (QB), 816–17:

> the land itself is one thing, and the estate in the land is another thing, for an estate in the land is a time in the land, or land for a time, and there are diversities of estates, which are no more than diversities of time, for he who has a fee-simple in land has a time in the land without end, or the land for time without end, and he who has land in tail has a time in the land or the land for time as long as he has issues of his body, and he who has an estate in land for life has no time in it longer than for his own life, and so of him who has an estate in land for the life of another, or for years.

Section 1 of the LPA 1925 reduced the number of freehold estates to one, the **fee simple absolute in possession** (see Chapter 6); freehold estates of limited duration can now only be created as **beneficial interests** in land. Leases were first treated as estates (rather than purely **personal rights**) during the fifteenth century and retained this status under the scheme of 1925.

2.2.1 The legal estates

The nearest concept to actual ownership of land in English law is the doctrine of the estate. All other types of interest in land are created out of a legal estate. The word 'estate' has a long lineage and refers to the duration of the owners' interest in the land. Since 1925 there have been two estates capable of existing as legal estates:

Law of Property Act 1925:
s 1(1) The only estates in land which are capable of subsisting or of being conveyed or created at law are:
    (a) An estate in fee simple absolute in possession [a freehold];
    (b) A term of years absolute [a lease].

The characteristics of the **freehold** estate (the estate of indefinite duration) are considered in Chapter 6. Leases are considered in Chapters 7 and 8.

2.2.2   The legal interests

The royal courts of common law recognised various interests in land less than an estate. Because **property rights** in land automatically affected anyone who subsequently acquired that land, the courts of common law restricted the classes of interests in land to rights that were relatively certain and easily discoverable. In most cases, this required certain formalities to be complied with when the rights were created, although the doctrine of **adverse possession** (see Chapter 16) and the acquisition of **easements** by **prescription** (see Section 10.7.6) are significant exceptions to this rule.

The Law of Property Act 1925 originally set out five interests capable of existing at law, although amendments to the Act have effectively reduced this number to four:

> s 1(2)   The only interests or charges in or over land which are capable of subsisting or of being conveyed or created at law are:
>
> (a) An easement, right, or privilege in or over land for an interest equivalent to an estate in fee simple absolute in possession or a term of years absolute [rights of way, for example];
> (b) A rentcharge in possession issuing out of or charged on land being either perpetual or for a term of years absolute [a periodical payment secured on freehold land, which does not arise out of a lease or a mortgage];
> (c) A charge by way of legal mortgage …
> (e) Rights of entry exercisable over, or in respect of, a legal term of years absolute [a lessor's right to end a lease].

Easements and **profits** (paragraph (a)) are considered in Chapter 10; **mortgages** (paragraph (c)) in Chapter 11; and **rights of entry** (also known as **forfeiture**) as part of Section 8.6. A **rentcharge** is the right to the payment of a periodic sum secured on **freehold** land (not to be confused with the **rent** payable under the terms of a **lease**). Their scope was severely restricted by the Rent Charges Act 1977, and, except for the estate rentcharge (see Section 12.6.3), they lie outside the scope of this book.

2.2.3   Equitable interests

Section 1(3) of the LPA 1925 provides that:

> All other estates, interests, and **charges** in or over land [that is, those not listed in sections 1(1) and 1(2)] take effect as **equitable** interests.

Historically, equity has recognised some interests that have never been recognised by the common law. Equity has also been prepared to recognise interests that could have been legal, but which failed to meet the strict requirements of the common law. For example, the interest may have been created without complying with the necessary formalities. Most legal interests must now be created by **deed** and completed by registration. Writing alone is usually sufficient to create an express equitable interest, although it will usually need to be protected by some form of registration if it is to be binding on third parties (see Sections 4.5 and 5.4). The distinction between creation and registration will, for all practicable purposes, become obsolete if electronic conveyancing is ever extended to cover such interests (see Sections 4.2.1 and 4.11).

2.2.3(a) *The trust*

The **trust** allows the ownership of land to be separated from the right to enjoy the land or any income generated by it. The history of how the courts of equity developed the trust is a long one, and detailed accounts can be found in most of the standard works on equity and trusts. In the simplest form of a trust, a settler transfers the legal **title to trustees** to hold for the benefit of the **beneficiary** or beneficiaries (Figure 2.2). However, trusts can also be created by statute and through the operation of law.

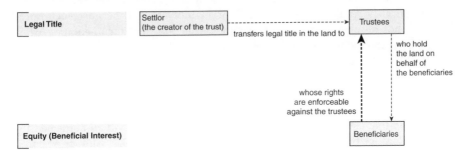

Figure 2.2   The trust

An example of a trust can be found in the case of *Bull v Bull* [1955] 1 QB 234 (CA), in which a son and his mother had both contributed to the purchase of a house on the outskirts of London. However, only the son's name appeared on the conveyance (that is, the deed transferring legal title in the land), so he alone became the new legal owner of the house. Mr Bull then married and, since his wife and his mother could not get on with each other, he tried to evict his mother. The Court of Appeal held that he could not simply turn her out. The mother's contribution to the purchase price meant that the beneficial entitlement to the house was divided between her and her son. Mr Bull held the legal title on trust for himself and his mother and had, therefore, to respect his mother's rights in the land. Another way to express this is to say that Mr Bull was a trustee for himself and his mother. This is shown diagrammatically in Figure 2.3.

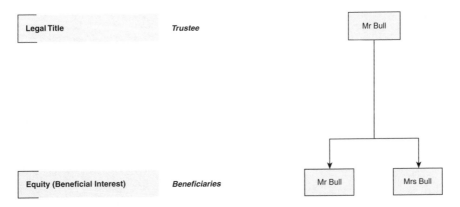

Figure 2.3   The trust relationship in *Bull v Bull* [1955] 1 QB 234 (CA)

The trust is a useful and very common device by which land can be shared. Sections 34–6 of the LPA 1925 provide that any land that is transferred to two or more people is automatically held on trust (the legal owners holding as trustees for themselves as beneficiaries; see Chapter 13). The duties of a trustee are contained in the general rules of equity and in statute. In the case of trusts of land, most of the relevant rules are contained in the Trusts of Land and Appointment of Trustees Act 1996 (see Chapter 14).

A **beneficiary**'s entitlement to land is an equitable interest in the land. However, the framers of the 1925 reforms to land law were concerned that **beneficial interests** seriously compromised the free marketability of land because such interests would not necessarily be apparent either from the title documentation or from an inspection of the property. They chose the doctrine of **overreaching** in an attempt to balance the interests of buyers (and the economic importance of keeping the process of transferring land relatively quick and cheap) with the interests of beneficiaries. Provided that the buyer of any legal estate in land pays the purchase price to at least two trustees (or a trust corporation), any beneficial interests under a trust in that estate are automatically detached from the land and attached to the purchase price by virtue of sections 2 and 27 of the LPA 1925. Most trust corporations are companies set up by banks or law firms to administer trusts and act as executors under wills. The doctrine of overreaching is considered in more detail in Section 14.6.1.

2.2.3(b) Other equitable interests

The trust is not the only creation of the Court of Chancery that is important to land lawyers. Other significant examples include:

- *restrictive freehold covenants*, which first became enforceable against third parties as a property right in the nineteenth century (see Chapter 12);
- the *equitable right of redemption*, which is the foundation of the modern law of mortgages (see Chapter 11); and
- *estate contracts*, where a person with a valid contract for the purchase of land is treated as having an equitable interest in the land (see Section 15.3).

More recently, the rights arising out of **proprietary estoppel** (see Chapter 18) have been recognised as having proprietary status by section 116 of the LRA 2002.

2.2.4   Did Mrs Boland have an interest in the land?

In order to determine whether Mrs Boland had a property interest in the house at 11 Ridge Park, each of the types of interest in land needs to be considered in turn.

- The land had been transferred to Mr Boland in his sole name. This meant that Mr Boland alone owned the *legal estate* in the land (the fees simple absolute in possession). Mrs Boland did not have a legal estate in the land.
- She did not claim to have any of the *legal interests* listed in section 1(2) of the LPA 1925. The bank's **mortgage** was, however, a legal interest (LPA 1925, s 1(2)(c)).

- Mrs Boland had contributed to the cost of the land. Consequently, she did have an *equitable interest* in the land (the same type of **beneficial interest** that arose in *Bull* v *Bull* [1955] 1 QB 234 (CA)).
- As the mortgage advance had been paid to Mr Boland as sole **trustee**, and not to two trustees, Mrs Boland's beneficial interest had not been overreached into the mortgage moneys (ss 2(1)(ii) and 27 of the LPA 1925).

On the face of it, therefore, Mrs Boland seemed to be in a good position. She certainly had a much stronger defence to the bank's claim than Mrs Ainsworth, who, in *National Provincial Bank Ltd* v *Ainsworth* [1965] AC 1175 (HL), had only her status as a wife to rely upon (see Section 1.4.2). However, Mrs Boland still needed to show that her equitable interest took priority over the legal interest claimed by the bank. This depended upon the rules of **title** and, in particular, the rules of **registered** land (see Sections 2.3.4 and 4.6.2).

2.3　Title and the rules of priority

Land lawyers had mastered 'virtual reality' before the term even existed, at least in its modern sense. They do not work directly with the physical world, but resolve issues by manipulating the various abstract legal and **equitable** interests that can exist in land. They are not unlike the computer programmers who, by devising routines in seemingly incomprehensible computer code, produced the word processing application with which this book was written. Being able to work in this way means knowing not only the different tools available (the legal and equitable interests in land), but also the relationship between them (how they interact with one another). In particular, what are the rules for determining which of two competing rights takes priority over the other?

It might be expected that anyone who buys or inherits land (or any interest in it) will own it subject to any interests which have been created by previous owners of the land. As a general rule, this is true. However, there have always been exceptions. For example, the court of Chancery has always been reluctant to enforce equitable rights against an innocent and honest legal purchaser who had no reasonable prospect of discovering the rights in advance (see Section 5.2.2). The detailed rules (what might be referred to as the grammar of land law) now depend upon whether title to the land concerned is **registered**.

2.3.1　Title

The term **title** refers to the right to hold an **estate** in land; it is also used when referring to how someone proves their ownership of such a right. So, for example, the potential purchaser of a plot of land will want to be sure that the seller has good title to the land (that is, they are entitled to sell what they are offering for sale).

There are two systems for proving title in England and Wales:

- **unregistered title** (sometimes referred to as 'unregistered land', or 'not yet registered land'); and
- **registered title** (or, less precisely, 'registered land').

Each system is distinct from the other, with its own set of rules for determining how interests in land are created and transferred and how disputes about those interests are resolved. These rules will be explained in detail as they become relevant in the chapters that follow (see, especially, Chapters 4 and 5). For the moment, however, it is useful to identify some of the main differences between the two systems. The meaning and significance of these differences should become more apparent as your study of land law progresses. The main differences are set out in Table 2.1.

Table 2.1   A comparison between unregistered and registered title

	Unregistered	Registered
Underlying nature	Private	Public
Basis of title (ownership)	Possession	Entry in Land Register Title is guaranteed by the State
Evidence of title	Title deeds	Official copy of the register
Types of interest	Legal estates Legal charges Other legal interests Equitable interests	Registrable estates Registrable charges Interests completed by registration Interests subject to registration Interests capable of overriding the register
Discovery of interests in the land	Deeds Land Charges Register Notice (including inspection of the land)	Register Inspection of the land for interests capable of overriding the register

2.3.2   Unregistered title

The system of **unregistered title** is based upon rules dating back many centuries under which establishing title to an **estate** depends upon being able to prove that your entitlement to it is better than that of the person claiming it from you. The best proof of title is a chain of **deeds** that demonstrate how the title has passed to the present owner. Historically, the general rule was that legal interests in an estate were effective against anyone who owned that estate, regardless of whether they knew or could have known about the legal interest when acquiring the estate. However, while **equitable** rights would bind some people, they were not enforceable against a purchaser without 'notice' of them (or 'Equity's Darlings': see Section 5.2.2). As part of the legislative reforms directed at making conveyancing simpler in 1925, the **doctrine of notice** was significantly modified, with most, but not all, equitable interests needing to be entered in a register of **land charges**. The rules (most of which are now found in the Land Charges Act 1972) are considered in Chapter 5. These rules are of diminishing importance as an increasing proportion of titles become registered. By the middle of 2018, there were over 25 million **registered titles** in England and Wales, amounting to some 85 per cent of the total land mass of England and Wales. Up-to-date figures can be found in the publications available from the Land Registry's website (www.gov.uk/government/organisations/land-registry).

2.3.3 Registered title

When title to land is registered, the question of whether an interest will affect someone acquiring the land is determined by the rules set out in the Land Registration Act 2002. The aim of those who drafted the LRA 2002 (and its 1925 predecessor) was for as many interests in land as possible to be entered on the **Register of Title** to the **estate** affected. The general rule is that any interest that appears on the register will normally be binding on whoever acquires for value the estate concerned or another interest over that estate. However, it would be unjust, and impracticable, to insist that every interest in the land must be registered if it is to be enforceable against the owner of the land. Consequently, the LRA 2002 (again, like the LRA 1925) lists a limited number of interests that are capable of binding the owner of a registered estate even though they do not appear on the Register of Title. These interests are commonly referred to as being capable of *overriding* the register, or '**overriding interests**'. Some of these interests are legal, others **equitable**. The rules relating to registered title are considered in Chapter 4.

The significance of the rules of unregistered title
A significant majority of titles to land in England and Wales are already registered. In most cases, therefore, the priority of any interests in land will fall to be determined using the rules considered in Chapter 4. However, there are a number of reasons why some understanding of the rules of unregistered land can be helpful.

- ▶ The rules are of practical importance because they:
  - ▶ apply to any dispute concerning land to which the title is still unregistered; and
  - ▶ are relevant to determining what interests were capable of binding the title at the date of first registration (see Section 4.7).
- ▶ The rules equip the land lawyer to better understand and evaluate important doctrines and concepts because:
  - ▶ they are the legal context in which most of the basic doctrines of land law first developed; and
  - ▶ they provide an alternative against which, through comparison, to illuminate and test the rules of registered title.

2.3.4 Does Mrs Boland's interest take priority over the bank's charge?

The first question to ask is whether title to the land concerned was registered or unregistered. It was registered. Consequently, the priority of Mrs Boland's interest must be determined using the rules in the Land Registration Act. At the time of Mrs Boland's case, the relevant act was the LRA 1925, but the outcome would almost certainly be the same under the present rules, contained in the LRA 2002. The House of Lords held that Mrs Boland's **beneficial interest** was capable of **overriding** the register (giving it priority over the bank's registered **legal charge**) because she was in actual occupation of the land for the purposes of section 70(1)(g) of the LRA 1925 (this aspect of the case is considered in more detail in Section 4.6.2). The bank could only enforce its **mortgage** against Mr Boland's beneficial interest in the house.

Important questions to ask when approaching a land law problem

A common way of examining land law students is to use problem questions in which the student is asked to advise of the legal implications of a fictional scenario. To deal quickly and efficiently with land law problems, it is crucial to develop an instinct for the various interests, so that you can immediately say, for example, 'This looks like an easement.' Consequently, the first question to ask in problem solving is:

▶ *What legal or equitable interests may exist here?*

The criteria for recognising the various types of interests are set out in the relevant chapters of this book.

After establishing that there may be a particular legal or equitable interest, it will be necessary to ask:

▶ *If the interest is a beneficial interest under a trust, has it been overreached?*

That is, has it ceased to be an interest in the relevant land? If not, further consideration of the problem will depend upon whether the title to the land concerned is *registered* or *unregistered*. The distinction between registered and unregistered titles is introduced in Section 2.3.

If the title is *registered* (see Chapter 4):

▶ *Is the interest entered on the register?*
▶ *If not, does it override the register?*

If the title is not yet registered (see Chapter 5):

▶ *Does the interest fall within the scope of the Land Charges Act 1972?*
▶ *If not, is the interest legal?*
▶ *If neither, did the purchaser have **notice** of the interest?*

This basic framework for approaching a question is shown in diagram form in Figure 2.4. One of the skills of a good lawyer is to be able to identify which of the various elements are the key issues that need to be addressed when tackling a specific question, and which are of less importance, or not relevant.

Summary

2.1 There are two important questions when considering a claim over land: is it a property right (an interest in land), and if so does it have priority over any other property interests in the same land?

2.2 Only a limited number of rights are recognised as capable of being interests in land. There are three main types of interest: legal estates, legal interests and equitable interests. The two major interests are the freehold and leasehold estate. All other interests are carved out of a legal estate.

2.3 When determining whether an interest is binding on a particular estate, or has priority over another interest in the same estate, regard must be had to the relevant rules governing the title. Titles to land are either registered or unregistered. Most titles are now subject to the rules in the Land Registration Act 2002.

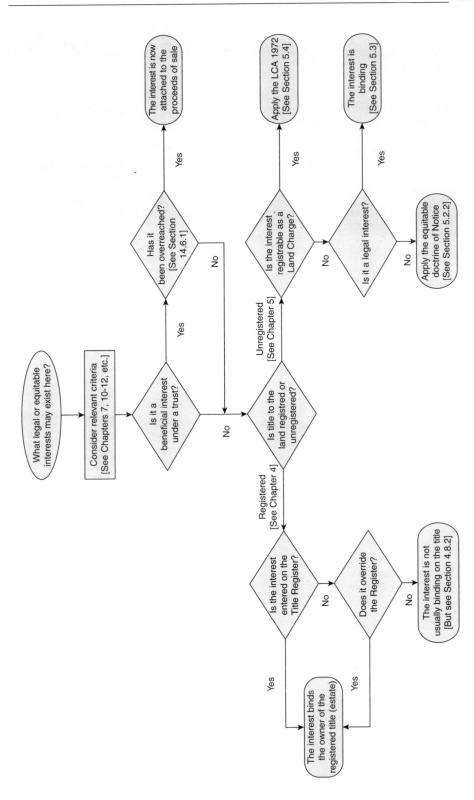

Figure 2.4 Approaching land law questions

Exercises

  2.1 Complete the online quiz on the topics covered in this chapter on the companion
website.

2.2 What are legal estates? Why are they so significant in modern English land law? How do
they differ from other types of interest in land?

    You can find a suggested answer plan to exercise 2.2 on the companion website.

Further reading

Bright, 'Of Estates and Interests: A Tale of Ownership and Property Rights' in Bright and Dewar
(eds), *Land Law Themes and Perspectives* (Oxford University Press 1998) 529

Burn and Cartwright, *Cheshire and Burn's Modern Law of Real Property* (18th edn, Oxford
University Press 2011) ch 1

Hayton, 'The Development of Equity and the "Good Person" Philosophy in Common Law Systems'
(2012) 76 Conv 263

Simpson, *History of the Land Law* (2nd edn, Clarendon Press 1986)

Thompson, 'Possession Actions and Human Rights' (2011) 75 Conv 421

Chapter 3

What is 'land'?

Key concepts

- **Chattel** – physical property other than land.
- **Fixture** – an object that is treated as part of the land to which it is attached or upon which it rests.

3.1 The case of the Welsh chalets

For most of the twentieth century, Holtsfield, near Swansea in South Wales, was the site of a village of chalets (wooden bungalows). The chalets were built as holiday homes before the Second World War, but over the course of time, people began to occupy them on a permanent basis. One such person was David Morris, who, in 1971, acquired the chalet on Lot 6. This was a two-bedroom wooden structure that rested on, but was not attached to, a foundation of concrete blocks. There he lived, in return for the payment of an annual fee to the owner of the site, renewing and replacing his home as required.

Elitestone Ltd purchased Holtsfield in 1989 with a view to redeveloping the land as executive housing. Meanwhile, the company agreed to renew the annual agreements with the residents, but at a much higher fee than that charged previously. A massive campaign followed in an attempt to preserve the chalets on Holtsfield and the way of life of their residents. In August 2018, most of the campaign group's website was still visible at http://tlio.org.uk/holtsfield/.

There are a number of legal aspects to the Holtsfield saga. For example, should the chalets be preserved, or should a new development be allowed (planning law)? Were the chalets fit for human habitation (environmental health law)? From a land law perspective, the question was whether Mr Morris and his fellow residents had any interest in the land they occupied that was binding upon Elitestone Ltd as the owners of the field. Indeed, did they have any interest in the land at all, or merely the right to occupy their chalets until the end of the annual agreement? The answer given by the House of Lords (*Elitestone Ltd v Morris* [1997] 1 WLR 687 (HL) (see Section 3.6) illustrates:

- the way in which different aspects of land law (including case law and statute law) interact in any given case;
- the significance of the concepts considered in Chapter 2 to solving land law problems; and
- the importance of knowing what is (and what is not) land.

3.2 Land's special rules

Almost all legal systems have special rules about the ownership of land which do not apply to other types of property. This reflects the significance of land to human beings and its distinctive characteristics when compared with other types of resources.

At the most basic level, human beings need somewhere to put their bodies, a piece of land on which to 'be'. On the emotional plane, most humans need contact with land. Physically, they need air to breathe and space in which to move about, eat and shelter. All these are provided by land.

As a resource, land has other special characteristics. Except in the rare cases of land falling into, or being thrown up from, the sea, it is geographically fixed and immovable; it is also effectively indestructible. Its nature means that the boundaries between one piece of land and another are normally touching, so neighbouring owners are aware of one another's business. Further, to its occupant one piece is never exactly the same as another: each is unique. Even in apparently uniform tower blocks, each floor, each flat, has its own particular characteristics.

The permanence and durability of land are matched by its flexibility. It is three-dimensional space that can be split into an almost infinite number of layers. A plot of land can also be used by a number of people in different ways simultaneously: one person can invest their money in it, while two or more live there, a fourth tunnels beneath to extract minerals and half a dozen more use a path over it as a shortcut, or graze their cattle on a part of it.

Land can be shared consecutively as well as simultaneously; that is to say, people can enjoy the land one after another. The great landowning families traditionally created complicated **settlements** of their estates, whereby the land would pass through the succeeding generations as the first owner desired. Each 'owner' only had it for a lifetime and could not leave it by will because, at death, it had to pass according to the directions in the **settlement**. In this way, the aristocratic dynasties preserved their land, and consequently their wealth and their political power.

All of these characteristics have contributed to almost all legal systems developing special rules relating to property in land. It is important, therefore, to know whether a particular object or resource is land (**real property**). If it is not, it is a **chattel** (personal property). The rules for determining this are considered in Section 3.5. Note how in English law, the word 'personal' is used to describe both a type of right (see Section 1.3) and a type of property. It is possible to have **personal rights** over land (for example, many of the **licences** discussed in Chapter 9) and **property rights** (ownership) over personal property.

3.3 Definitions of land

At common law, 'land' means the soil, the rocks beneath and the air above. Various statutes contain their own version of this definition. For example:

▶ section 132(1) of the Land Registration Act (LRA) 2002:

'Land' includes
(a) buildings and other structures,
(b) land covered with water, and
(c) mines and minerals, whether or not held with the surface.

▶ section 205(1)(ix) of the Law of Property Act (LPA) 1925:

'Land' includes land of any tenure, and mines and minerals ... buildings or parts of buildings ... and other corporeal hereditaments, also ... a rent, and other incorporeal hereditaments, and an easement right, privilege, or benefit in, over, or derived from land.

The word-saving provisions of sections 62(1) and 62(2) of the LPA 1925 (see Section 1.3.3) are also important in this context, because they set out what is deemed to be included (in the absence of express provision to the contrary) whenever 'land' is transferred or mortgaged.

Examining these provisions reveals some important characteristics of land as understood by the law of England and Wales. Firstly, land law cannot quite decide whether to treat land as a physical entity or solely as a bundle of abstract rights and interests. This is, perhaps, most apparent in the definition in section 205 of the LPA 1925, which expressly includes both *corporeal* and *incorporeal* **hereditaments**. The term 'corporeal hereditaments' is an ancient way of referring to the physical aspects of land, while 'incorporeal hereditaments' are the invisible interests in land, such as **leases**, **mortgages** and **easements** (rights of way, for example). Thus, both a person who takes a lease (that is, becomes a leaseholder or a tenant) and a person who acquires a right of way over their neighbour's land gain an interest in land.

The second factor that should be apparent from the various definitions is that the term 'land' is not limited to the surface of the Earth. If land includes buildings as well as things growing on the land and things, such as minerals, underneath the land, then the land lawyer is not concerned with two-dimensional areas of ground (as it might appear on a map or plan), but with three-dimensional blocks of space. One of the consequences of this is that land can be divided horizontally, into strata (such as different floors in an office block), as well as vertically. However, it also means that land law has to find answers to two important questions:

▶ how high (and how low) any particular interest in land extends; and
▶ how to distinguish between the land itself and objects placed in or on the land.

3.4 How high, how low?

The oft-cited Latin maxim is *cuius est solum, eius est usque ad coelum et ad inferos*, or, 'the one who owns the surface owns up to the heavens and down to hell'. Its origin is obscure, and there have long been doubts about whether it is an accurate summary of English Law. In the Privy Council case of *Comr for Railways v Valuer General* [1974] AC 328 (PC), Lord Wilberforce reviewed the authorities, before concluding at 351–2:

> In none of these cases is there an authoritative pronouncement that 'land' means the whole of the space from the centre of the earth to the heavens: so sweeping, unscientific and unpractical a doctrine is unlikely to appeal to the common law mind.

In the case of **freehold** land, the **estate** usually includes the airspace above the surface of the land necessary to allow the reasonable enjoyment of the surface of the land and any buildings on it. So held Griffiths J in *Bernstein of Leigh (Baron) v Skyviews & General Ltd* [1978] QB 479 (QB). The defendant company was a small family business that took photographs of people's houses from the air and offered them for sale to the house owners. When they offered to sell Lord Bernstein the photograph they had taken of his country house in Kent, he took exception to what he believed to be a gross invasion of privacy. An unfortunate series of events led to a high court judge having to determine whether, as the owner of the house and grounds, Lord Bernstein had the right to prevent the company flying over them. An interesting twist to the case was that Lord Bernstein was the chairman of a television company that had just made a series of educational films for which helicopters had photographed a great deal of land without having sought the consent of its owners or occupiers. Griffiths J said, at 487–8:

> I can find no support in authority for the view that a landowner's rights in the air space above his property extend to an unlimited height. ... The problem is to balance the rights of an owner to enjoy the use of his land against the rights of the general public to take advantage of all that science now offers in the use of air space. This balance is in my judgment best struck in our present society by restricting the rights of an owner in the air space above his land to such height as is necessary for the ordinary use and enjoyment of his land and the structures upon it, and declaring that above that height he has no greater rights in the air space than any other member of the public.

What constitutes sufficient airspace for these purposes would seem to depend upon the context. Rules made under the Civil Aviation Act 1982 suggest that is likely to lie somewhere between 500 and 1,000 feet (the latter being the usual minimum height for aircraft flying over congested areas).

The freehold owner of the surface of the land also owns the strata beneath the surface (including any minerals) unless the strata have been separated from the surface in some way. Precisely how far down ownership can extend remains undetermined, but according to the Supreme Court case of *Bocardo SA v Star Energy UK Onshore Ltd* [2011] 1 AC 380 (SC) it is not limited to the depth necessary for the reasonable enjoyment of the surface. Lord Hope, at [26], was less dismissive of *cuius est solum, eius est usque ad coelum et ad inferos* than some of his predecessors:

> In my opinion the brocard still has value in English law as encapsulating, in simple language, a proposition of law which has commanded general acceptance. It is an imperfect guide, as it has ceased to apply to the use of airspace above a height which may interfere with the ordinary user of land.

In the case of a **leasehold** estate, the extent of the airspace and subsoil demised (if any) will depend upon the nature (and the wording) of the lease. In *Davies v Yadegar* (1990) 22 HLR 232 (CA), at 235 Wilberforce LJ concluded, in circumstances where the **demise** included the whole roof and top floor of the building:

> the logical intent would be that the airspace above should be included in that demise. Were the position otherwise, one can easily see that all sorts of absurd results would follow: if the tenant of the upper flat wished to ... change the flue on the roof because of changes in building practices he would not be in a position to do so without the consent of the lessor, and the lessor would have completely unfettered discretion to refuse the consent.

However, in *Rosebery Ltd v Rocklee Ltd* [2011] EWHC 2947 (Ch), L & TR 21 (CA) [43], Mr N. Strauss QC, sitting as a deputy judge of the High Court, concluded that there is no general rule that a lease of, or including, a roof 'extends upwards to the full height of the airspace available to the **lessor**'. He felt able to distinguish *Davies v Yadegar* because the lease before him concerned only a small part of the roof of the entire building and the use of the space above it would affect tenants on other floors. *Gorst v Knight* [2018] EWHC 613 (Ch) concerned a long lease of a ground-floor flat and cellar in London. The tenant wished to dig down into the subsoil to make the cellar tall enough to use as a habitable room (which would have added considerable value to the flat). HHJ Paul Matthews (sitting as a Judge of the High Court) concluded at [37] that, at least so far as this particular type of lease was concerned:

it is not a question of presumption (or not) that the grant of the leasehold interest in land includes the subsoil. The question is rather what the construction of the grant, given what was available to be granted, and in the context, reveals the intentions of the parties to have been.

3.5   Fixtures and chattels

There are a number of situations in which it is important to determine the status of an object situated on a piece of land, the main examples of which are set out in Table 3.1. Most cases are concerned with the question of who is entitled to remove a particular object from the land, although an important group of cases concern whether different types of structure are 'land' included within the grant of a **tenancy**.

Table 3.1 The significance of the distinction between fixtures and chattels

Circumstances	Comment
I am buying or selling the land.	'Fixtures' are included in section 62 of the Law of Property Act 1925 as automatically passing on the conveyance of land, unless expressly excluded. In most cases the presumptions in section 62 are replaced by a detailed list of items included with the sale. In cases of uncertainty the courts will have to decide on whether a particular object was included in the sale (see, for example, *Berkley* v *Poulett* [1977] 1 EGLR 86 (CA)).
I have granted a mortgage over my land.	If I default on my mortgage, what objects can I remove from my house? All the fixtures automatically pass to the lender (see, for example, *Holland* v *Hodgson* (1871–72) LR 7 CP 328 (ExCh)).
My interest in the land is limited.	If, for example, I have a lease of the land rather than owning the freehold. Special rules apply to tenants wishing to remove trade fixtures, ornamental and domestic fixtures, and agricultural fixtures.
My claim is dependent upon my having an interest in land.	For example, in *Elitestone Ltd* v *Morris* [1997] 1 WLR 687 (HL), Mr Morris needed to have a lease of a dwelling-house to be protected by the Rent Act 1977.

3.5.1   A question of terminology

Traditionally, all objects fixed to the land have been referred to as '**fixtures**', while objects not attached to the land are referred to as '**chattels**'. However, this terminology can be confusing, because, as Lord Lloyd observed in the case of *Elitestone Ltd* v *Morris* [1997] 1 WLR 687 (HL), at 690–1:

▶ the legal meaning of the word 'fixture' is not limited to something fixed to a building in the usual sense (for example, it can include parts of a building, such as plate glass windows, and even structures not physically attached to the land at all, as in *Elitestone*); and

▶ 'fixture' suggests permanence, whereas many fixtures can, and are, removable by an appropriate person (the freeholder, or, in certain circumstances, a tenant at the end of their **lease**).

Lord Lloyd preferred the threefold distinction, originally set out in the major, loose-leaf text used by legal practitioners, Woodfall, *Landlord and Tenant* (likely Release 36 (1994) vol. 1, p. 13/83, para 13.13). Under this scheme, objects on land are:

(a) chattels;
(b) fixtures; or
(c) part and parcel of the land itself.

Objects in categories (b) and (c) are both part of the land, but the term 'fixture' is confined to objects that can, in certain circumstances, be detached from it. However, although this use of the word 'fixture' is closer to its everyday meaning, there is little evidence of the threefold classification being widely adopted by the courts since *Elitestone* (see Luther (2008) 28 LS 574).

3.5.2 The two-stage test

Although it is generally true to say that 'whatever is attached to the land becomes part of it', this has not proved to be a precise enough rule by which to distinguish between fixtures and chattels. Instead, it is best to start with the so-called 'two-stage test' adopted by the House of Lords in *Elitestone Ltd* v *Morris*. This test is based on questions identified by Blackburn J in *Holland* v *Hodgson* (1871–72) LR 7 CP 328 (ExCh):

(a) First, to what degree was the item annexed (attached) to the land?
(b) Second, for what object or purpose had it been annexed?

3.5.2(a) Degree of annexation

The importance of the degree of annexation depends upon the nature of the object concerned. In *Holland* v *Hodgson* looms fixed to the floor by wooden pegs or nails were held to be fixtures, and in *Elitestone*, although the chalet was not attached to the land, the test was deemed satisfied because it was heavy enough to rest on the ground by its own weight. However, in *Chelsea Yacht & Boat Co Ltd* v *Pope* [2000] 1 WLR 1941 (CA) a houseboat that was easily detachable from its moorings and the connections providing electricity was held not to be sufficiently annexed to the land.

3.5.2(b) Object (purpose) of annexation

The question of the purpose of annexation must be determined objectively on the facts. As Lord Lloyd explained in *Elitestone Ltd* v *Morris* (at 993):

> the intention of the parties is only relevant to the extent that it can be derived from the degree and object of the annexation.

In other words, the parties cannot agree between themselves that something is a chattel, if the circumstances reveal it to be a fixture (or *vice versa*). *Melluish* v *BMI (No 3) Ltd* [1996] AC 454 (HL) concerned the status of heating equipment that had been incorporated into homes and buildings erected by local authorities. In each case, the defendant company had agreed with the local authority that the equipment was only leased to the authority, and that it remained the personal property of the defendant. Lord Browne-Wilkinson said at 473B:

> The equipment in these cases was attached to the land in such a manner that, to all outward appearances, it formed part of the land and was intended so to do. Such fixtures are, in law, owned by the owner of the land. ... terms expressly or implicitly agreed between the fixer of the chattel and the owner of the land cannot affect the determination of the question whether, in law, the chattel has become a fixture and therefore in law belongs to the owner of the soil.

When considering the purpose of annexation, the court must establish what was intended at the time the object was installed, and not what is indicated by the circumstances at the date of trial. *Mew* v *Tristmire* [2012] 1 WLR 852 (CA) concerned two houseboats resting on piers sunk into the foreshore. According to Patten LJ, at [21]:

> Although it is unlikely that they could now be removed without breaking up, that is not material to the question whether they became affixed to the land. That question has to be answered by reference to their condition at the time when they were placed on to the supporting structures.

The questions that need to be asked in order to determine the purpose of annexation will also depend upon the type of object concerned. Where the item concerned is a substantial structure, its character and the nature of its construction are likely to be major factors in determining the purpose of annexation. For example, in *Elitestone Ltd* v *Morris*, the fact that the chalet could not be moved without destroying it (that is, it could only be enjoyed on the site where it was) indicated that it was part and parcel of the land. In contrast, *Botham* v *TSB Bank plc* (1997) 73 P & CR D1 (CA) (see Haley, 1998) concerned the status of items in a flat, including bathroom and kitchen equipment. Lord Justice Roch suggested that the following factors indicated, but did not confirm, that an object is a chattel:

- in instances where the item is ornamental, the attachment is simply to enable the item to be displayed;
- there is the ability to remove an item or its attachment from the building without damaging the fabric of the building; and
- the items were installed by the original builder.

Objects that form part of an overall architectural design have been considered fixtures, as was the case in *D'eyncourt* v *Gregory* (1866–67) LR 3 Eq 382 (Ch) which concerned, among other items, carved figures and sculpted marble vases in the great hall of a stately home. However, in *Re de Falbe* [1901] 1 Ch 523 (CA), the Court of Appeal decided that tapestries fixed to the wall of a drawing-room of another large house were there to be enjoyed as ornaments and that they were not, therefore, fixtures. The dispute in *Berkley* v *Poulett* [1977] 1 EGLR 86 (CA) (another stately home case) included the status of a statue on a plinth on the west lawn in front of the main house. Lord Justice Scarman concluded that the statue was a chattel because (at 89):

> The best argument for the statue being a fixture was its careful siting in the West Lawn so as to form an integral part of the architectural design of the west elevation of the house. The design point is a good one so far as it goes: it explains the siting of the plinth, which undoubtedly was a fixture. But what was put upon the plinth was very much a matter for the taste of the occupier of the house for the time being.

In the case of *London Borough of Tower Hamlets* v *London Borough of Bromley* [2015] EWHC 1954 (Ch), Norris J decided that a large bronze sculpture, known affectionately as 'Old Flo', was a chattel, because ([17]):

> It rested by its own weight upon the ground and could be (and was) removed without damage and without diminishing its inherent beauty. It might adorn or beautify a location, but it was not in any real sense dependant upon that location.

3.5.3 Tenant's fixtures

It has long been accepted that certain classes of occupiers of land are entitled to remove at least some of the objects that they affix to the land. In particular, tenants are allowed to remove items attached to the land for the purpose of their trade or business and certain classes of ornamental and domestic fixtures. However, the objects must be removed during the **tenancy** or within a reasonable time after it has come to an end, otherwise they will become the property of the **landlord**. This proved to be the case with the petrol pumps that were the subject of *Smith* v *City Petroleum Co Ltd* [1940] 1 All ER 260 (Assizes). The original tenant left the petrol pumps that he had installed on the land when his tenancy came to an end. Consequently, the pumps became the property of the landlord, and the new tenant of the land was not entitled to remove them.

In *Wessex Reserve Forces and Cadets Association* v *White* [2006] 1 P & CR 22 (QB), Mr Michael Harvey QC, sitting as a deputy judge of the High Court, had to decide on the status of six structures at the end of a tenancy. Paragraphs [25]–[60] of his judgment provide an excellent example of how to apply the principles for distinguishing between a fixture and a chattel to the facts of an individual case or problem question, as well as illustrating the difference between the tenant's fixtures (two of the structures); chattels belonging to the tenant (three of the structures); and a stone shed that formed part of the **demise**.

3.6 Bringing it together: *Elitestone Ltd* v *Morris*

Elitestone Ltd owned the **freehold** of Holtsfield and brought possession proceedings against Mr Morris and the other residents. To successfully resist these proceedings, Mr Morris needed to establish that he had an interest in the land occupied by his chalet and that this interest was binding upon the freeholder.

- One possibility was that he occupied the land as an annual licensee (see Chapter 9). This would not give him an interest in the land, and any such rights would terminate at the end of the present **licence** period.
- The alternative was that Mr Morris had an annual **lease** of Lot 6. If he could establish this, he would have an interest in the land (a lease is capable of being a legal **estate**; LPA 1925, s 1(1)(b)). However, this would not protect Mr Morris beyond the end of the present year of the lease. By definition, the leasehold estate can only be enjoyed during the term of the lease.
- If Mr Morris had an annual lease of a *dwelling-house*, he would be protected by the provisions of the Rent Act 1977, which would entitle him to a new lease at the end of each year at a fair rent. The lease of a plot of land alone would not be sufficient to fall within the Act.

▶ It is not possible to have a lease of a chattel. Consequently, Mr Morris would only have a lease of a dwelling-house if his chalet formed part of the land that he was leasing. His case turned, therefore, on whether the chalet was a chattel or a fixture.

At first instance, the Assistant Recorder held that the chalet was part of the land, but the Court of Appeal reversed his decision. The House of Lords held that a house built in such a way that it could not be removed except by destroying it could not have been (objectively) intended to be a chattel and must, therefore, have become part and parcel of the land (distinguishing this case from *Deen* v *Andrews* (1986) 52 P & CR 17 (QB), where a substantial, but moveable, greenhouse had been held to be a chattel).

Summary

3.1 Many types of law are relevant to how land is used and shared. This book is primarily concerned with the interests that can be enjoyed in land, and their rules.

3.2 Although land is just one type of property, English law, like most other legal systems, has a distinct set of rules that apply to land.

3.3 'Land' includes the airspace above the surface of the ground and that which lies beneath the ground. It also includes any incorporeal interests in the land.

3.4 Ownership of freehold land usually includes the airspace above the surface of the land necessary to allow the reasonable enjoyment of the surface of the land and any buildings on it.

3.5 Land also includes any objects that are annexed to the land (traditionally known as 'fixtures'). Whether an object is a 'fixture' is a question of fact, discernible from the degree of annexation of the object and the purpose of its annexation.

Exercises

 3.1 Complete the online quiz on the topics covered in this chapter on the companion website.

3.2 Waheeda has bought Jack's house. When she first viewed the house, she was particularly taken with the garden, which contained an ornamental pond with a statue of a mermaid set on a plinth in its centre. She was also pleased that she would be getting a large garden shed which rested on a concrete base.

When she moved in, she was horrified to discover that Jack had taken away both the statue and the shed. The fitted carpets in the house had also been removed. Waheeda checked the contract for the sale, but found that it made no mention of any of these items.

Advise Waheeda, who also tells you that she cannot understand how Jack managed to remove the shed, since he would have had to dismantle it completely to do so.

 You can find a suggested answer plan to exercise 3.2 on the companion website.

Further reading

Haley, 'The Law of Fixtures: An Unprincipled Metamorphosis?' [1998] Conv 137

Iljadica, 'Is a Sculpture "Land"?' (2016) 80 Conv 242

Luther, 'The Foundations of *Elitestone*' (2008) 28 LS 574

Part II

Title

Chapter 4

Registered title

Key concepts

- ▶ **Overriding interests** – interests that are capable of binding a person with an interest in registered land, even though they do not appear in the register of the title concerned.
- ▶ **Registered interests** – subordinate interests in land entered in the Charges Register of a registered estate.
- ▶ **Registrable estates** – interests capable of being substantively registered with their own title number.
- ▶ **Title by registration** – a system in which proof of title to estates in land is based on entries in a register controlled by the State.

4.1 Title

Ownership of land in England and Wales is based upon the concept of the legal **estate**. As is explained in Chapter 2, land owners do not actually own the physical land. Instead they own the entitlement to that land for a period of time: that is, they own one of the two legal estates of **freehold** and **leasehold**. Similarly, all other **property rights** over land are not granted over the physical land as such, but are derived from an estate in that land. The main interests are considered in Chapters 10–14. Any one estate may be subject to a large number of different interests, as Figure 4.1 illustrates.

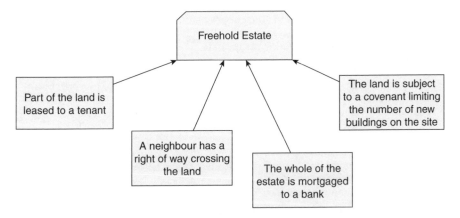

Figure 4.1 An example of interests that may affect a freehold estate in land

One of the tasks of land law is to provide criteria by which the various estates and interests in land can be recognised. These criteria form the subject matter for most of the remaining chapters in this book. However, another requirement for a successful system of land law is a set of coherent rules that enable people to determine:

- who owns any particular estate in land;
- what **property rights** that estate is subject to; and
- the order of priority of those interests.

This latter set of rules comes under the broad heading of title.

The rules relating to title will most obviously be relevant if a landowner wishes to sell their estate in land. The purchaser will wish to be sure that the seller owns what they claim to own. In the same way, a lender or a **tenant** will want to be sure that the borrower or **landlord** has good title to the land out of which the interest is being granted. Another problem that may arise is a conflict between people with different interests in the same estate. For example, the **mortgagee** in Figure 4.1 will need to know where its rights rank compared to the other interests that have been created. If the mortgagee can sell the land free from any tenant and from building restrictions (a **restrictive covenant**) it may well get a higher price than if these other interests take priority over the mortgage.

There are two separate sets of rules for establishing title in England and Wales. A significant majority of the country (both in terms of the number of titles and in terms of surface area) falls under the rules in the Land Registration Act 2002. These rules are considered in this chapter. There are, however, still some titles that have yet to be transferred to the Register. The rules relating to such titles (often referred to as **unregistered land**) are based upon proving title through a chain of **deeds**: these rules are considered, in outline, in Chapter 5.

Disputes and priorities

There are several types of disputes that can arise out of the ownership of land and interests in land. The rules for dealing with disputes between landlords and tenants are considered in Chapter 8, and the resolution of disagreements between co-owners of land are explored in Chapter 14. The present chapter and the chapter that follows are concerned with the rules that are used for determining disputes about the relative priority of different interests and estates in land.

In many cases, such disputes will arise when the estate changes hands and there is a conflict between the new owner of the land and a person who owns another, pre-existing interest in the land, such as an **easement**. However, not all disputes are triggered by a sale; for example, they can also arise because of a breakdown in the relationship between neighbours or when a **mortgagee** enforces its security. In fact, relatively few practising land lawyers are concerned with solving disputes that have actually arisen. In this branch of law, practitioners are usually more concerned with ensuring that no disputes arise, or, if they do arise, that the outcome is relatively straightforward. For example, one of the tasks of lawyers handling the purchase of land is to identify any potential problems and resolve them prior to the transfer of the land to the new owner.

Resolving a dispute about conflicting interests in land involves deciding:

- what interests actually exist in the land; and
- the order of *priority* of any such interests.

Whether or not a particular right is an interest in land will depend upon whether it meets the criteria established by law or equity for the type of property right being claimed. Once the proprietary nature of the right is established, the next question to ask is: *is the title registered or unregistered?* The relevant rules can then be applied.

4.2   Introducing registered title

4.2.1   Registered title in England and Wales

The idea of a register of land ownership was promoted in the nineteenth century by Robert Torrens, who worked in a **deeds** registry in South Australia. He was dismayed by the complexity of traditional **unregistered** conveyancing based on proving **title** by reference to a number of private documents (the title deeds) usually in the possession of the landowner or a **mortgagee**. Not only might it be necessary to find and refer to many such deeds each time there was any dealing with the land, but they could easily be lost or misplaced. Torrens devised a system in which the titles to individual **estates** in land are recorded and ownership depends not upon deeds but upon the entries in the centrally held register. His scheme, which worked efficiently in Australia, gradually spread through the common law world, although title registration has yet to be widely accepted in the United States.

The earliest attempts to introduce a system of voluntary land registration in England can be found in the Land Registry Act 1862 and the Land Transfer Act 1875, although the first real success was achieved when the Land Transfer Act 1897 made registration compulsory within the County of London. A more effective scheme (although not the Torrens system) was introduced by the LRA 1925. The plan was for the system of registration to be gradually extended across England and Wales, district by district. This took somewhat longer than originally anticipated, with all districts of England and Wales eventually becoming areas of compulsory land registration in 1990. Originally title had to be registered if the **freehold** estate or a **lease** for a term exceeding 21 years was transferred for value and upon first creation of such a lease. However, the triggers for first registration of title have been extended on a number of occasions (see Section 4.7 for the present list). Landowners could also register their title voluntarily, without the need for a triggering event.

Although the Land Registry and the courts worked hard to make the 1925 scheme work, the LRA 1925 had serious shortcomings. A number of amendments to the 1925 Act were introduced. By the end of the twentieth century the scheme comprised the Land Registration Acts 1925–1997, supplemented by the Land Registration Rules. However, by the 1990s it was clear that wholesale revision was needed, especially if there was to be any prospect of moving from a paper-based system to an electronic system of conveyancing. *Land Registration for the Twenty-First Century* (Law Com No 254), published by the Law Commission and Land Registry together in 1998, contained a summary and critique of the existing law along with initial proposals for its radical reform. A draft Bill was published in Law Com No 271 in 2001, which was enacted as the Land Registration Act 2002. Most of the LRA 2002 came into force on 13th October 2003, replacing the LRA 1925. The new scheme introduced by the 2002 Act is supported by the regulatory framework contained in the Land Registration Rules 2003.

Although the 2002 Act addressed many of the shortcomings inherent in the 1925 scheme, it soon became clear that the new scheme was not problem free. Additionally, as the Law Commission noted in its 2016 Consultation Paper (Law Com CP No 227, 2016) at para 1.6:

> The landscape within which land registration operates has changed considerably since the LRA 2002 came into force. We have seen an increase in incidents of registered title fraud, the legal consequences of which have proved difficult to resolve, while technology has

not developed in the way that was predicted at the time of the legislation. We have also witnessed the global economic crisis and a domestic recession, which impacted significantly on the property market.

The Law Commission's report *Updating the Land Registration Act 2002* (Law Com No 380), published in June 2018, contains recommendations designed to improve the operation of the scheme contained in the 2002 Act.

One of the most heralded benefits of the LRA 2002 was that it would enable the progressive introduction of electronic conveyancing, leading to the holy grail of simultaneous completion and registration of a transfer of land. Progress was much slower than anticipated, and in 2011 the Land Registry announced that it had no immediate plans to extend electronic completion beyond creating and discharging mortgages. At the beginning of 2018, the Land Registration Rules 2003 were amended to allow for entirely electronic documents, including the use of electronic signatures, but the actual implementation of paper-free registration still lies in the future. More significantly, in Chapter 20 of Law Com No 380, the Commission has recognised as a 'strait-jacket' the requirement (LRA 2002, s 93) for simultaneous electronic completion and registration before the introduction of compulsory electronic conveyancing and recommends that the goal of compulsory electronic conveyancing be divorced from the quest for simultaneity.

4.2.2   The underlying principles of registered title

Theodore Ruoff, who was Chief Land Registrar from 1963 until 1975, is credited with identifying three key elements of title registration.

- *The mirror principle*: The Register should *mirror* the actual structure of title and third-party rights in the land. It should be possible to discover who owns the land and who else has an interest in it simply by reading the Register. The uncertainties of deeds-based conveyancing, and especially the doctrine of **notice** (see Section 5.2.2), should have no place in a system of registered title.
- *The curtain principle*: There should be no need to go behind the statement or certificate of title provided by the Land Registry; a *curtain* should be drawn between the purchaser of the legal title and anything that has occurred off the register. In particular, a purchaser should not have to be concerned about any **trusts** affecting the land.
- *The insurance (or guarantee) principle*: To ensure that everyone has confidence in the system, the State must *guarantee* the accuracy of the titles on the Register and indemnify anyone who suffers loss as a result of any mistake on it.

When applied strictly, the result of these three principles is that a title that has been registered will be **indefeasible**; that is, incapable of being defeated and immune from all claims that are not referred to in the Register. The degree to which titles registered under the LRA 2002 are (and should be) indefeasible is, in 2018 at least, one of the live land law issues so far as both academics and judges are concerned (see Sections 4.9 and 4.10).

Although the three principles provide a useful benchmark against which the scheme of the LRA 2002 can be assessed, it should be remembered that there is no objective standard for land registration: the 2002 Act, like any other scheme, must be judged against the expectations of the society which it serves. No system of land registration has been able to achieve completely the three principles in practice. Any system that did so would uncritically favour certainty over justice, whatever the circumstances and fairness of a particular case. The appropriate question is not whether the 2002 Act completely embodies the three principles of land registration, but whether it properly balances the need for certainty, transparency and security against the need for justice to be done.

Solving problems of priority with the LRA 2002
When approaching a question that concerns the priority of interests in a registered title, the main things to remember are:

▶ A registered proprietor (the owner of the estate) and a person acquiring an estate or interest from a registered proprietor (except as a gift) are usually bound only by:
  ▶ interests that appear in the Register; and
  ▶ interests that are capable of **overriding** the Register.
▶ The relevant provisions in the LRA 2002 (and the list of interests capable of overriding the Register) depend upon whether you are advising the first registered proprietor immediately after the first registration of the title or whether there have been any subsequent dealings with the land.

The detailed rules are considered in the sections that follow. A detailed guide to applying the relevant rules following the **disposition** of an already registered title can be found in Figure 4.3.

4.3 The Register

The Register, the mirror of the **title** to the land, is held as a computerised record at one of a number of District Land Registries. It is now an open record and, for a small fee, anyone can easily get a copy of an individual Register (the quickest way to do this is electronically, from the Land Registry website). Each individual Register is divided into three sections: the *Property Register*, the *Proprietorship Register* and the *Charges Register*. These three *registers* combine to make one **Register of Title**. It is important to realise that the *Charges Register* referred to here is not the same as the Land Charges Register (see Section 5.4). The Land Charges Register has *no connection* with registered title.

4.3.1 The Property Register

This part of the Register describes:

▶ the title to the land (**freehold** or **leasehold**); and
▶ any benefits attached to it (such as the benefit of an **easement**).

The property is identified by its address and by reference to a plan on which the plot of land is outlined in red. Note, however, that the Register is a register of title, not a 'plot-based' register. One plot of land may have several registered titles, such as the **freehold** and one or more long **leases**. Each registrable **estate** in the land has its own title number and entry in the Register.

4.3.2　The Proprietorship Register

The Proprietorship Register states:

- the class (or status) of the title under the registration system (the various classes of title are considered at Section 4.4.1);
- the name and address of the owner, who is called 'the registered proprietor'; and
- any **restrictions** which limit the power of the registered proprietor to deal with the land, due, for example, to a **trust** or personal **covenant** (see Section 4.4.2).

The Proprietorship Register will usually also include details of the last price paid for the title concerned.

4.3.3　The Charges Register

This part of the Register contains details of burdens on the land such as **mortgages** and **restrictive covenants** (see Section 4.5.1).

4.4　Registrable estates

The **Title Register** is an **estate**-based register. This means that all qualifying estates are allocated a separate Register of Title, with a unique title number. The owner of a registrable estate may apply for registration at any time (LRA 2002, s 3), but is obliged to do so if any of the events listed in section 4 occur (see Section 4.7).

The interests in land that can be registered in their own right are listed in section 3 of the LRA 2002. The most important are:

- all **freehold** estates in land, and
- **leasehold** estates in land for a term of which more than seven years are unexpired (s 3(3)) or where the right to possession by the **tenant** is discontinuous (s 3(4)).

Section 118 of the LRA 2002 makes provision for the period of seven years to be reduced in the future. In 2018, the Law Commission concluded that it would be inappropriate to reduce the seven-year requirement for the time being (see *Updating the Land Registration Act 2002* (Law Com No 380, 2018), paras 3.161–3, 3.164).

4.4.1　Classes of title

In **unregistered land**, some titles, such as a title obtained by **adverse possession**, are not as secure as others. When the owner of such a title applies for it to be registered, it is important that the Register reflects the actual state of the title to the land. This is done by placing the title in one of four possible classes (ss 9(1) and 10(1) of the LRA 2002) which are explained in Table 4.1. The vast majority of titles will be registered with **absolute title**. Section 62 of the LRA 2002 makes provision for weaker titles to be upgraded where this becomes possible.

Table 4.1 The classes of title available under sections 10 and 11 of the LRA 2002

Absolute title	Absolute freehold or leasehold title is the strongest class of title available. The registered proprietor with absolute title has a better right than anyone else to the land (although there are still circumstances where the title might be open to alteration by the courts or the Registrar; see Section 4.9). A registered proprietor with title absolute is subject only to: ▶ third-party interests protected on the Register; ▶ interests which have overriding status (Section 4.6); ▶ the terms of any trust upon which they hold the title; and ▶ the covenants in the lease if the title is leasehold.
Good leasehold title	Good leasehold title is given to a leasehold estate when the Registrar is unable to guarantee that the freeholder had the right to grant the lease because the freehold has not yet been registered.
Possessory title	Possessory titles are granted by the Registrar when the alleged owner's title is based only on possession, not on title deeds. The Registrar guarantees the title only as far as dealings after first registration are concerned. No promises are made concerning the right of the first registered proprietor to the land. Such titles are very rare.
Qualified title	Qualified titles are granted only if the Registrar has some specific reservation about the title. They are almost unheard of.

4.4.2 Restrictions

The general rule is that a registered proprietor may deal with the land in any way that is permitted by law. However, it is possible to restrict an owner's power of **disposition** by entering a restriction in the Proprietorship Register of the relevant title (LRA 2002, ss 40–7). Once entered, a restriction does not directly protect an interest in the land, but prevents the registered proprietor dealing with the title unless the conditions set out in the restriction are met (LRA 2002, s 40). The most commonly encountered restriction is that used to protect beneficiaries under a **trust** by requiring payment to two **trustees** before a sale or other disposition will be registered (Land Registration Rules 2003, r 94). This restriction, combined with the rule that **beneficial interests** are not referred to on the Register, ensures that the 'curtain' of the Register is drawn across such beneficial entitlements (see Section 4.2.2). Restrictions can also be used to protect personal obligations, and to ensure that the terms of a lease or mortgage are complied with. The use of restrictions to protect personal obligations has increased significantly since the LRA 2002 came into force, prompting attention from the Law Commission at paras 10.13–10.85 of *Updating the Land Registration Act 2002* (Law Com No 380, 2018), albeit with no major proposals for reform. A long list of standard form restrictions can be found in Schedule 4 of the Land Registration Rules 2003.

4.5 Interests in registered land

The normal range of legal and **equitable** interests exist in registered land. However, the LRA 2002 superimposes a new set of categories onto the traditional structure. These are summarised in Table 4.2.

Table 4.2   A classification of interests in registered estates

Interests which are completed by registration (see Section 4.5.2)	The interests listed in section 27 of the LRA 2002 can only operate at law if they are completed by being entered on the Register. The most important of these are expressly created legal easements (s 27(2)(d)) and legal charges (s 27(2)(f)). At present, failure to register such interests means that they are unprotected equitable interests.
Other interests which are subject to an entry on the Register (see Section 4.5.1)	Almost all property interests in land can be protected by entering them on the Register (the list of exceptions is in LRA 2002, s 33). Unless an interest is capable of overriding the Register, it will normally only be binding upon a transferee for value of the registered estate if it is noted on the Register (LRA 2002, s 29).
Interests that cannot be protected by an entry on the Register	The only interests that cannot be protected by registration are those listed in section 33 of the LRA 2002. The most important of the interests that cannot be protected by registration are: ▶ trusts of land; ▶ leases for a term of three years or less; and ▶ covenants made between a lessor and a lessee.
Interests capable of overriding registration (see Section 4.6)	These interests are binding on everyone who gains a later interest in the land even if they are not protected by entry on the Register. The rules for determining whether a particular category of interest is capable of overriding the first registered proprietor (LRA 2002, Sch 1) differ from the rules that apply after any subsequent dealing with the registered title (LRA 2002, Sch 3).

4.5.1   Protection by entering a notice

A notice is an entry in the Charges Register recording the burden of an interest that affects the land, such as a registered **charge (mortgage)**, **easement** or **restrictive covenant** (LRA 2002, s 32). The only interests in land that cannot be protected by notice are those listed in section 33 of the LRA 2002.

The most important are:

▶ **trusts** of land;
▶ **leasehold estates** for a term of three years or less (unless they are required to be registered by another section of the LRA 2002); and
▶ restrictive covenants between a **lessor** and **lessee** that relate to the premises demised by the lease.

Interests that are not (or cannot) be protected by registration will only be binding on a registered proprietor if they fall within one of the categories of interests capable of overriding the Register (see Section 4.6). The fact that a notice of an interest has been entered on the Register does not necessarily mean that the interest itself is valid (LRA 2002, s 32(3)); this will depend upon the rules relating to that type of interest.

Under the 2002 regime, notices can be entered with the agreement of the registered proprietor or unilaterally by the person claiming the interest to be protected (LRA 2002, s 34(2)). The Land Registrar must inform the registered proprietor of the relevant **estate** of any unilateral notices registered against it (LRA 2002, s 35(1)). The registered proprietor may apply to have a unilateral notice cancelled. If the person who registered the notice does not agree to this, the matter is determined by the Registrar, with an appeal (since 1st July 2013) to the Land Registration division of the Property Chamber, First-tier Tribunal.

In the 1925 scheme, the interests that needed to be protected by an entry on the Register were known collectively as 'minor interests'. This term is not found in the LRA 2002, but will still be encountered in some of the older cases and articles.

4.5.2   Registrable dispositions

Section 27 of the LRA 2002 contains a list of six transactions concerning registered titles (the term used in the Act is 'dispositions') that must usually be completed by the relevant type of entry on the Register in order to take effect at law. The only exceptions are in the circumstances set out in section 27(5), (5A), and (7). In other words, these legal interests or dispositions cannot occur without them being entered on the Register. Failure to complete these dispositions by registering them means that they will be, at best, **equitable** interests, and, therefore, binding on the registered proprietor only if they are protected by a notice, or fall within one of the categories of interest capable of overriding the Register (see Section 4.6). (The only formality usually required for comparable dispositions of an **unregistered title** is a **deed,** unless, of course, the transaction triggered first registration under section 4 of the LRA 2002.)

One of the consequences of section 27 is that certain interests can now only exist as legal interests if entered on the Register (in addition to complying with any other formalities required, such as the need for a deed). The main examples are:

- the creation of a legal **easement** by express grant or reservation (s 27(2)(d)); but not one created by virtue of section 62 of the LPA 1925 (LRA 2002, s 27(7); see Section 10.7.5); and
- the creation of a legal **mortgage** (s 27(2)(f)).

The need to register **legal charges** (that is, mortgages) is uncontroversial, but the requirement to register expressly created legal easements is not without its problems. First, this was a major departure from the scheme in the LRA 1925; however, rather than impose a retrospective obligation to register all the easements that already existed when the 2002 Act came into force on 13th October 2003, their validity is preserved by the transitional provisions in paragraph 9 of Schedule 12 of the LRA. A second problem is that section 27 contains no exemption for easements granted as part of a short-lease of registered land. A lease not exceeding seven years does not need to be protected by registration, and a lease not exceeding three years cannot be protected by registration (paragraph 1 of Schedule 3 and section 33 of the LRA 2002). However, the effect of section 27(2)(d) is that any easements granted over registered land by such a lease must be completed by entering a **notice** on the Register. The Law Commission has recommended that where a lease is not a registrable disposition there should be no need to register any easements that it contains for them to operate at law (*Updating the Land Registration Act 2002* (Law Com No 380, 2018), paras 6.44, 6.77).

Students may come across references to 'cautions' and 'inhibitions' when reading cases and articles referring to the 1925 Act. These are two forms of entry on the Register previously available under the LRA 1925 which did not survive as separate entities in the terminology of the 2002 Act, leading to the, now somewhat old, law-yers' joke that, 'With the 2002 Act, the Land Registry threw *cautions* to the wind and abandoned its *inhibitions*.'

4.6   Interests capable of overriding the Register

One of the main principles of a system of **title** registration is that its register should be an accurate reflection of the title itself. From this perspective, in an ideal system the buyer of a registered title would not be bound by any rights that did not appear on the Register. However, as has already been noted at Section 4.2.2, such a system is unlikely to be either completely practicable or completely just. Justice requires certain interests to be capable of binding the title, even if not registered. The tradi-tional explanation given for the existence of interests that can 'override' the Register is that people who have the benefit of the particular rights given this status by the LRA 2002 cannot reasonably be expected to protect their interest through registration. By their very nature, some interests do not lend themselves to protection by entry on the Register, including, for example, **easements** created through **prescription** or by implication or the rights of people in actual occupation of the land. The 1925 scheme also gave overriding status to several other types of interest that could be expected to be reasonably apparent to any purchaser, including expressly created legal easements and legal **leases** for 21 years or less. This helped to reduce the amount of information held at the Land Registry to practicable proportions in a pre-computer age. By the end of the twentieth century, the Law Commission and the Land Registry were agreed that the list of potential overriding interests should be rationalised (Law Com No 271, 2001, para 2.25), and the 2002 Act reduced the number and scope of these inter-ests. However, the fact remains that any interests that do not need to appear on the Register are potentially a considerable crack in the 'mirror' of title (see Section 4.2.2).

The LRA 2002 contains two lists of interests capable of overriding the Register. The first list, in Schedule 1, applies to the first registered proprietor immediately after first registration of the title (ss 11(4) and 12(4)); the list in Schedule 3 applies upon any subsequent dealing with the registered title for valuable considera-tion (ss 29 and 30)). The key provisions of the two Schedules are summarised in Table 4.3.

The most important overriding interests recognised in the 2002 Act are:

- short-term leases;
- the rights of people in actual occupation; and
- legal easements and **profits**.

In determining whether a particular interest is, in fact, overriding, all the require-ments of the relevant paragraph of the relevant schedule must be applied in turn. Only if the interest meets *all* of the relevant requirements set out in the LRA 2002 will it be binding over the registered title. At first sight, the rules in Schedule 1 seem to encompass a much wider range of interests than those in Schedule 3, where a num-ber of significant provisos apply (compare, in particular, the respective paragraphs 2 and 3). However, in practice, the difference is less significant than it might appear. This is because the first registered proprietor can only be bound by interests that

Table 4.3 The main unregistered interests capable of overriding the register

	First registration (Schedule 1)	Disposition of registered land (Schedule 3)
Para 1	*Legal leases for a term not exceeding seven years, except for* a lease falling within the categories set out in LRA 2002, s 4(1)(d–f). Note that: ▶ leases falling within the categories set out in LRA 2002, s 4(1)(d–f) are not capable of overriding and must be protected by registration (the most important example is a reversionary lease taking effect more than three months after the date of the grant); and ▶ legal leases with a term of between three and seven years may be protected by entering a notice (see LRA 2002, s 33(b)).	*Legal leases for a term not exceeding seven years, except for:* ▶ a lease falling within the categories set out in LRA 2002, s 4(1)(d–f); and ▶ a lease which is a registrable disposition for some other reason (see LRA 2002, s 27(2)(b)).
Para 2	*Interests of persons in actual occupation of the land concerned*	*Interests of persons in actual occupation of the land concerned, unless:* ▶ the occupier did not disclose their right when asked about it, when they could reasonably have been expected to do so (para 2(b)); or ▶ the occupation was not obvious on a reasonably careful inspection of the land, and the purchaser did not have actual knowledge of the interest (para 2(c)); or ▶ the interest being claimed is a reversionary leasehold estate which takes effect in possession after three months from the date of the grant and which had not taken effect at the date of the disposition (para 2(d)).
Para 3	*Legal easements and profits à prendre*	*Legal easements or profits à prendre, unless:* ▶ the new proprietor did not actually know about it (para 3(1)(a)); and ▶ its existence was not apparent on a reasonably careful inspection of the land (para 3(1)(b)). However, even if these conditions are not satisfied, an informally created easement or profit can still override the disposition if the person entitled to it can prove that it had been exercised in the year before the disposition was made (para 3(2)).
	Note that only *legal* easements are now capable of overriding the Register. The LRA 2002 effectively reversed the controversial case of *Celsteel Ltd v Alton House Holdings Ltd (No 1)* [1986] 1 WLR 512 (CA), which held that equitable easements were overriding interests within the 1925 scheme.	

were valid under the rules of unregistered conveyancing (see Chapter 5). For example, whether the interests of persons in occupation survive the transfer (that is, are capable of binding the newly registered title) will depend upon whether the interests were properly protected at the time of the transfer by registration as a **Land Charge** (see Section 5.4.5) or under the doctrine of **notice** (see Section 5.2.2).

Many (although not all) interests capable of overriding the Register can be protected by entering a **notice** on the Register (a lease with a term of between three and seven years, for example). The Land Registration Rules 2003 impose a duty on anyone applying for registration to disclose any unregistered interests which they are aware of that override registered dispositions (rules 28 and 57). However, failure to disclose such an interest does not appear to prevent it from continuing to override the Register. Once an interest capable of overriding has been entered on the Register, it will cease to be overriding, even if the notice is subsequently deleted from the Charges Register (LRA 2002, s 29(3)).

It is common to refer to the interest considered in this section as 'overriding interests'. Although this term does not appear as such in the LRA 2002, its convenience means that it has outlasted the 1925 Act from whence it came into general use.

4.6.1 Short leases

Leases granted for more than seven years are substantively registrable (see Section 4.4). Most legal leases granted for seven years or less override on first and subsequent registration, and a purchaser will be bound by them. However, there are certain special types of lease of seven years or less that do not have overriding status and must, therefore, be substantively registered (s 4(1)(d–f)). The most important example is a **reversionary lease** taking effect more than three months after the date of the grant.

4.6.2 The interests of occupiers

The LRA 2002 recognises the need to protect the third-party interests of people who are in actual occupation of land who have not protected their rights in the land by registration. This may occur because the right arose informally or because the person with the right thought that the mere fact of their occupation was enough protection against a purchaser (Law Com No 254, 2001, para 5.61). The provisions in the LRA 2002 replace section 70(1)(g) of the LRA 1925, which was, perhaps, the most contentious (and certainly the most litigated) of the overriding interests under the 1925 Act. Much of the case law concerning section 70(1)(g) remains relevant. However, care must be taken when referring to this earlier case law as the provisions of the 2002 Act modify the old law in several important respects. For this reason, a brief comparison of the provisions is set out in Table 4.4.

To override the Register, Schedules 1 and 3 provide that the right claimed must be:

- an interest other than a **settlement** under the Settled Land Act 1925 (see Section 14.1);
- belonging to a person in actual occupation; and
- in the case of a disposition of a registered title, an interest that does not fall within paragraph 2 (b), (c), or (d) of Schedule 3.

Where these requirements are met, Schedule 1, paragraph 2 and Schedule 3, paragraph 2 provide that the interest will be binding only upon the part of the registered title that the person is actually occupying. This reverses the decision in *Ferrishurst* v *Wallcite* [1999] Ch 355 (CA), under the 1925 scheme.

Table 4.4 Comparison of Land Registration Act 1925, s 70(1)(g) with Land Registration Act 2002, Sch 1, para 2 and Sch 3, para 2

	LRA 1925	LRA 2002	
	s 70(1)(g)	Sch 1, para 2	Sch 3, para 2
Who is protected?	A person: (i) in actual occupation; or (ii) in receipt of rents and profits.	Only a person in actual occupation.	
What land is affected?	All land over which the interest is claimed.	Only the land actually occupied by the claimant.	
Main exceptions	Enquiry was made of the person in occupation, and the rights were not disclosed.	An interest under a settlement under the SLA 1925 (see below). Note, however, that the right being claimed must survive the disposition that triggered first registration if it is to be an interest in the land, which will depend upon the rules relating to unregistered land.	(i) An interest under a settlement under the SLA 1925 (see below). (ii) If enquiry was made of the person in occupation, and they failed to disclose the right when they could reasonably have been expected to disclose it. (iii) The purchaser did not actually know about the interest, and the interest would not have been obvious on a reasonably careful inspection of the land.
		Settlements under the SLA 1925 (see Section 14.1) are now rare. Settled land is not considered in detail in this book.	

4.6.2(a) Interest

An interest will be an interest for the purposes of the two paragraphs 2 if it is 'an adverse right affecting the title to the estate or charge' concerned (per Lord Collins JSC, *Southern Pacific Mortgages Ltd* v *Scott* [2015] AC 385 (SC), [59]). That is to say, the interest must be a proprietary interest in the land. Occupation alone cannot attach what is otherwise a purely **personal right** or obligation to the land. Since most **licences** to occupy land are **personal rights** (see Chapter 9), they will not fall within the scope of paragraph 2 unless they affect the conscience of the buyer in such a way as to give rise to a **constructive trust** or an **estoppel**. This proved not to be the case in *Southern Pacific Mortgages Ltd* v *Scott*.

Southern Pacific Mortgages Ltd **v** *Scott* **[2015] AC 385 (SC)**
Mrs Scott was just one of nearly a hundred people threatened with losing their homes as the result of the activities of a nebulous entity called North East Property Buyers (NEPB) in the north of England. After falling into financial difficulties in 2005, Mrs Scott sold her home to a Ms Wilkinson, a nominee of NEPB, in return for a cash sum (less than the market value, although this was not apparent on the face of the transfer) and a

promise that Mrs Scott could continue to live in the house for as long as she wished. This is just one form of what are commonly referred to as 'equity release schemes' designed to help people access the capital value locked up in their homes. Unfortunately for Mrs Scott, this particular scheme was a scam. NEPB financed each individual purchase with an acquisition mortgage which was registered at the same time as the transfer of the freehold title. None of the lenders was aware of the promises made to allow the sellers to continue to occupy their homes, and the terms of the mortgages prohibited the properties concerned being occupied in this way. The scam came to light when NEPB defaulted on the mortgages and the various lenders began to try to realise their security against Mrs Scott and the other sellers. Neither Mrs Scott nor Southern Pacific were directly responsible for the fraud: both had been duped by NEPB. The question of who would bear the cost of the fraud fell to be determined within the framework of paragraph 2 of Schedule 3 of the LRA 2002.

To succeed in keeping her home, Mrs Scott needed to demonstrate that:

- she had an interest in the registered title concerned; and
- it was valid and binding at the date of the creation of the lender's charge (that is, the date of the sale to the nominee purchaser).

All that Mrs Scott could rely upon was the assurance given to her that she would be able to stay in the house for as long as she wished, which predated the transfer of the legal estate to Ms Wilkinson. The Supreme Court held that a purchaser of property could not grant 'equitable rights of a proprietary character' prior to acquisition of the legal estate. Consequently, any rights that Mrs Scott had against Ms Wilkinson were purely personal rights which could not override the registered charge in favour of Southern Pacific.

In his casenote, at (2015) 79 Conv 245, Nicholas Hopkins suggests that the Supreme Court reached the correct result, but for the wrong reasons. According to Hopkins, the fundamental problem with Mrs Scott's case is not that a purchaser cannot grant equitable rights prior to completion as such, but that the LRA 2002 requires those rights to be granted over a registered estate if they are to fall within paragraph 2. At the relevant time, Ms Wilkinson had no such estate. Hopkins argues that that outcome is inevitable if one treats the rules in the LRA 2002 as substantive land law. Baroness Hale, in contrast, regards the provisions of the LRA 2002 as 'merely conveyancing machinery' (at [96] of her judgment). The tension between these two approaches to the LRA 2002 is considered further in Section 4.10.

Examples of interests that would meet this criterion include:

- possessory rights arising out of a period of **adverse possession**;
- an **estate contract**;
- a **beneficial interest** under a **trust** of land, provided that it has not been overreached (*Williams & Glyn's Bank Ltd* v *Boland* [1981] AC 487 (HL) and *City of London Building Society* v *Flegg* [1988] AC 54 (HL), discussed in detail in this section); and
- a right arising out of an **estoppel** (LRA 2002, s 116).

However, some rights that are arguably proprietary are expressly excluded by statute, including rights of occupation under the Family Law Act 1996, rights under the Access to Neighbouring Land Act 1992 and an original **tenant's** right to an **overriding lease** under the Landlord and Tenant (Covenants) Act 1995.

The need for an interest in the registered estate means that a beneficial interest that has been overreached by a sale or **mortgage** (see Section 14.6.1) cannot override the Register by virtue of paragraph 2 of Schedule 1 or 3. In *City of London Building Society* v *Flegg* Mr and Mrs Flegg had unprotected beneficial interests under a **trust** in their home, named 'Bleak House', which they shared with the two registered proprietors, their daughter and son-in-law, Mr and Mrs Maxwell-Brown. Both registered proprietors had been party to a mortgage in favour of the defendant. Despite the fact that the Fleggs were in actual occupation, and no enquiry had been made of them, the building society was able to defeat their interests. Under the doctrine of **overreaching**, payment of the proceeds of sale or of a mortgage to two or more **trustees** automatically transfers the rights of the beneficiaries from the land to the money paid for it. The House of Lords held that, from the moment that the lender overreached the beneficial interests by paying the mortgage money to two trustees, the beneficiaries no longer had any interest in the land but merely a right to share in the proceeds of the mortgage advance. Lord Templeman said at [73–4]:

> The right of the [beneficiaries] to be and remain in actual occupation of Bleak House ceased when [their] interests were overreached by the legal charge ... There must be a combination of an interest which justifies continuing occupation plus actual occupation to constitute an overriding interest. Actual occupation is not an interest in itself.

In contrast, if the mortgage advance is paid to a single registered proprietor (as in *Williams & Glyn's Bank Ltd* v *Boland*), the **beneficiary** is safe for as long as they remain in actual occupation, subject to the provisos in paragraph 2 of Schedule 3 of the 2002 Act.

City of London Building Society v *Flegg* was applied in *State Bank of India* v *Sood* [1997] Ch 276 (CA), where the interests of the five beneficiaries were overreached on execution of the charge to the bank, even though no capital money was payable (the mortgage was granted to secure an existing debt). In the more recent case of *Mortgage Express* v *Lambert* [2017] Ch 93 (CA), the Court of Appeal held that rights arising out of an equity, which is an interest in this context because of section 116 of the LRA 2002, could also be overreached, at least if there is the potential to trace the interest into the proceeds of sale.

4.6.2(b) Actual occupation

According to Lloyd LJ, *Chaudhary* v *Yavuz* [2013] Ch 249 (CA) (at [32]):

> Occupation must be, or be referable to, personal physical activity by some one or more individuals.

Since *Williams & Glyn's Bank Ltd* v *Boland* [1981] AC 487 (HL), whether a person is 'in actual occupation' is a question of fact, not of law. In the words of Lord Wilberforce (at 505), 'physical presence, not some entitlement in law' is what is required. One of the arguments used by the bank in that case was that Mrs Boland could not occupy the house in her own right because, despite her beneficial interest, her occupation was 'nothing but a shadow of her husband's'. Lord Wilberforce declared this doctrine, based on the perceived unity of husband and wife, obsolete. What constitutes 'actual occupation' in any given case will depend on the nature of the land concerned.

In *Link Lending Ltd* v *Bustard* [2010] EWCA Civ 424, Mummery LJ cited, with approval, the judgment of Lewison J in *Thompson* v *Foy* [2010] 1 P & CR 16 (Ch), which contains the following five-point summary of the principles of 'actual occupation'.

Actual occupation
Thompson v *Foy* [2010] 1 P & CR 16 (Ch) (at [127]):

(i)   The words 'actual occupation' are ordinary words of plain English and should be interpreted as such. The word 'actual' emphasises that physical presence is required: *Williams & Glyn's Bank* v *Boland* [1981] AC 487 per Lord Wilberforce at 504;

(ii)   It does not necessarily involve the personal presence of the person claiming to occupy. A caretaker or the representative of a company can occupy on behalf of their employer: *Abbey National BS* v *Cann* [1991] 1 AC 56 per Lord Oliver at 93;

(iii)   However, actual occupation by a licensee (who is not a representative occupier) does not count as actual occupation by the licensor: *Strand Securities Ltd* v *Caswell* [1965] Ch 958 per Lord Denning MR at 981;

(iv)   The mere presence of some of the claimant's furniture will not usually count as actual occupation: *Strand Securities Ltd* v *Caswell* [1965] Ch 958 per Russell LJ at 984;

(v)   If the person said to be in actual occupation at any particular time is not physically present on the land at that time, it will usually be necessary to show that their occupation was manifested and accompanied by a continuing intention to occupy: compare *Hoggett* v *Hoggett* (1980) 39 P & CR 121, per Sir David Cairns at 127.

Although this summary is helpful, it must be used with care. As Mummery LJ explained during his judgment in *Link Lending Ltd* v *Bustard* (at [27]):

> The trend of the cases shows that the courts are reluctant to lay down, or even suggest, a single legal test for determining whether a person is in actual occupation. The decisions on statutory construction identify the factors that have to be weighed by the judge on this issue. The degree of permanence and continuity of presence of the person concerned, the intentions and wishes of that person, the length of absence from the property and the reason for it and the nature of the property and personal circumstances of the person are among the relevant factors.

Lord Oliver had expressed similar caution in the earlier case of *Abbey National Building Society* v *Cann* [1991] 1 AC 56 (HL), at 93 when he said that:

> 'occupation' is a concept which may have different connotations according to the nature and purpose of the property which is claimed to be occupied. It does not necessarily, I think, involve the personal presence of the person claiming to occupy. A caretaker or the representative of a company can occupy, I should have thought, on behalf of his employer. On the other hand, it does, in my judgment, involve some degree of permanence and continuity which would rule out mere fleeting presence. A prospective tenant or purchaser who is allowed, as a matter of indulgence, to go into property in order to plan decorations or measure for furnishings would not, in ordinary parlance, be said to be occupying it, even though he might be there for hours at a time.

4.6.2(b)(i) Physical presence   In *Chaudhary* v *Yavuz* [2013] Ch 249 (CA), the court held that the passage to and fro of tenants and their visitors on a shared staircase did not amount to occupation for the purposes of paragraph 2 of Schedule 3. It seems to be common sense, however, that a person can be in actual occupation of land without having to be physically present on it without any interruption. For example, most people leave their homes for at least a few minutes, and in most cases several hours, each day for work or leisure. Many will go on holiday for several days, even weeks each year. At what point does such absence cease to be 'actual occupation'?

As Robert Walker J explained in the unreported case of *Stockholm Finance Ltd* v *Garden Holdings Inc* [1995] LTL (26 October 1995):

> Whether a person's intermittent presence at a house which is fully furnished, and ready for almost immediate use, should be seen as continuous occupation … is a matter of perception which defies deep analysis. Not only the length of any absence, but also the reason for it, may be material … But there must come a point at which a person's absence from his house is so prolonged that the notion of his continuing to be in actual occupation of it becomes insupportable …

He went on to hold that the point had certainly been passed on the facts before him, where the alleged occupant, a Saudi princess, had been living with her mother in Saudi Arabia for over a year.

The case of *Chhokar* v *Chhokar* [1984] FLR 313 (CA) concerned a wife with a **beneficial interest** in a house registered in the sole name of her husband. Unbeknown to Mrs Chhokar, her husband sold their matrimonial home to Mr Parmar, formal completion of the sale taking place while Mrs Chhokar was absent from the house, in hospital having a baby. She eventually managed to gain access to the house, where, ultimately, a very contrite Mr Chhokar joined her. The question before the Court of Appeal was whether she had been in actual occupation of the house at the time the transfer to Mr Parmar was completed. The court held, perhaps unsurprisingly, that Mrs Chhokar had not ceased to be in actual occupation during her temporary stay in hospital; most of her belongings were in the house and she clearly intended to return there.

The more recent Court of Appeal case of *Link Lending Ltd* v *Bustard* [2010] EWCA Civ 424 arguably pushes the boundary of 'actual occupation' to somewhere near its limit. Mrs Bustard suffered from a severe medical condition which affected her understanding, memory, insight, cognitive faculties and judgement, and which resulted in prolonged periods of in-patient hospital treatment. In 2004 Mrs Bustard was persuaded to transfer the legal title of her home to a Mrs Hussain. Although the transfer referred to a price of £100,000, no money was actually paid. The status of the transfer was relatively uncontentious: because Mrs Bustard (to Mrs Hussain's knowledge) did not have sufficient mental capacity to enter into the transfer, she had an equity in the property entitling her to have the transfer set aside. However, Mrs Hussain had granted a **legal charge** to Link Lending Ltd who had no knowledge of the circumstances of the original transfer. The question was whether Mrs Bustard's equity was capable of overriding Link Lending's registered charge. Such an equity is an interest in the land for the purpose of paragraph 2 of Schedule 3 (and Schedule 1) by virtue of section 116 of the LRA 2002. However, Mrs Bustard was a long-term residential hospital patient at the time of the grant of the charge. Her belongings were in the house, she frequently returned to it under supervised visits, and she certainly wished to return there permanently, although there seems to have been no reasonable prospect of her being able to do so. Lord Justice Mummery concluded (at [27]) that the factors to be weighed by the court include:

> The degree of permanence and continuity of presence of the person concerned, the intentions and wishes of that person, the length of absence from the property and the reason for it and the nature of the property and personal circumstances of the person …

In a judgment with which the rest of the court concurred, he held that Mrs Bustard satisfied the test for being in actual occupation at the date of the grant of the legal charge.

4.6.2(b)(ii) Intermediate lessors   A tenant who has sublet all or part of their land is not in actual occupation of the land for the purposes of Schedule 1 and Schedule 3 of the LRA 2002. Intermediate **lessors** must, therefore, protect their **leasehold** interest by registration against the **freehold** title, unless the lease itself is capable of overriding the Register (that is, as a legal lease for seven years or less (see Section 4.6.1)). This is a change from the situation under the 1925 scheme, which gave overriding status to the interests of a landowner who was 'in receipt of rents and profits'. The 2002 Act removed this protection except where the landowner's interest existed and was protected under section 70(1)(g) before 13th October 2003.

4.6.2(b)(iii) The timing of actual occupation   In *Abbey National Building Society* v *Cann* [1991] 1 AC 56 (HL), the House of Lords held that a mother whose belongings were moved into her new house some 35 minutes before completion of the purchase (and the mortgage that financed the purchase) was not in actual occupation at that time because her occupation lacked the necessary degree of 'permanence and continuity'. This was enough to decide the case, but the House of Lords also considered what the consequences would have been if the mother had been in actual occupation at the time of completion. It concluded that both the right and the occupation must exist at the moment the transfer is executed, rather than at the time of registration (as the LRA 1925 seemed to indicate). Further, if the transfer was financed by a contemporaneous mortgage, the transfer and mortgage should be treated as a single, indivisible transaction with no *scintilla* of time between them in which occupation can take place. The Supreme Court considered the same question, in relation to the 2002 Act, in *Southern Pacific Mortgages Ltd* v *Scott* [2015] AC 385 (SC) (although, as in *Cann*, the point is strictly *obiter*), and accepted the reasoning in *Cann* (at least in this respect). Where a transfer of land is financed by a contemporaneous mortgage, there is no *scintilla temporis* during which the purchaser holds the legal estate unaffected by the lender's charge over it.

4.6.2(b)(iv) The physical extent of the occupation   Where a person has a right over land, but is only occupying part of the land concerned, only the land actually occupied will be subject to the overriding interest. The express provisions to this effect in Schedule 1, paragraph 2 and Schedule 3, paragraph 2 reverse the decision in *Ferrishurst* v *Wallcite* [1999] Ch 355 (CA).

4.6.2(c) The discoverability of occupation

Paragraph 2 of Schedule 3 of the 2002 Act contains a number of conditions that are not found in the equivalent paragraph in Schedule 1, nor, at least not in this form, in the jurisprudence of the 1925 Act. If Schedule 3 applies (as it will in all cases except immediately after first registration), the provisos in subparagraphs (b) and (c) need to be addressed. Figure 4.2 illustrates one approach to doing so.

4.6.2(d) The significance of occupiers' interests

Paragraphs 2 of Schedules 1 and 3 protect those occupiers who have an otherwise unprotected interest in the land. *Williams & Glyn's Bank Ltd* v *Boland* represented the high point of protection for beneficial owner-occupiers in registered land. The effect of *Williams & Glyn's Bank Ltd* v *Boland* was that institutional lenders began, properly, to ensure that there were no resident beneficiaries with rights. Anyone who was

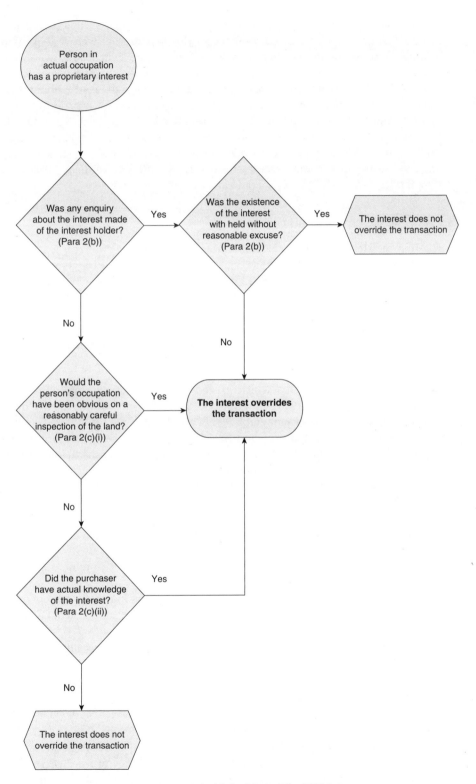

Figure 4.2 Discoverability in paragraph 2 of Schedule 3 of the 2002 Act

going to live in the house was required to agree that the mortgage would take priority over their interest, if any. As a result, occupying beneficiaries were less likely to be caught out by a secret mortgage or sale by their trustee. Beneficiaries who were aware of their rights in the land also began to insist on their names being placed on the legal title so that their co-owners could not mortgage the land without their agreement and, as in the case of *City of London Building Society* v *Flegg*, destroy their property rights. This, in turn, has almost certainly contributed to the considerable increase in the number of cases of undue influence in recent years, which itself has led the courts to develop principles which must be followed by mortgage lenders in order to prevent their commercial interests being defeated (*Royal Bank of Scotland plc* v *Etridge* (No 2) [2002] 2 AC 773 (HL) and Section 11.4.4).

4.6.3   Legal easements and profits

The first registered proprietor of a title holds the land subject to any legal **easements** and *profits à prendre* that survived the disposition that triggered the first registration (LRA 2002, ss 11, 12; Sch 1, para 3). The situation following subsequent dealings with the registered title is, however, more complicated. This is because of the underlying objective of trying to balance the competing demands of preserving important third-party rights with not burdening land with rights that a new owner could not have discovered. The consequences of paragraph 3 of Schedule 3 are as follows.

1. Any easements and profits which existed as overriding interests under section 70(1)(a) of the LRA 1925 before 13th October 2003 will continue to have overriding status by virtue of paragraph 9 of Schedule 12 of the LRA 2002. The LRA 1925 gave overriding status to a much wider class of easements and profits than the LRA 2002, including **equitable** easements. Paragraph 9 of Schedule 12 ensures that the benefit of these pre-existing rights is not lost.
2. No easement or profit *expressly created* out of a registered title after the LRA 2002 came into force on 13th October 2003 is capable of overriding a registered disposition of the land. This is because since the LRA 2002 came into force, an express easement or profit cannot operate at law unless it has been entered on the Register (LRA 2002, ss 27(1) and 27(2)(d)).
3. Any legal easements or profits registered under Part 1 of the Commons Act 2006 will be protected by the scheme contained in that Act.
4. Since 13th October 2006 (Sch 12, para 10) legal easements and profits (except those protected by Part 1 of the Commons Act 2006) will override a registered disposition of the land *unless* at the time of the disposition:
   (a) the disponee (purchaser) had no actual knowledge of the easement or profit (para 3(1)(a)); and
   (b) the easement or profit would not have been obvious on a reasonably careful inspection of the land (para 3(1)(b)); and
   (c) the easement or profit had not been exercised within the previous year (para 3(2)).

The important exception contained in paragraph 3(2) is designed to protect what Law Com No 271 terms 'invisible' easements, such as rights of drainage (para 8.70), which would otherwise be easily defeated. The overall policy of the 2002 scheme, however, is to encourage owners of easements which are used only intermittently to protect them by registration rather than rely on them being disclosed to the prospective purchaser during pre-contract enquiries (which provides actual knowledge of the interest).

4.6.4 Other rights which override the Register

For the sake of completeness, it is necessary to consider other rights which override. Perhaps the most important of these is the local land charge. Although they do not appear on the Register, anyone contemplating the purchase of land should check at the local authority's Local Land Charges Registry for any local land charges affecting the property. Other rights which will bind a purchaser on first registration and subsequent transfers of the land are customary rights, public rights, an interest in coal or a coal mine, and certain rights to other mines and minerals.

There is a further category of the old section 70(1) of the LRA 1925 overriding interests which had their origin in feudal **tenure**, which were only temporarily preserved by the LRA 2002. These interests, such as manorial rights, have been described as 'relics from past times' (Law Com 271, 2001, para 8.88). They ceased to be capable of overriding the Register on 13th October 2013 (ten years after the introduction of the 2002 Act). They have not necessarily disappeared altogether, since if they had, the State would, perhaps, be in breach of Article 1, Protocol 1 of the European Convention on Human Rights. Instead, their owners must now protect them by registration or, if the land is not yet registered, by a caution against first registration.

In exceptional circumstances, an otherwise unprotected interest may give rise to a **constructive trust** that will override the Register. This occurred in the case of *Lyus* v *Prowsa Developments Ltd* [1982] 1 WLR 1044 (Ch). Mr and Mrs Lyus had acquired an option to purchase a plot of land in a housing development. The developer went bankrupt, and the **mortgagee** sold the land to Prowsa. This first sale was expressly subject to the option, although it did not have to be, as the option was not an overriding interest (Mr and Mr Lyus were not in actual occupation) and there was no way in which the option could have been protected against either the mortgagee or their purchaser (Prowsa) by an entry on the Register. When Prowsa sold the land on, the question arose as to whether the option was enforceable. Dillon J imposed a **constructive trust** on the buyer because it would be a fraud if Prowsa were allowed to renege on its express undertaking to the mortgagee in favour of Mr and Mrs Lyus. It is important to note that the constructive trust that arises in these circumstances is based not upon the doctrine of notice (see Section 5.2.2) but upon whether 'the conscience of the estate owner is affected so that it would be inequitable to allow him to deny the claimant an interest in the property' (Sir Christopher Slade, *Lloyd* v *Dugdale* [2002] 2 P & CR 13 (CA) at [52]). *Lyus* v *Prowsa* was considered at length by Lloyd LJ in *Chaudhary* v *Yavuz* [2013] Ch 249 (CA). He concluded (at [68]) that the LRA 2002:

> does not exclude the possibility that the court may find an obligation binding on the registered proprietor personally, by way of, for example, a constructive trust, as a result of which an obligation which is not protected on the register is nevertheless effective. *Lyus* v *Prowsa Developments Ltd* is an example of that, and a rare one.

It is interesting to compare *Lyus* v *Prowsa* with decisions in **unregistered land** such as *Midland Bank Trust Co Ltd* v *Green (No 1)* [1981] AC 513 (HL) (see Section 5.4.5), where an unregistered **land charge** was held void, even though the purchaser knew about it and the purpose of the transaction seems to have been to defeat it. Although many people would say that justice was done in *Lyus* v *Prowsa*, the case created another blank spot on the mirror of the Register.

4.7 First registration of title

Section 3 of the LRA 2002 allows a landowner to apply voluntarily for the registration of an **unregistered title** at any time. However, certain events (set out in section 4 of the LRA 2002) trigger compulsory first registration. **Freehold** land and legal **leases** with a term of more than seven years remaining must be registered on:

- transfer (whether or not the transfer is for value);
- creation (in the case of a lease);
- the grant of a first legal **mortgage**;
- partition (that is, the division of jointly owned land between the co-owners); and
- the appointment of new **trustees** to a land holding.

The application to register the **title** must be made within two months of the triggering transaction (LRA 2002, s 6), otherwise it will be void so far as the transfer, grant or creation of the legal **estate** is concerned (s 7(1)). The precise consequences, which differ according to the type of transaction concerned, are set out in Table 4.5.

Table 4.5 The consequences of failing to apply for first registration within two months of a triggering event

The transfer of the legal freehold or legal lease exceeding seven years	The legal title (which has already vested in the new owner under the traditional unregistered procedure) reverts to the former owner who holds it on a bare trust for the new owner (s 7(2)(a)).
The creation of a new lease or the grant of a first legal mortgage	The transaction takes effect as if it were a contract for valuable consideration (s 7(2)(b)). The grantee will have the benefit of an equitable estate contract (see Section 15.3) and not a legal lease or mortgage.
The transfer of the estate to new trustees	The estate reverts to the person or persons in whom it was vested immediately before the transfer (s 7(2)(aa)).

Upon application for registration, each registrable estate (see Section 4.4) is allocated its own unique title number. A member of staff at the Land Registry will then check the application, make any further enquiries and searches that they feel are appropriate, and check to see whether the land is affected by any cautions against first registration lodged pursuant to section 15 of the LRA 2002. An owner of an unregistered freehold or long lease may lodge such a caution (to prevent someone else applying to register their property, whether due to accident or fraud), while someone with an interest in unregistered land can use a section 15 caution to make sure that their interest is not overlooked upon the first registration of the relevant title. If the caution is valid, the Registrar must inform the cautioner of any application for registration and of their right to submit objections to the Land Registry (s 16). The Land Registry examiner decides whether the title is good enough for **absolute title** or whether it should be given a weaker class of title (see Section 4.4.1). Any benefits and burdens that the examiner discovers will be entered in the relevant part of the new Register of Title, as will any burdens, such as **restrictive covenants** found in the Land Charges Register. Other relevant information, such as the title number of the freehold **reversion** of a lease, will also be noted in order to ensure that the Register really does mirror the title to the land. If Registry staff make a mistake, there are provisions for compensation in the form of an indemnity from the State (see Section 4.10).

Under the 1925 scheme, the new proprietor of the land was issued with a Land Certificate containing a copy of the Register, unless the land was subject to a mortgage, in which case the **mortgagee** would be sent a Charge Certificate. The Law Commission and the Land Registry considered these certificates unnecessary, and incompatible with electronic conveyancing. However, after consultation, and to reassure those who are not convinced by this policy, the Registry now issues 'title information documents' to the registered proprietor on completion of first registration and whenever the Register is changed.

Upon completion of first registration the new registered proprietor is subject *only* to the interests referred to in section 11(4) of the LRA 2002 if the estate is a freehold and *only* to the interests referred to in section 12(4) of the LRA 2002 if the estate is a lease exceeding seven years. These interests are summarised in Table 4.6. It is important to grasp that the legal or **equitable** status of any particular interest is not directly relevant to whether it binds the newly registered title: this is determined solely by the rules in sections 11 and 12 of the Act.

Table 4.6   Interests binding upon a first registered proprietor

	Freehold estate s 11(4), para...	Leasehold estate s 12(4), para...
Interests protected by an entry on the Register	(a)	(b)
Interests capable of overriding first registration (these are listed in Schedule 1)	(b)	(c)
The interests of anyone in adverse possession (see Chapter 16) of whom the registered proprietor has notice	(c)	(d)
The covenants and obligations contained in the lease		(a)

4.8   Dealings with registered titles

4.8.1   Dispositions of registered land

There are three main categories of transactions (the term in the LRA 2002 is 'dispositions') involving registered titles.

4.8.1(a) Registrable dispositions

The dispositions that must be completed by registration are listed in section 27(2) of the LRA 2002. The most important of these are:

- the transfer of the **title** or part of the title (s 27(2)(a));
- the grant of a **lease** for a term exceeding seven years, and certain other types of lease (s 27(2)(b));
- the express creation of an **easement** and the grant of a **legal charge** (s 27(2)(d),(f): see Section 4.5.2).

These transactions must be reported to the Land Registry using the appropriate form, together with the necessary fee. Until registered, any purchaser will, at best, have an **equitable** interest in the land: there is no two-month period of grace, as on first registration (LRA 2002, ss 5 and 6; see Section 4.7). This will mean, for example, that the assignee of a **reversion** is unable to serve notice to quit on the tenant of the lease until registration of the transfer of the reversion is complete (*Pye v Stodday Land Ltd* [2016] 4 WLR 168 (Ch)). The period between completion of the transaction and its registration is referred to as the 'registration gap'. One of the main goals of the provisions enabling electronic conveyancing in the LRA 2002 was the abolition of the registration gap by the simultaneous completion of the transaction and registration (s 93). Although this goal is not abandoned in *Updating the Land Registration Act 2002* (Law Com No 380, 2018), in Chapter 20 the Law Commission recommends that simultaneous registration should be seen as a separate goal to that of the compulsory digitisation of dispositions of land.

4.8.1(b) Dispositions that should be protected by an entry on the Register

Almost all other interests created over a registered title can be protected by registering a **notice** in the Charges Register to the relevant **estate**. The only exceptions are the types of interest listed in section 33 of the LRA 2002 (see Section 4.5.1). An interest that is not protected by registration will only be binding following a disposition of the registered estate for value if it falls within Schedule 3 of the LRA 2002; that is, if it is capable of overriding the Register (s 29(2)(a)(ii) of the LRA 2002 and Section 4.6).

4.8.1(c) Interests that are not capable of entry on the Register

The interests listed in section 33 of the LRA 2002 cannot be protected by an entry on the Register. It may be possible, in certain circumstances, to protect them indirectly by entering a **restriction** in the Proprietorship Register (see Section 4.4.2). However, in most cases such interests will only be binding if they are capable of overriding the Register by virtue of Schedule 3 of the LRA 2002 (see Section 4.6).

4.8.2 The priority of interests in registered land

The first question to ask when considering the priority of a registrable disposition of a registered **estate** or charge is, '*Was the disposition made for valuable consideration?*' Because so many transactions are made for value, it is all too easy to forget this question, but doing so risks applying the wrong set of rules concerning priority.

- ▶ If the disposition was made for money's worth (but not for marriage or merely nominal money consideration (LRA 2002, s 132(1)), its priority is determined by the rules in sections 29 and 30 of the LRA 2002.
- ▶ If the disposition was not for value (a gift, for example), then the basic common law rule of priority applies (s 28). This means any third-party interests are ranked in order of their creation, regardless of whether they are entered on the Register.

By virtue of sections 29 and 30, a registrable disposition of a legal estate or a **registered charge** *for valuable consideration* is subject only to:

- ▶ legal charges and other interests protected by a notice in the Charges Register at the date of the disposition;
- ▶ any interests which override registration at the date of the disposition (that is, those listed in Schedule 3 of the LRA 2002);

- any interest excepted from the effect of registration (that is, where the estate is registered with a title less than absolute (see Section 4.4.1)); and
- if the estate is **leasehold**, the terms of the lease that created the estate.

Note that sections 29(3) and 30(3) prevent an interest that has previously been protected by notice subsequently becoming capable of overriding the Register if the notice has been removed for any reason. A suggested approach to determining the priority of an interest in a registered **title** is outlined in Figure 4.3.

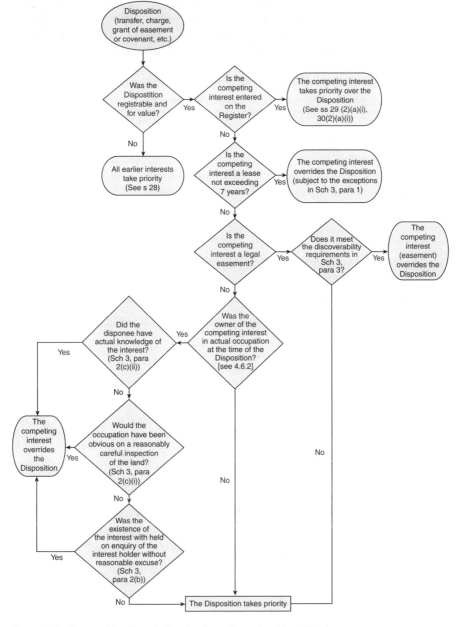

Figure 4.3 Approaching the priority of a disposition of registered land

4.9 Alteration of the Register

One of the purposes of schemes of **title** registration is to allow citizens to purchase interests in land conveniently and confidently. A purchaser needs to be able to rely on what is entered in the Register (albeit subject to the revelation of any overriding interests) without the fear of those entries being changed, or the prospect of their title being taken away from them. One way of expressing this is to say that Registered Estates should be **indefeasible**; that is, incapable of being defeated by claims that are not referred to in the Register. However, the benefits of indefeasibility need to be balanced with sufficient flexibility to allow justice to be done where the circumstances require it. Landowners may find themselves deprived of their land or interests through mistakes made by conveyancers or by the Land Registry; or they may be the victim of fraud. This is why the LRA 2002 includes the power for the Registrar or the court to alter the Register in section 65 and Schedule 4.

Schedule 4 of the LRA gives the Registrar and the court the power to alter the entries in the circumstances set out in Table 4.7. Most alterations made pursuant to Schedule 4 will be administrative and uncontroversial, but the power to correct a mistake requires special attention, because:

▶ the LRA does not provide a definition of what constitutes a mistake; and
▶ Schedule 4 imposes significant restrictions on when either the court or the Register can correct a mistake to the prejudice of the registered proprietor.

Table 4.7 Power to alter the Registy, Schedule 4 of the LRA 2002

Power	Registrar	Court
To correct a mistake on the Register	Para 5(a)	Para 2(1)(a)
To bring the Register up to date	Para 5(b)	Para 2(1)(b)
To give effect to any estate, right or interest excepted from the effect of registration	Para 5(c)	Para 2(1)(c)
To remove superfluous entries from the Register	Para 5(d)	n/a

These rules have received considerable judicial attention in recent years, not least because of the increased number of fraudulent land transactions, and because the correction of a mistake (or the decision not to do so) is a trigger for considering the payment of an indemnity under Schedule 8 (see Section 4.10).

4.9.1 'Mistake'

In the absence of a statutory definition, the question of what constitutes a mistake for the purposes of paragraphs 2(1)(a) and 5(a) of Schedule 4 has fallen to the courts to decide. In *NRAM Ltd* v *Evans* [2018] 1 WLR 639 (CA), at [49] and [51], Kitchin LJ cited with approval the explanation of 'mistake' provided in two major textbooks, which might be summed up as:

> *a mistake occurs when the Registrar would have done something different had he known the true facts at the date of making or deleting the relevant entry.*

He continued, at [52]:

> It will be noted that both of these formulations focus on the position at the point in time that the entry or deletion is made. That, so it seems to me, must be right. If a change in the register is correct at the time it is made it is very hard to see how it can be called a mistake.

One of the consequences of this is the importance of recognising whether the transaction concerned was void (as would be the case if a transfer had been forged, for example) or voidable. If the disposition was voidable (as in *NRAM Ltd* v *Evans*) there would have been no error at the date of its registration, as a voidable transaction is valid until it is rescinded ([59]). Consequently, registration of a merely voidable transaction does not constitute a mistake for the purposes of Schedule 4 and cannot, therefore, amount to **rectification** within the meaning of paragraph 1 (see Section 4.9.2). The conceptual integrity of *NRAM Ltd* v *Evans*, as well as some of the issues it leaves unanswered, are considered in more detail in Lees (2018).

Mistakes may arise because of some official or administrative error but, as will already be appreciated, they may also arise when the Registrar has been deliberately or accidentally misled. For example, in *Baxter* v *Mannion* [2011] 1 WLR 1594 (CA), Mr Baxter had successfully applied to be registered as proprietor of land owned by Mr Mannion on the basis of Mr Baxter's claim to ten years' **adverse possession** of that land. Mr Mannion had not opposed Mr Baxter's original application for registration. However, it was subsequently discovered that Mr Baxter had not actually been in adverse possession for the requisite period and he had not, therefore, been entitled to be registered as proprietor of the land. The Register was restored in Mr Mannion's favour. In *MacLeod* v *Gold Harp Properties Ltd* [2015] 1 WLR 1249 (CA) two **leasehold** titles had been closed by the Land Registry after the **lessor** filed evidence of them having been terminated. It was subsequently held that the leases had not in fact been terminated, and that the titles should be restored to the **tenants**.

4.9.2   Rectification

'Rectification' is the most significant type of alteration to the Register permitted by the 2002 Act. It is defined in Schedule 4, paragraph 1 of the Act as:

- the correction of a *mistake*
- that will *prejudicially affect the title of the registered proprietor*.

No rectification may take place against the title of a registered proprietor in possession without their consent unless the conditions in paras 3(2) and 6(2) are satisfied; that is, unless:

- the registered proprietor has substantially contributed to the mistake through fraud or carelessness, or
- it would be unjust for any other reason not to correct the Register (paras 3(2) and 6(2)).

The question of when it is 'for any other reason unjust for the alteration not to be made' for the purposes of paras 3(2) and 6(2) was considered by the Court of Appeal in *Baxter* v *Mannion* (the facts of which are set out in Section 4.9.1). The court held that it would be unjust not to order rectification, because the loss of the title would be disproportionate to Mr Mannion's 'mere failure to operate bureaucratic machinery' (at [42]). On this reasoning, it is difficult to see many circumstances in which rectification will not be ordered once a mistake has been proved, unless there has been some dealing with the registered title since the mistake occurred.

Walker v *Burton* [2014] 1 P & CR 9 (CA) concerned manorial rights. The Burtons had been registered as proprietors of 362 acres of moorland known as Ireby Fell, following, erroneously as it turned out, their recognition as the lords of the Lancashire manor of Ireby. The question before the Court of Appeal was whether the register should be rectified by the cancellation of the registration of title to the **freehold** of the Fell. Mummery LJ, who gave the only substantial judgment, held (at [100]) that:

> Whether or not there would be an injustice is an assessment to be made by the fact-finding tribunal in the light of all the relevant data. An appellate court should not interfere with that assessment, unless there has been a self-misdirection of law, or an error of principle, or the assessment is one which no reasonable Adjudicator, properly directing himself, would have made.

In particular, just because the mistake was consequential on a mistake that had been corrected (the erroneous registration of title to the lordship of the manor of Ireby) did not automatically mean that it would be unjust not to alter the registered title to the Fell. In *Sainsbury's Supermarkets Ltd* v *Olympia Homes Ltd* [2006] 1 P & CR 17 (Ch), Mann J held that it would be unjust not to order rectification against the registered proprietor because it had been aware of the right being claimed when it acquired the land and had, until relatively late in the day, believed itself to be bound by that right. Not to order rectification would give the registered proprietor an unexpected windfall.

4.10 Indemnity

Section 103 of the LRA 2002 provides that State compensation is payable by the Registrar in the circumstances set out in Schedule 8. The most significant of such claims are likely to be those from people who suffer loss as the result of **rectification** or failure to rectify the Register, although the indemnity rules extend to mistakes in information provided by the Land Registry and some other circumstances (Sch 8, para 1).

Swift 1st Ltd v *Chief Land Registrar* [2015] Ch 602 (CA) concerned the consequences of a **mortgage** fraud. Mrs Rani was the registered proprietor of 15 Elmstead Road, in Ilford. Unbeknown to Mrs Rani, someone forged her signature on a **legal charge** over the house which was subsequently properly protected by registration. A month later this first charge was paid off using the proceeds of a second fraudulent mortgage in favour of Swift 1st Ltd, which was also properly registered. Mrs Rani only became aware of the situation when Swift began possession proceedings. When the fraud came to light, Swift accepted that the forgery meant that it had no enforceable legal charge and a consent order was made requiring the Land Registry to rectify the **title** by deleting the relevant entry in the charges register. Swift then began proceedings against the Registrar, seeking indemnity for the money it had lost as a result of the transaction (presumably because it saw no realistic prospect of recovering the money from the fraudster, even if they could be found). The case turned on the interpretation of the word 'loss' in paragraph 1(2)(b) of Schedule 8. In *Chowood Ltd* v *Lyall* (No 2) [1930] 2 Ch 156 (CA), the Court of Appeal had held that there was no loss where the Register had been rectified (in that case under the very different provisions of the LRA 1925) to give effect to an overriding interest already binding on the title. Patten LJ, who gave the main judgment in *Swift 1st Ltd*, accepted that the right to seek **rectification** amounted to an overriding interest (at [45]), but went on to hold that the wording of paragraph 1(2)(b) meant that Swift was deemed to suffer loss by virtue of the statute and was entitled to indemnity pursuant to Schedule 8.

Indefeasibility, rectification and overriding interests

Swift 1st Ltd v *Chief Land Registrar* [2015] Ch 602 (CA) has received considerable attention from commentators on land law, not least because it seems to restore the principle of **indefeasibility** to the 2002 scheme. This principle had been significantly undermined, in the view of many of the same commentators, by the earlier decision in *Fitzwilliam* v *Richall Holdings Services Ltd* [2013] 1 P & CR 19 (Ch), in which Newey J had held himself to be bound by the reasoning in *Malory Enterprises Ltd* v *Cheshire Homes (UK) Ltd* [2002] Ch 216 (CA), a case concerning the 1925 Act.

In all three cases the question that needed to be answered was:

> *where a registered proprietor is entered on the Register as the result of fraud, who actually owns the land in the period between the registration and its rectification?*

The answer to this question is important because it has consequences for those who use the land, or are granted rights over it, during the pertinent period. For example, in *Malory Enterprises Ltd* v *Cheshire Homes (UK) Ltd* [2002] Ch 216 (CA), Cheshire Homes (UK) Ltd did not dispute that the Register should be rectified, but wished to establish that it was entitled to possession of the land between the date of registration and the date of rectification so as to avoid any liability for trespass and to safeguard its ability to claim an indemnity from the Land Registry. In *Malory*, the Court of Appeal had held that the effect of a fraudulent transfer was to separate the registered (legal) title from the beneficial interest. Although section 69 of the LRA 1925 guaranteed the legal title of the registered proprietor, it did not also guarantee the beneficial title. Consequently, although title had been vested in Cheshire Homes (UK) Ltd, that company held the land on bare trust for the claimants ([2002] Ch 216 (CA), [65]). In *Fitzwilliam* v *Richall Holdings Services Ltd*, Newey J concluded that the relevant provisions in the 2002 Act (the title guarantee is found in section 58) were sufficiently similar to those considered in *Malory Enterprises Ltd* for him to be bound by that decision. As Emma Lees explains in her casenote in (2015) 131 LQR 515, at 516, the reasoning in *Malory* is subject to two major criticisms:

> First, the case fatally undermined the point of registration, since it meant that only bare legal title could ever be conferred by registration, robbing the guarantee of title provided by the register of any value … Secondly, it was problematic because of the mechanism by which the equitable interest was said to arise … There was nothing which could be said to trigger the imposition of the trust …

Martin Dixon in his book *Modern Land Law*, 8th edition, p. 44, footnote 6 (quoted by Patten LJ in his judgment in *Swift* at [37]) explains that:

> Acceptance of the Malory approach would be to import principles of unregistered conveyancing into registered land and this would wholly contradict the system of registration of title and the move to e-conveyancing that the LRA 2002 is designed to facilitate.

In other words, the approach in *Malory* seems to be that the court starts by working out a suitable solution based on the rules of general land law before trying to fit that conclusion within the scheme of the LRA. *Malory* is far from unique in this respect: see, for example, the words of Lady Hale (at [96]) in *Southern Pacific Mortgages Ltd* v *Scott* [2015] AC 385 (SC) (see Section 4.6.2(a)).

The Court of Appeal decision in *Malory* would normally be binding upon the Court of Appeal as constituted to hear *Swift*. One option open to the later court was to distinguish *Malory* on the basis of the wording of the 2002 Act compared with that of 1925 (*Fitzwilliam* being a decision of the High Court, and not binding on the Court of Appeal). The court chose, instead, to hold that the decision in *Malory* was *per incuriam*, having been made without reference either to the binding decision in *Argyle Building Society* v *Hammond* (1985) 49 P & CR 148 (CA) or section 114 of the LRA 1925.

The result of *Swift* is that section 58 of the LRA 2002 can be treated as the guarantee of title that it was almost certainly always intended to be. However, the decision is not without its difficulties. In particular, Patten LJ accepted the assumption, itself derived from *Malory*, that a right to rectification is automatically capable of taking effect as an overriding interest. This concession seems to have been made without explaining how a right to rectification has been added to those interests capable of being protected by occupation. Not all 'mistakes' giving rise to the possibility of rectification create the recognised interest in land which is what is required for the purposes of paragraphs 2 in Schedules 1 and 3. Further, if all rights to rectification are also overriding interests, the general principle that there is no loss where the register is rectified to give effect to an overriding interest (*Chowood Ltd* v *Lyall* (No 2) [1930] 2 Ch 156 (CA)) remains for cases falling outside para 1(2)(b) of Schedule 8. In other words, no fraud, no indemnity. Perhaps unsurprisingly, the Law Commission has recommended that the LRA 2002 should be amended to explicitly provide that the ability of a person to seek alteration or rectification of the register is not, in itself, a property right (Law Com No 380, 2018, para 13.32).

4.11 Looking back and looking ahead

The 2002 Act has had fundamental consequences for the way lawyers think about and deal with land. One of the main objectives of the scheme of registration was to do away with the difficulties caused by the doctrine of **notice** (discussed in more detail in Sections 5.2.2 and 5.6). Law Com No 271 stated that the doctrine 'as a general principle … has no application whatever in determining the priority of interests in registered land' (para 5.16). The report recognised, however, that on first registration the new proprietor should take the land subject to any rights under the Limitation Act 1980 of which they had notice. It also recognised that something similar to notice is relevant in two further categories of interests that have overriding status: the interests of those in actual occupation and certain legal **easements**. However, the report was at pains to point out that 'knowledge' in these circumstances is not the same as the old doctrine of notice in **unregistered land**, but comes from a conveyancing rule which requires a seller to disclose to the buyer any burdens on the land which would not be obvious on a reasonable inspection and which the buyer does not know about.

Another major shift in legal thinking, reflected in the 2002 Act, is the acceptance by the Law Commission and many of the judiciary that registered and unregistered title are two distinct systems. See, for example, (1998) Law Com No 254, para 1.6:

> there seems little point in inhibiting the rational development of the principles of property law by reference to a system that is rapidly disappearing, and in relationship to which there is a diminishing expertise amongst the legal profession … both the computerisation of the

register and the move to electronic conveyancing make possible many improvements in the law that cannot be achieved with an unregistered system.

This is quite a change from the approach taken by Judge Finlay QC in *Kingsnorth Finance Co Ltd* v *Tizard* [1986] 1 WLR 783 (Ch) who seems to have assumed that the outcome (and the underlying rules) should be the same regardless of whether the title to the land is registered or unregistered. However, it should be noted that both Arden LJ in *Malory Enterprises Ltd* v *Cheshire Homes (UK) Ltd* [2002] Ch 216 (CA) and, more recently, Baroness Hale in *Southern Pacific Mortgages Ltd* v *Scott* [2015] AC 385 (SC) seem to assume that the LRA is concerned with the practicalities of conveyancing rather than with substantive rules of land.

The LRA 2002 did much to pave the way for the introduction of compulsory electronic conveyancing, but this has proved much more difficult to deliver than was anticipated. There are various reasons for this, including the technical challenges and concerns about the security of electronic transactions. While the Land Registry has continued to develop its digital services, and the Land Registration Rules 2003 have been amended to provide for the possibility of paperless transactions in the future, it is clear that the holy grail of simultaneous completion and registration, and with it the elimination of the 'registration gap', is still some years away (Law Com No 380, 2018, Chapter 20).

The Land Registry's aim of completing the Register means that it must continue to find ways of encouraging landowners to register unregistered titles. Much progress has been made, but some landowners remain reluctant to have their titles open to public inspection, and others do not wish to pay the fees associated with registration. The Act encourages landowners to register their titles by offering significant protection against adverse possessors (see Section 16.5.2). In addition, section 79 of the LRA 2002 makes specific provision for the Queen to grant herself **freehold** title out of her demesne land, which she must then register. Demesne land is land which the Crown holds for itself as the 'ultimate feudal overlord' and which is not therefore held on a fee simple or term of years.

Although some may regret the passing of unregistered conveyancing, registration of title to land is generally considered 'A Good Thing'. Nonetheless, it is important to consider its failings and limitations (as the Law Commission has done in *Updating the Land Registration Act 2002* (Law Com No 380, 2018)). Only then is it possible to decide whether, as is usually assumed, registration of title really is of benefit to all buyers and sellers of land. For example, title registration does not, of itself, solve the conflicts of interests that arise between people with different interests in (and hopes for) the same parcel of land. The Land Register was originally introduced to simplify conveyancing by removing the need for repetitive examinations of title deeds. One of the main driving forces behind the 2002 Act was the need to simplify the process further, and to make the Register as far as possible a perfect mirror of title, in readiness for the electronic revolution to come. Should simplification of the conveyancing process be the dominant rationale behind all land law? What is the place of other important principles, such as security of occupation? Are **equitable** doctrines such as **estoppel** robust enough to protect the person who, through no fault of their own, fails to comply with the formalities prescribed by the LRA 2002?

Summary

4.1 Registration of title to land is designed to offer a simple and efficient form of conveyancing, by providing a guaranteed mirror of most rights in the land and promising State compensation for loss.

4.2 The rules needed to determine when an owner of registered land (the registered proprietor) will be bound by other people's interests in their land are contained in the LRA 2002.

4.3 The Register of Title is divided into three sections: property, proprietorship and charges. Each part of the Register contains specific information about the land, the title and the burdens on the land.

4.4 The Register is an estate-based register. The main interests registered in their own right are freehold estates and leases with an unexpired term exceeding seven years.

4.5 Most interests in land that is registered can be protected by registering a notice. Those that cannot are listed in section 33 of the LRA 2002. The dispositions listed in section 27(2) of the LRA 2002 will only take effect at law if completed by the relevant entry on the Register.

4.6 A limited number of interests are capable of overriding the Register. These are listed in Schedules 1 and 3 of the LRA 2002 (depending on whether it is a first registration or a subsequent registered disposition) and include easements, leases and the interests of people in actual occupation of land. Overriding interests override any buyer of an interest in registered land.

4.7 Almost all dealings with legal estates (except for leases not exceeding seven years) trigger first registration of title. The consequences of first registration of title are set out in sections 11 and 12 of the LRA 2002.

4.8 Where there is a disposition of a registered estate or legal charge for value, it will be subject only to the interests set out in the relevant sections of the LRA 2002.

4.9 The LRA 2002 allows for the Register to be altered, in certain circumstances, even against a registered proprietor in possession (rectification).

4.10 The State may provide compensation where someone suffers loss by reason of rectification, lack of rectification, and in other limited circumstances.

Exercises

 4.1 Complete the online quiz on the topics covered in this chapter on the companion website.

4.2 'The register of title of any particular registered estate is ... intended to operate as a mirror, reflecting to potential disponees (and to any other interested persons) the full range of the proprietary benefits and burdens which currently affect the land' (Gray and Gray, *Elements of Land Law* (5th edn, Oxford University Press 2009) para 2.2.24).

4.3 Jake was the registered proprietor with absolute title of Albatross Cottage. He agreed by deed to sell it to Agnes, aged 80, for £140,000. Agnes paid Jake the price and moved in but failed to register the transaction at the Land Registry because she did not believe in lawyers. Soon afterwards, Jake brought Maria to see the cottage. Maria met Agnes briefly in the kitchen and asked her what she was doing there. Agnes replied that she was just having a cup of tea. Maria liked the cottage so much that she offered Jake £160,000 for it. Jake agreed to sell it to her.

Exercises (continued)

Maria paid Jake the price and registered the transfer. Jake gave her the keys, and she moved in when Agnes was in Majorca for a month. Agnes has now returned and has asked you to advise whether she is entitled to be registered as the proprietor of the cottage.

How would your answer differ if Jake and his sister Josephine were joint registered proprietors?

You can find suggested answer plans to exercises 4.2 and 4.3 on the companion website.

Further reading

Battersby, 'More Thoughts on Easements under the Land Registration Act 2002' (2005) 69 Conv 195

Bogusz, 'Defining the Scope of Actual Occupation under the Land Registration Act 2002: Some Recent Judicial Clarification' (2011) 75 Conv 268

Cooke, 'The Register's Guarantee of Title' (2013) 77 Conv 345

Dixon, 'Proprietary Rights and Rectifying the Effect of Non-Registration' (2005) 69 Conv 447

Gardner, 'Alteration of the Register: An Alternative View' (2013) 77 Conv 531

Gravells, 'Getting Your Priorities Right' (2010) 74 Conv 169

Law Commission, *Land Registration for the Twenty-First Century* (Law Com No 254, 1998)

Law Commission, *Land Registration for the Twenty-First Century: A Conveyancing Revolution* (Law Com No 271, 2001)

Law Commission, *Updating the Land Registration Act 2002 A Consultation Paper* (Law Com CP No 227, 2016)

Law Commission, *Updating the Land Registration Act 2002* (Law Com No 380, 2018)

Lees, 'Registration Make-Believe and Forgery – *Swift 1st Ltd v Chief Land Registrar*' (2015) 131 LQR 515

Lees, '*NRAM* v *Evans*: there are mistakes and mistakes ...' (2018) 82 Conv 91

Chapter 5

Unregistered land

Key concepts

- ▷ **Land charges** – interests in unregistered land capable of protection through registration in the Land Charges Register.
- ▷ **Notice** – the rule, now of limited application, which governs whether a purchaser of an unregistered legal estate for value takes the title subject to any equitable interests in the land.
- ▷ **Overreaching** – transferring the beneficial interest from the land that was subject to the trust to the proceeds of sale (or mortgage) of the land.

5.1 The case of the disappearing husband

In 1978, Mr and Mrs Tizard purchased a plot of land at Lechlade, on the edge of the Cotswolds and just north of the river Thames. Although they effectively contributed to the purchase in equal shares, legal **title** to the land was in Mr Tizard's name alone. There they built Willowdown, to be home to them and their two children. Unfortunately, their relationship became strained, and sometime in 1982 Mrs Tizard moved into the spare bedroom. Eventually, she began to spend some nights away from the house, but early each morning she would drive to Willowdown to give the children breakfast, and she returned there each evening so that she and the children could eat their evening meal together. On the frequent occasions when Mr Tizard did not spend the night at the house, Mrs Tizard would stay at Willowdown overnight. Most of her clothes, toiletries and nightwear were there. In April 1983, Mr Tizard obtained a three-month loan of £66,000 secured by way of **mortgage** on Willowdown. Two months later, Mrs Tizard arrived at the house to find a note from Mr Tizard saying that he was going on holiday abroad with one of the children. Neither returned. The loan was not repaid, and the lender sought possession of the house.

Kingsnorth Finance Co Ltd v *Tizard* [1986] 1 WLR 783 (Ch) is one of a number of significant cases from the 1980s in which the court had to balance the interests of an institutional lender against those of an innocent person claiming a **beneficial interest** in mortgaged land. Most of these cases, the most important of which is *Williams & Glyn's Bank Ltd* v *Boland* [1981] AC 487 (HL), concerned **registered land** and turned on whether the interest of a **beneficiary** was capable of **overriding** the mortgage (see Section 4.6.2(a)). However, in 1983 the title to Willowdown was still unregistered. Consequently, it fell to Judge John Finlay QC, sitting as a judge of the High Court, to determine whether the finance company could enforce its **charge** against Mrs Tizard's share of the land. Would the rules of unregistered land produce a similar result to that in *Williams & Glyn's Bank Ltd* v *Boland*? The answer to this question can be found in Section 5.7.

5.2   Unregistered land: the general framework

The main differences between **registered** and unregistered title are summarised in Section 2.3 and in Table 2.1. Fundamentally, in unregistered land, title is established by producing the title deeds, whereas in registered land it is the registration of ownership at the Land Registry that counts.

5.2.1   The rules since 1925

> **The basic rules of unregistered land**
> A buyer in good faith and for money or money's worth of a legal estate is bound by:
>
> ▶ any pre-existing legal interest (except an unregistered *puisne* **mortgage**; see Section 5.4.2(a)); and
> ▶ any interest which must be registered under the Land Charges Act 1972, and is properly registered; and
> ▶ any other interest:
>   ▶ which could not have been registered under the Land Charges Act 1972; and
>   ▶ which has not been overreached within the statutory limits imposed in 1925; and
>   ▶ of which the buyer has actual, imputed or constructive **notice**.
>
> A buyer of an **equitable** interest is bound by almost all pre-existing legal and equitable interests.

5.2.2   The doctrine of notice

It can be seen from the summary of the basic rules above that the doctrine of notice now plays only a residuary role in determining disputes concerning unregistered land. The doctrine is used only when none of the other sets of rules apply. However, until the reforms introduced by the 1925 legislation, the doctrine of notice was of much greater importance. Prior to 1926, the buyer of a legal interest in land was bound by any equitable interests of which they had, or was deemed to have, notice. One of the objectives behind the 1925 legislation was the desire to protect both the buyer of the land and the holders of equitable interests by releasing them from the uncertainties of the doctrine of notice. It is helpful, therefore, to summarise the equitable doctrine of notice before considering the post-1925 rules in more detail.

Under the doctrine of notice, an equitable interest will not bind the *bona fide purchaser of a legal estate for value without notice* (actual, imputed or constructive) of the interest. Such a person is known as 'Equity's Darling'. Each of the components of Equity's Darling (with the possible exception of the first) has its own significance.

Bona fide	in good faith (although it is difficult to see when a purchaser would be acting in 'bad faith' if the term has the same meaning as it was given in the slightly different context of *Midland Bank Trust Co Ltd* v *Green (No 1)* [1981] AC 513 (HL)).
Purchaser	includes a person who buys land or receives land as a gift, a tenant on the grant of a lease, and a mortgagee, but not a person who acquires an interest in the land by virtue of an intestacy or bankruptcy (LPA 1925, s 205(1)(xxi)).
of a legal estate	not an equitable estate.
for value	money, money's worth, or a future marriage.
without notice	actual, constructive or imputed (see Table 5.1).

Table 5.1 The three types of notice

Actual notice	Has the mind of the purchaser 'been brought to an intelligent apprehension of the nature of the incumbrance which has come upon the property so that a reasonable man, or an ordinary man of business, would act upon the information and would regulate his conduct by it' (per Lord Cairns LC, *Lloyd* v *Banks* (1867–68) LR 3 Ch App 488 (ChApp), 490)?
Constructive notice	'Constructive notice is the knowledge which the courts impute to a person … either from his knowing something which ought to have put him to further inquiry or from his wilfully abstaining from inquiry, to avoid notice' (per Farwell J, *Hunt* v *Luck* [1901] 1 Ch 45 (Ch), 52). Constructive notice will only extend to the facts which would have been discovered had the necessary further enquiries been made.
Imputed notice	Purchasers are deemed to have the same actual or constructive notice as their professional advisors (LPA 1925, s 199(1)(ii)(b)).

The difficulty with the doctrine of notice is that someone with an **equitable** interest in land cannot be sure that it will survive the sale of a legal **estate** in that land. Nor can a buyer ever be completely sure that they have done enough to be free from constructive notice of all the equitable rights that might exist over the land they are purchasing. For example, in the nineteenth-century case of *Hervey* v *Smith* (1856) 52 ER 1123 (Ch), the defendant had bought a house with 12 flues in it, but 14 chimney pots. Sir John Romilly MR concluded (at 1125):

> The question is, was he not bound to see that he alone had twelve out of the fourteen, and does it not follow that two must have been used by the adjoining neighbour? He might not have thought fit to count them, or look at them, but I think he was put on inquiry, and that he cannot now say that he had no notice of the agreement by which [the neighbouring house used the other two chimneys].

5.3 Legal interests

Almost all legal interests are binding on a purchaser whether or not they were aware of them on the date of the **conveyance** of the land. The only exception is a *puisne* mortgage; that is, a legal **mortgage** not protected by the deposit of **title** deeds. Legal interests are normally discovered during the enquiries made before purchase. However, even if they are not discovered until later, the buyer is still bound by them, although the seller would be liable in damages if they have failed to deliver the unburdened land they promised. The reason why the drafters of 1925 legislation made an exception for legal *puisne* mortgages is that they can be especially difficult to discover because any documentation is likely to be separate from the main title deeds to the land, which will probably be held by the first (non-*puisne*) **mortgagee**.

5.4 The Land Charges Register

5.4.1 Introduction

The introduction by the 1925 legislation of the need to register certain interests in land was intended to release both the buyer of the land and the holder of the interest in it from the uncertainties of the doctrine of **notice**. Registering an interest in the appropriate register is now deemed to be 'actual notice' of the charge, and so it binds the buyer (LPA 1925, s 198). The Land Charges Department is responsible for five separate registers under the Land Charges Act (LCA) 1972 (which replaced the Land Charges Act 1925). The most important of these is the Land Charges Register. Failure to register a land charge usually means that the interest does not bind the buyer (LCA 1972, s 4; see Section 5.4.5).

Table 5.2   Interests registrable in the Land Charges Register under section 2 of the LCA 1972.

Class	Interest
A	Charges created by a person making an application for them under a statute (for example, the costs of certain works carried out by a public authority, but payable by the landowner).
B	Charges created automatically by a statute (for example, a charge on land in respect of unpaid contributions towards legal aid relating to the recovery of that land).
C(i)	**A legal mortgage where the borrower did not deposit the title deeds with the lender (a _puisne_ mortgage).**
C(ii)	A limited owner's charge; this arises where an owner's interest is limited by a trust: if they pay a tax bill themself instead of mortgaging the land to pay it, they own this equitable interest.
C(iii)	**A general equitable charge (this seems to cover, for example, an equitable mortgage of a legal estate without deposit of title deeds, and certain annuities).**
C(iv)	**An estate contract: a contract to transfer a legal interest in land.**
D(i)	An Inland Revenue charge: a charge on land arises automatically if the tax due on an estate at death is not paid.
D(ii)	**A restrictive covenant _created since 1925_, excluding leasehold covenants.**
D(iii)	**An equitable easement _created since 1925_.**
E	Annuities (now obsolete).
F	**A right of occupation in the family home due to civil partnership or marriage.**

The most important interests are shown in **bold**.

Land charges are burdens on land. They are divided into 11 'classes', A to F (see Table 5.2) and, in theory, comprise those interests which are otherwise difficult for the buyer of land to discover. The registrable interests are mostly **equitable** and are often described as 'commercial' interests. Since 1925, **trusts**, which are not registrable interests and are referred to as 'family' interests, have been dealt with by **overreaching** (see Section 14.6.1).

Many students find the presence of a register within a system called 'unregistered land' confusing and counter-intuitive. It is important to remember, however, that the question of whether land is registered or unregistered refers to the status of the **title** to the land (that is, how ownership is proved), rather than how particular interests in the land are protected. The Land Charges Register must not be confused with the registers of title to registered land (see Chapter 4). Neither should it be confused with the register of local land charges held by each local authority under the Local Land Charges Act 1975. The register of local land charges records other types of burdens on land falling within the jurisdiction of the relevant local authority, including financial matters (resulting, for example, from non-payment of council tax) and planning matters, including planning consents and tree preservation orders.

5.4.2 The important registrable charges

5.4.2(a) C(i): puisne mortgages

Puisne mortgages are legal **mortgages** that have not been protected by requiring the borrower to deposit the title deeds of the property with the lender. This will usually occur when the mortgage is not the first loan secured on the land, as the title deeds will remain in the hands of the first **mortgagee**. If *puisne* mortgages were automatically binding on a purchaser (as is normally the case with legal interests), there would be a significant risk that a purchaser would not discover the existence of such a charge until it was too late. Consequently, since 1925, buyers have been protected from undisclosed *puisne* mortgages by the requirement that the lender register them as a Class C(i) land charge.

5.4.2(b) C(iii): general equitable charges

This residuary category of **equitable** land charge is actually more limited than its title suggests. Section 2(4) of the LCA 1972 provides that it does not extend to interests arising under a trust. Neither does it appear to include interests arising by way of **proprietary estoppel**, since, according to *ER Ives Investment Ltd* v *High* [1967] 2 QB 379 (CA), the doctrine of **estoppel** is too recent to have been within the contemplation of Parliament during the passage of the original Land Charges Act in 1925 (see Section 5.4.2(e)).

5.4.2(c) C(iv): estate contracts

> [An] estate contract is a contract by an estate owner … to convey or create a legal estate, including a contract conferring … a valid option of purchase, a right of pre-emption or any other like right (LCA, s 2(4)(iv)).

As shown in Section 15.3, a buyer of land (whether of a fee simple or a **lease** or some other interest) is normally recognised as having some equitable interest in the land as soon as there is a valid contract. This right is an **estate contract**. Most solicitors do not bother to register such estate contracts because the contracts are nearly always successfully completed within a week or a fortnight. However, some types of contract should always be registered, including:

- *Options to purchase.* An option to purchase will bind a purchaser only if protected by registration in the Land Charges Register.
- *Rights of pre-emption.* A right of pre-emption is the right to be given first refusal if the landowner decides to sell the land. In the case of *Pritchard* v *Briggs* [1980] Ch 338 (CA) it was held that no interest in land can arise until the decision to sell is made. Consequently, such rights can only be registered after the landowner has decided to sell. The decision in *Pritchard* has been heavily criticised and was distinguished in *Dear* v *Reeves* [2002] Ch 1 (CA) (although that case was not about the LCA 1972).
- *Equitable leases* that are also estate contracts must be registered. In *Hollington Brothers Ltd* v *Rhodes* [1951] 2 All ER 578n (Ch), the owner of the equitable lease failed to protect it by registration. It was therefore held void against the buyer of the **freehold reversion**, even though the buyer of the **freehold** had known about the equitable lease from the outset and had paid less for the land because of it.
- A **tenant's** *option to renew a lease or to buy the freehold.* These options are registrable interests within this class. This is so even if the option is contained within a legal lease and was known about by all parties (*Phillips* v *Mobil Oil Co Ltd* [1989] 1 WLR 888 (CA)).

5.4.2(d) D(ii): restrictive covenants

The registration requirement only applies to **restrictive covenants** created after 1925.

5.4.2(e) D(iii): equitable easements

This is:

> an easement, right or privilege over or affecting land created on or after 1st January 1926 being merely an equitable interest (LCA, s 2(5)(iii)).

Unfortunately, this definition is not as simple as it appears. An equitable **easement** often arises out of an informal arrangement which no one would think of seeing a solicitor about, in which case it is unlikely to be protected by registration. In *ER Ives Investments Ltd v High* [1967] 2 QB 379 (CA), a block of flats was being built on a bomb site, when it was discovered that the foundations trespassed on the neighbouring plot. Mr High, the owner of that plot, agreed (unfortunately not by **deed**) that he would allow the foundations to remain there if he could use a drive over the developer's land. He then built a garage on his own land at the end of the drive. This arrangement was clearly an equitable easement. However, it was never protected by registration as a Class D(iii) land charge. Both plots of land changed hands, and the new owners of the flats decided they wanted to stop their neighbour's use of their drive. They argued that the equitable easement was void for non-registration. The Court of Appeal decided that the LCA 1925 (the case preceded the 1972 Act) 'was not the end of the matter' since there were rights arising from the mutuality principle and from estoppel which were not affected by the failure to register. Mutuality is an ancient principle: a person cannot reject a burden, the neighbour using the drive, so long as they want to enjoy a related benefit, in this case the trespass of the foundations (see Section 12.6.2). The estoppel (see Chapter 18) arose because the landowner had allowed Mr High to spend a considerable amount of money on building the garage, knowing that Mr High believed himself to have a legal right to use the drive. Mr High was, therefore, allowed to continue to use the drive so long as the foundations of the flats remained on his land. *ER Ives Investments Ltd v High* represents one of the very few examples of a court finding a way around the LCA in order to arrive at a just result.

5.4.2(f) F: rights of occupation for spouses and civil partners

Section 30 of the Family Law Act (FLA) 1996 (as amended by the Civil Partnership Act 2004) gives a spouse or civil partner who is not already a co-owner a statutory right to occupy the dwelling house owned by the other spouse. This right of occupation, available to either party to the marriage or civil partnership, was originally created under the Matrimonial Homes Act 1967 in an attempt to solve some of the problems which can arise when one party to the relationship (historically, usually the husband) is the sole legal owner of the home. Under the pre-1967 law, he could sell it and disappear whenever he liked, and the deserted partner could not protect herself and their children in advance (*National Provincial Bank Ltd v Ainsworth* [1965] AC 1175 (HL)). In theory, the Class F charge is a simple, cheap and efficient solution. In *Wroth v Tyler* [1974] Ch 30 (Ch), the contracts were exchanged for the sale of the family home, which was in Mr Tyler's sole name. A day later, Mrs Tyler registered a Class F land charge. This prevented Mr Tyler from being able to transfer the house to the buyers with vacant possession. In the circumstances, however, the court refused to grant the claimants the equitable remedy of specific performance because this would force

Mr Tyler to begin proceedings against his wife. Instead, the court awarded the claim-ants damages calculated to place them in the same financial position that they would have been in had the sale been completed.

Wroth v *Tyler* is somewhat unusual. Many non-owning partners do not discover the possibility of registering a Class F charge until it is too late, and it is of no use to people living together who are not married or in a civil partnership. Although the right of occupation is binding on a purchaser if it has been protected by registration, the court has discretion to terminate the rights against a purchaser where it is just and reasonable to do so (FLA 1996, s 34(2)).

5.4.3   Registering and searching for a charge

Registering an interest is a simple matter. The owner of the interest fills in a short form giving their own details, the nature of the charge and the name of the owner of the land which is subject to the charge (the estate owner). All charges are registered against the name of the estate owner and not against the land itself. Such a name-based register causes all kinds of problems, not least because people who fill in forms make typing errors. Apparently, the Register contains charges registered against peo-ple with first names like Nacny, Brain and Farnk. If the wrong name is given on the charge registration form, and the purchaser searches against the correct name, the purchaser will normally take free from the charge. In the extraordinary case of *Oak Cooperative Building Society* v *Blackburn* [1968] Ch 730 (CA) where both the regis-tration and the search were against different incorrect names, the land charge was held to be valid against a mortgagee who had taken two years from its discovery of the mistake before taking action.

Although it is possible to register ineffective charges on the Register, registration alone does not make the charge valid. For example, a prospective purchaser will need to ensure that the benefit and burden of any registered **restrictive covenants** have run with the land. The Registrar has the power to 'vacate the Register' (that is, to remove invalid charges). In fact, many charges in the Register are a waste of space, including the many **estate contracts** which have been completed and the many *puisne* **mortgages** which have been redeemed. The Register thus tends to increase, rather than reduce, the apparent burdens on title.

Anyone can search the Register, but it is usual, and safer, to have an official search carried out by the staff at the Registry using a form giving the names of the people who have owned the land, and paying the appropriate fee. Legal professionals can make searches. The staff at the Registry search against the estate owners' names as requested and send back a form giving details of any charges they discover. In prac-tice, these are often already known to the buyer from the investigations made before contracts are exchanged (see Section 15.1).

The official certificate of search is conclusive (LCA 1972, s 10). If it fails to give details of a charge, the charge is void, despite the fact that the charge appears on the Register (the owner of the charge will receive compensation for the negligence of the Registry). The official certificate also gives the person who requested the search 15 working days' protection from having any further charges registered (LCA 1972, s 11). Thus, once the official search has been made, the buyer is safe, provided the sale is completed within the 15 days.

One of the problems with using the Land Charges Register is that it is possible that a charge was registered against the name of the correct estate owner, but that the buyer of the land is unable to discover the name of that owner because it is hidden behind the root of the title. A seller of unregistered land must provide a **deed** (the 'root of title') proving that they have a good legal title going back only at least 15 years (LPA 1969, s 23). The buyer cannot insist that the seller produce any documents earlier than the root of title. However, the buyer is deemed to have notice of, and to be bound by, any charge that was registered before the date of the root of title, even though no amount of prudence could have uncovered it. In these circumstances, the buyer can claim compensation (LPA 1969, s 25). As time passes, more and more charges lie behind the root of title. Wade (1956) described this problem as a 'Frankenstein's monster' which grows more dangerous and harder to kill as the years pass. His fears have yet to be realised.

5.4.4   The effect of registering a charge

Section 198 of the LPA 1925 (as amended) states that:

> The registration of any instrument or matter in any register kept under the Land Charges Act 1972 ... shall be deemed to constitute actual notice ... to all persons and for all purposes connected with the land affected.

The land charges system is, therefore, a statutory way of giving notice of an interest to a buyer of land. Registration of a charge binds everyone because registration is 'actual notice'. Consequently, the pre-1926 rules of actual, constructive and imputed notice (see Section 5.2.2) are not relevant to interests that are caught by the LCA 1972. A prudent buyer cannot now protect themself through diligent enquiries alone, because they have actual notice of any properly registered charge, whether or not they could ever have found it in the Register. The only exception to the rule that registration is actual notice is where the official search certificate fails to mention a charge that has been properly registered (see Section 5.4.3). It is therefore effectively the official certificate of search which counts as notice, not the Register.

5.4.5   The effect of failing to register a charge

As shown in *Hollington Brothers Ltd* v *Rhodes* [1951] 2 All ER 578n (Ch), an unregistered **estate contract** does not bind the buyer: it is void. However, different classes of land charge are void in slightly different circumstances. The detailed rules are contained in section 4 of the LCA 1972.

Classes A, B, C(i), C(ii), C(iii), F	are void against anyone who gives 'value' for *any interest* in land (legal or equitable; LCA 1972, s 4(2), (5) and (8)).
Classes C(iv), D(i), D(ii), D(iii)	are void against anyone who gives 'money or money's worth' for a *legal* estate (LCA 1972, s 4(6)).

Value means money, money's worth or an agreement to convey land in consideration of marriage. In *registered* land, marriage has ceased to be valuable consideration. The Law Commission ((1998) Law Com No 254, at para 3.43) was of the view that:

> marriage consideration is an anachronism and should cease to be regarded as valuable consideration in relation to dealings with registered land. A transfer of land in consideration of marriage is in substance in most cases a wedding gift.

Money's worth means anything that is worth money, such as other land or company shares. An unregistered charge within Class C(iv), D(i), D(ii) or D(iii) is, therefore, not void against someone who is buying only an **equitable** interest in the land or who is getting married as consideration (that is, not paying money or money's worth). Whether such a person is bound by the unregistered interest will still depend upon the doctrine of notice (see Sections 5.2.2 and 5.6).

It is only when the burdened land changes hands that a charge becomes void for non-registration. Between the original parties the charge is enforceable, and damages for breach of contract may still be available, even if a charge is void against a later buyer of the land. Anyone who gains land through **adverse possession** or as a gift will also be bound by all interests in the land, whether or not protected by registration, because they are not a buyer.

Section 4 of the LCA 1972 is given even more force by section 199 of the LPA 1925, which provides that an unregistered charge is void even if the buyer actually knew about it:

> A purchaser shall not be prejudicially affected by notice of ... any instrument or matter capable of registration under the provisions of the [LCA 1972] ... which is void or not enforceable against him under that Act ... by reason of the non-registration thereof.

This section has been ruthlessly interpreted by some judges, as in *Hollington Bros* v *Rhodes*, where express notice in writing of an unregistered estate contract (an option to renew a lease) was held to be irrelevant. This was taken even further in *Midland Bank Trust Co Ltd* v *Green (No 1)* [1981] AC 513 (HL). A father had granted his son a ten-year option to purchase his farm, which the son was managing and occupying with his family. This was an estate contract, registrable as a Class C(iv) land charge, but the son failed to register it. Later the father changed his mind about the option and discovered that, if he were to sell the legal estate in the land to 'a purchaser for money or money's worth', the son's estate contract would be void. He did just that: he sold the land to his wife, the mother of the owner of the unregistered charge. She knew about the father's scheme and paid far less than the market value of the land. One after another, those concerned in the conflict died, and the executors had to sort out who was now entitled to what interest in the land. The House of Lords (reversing the Court of Appeal) held that the unregistered charge was void against the mother. She was the purchaser of the legal estate for money, and that was all that was needed. According to Lord Wilberforce, at 528:

> The case is plain: the Act is clear and definite. Intended as it was to provide a simple and understandable system for the protection of title to land, it should not be read down or glossed; to do so would destroy the usefulness of the Act.

Unlike the position in registered land (see Section 4.6.2), the LCA 1972 makes no special allowance for a person in occupation of the land. It seems that the 1925 legislation was intended to give occupants some degree of protection, since section 14 of the LPA 1925 expressly provides that:

> This part of this Act shall not prejudicially affect the interest of any person in possession or in actual occupation of land to which he may be entitled in right of such possession or occupation.

Unfortunately, however, section 14 is in Part I of the LPA 1925, which means that it cannot affect either section 199 of the LPA 1925 or the LCA 1972 (neither of which are in Part I of the LPA 1925).

In *Lloyds Bank plc* v *Carrick* [1996] 4 All ER 630 (CA), an estate contract to buy a long **lease** of a maisonette was void for non-registration against a later **mortgagee**. Although the terms of the contract were not recorded in writing, Mrs Carrick had paid the full price to the seller, her brother-in-law, and had moved in. As the contract, made in 1982, predated the Law of Property (Miscellaneous Provisions) Act 1989 (see Section 15.4.1), these acts were sufficient to make the contract enforceable. However, the title to the lease was never actually transferred to Mrs Carrick. The brother-in-law subsequently secretly mortgaged the property to Lloyds Bank, which, when he defaulted on the repayments, sought possession. Mrs Carrick argued that her brother-in-law held the property either on a bare trust for her (as any seller does between exchange of contracts and completion) or under a **constructive trust** (see Section 17.3) or through **estoppel** (see Chapter 18). If the trust arguments had found favour with the Court of Appeal, then Mrs Carrick's rights against the bank would have depended on the doctrine of **notice**: since she was in occupation, the bank would have had constructive notice of her interest. However, the Court held that her rights arose as a consequence of the contract, and her failure to protect it by registration as a land charge meant that it was void against the bank.

The harsh simplicity of these cases, where the buyer either knew or could easily have discovered the interest of the occupier of land, is the sort of thing that makes people cynical about lawyers and their justice. Just as in *Midland Bank Trust Co Ltd* v *Green (No 1)* [1981] AC 513 (HL), the opposite result would have been reached in *Carrick* (as Morritt LJ observed) if the rules of registered land had applied. Registered title offers protection to occupiers who have rights in the land (see Section 4.6.2), so if the titles had been registered, the farmer's son would have been able to exercise his option, and Mrs Carrick would have kept her home.

5.5　Overreaching

In order to simplify the process of buying and selling land subject to a **trust**, it was intended by the framers of the 1925 scheme that trust interests should all be capable of being overreached (LPA 1925, ss 2 and 27). The doctrine of overreaching operates when the purchase price is paid to two or more **trustees** or a trust corporation. In such circumstances, the beneficiaries' interests are transferred from the land into the proceeds of sale (now in the hands of the trustees). Overreaching is considered in detail in Section 14.6.1.

None of the LCA 1972 interests, such as **equitable** charges, **restrictive covenants** and **estate contracts**, can be overreached. As Robert Walker LJ pointed out in *Birmingham Midshires Mortgage Services Ltd* v *Sabherwal* (2000) 80 P & CR 256 (CA), at 263:

> The essential distinction is ... between commercial and family interests. [A commercial interest] cannot sensibly shift from the land affected by it to the proceeds of sale. [A family interest] can do so ... since the proceeds of sale can be used to acquire another home.

5.6　The doctrine of notice

If an interest cannot be registered because it does not fit into the categories set out in the LCA 1972, the next step is to decide whether the interest can be overreached. If it cannot be overreached (or if it has not been, because, for example, there was only one **trustee**), then any conflict between the buyers and the owners of pre-existing interests must be resolved by the pre-1925 rules of notice. Table 5.3 shows the main interests to which the doctrine of notice is still relevant. It must be stressed that this is a residual, open-ended category that will catch any equitable interest in unregistered land that is not governed by the rules of the LCA 1972.

Table 5.3 The doctrine of notice in unregistered land

Type of interest	Section/case
Restrictive covenants created before 1926	Section 2(5)(ii) LCA 1972
Equitable easements created before 1926	Section 2(5)(iii) LCA 1972
Estate contracts, and Class D charges against purchasers other than of a legal estate for money or money's worth	Section 4(6) LCA 1972
Equitable easement arising out of mutual rights, estoppel	*ER Ives Investments Ltd* v *High* [1967] 2 QB 379 (CA)
Contractual licence	*Binions* v *Evans* [1972] Ch 359 (CA)
Equitable lessor's right of re-entry	*Shiloh Spinners Ltd* v *Harding* [1973] AC 691 (HL)
An equitable interest behind a trust that has not been overreached	*Kingsnorth Finance Co Ltd* v *Tizard* [1986] 1 WLR 783 (Ch)

In *Kingsnorth Finance Co Ltd* v *Tizard* [1986] 1 WLR 783 (Ch) (the facts of which are set out in Section 5.1) Mrs Tizard's **equitable** interest in the house had not been overreached because the **mortgage** advance had been paid to only one trustee, her husband (LPA 1925, s 2). Judge Finlay QC held that the finance company had constructive or imputed notice of Mrs Tizard's equitable rights because she was, on the facts, 'in occupation'. The bank's agent should have made more enquiries about the wife because the agent knew that Mr Tizard was married, even though he had described himself as 'single' on the mortgage application form. As the judge explained at 794:

> the plaintiffs had, or are to be taken to have had [through their agent], information which should have alerted them to the fact that the full facts were not in their possession and that they should make further inspections or inquiries; they did not do so and in these circumstances I find that they are fixed with notice of the equitable interest of Mrs Tizard.

What a prudent buyer ought to do depends on the facts of each case. There is no need to open drawers and wardrobes to examine clothes and belongings, but in suspicious circumstances an unannounced visit should probably be made. In this case, there should have been further enquiries, and Mrs Tizard should have been interviewed.

5.7 Applying the rules to *Tizard*

Figure 5.1 sets out, in diagrammatic form, one suggested way of approaching problems concerning interests claimed over an unregistered title. This is not the only order in which the questions could be approached, and, of course, a **beneficial interest** that has been overreached is not actually an interest in land at all. However, a systematic answer to a problem question will need to consider all of the different avenues identified in this diagram.

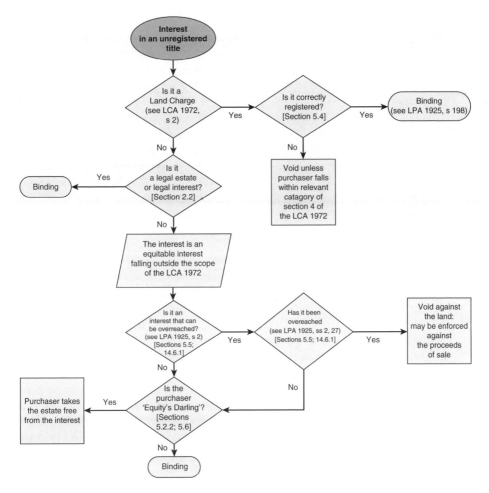

Figure 5.1 Approaching an interest in an unregistered title

Using the diagram to analyse *Tizard*:

▸ Mrs Tizard was claiming a beneficial interest under a **trust** of the land: such an interest is excluded from the scope of the Land Charges Register by section 2(4) (iii)(b) of the Land Charges Act 1972.

▸ A beneficial interest is not a legal interest. The situation would have been different, however, had the house been purchased in joint names.

▸ The **mortgage** advance had been paid to Mr Tizard alone. Without a receipt signed by at least two **trustees,** Mrs Tizard's beneficial interest was not overreached by the mortgage and remained, therefore, an interest in the land.

▸ The lender had given value for the mortgage of the legal **estate** in the form of the mortgage advance. However, on the facts the lender had not completed all the enquiries it should have made and was held to have notice of Mrs Tizard's interest.

One of the interesting features of the judgment in *Tizard* is that Judge Finlay QC assumed that the outcome should have been the same as in the **registered** land case of *Williams & Glyn's Bank Ltd* v *Boland* [1981] AC 487 (HL). This illustrates the once common, but now widely doubted, view that the two types of title were merely two different ways of administering the same rules. The result in *Tizard* is that the registered land concept of 'occupation' (Land Registration Act (LRA) 1925, s 70(1)(g), now LRA 2002, Sch 3, para 2) is imported into the unregistered land doctrine of **notice**. The generous view taken of occupation in this case applies to all cases of constructive notice. In the *Tizard* case, it was probably the right decision, although the wife's occupation was borderline. Of course, if the finance company had paid two **trustees**, Mrs Tizard's interest would have been overreached, and she would have had to leave the house.

5.8 Unregistered land: a retrospective

The 1925 modifications to the rules that applied to unregistered land, and the Land Charges Register in particular, were a temporary measure to facilitate the gradual introduction of **title** registration. However, it took much longer than had been expected to introduce compulsory registration to the whole of England and Wales, and universal registration has still not quite been achieved. By the 1950s, the Land Charges Register was under considerable strain. The main problem was that the Register was name based, and as the years passed it became increasingly difficult for purchasers and lenders to discover the names of all the former estate owners against whom they needed to search. Another major concern was that, contrary to the aim of the 1925 drafters, buyers could destroy the unregistered interests of occupiers of the land even though the buyer knew, or ought to have known, about them before buying the land. In contrast, protection was given to occupiers of registered land, and even, in certain circumstances, to the owners of **beneficial interests** in unregistered land (such as Mrs Tizard). Other problems with the Land Charges Register included the narrow definitions of the registrable interests and the illogical difference between the consequences of non-registration of interests falling within different classes. Various reforms were suggested over the years, but the final answer seems to be that of the 1956 Report on Land Charges (Cmnd 9825), which, in the words of H.R.W. Wade (Wade, 1956, 234), confessed that:

> to rectify the 1925 machinery of registration, now that it is more than thirty years old, is a task beyond the wit of man.

It is, as Wade goes on to observe at 234, much to the credit of the actual custom and practice of conveyancers that 'fortunately, none of these deficiencies seem to matter in real life'.

The final burial of the Land Charges Register is still some years away, but with universal registration of title in sight, the difficulties of unregistered land now only concern a relatively small number of landowners and their lawyers. However, it would be over-optimistic to expect that universal registration of title will solve all the problems encountered by buyers and sellers of land. The story of the tensions between the rights of people with interests in land and those of the buyers of that land (often a bank or building society lending money on the security of a **mortgage**) will continue, as the previous chapter shows only too clearly.

Summary

5.1 The rules for determining whether the owner of a legal estate in land is bound by another person's interest in that land depend upon whether title to the land is registered or unregistered.

5.2 Nearly all legal interests are automatically binding on the purchaser of an interest in unregistered land. The status of other types of interest depends upon the rules of the Land Charges Act 1972, the doctrine of overreaching and the doctrine of notice.

5.3 The only legal interest in land that does not bind the purchaser (regardless of whether or not they are aware of it at the time of the conveyance) is a legal charge not protected by the deposit of title deeds.

5.4 The interests listed in the Land Charges Act 1972 should be registered at the Land Charges Registry; failure to do so (or to do so correctly) will almost always result in them failing to bind any buyer of unregistered land.

5.5 'Family' (trust) interests are not registrable but can be overreached by a buyer who pays two trustees.

5.6 If an equitable interest is not registrable and has not been overreached, the rights of a buyer of a legal interest in unregistered land depend on the doctrine of notice; the buyer of an equitable interest is probably bound by any existing equitable interests.

5.7 A diagram setting out a suggested approach to problem questions concerning unregistered titles can be found at Figure 5.1.

Exercises

 5.1 Complete the online quiz on the topics covered in this chapter on the companion website.

5.2 Hilary is the sole legal owner of a four-storey house, title to which is unregistered, and which is subject to a restrictive covenant that it should be used as a private dwelling house only. She lives on the first floor, and her aged mother, Lucy (who contributed a quarter of the cost of the house when it was bought), occupies the ground floor.

Hilary is a compulsive gambler on the Stock Exchange and recently lost a good deal of money. She met Emma at the hairdresser's, and in the course of a chat they agreed that Emma should rent the basement of Hilary's house for three years. Emma moved in and has paid rent regularly. Hilary then accepted £2,000 from Clive, a colleague, as a deposit on a ten-year lease of the top floor of her house. Nothing was put in writing for tax reasons.

Six weeks later, Hilary decided to emigrate. Clive has discovered that she has made an agreement in writing to sell the whole house to Dee.

Clive, Lucy and Emma seek your advice.

 You can find a suggested answer plan to exercise 5.2 on the companion website.

Further reading

Harpum, 'Purchasers with Notice of Unregistered Land Charges' (1981) 40 CLJ 213

Thompson, 'The Purchaser as Private Detective' [1986] Conv 283

Wade, 'Land Charge Registration Reviewed' [1956] CLJ 216

Yates, 'The Protection of Equitable Interests under the 1925 legislation' (1974) 37 MLR 87

Part III

The estates and interests

Key concepts

▶ **Commonhold** – a statutory form of registered freehold that can be used to divide the ownership of a building or estate with shared common parts.
▶ **Freehold** – the most complete form of ownership of land recognised by English law.

6.1 Who owns the land?

Is it true that only the monarch can own land in England and Wales? This is the sort of question that is sometimes asked of the land lawyer at certain types of party. Unfortunately, there is not a simple 'yes' or 'no' answer, and, even more unfortunately, many partygoers are not prepared to linger long enough to discover the full truth. One fairly concise answer to the question can be found on the Crown Estate's website as part of the answer to 'What is an escheat?' (www.thecrownestate.co.uk/en-gb/resources/faqs):

> Under our legal system, the Monarch (currently Queen Elizabeth II), as head of state, owns the superior interest in all land in England, Wales and Northern Ireland. In most cases, this is usually irrelevant but it can become relevant if a freehold property becomes ownerless. If this happens, freehold land may, in some circumstances, fall to the monarch as the owner of the superior interest. This process is called 'escheat'.

Any attempt to answer the question must, of course, examine what is meant by the word 'ownership'. Some of the relevant issues were introduced at Sections 1.4 and 3.2 when considering social attitudes to land and the meaning of the word 'property'. Linked to this is the question of how the various rights that are normally accorded to an owner are distributed between the monarch (as outright owner) and the immediate owner. If the immediate owner has effective control of the land, the monarch's superior interest will rarely matter.

Since 1925, English law has recognised two main 'ownership' interests in land that can be enjoyed by those people who are not the head of state: the freehold and the **leasehold** (Law of Property Act (LPA) 1925, s 1(1); see Section 2.2.1).

▶ *a freehold* is a holding for an indefinite period (providing there is someone able to inherit the land under a will or through the rules of intestacy on the freeholder's death);
▶ *a leasehold* is a holding for a fixed time (the maximum possible duration of the **lease** must be certain when the lease is granted; the detailed rules, including the possibility of periodic tenancies, are considered in Section 7.5.2).

All other interests in land are granted out of these **estates** (rather than over the land itself).

The legal freehold estate is the foundation of land ownership in both **registered title** and **unregistered land**. This chapter considers what a freehold estate comprises, and the rights enjoyed by someone who owns a freehold. Leases are considered in Chapters 7 and 8.

6.2 Definition of the freehold estate

The 'fee simple' is the only surviving legal freehold estate; its proper name is *fee simple absolute in possession* (LPA 1925, s 1(1)(a)). Each of the words in this title is significant.

Fee	This word comes from 'fief' (*feudum* in Latin), the basic concept of the feudal system. By the sixteenth century, a fee had come to be recognised as an **estate** that could be inherited (instead of automatically returning to the feudal lord when the **tenant** died).
Simple	The fee is 'simple' because it does not suffer from the complications of the **fee tail** (also known as the 'entail'). The fee simple can be inherited by anyone the owner wishes, whereas the fee tail must pass to a direct descendant (for example, a child or grandchild) and, in some cases, only to a certain class of descendant. For example, a 'tail male' could only be inherited by a male. It has not been possible to create new entails since 1997 (Trusts of Land and Appointment of Trustees Act 1996, Sch 1, para 5), but entails created before 1997 remain valid.
Absolute	The word 'absolute' distinguishes this fee simple from others that are limited in some way. One type of limited fee is the 'determinable fee simple'. An example of a determinable fee would be where a mother gives land to her son 'until he marries a solicitor', at which point the land will go to his cousin. A determinable fee must be distinguished from another type of fee, the 'conditional fee simple'. Conditional fees are created by words such as 'but if he marries a solicitor'. The difference is very subtle but important, because although only the fee simple absolute can be a legal estate (LPA 1925, s 1(1)), a special exception was made in 1926 for conditional fees simple (LPA 1925, s 7(1), as amended). Conditional fees can now be legal, but the other limited fees simple (including determinable fees) can only exist in equity.
In possession	All interests in land can be 'in possession', 'in **remainder**' or 'in **reversion**'. 'In possession' means that the owner is entitled to enjoy the interest now by occupying the land or collecting the **rent** (LPA 1925, s 205(1)(xix)); the other two mean that the owner will have the right to enjoy the interest after another interest (for example, an interest for life) has ended. In the example above, the son has a conditional fee simple in possession, and the cousin has a fee simple absolute *in remainder*. However, if the mother gave land to her son on the condition that it would return to her if he married a solicitor, the mother would have a fee simple absolute *in reversion*.

6.3 Legal and equitable freeholds

Of all the possible estates of indefinite duration, only the fee simple absolute in possession can be a legal estate (subject to the exception for conditional fees), because of section 1 of the LPA 1925 (see Section 2.2.1). Other types of estate, such as **entails** and life interests, can only be **equitable**; that is, held as **beneficial interests** behind a **trust**.

6.4   The rights of the freeholder

In theory, at common law the owner can do whatever they like with their land, subject, of course, to any interests such as **mortgages**, **easements** and **restrictive covenants** that have already been granted. In 1885, Challis wrote that ownership of the fee simple 'confers … the lawful right to exercise over, upon, and in respect of the land, every act of ownership which can enter into the imagination' (Challis, *The Law of Real Property, Chiefly in Relation to Conveyancing* (3rd edn by Sweet, Butterworth 1911), 218). However, even in 1885 this was not true. For example, the law of tort could be used to prevent a landowner unreasonably interfering with their neighbour's enjoyment of their land (the doctrine of nuisance). In the old case of *Christie v Davey* [1893] 1 Ch 316 (Ch), Mrs Christie, one of the claimants, was a music teacher who taught some pupils at her home. Mr Davey, who occupied an adjoining house, complained about the frequent music practices. Shortly after Mr Davey's complaint, a series of unusual and loud noises from within his house began to significantly interfere with the comfort of Mrs Christie's pupils. Mr Justice North granted an **injunction** requiring Mr Davey to cease from his vindictive noise-making, saying (at 327), that he was:

> persuaded that what was done by the Defendant was done only for the purpose of annoyance, and in my opinion it was not a legitimate use of the Defendant's house to use it for the purpose of vexing and annoying his neighbours.

North J refused to impose a similar injunction on Mr and Mrs Christie as he considered that their use of their house did not constitute actionable nuisance. However, he did suggest instrument practice should finish by 11 o'clock each evening (at 328).

Today, legislation has imposed great limitations on the owner of land, so that, for instance, they cannot prevent aeroplanes from flying above their land and they may not mine coal, demolish a listed building, kill protected species or pollute water; they must also observe building regulations and licensing laws. The Town and Country Planning Acts impose probably the best-known limitation on landowners. When the Town and Country Planning Act 1947 established the foundations of our present system of planning law, it was suggested by some that the fee simple had been destroyed by the powers taken by the government to control land use. Today, most landowners appreciate the fact that the value of their land is maintained for them by the local authority ensuring that the use and development of neighbouring land reflect the needs and character of the area as a whole.

6.5   Commonhold

Although freehold is the most extensive of the two **estates**, it has its limitations. Historically, English law has been highly suspicious of so-called 'flying freeholds'; that is, a freehold estate that does not include the surface of the land. Further, as will become evident in Chapter 12, in freehold land it is frequently not possible to enforce **covenants** against successors of the original **covenantor**. However, being able to enforce a covenant against a successor in **title** will be very important in certain circumstances. Consider, for example, the owner of a flat in a block of flats. In order to protect the structural integrity of their own property they, or the owner of the whole building, might wish to seek to enforce a repairing covenant against their neighbour.

Until recently, the only answer has been for all the flats in a block to be held on long **leases**, since, as is explained in Chapter 8, leasehold covenants are enforceable against successors in title. However, the use of leases in this situation is not without its own difficulties. The most obvious is that because a lease runs for a defined period it is a diminishing asset (see Section 7.2.2). A lease will often become unmarketable well before its term is due to expire because **mortgage** lenders are unwilling to lend on leases with less than 60 years to run. A further difficulty may be the inability of the **tenants** to get the **lessor** to manage the building and carry out its obligations to repair and maintain the common parts while keeping the tenants' financial contributions at a reasonable level. These problems have been addressed at various times by Parliament, but no entirely satisfactory solution has been found. The latest attempt is found in Part 2 of the Commonhold and Leasehold Reform Act 2002, which gives qualifying tenants of long residential leaseholds the right to take over management of the property from the lessor, even if the latter is not at fault.

In the final decades of the twentieth century, there was considerable discussion about proposals to introduce a new form of land holding called 'commonhold', based on strata title in Australia and condominium title in the United States. After a good deal of uncertainty and procrastination, these proposals were enacted in the Commonhold and Leasehold Reform Act 2002. Part 1 of the Act, which came into force on 27th September 2004, introduced the 'freehold estate in commonhold land' to English law.

A property to be owned on a commonhold basis (for example, a block of flats or an industrial estate) is **registered** at the Land Registry by the freehold owner as a 'freehold estate in commonhold land'. The property is divided into 'units', each held by the unit owner on a freehold basis. The owner of each unit becomes a member of the Commonhold Association, a private company limited by guarantee, which owns and has responsibility for the upkeep of the common parts of the building. Under the regulations in the Commonhold Community Statement (CCS), each unit owner has obligations (for example, to maintain their unit in good repair and to contribute to the commonhold expenditure), binding on their successors and enforceable by the Association – a kind of private local community law. The enforcement of the rules in the CCS takes place initially through an internal complaints procedure, and then, depending on regulations introduced through secondary legislation, through some form of mediation or arbitration or through an ombudsman, before finally moving towards formal legal proceedings.

The advantage of the commonhold scheme is that all the obligations in the CCS are binding on all unit holders at all times, so there is no longer any need to use the unsatisfactory device of a long lease in order to buy an interest in a shared building. The scheme should also remove the associated problems of 'unreasonable and oppressive behaviour by unscrupulous landlords' (Commonhold and Leasehold Reform Consultation Paper, Cm 4843, 2000, 107) and the difficulties of getting mortgage finance in the later years of a lease. Of course, as the Law Commission has remarked, the scheme will not solve the problems by itself: neighbours will not always cooperate, and buildings cannot be repaired for ever. Nevertheless, commonhold offers land developers a new flexibility when building new blocks of flats or developing industrial areas. Despite this, the years since 2004 have seen only a handful of commonhold schemes established. This seems to be a case of developers and the banks, which provide the mortgage finance for developments and the purchase of individual flats, preferring the devil they know (or, perhaps, their lawyers doing so). However, it seems that not everyone has given up on commonhold. In February 2018 the Law Commission launched a consultation to try to discover the specific reasons why commonhold had proved so unattractive to homeowners and the wider property sector with a view to preparing proposals that would address the issues raised.

6.6   Conclusion

In English land law, the predominant method of owning land is to hold the freehold estate. At this point, the ancient historical roots of modern English land law show through the ground: the origins of freehold land can take lawyers straight back to the conquest of England by William of Normandy in 1066. In theory, all the land in England and Wales is still owned by the Crown, with individuals holding interests in the Queen's land. However, although twenty-first-century lawyers may use the same words as lawyers in the eleventh or fifteenth centuries, the meaning and context are quite different. Our forebears might recognise the terms, but they would not understand our law.

This is just one illustration of how land law has developed and continues to develop in response to changing social, economic and political conditions. Whenever a case or statute appears to result in inappropriate or merely technical rules, it is worth taking a step back from the law to consider the conditions in which those rules first developed. One of the tasks of the lawyer is to consider whether and how those rules can be used to meet contemporary needs – or whether the time has come for them to be replaced and to campaign accordingly.

Summary

6.1 The foundation of ownership in modern land law is the legal freehold estate.

6.2 'Fee simple absolute in possession' means an interest in land which can be inherited by anyone, is not restricted by some future event and is enjoyed at the moment.

6.3 Other types of fee can only exist as equitable interests.

6.4 Although it has been asserted that the owner of fee simple absolute in possession has unlimited powers over their land, both common law and statute have greatly restricted their freedom of action.

6.5 A new form of land ownership, commonhold (a special type of freehold estate), was introduced in 2004, but it has not been widely adopted.

Exercises

 6.1 Complete the online quiz on the topics covered in this chapter on the companion website.

Further reading

Bright, 'Of Estates and Interests: A Tale of Ownership and Property Rights' in Bright and Dewar (eds), *Land Law Themes and Perspectives* (Oxford University Press 1998) 529

Burn and Cartwright, *Cheshire and Burn's Modern Law of Real Property* (18th edn, Oxford University Press 2012) 48–60

Clarke, 'The Enactment of Commonhold – Problems, Principles and Perspectives' [2002] Conv 349

Harpum, Bridge and Dixon, *Megarry & Wade: The Law of Real Property* (8th edn, Sweet & Maxwell 2012) Ch 3

Chapter 7

The leasehold estate

Key concepts

▶ **Certainty of term** – the rule requiring that the maximum possible duration of a lease must be ascertainable with certainty at the beginning of the lease.

▶ **Exclusive possession** – the right to exclude other people, including the landlord, from the land.

▶ **Lease** – a contractual arrangement giving rise to the relationship of landlord and tenant.

▶ **Tenancy** – another word for 'lease'.

7.1 The case of the dilapidated flats

Oval House is a three-storey Victorian mansion block typical of those found in Rushcroft Road, London SW2. The London Borough of Lambeth purchased many of the properties in the area in the 1970s, intending to level them to make way for a new residential development. However, the scheme was delayed, and many of the buildings were occupied by members of a 'vibrant squatting community' (something of its story was told at www.urban75.org/brixton/features/rushcroft.html). In 1986, the council agreed that London & Quadrant Housing Trust could use Oval House to provide short-term accommodation for people in urgent need of housing. The agreement between the council and the Trust was called 'a **licence**'. There was no question of it being a lease: in these circumstances, a lease could only have been created with the express consent of the Secretary of State under section 32(3) of the Housing Act 1985 and no such consent was obtained.

In early 1989, the Trust agreed to allow Mr Bruton to occupy a flat in Oval House. The terms were similar to those that the Trust had used many times before.

> Occupation of short-life accommodation at 2, Oval House, Rushcroft Road, SW2 on a temporary basis. As has been explained to you, the above property is being offered to you by [the Trust] on a weekly licence from 6 February 1989. The trust has the property on licence from [the council] who acquired the property for development ... and pending this development, it is being used to provide temporary housing accommodation. It is offered to you on the condition that you will vacate upon receiving reasonable notice from the trust, which will not normally be less than four weeks. You understand and agree that while you are living in the property, you will allow access at all times during normal working hours to the staff of the trust, the owners and agents for all purposes connected with the work of the trust.

Perhaps unsurprisingly, the flats were in a relatively poor state of repair. The only reason that they were available for the Trust to use to help the homeless at all was the fact that they were due to be demolished. However, in 1995, Mr Bruton brought proceedings in the Lambeth County Court, claiming that the Trust was in breach of a **covenant** (implied by section 11 of the Landlord and Tenant Act 1985) to keep the premises in repair. As section 11 only applies to leases, the case turned on whether the Trust's agreement with Mr Bruton created a lease or a contractual **licence**. The main issues, therefore, were:

- What are the ingredients of a lease?
- Which of these ingredients distinguish a lease from a contractual licence?
- Were all the ingredients required for a lease present in Mr Bruton's case?
- What was the significance of the fact that the agreement with Mr Bruton described itself as a 'licence'?
- Could the Trust grant a lease to Mr Bruton when it did not own the **freehold** or have a lease of the land itself? The Trust had only been given a licence to use the land, which is not a property interest (see Chapter 9).

These questions were answered by the House of Lords in *Bruton v London & Quadrant Housing Trust* [2000] 1 AC 406 (HL) and in a number of related cases, including *Kay v Lambeth LBC* [2006] 2 AC 465 (HL). *Bruton* is considered at various points in this chapter, and especially at Sections 7.4.8, 7.5.1 and 7.5.3.

7.2 Leaseholds in context

7.2.1 Leases as property rights

A lease was originally a contract for the occupation of land. It was only in the sixteenth century that leases were recognised as interests in land, so that the rights and duties of the parties were no longer merely contractual, but became attached to the land. Now leaseholds are one of only two interests that are capable of being legal **estates** in land (LPA 1925, s 1(1); see Section 2.2.1). However, much of the law of leases is still based on contract law, albeit with overarching statutory provisions controlling residential, business and agricultural tenancies. As Lord Browne-Wilkinson explained in the case of *Hammersmith & Fulham LBC v Monk* [1992] 1 AC 478 (HL) at 491:

> In certain cases a contract between two persons can, by itself, give rise to a property interest in one of them. The contract between a landlord and a tenant is a classic example. The contract of tenancy confers on the tenant a legal estate in the land: such legal estate gives rise to rights and duties incapable of being founded in contract alone.

At times, the courts have tended to emphasise the proprietary nature of leases (as in *Street v Mountford* [1985] AC 809 (HL)). More recently, judges have favoured a more contractual approach, as in *National Car Parks Ltd v The Trinity Development Co (Banbury) Ltd* [2002] 2 P & CR 18 (CA) (see Section 7.5.1) and *Bruton v London & Quadrant Housing Trust* [2000] 1 AC 406 (HL) (see Sections 7.1 and 7.5.3).

7.2.2 The advantages (and disadvantages) of leases

The commercial advantages of the lease are obvious. A landowner can let other people use their land for a certain period of time (for example, to farm, mine for gravel or dwell) in exchange for a regular income. They can make rules about the kinds of things that are (or are not) to be done on the land, and, at the end of the period, they will get the land back. The wealth of the powerful landowning families came, to a large extent, from rental income. Great cities such as London were developed in the eighteenth and nineteenth centuries through building leases. The ancestors of the Duke of Westminster owned large estates in London and granted long leases to speculative builders, subject to strict rules about the density and type of housing. The builders made their profit, the dukes enjoyed the **rent**, and at the end of the period the valuable housing estates reverted to the descendants of the first duke. Thus, London and other cities grew through the carefully planned, high-quality developments of far-sighted landowners and also, of course, through get-rich-quick rented slums.

There are also many other tenants, those who are unable to or do not wish to climb on to the so-called 'property ladder', with much shorter leases. Short leases for housing have been greatly affected by Acts of Parliament since 1915 because of the social and economic importance of decent housing for the community as a whole. Statutes on rent control, security and repairs were intended to protect poor tenants with little bargaining power against more powerful landlords. However, much of this protection, latterly found in the Rent Act 1977, has been removed in recent years (especially by the Housing Act 1988) in order to provide realistic commercial opportunities for private **landlords**. The detail of this area of the law is usually outside the scope of land law courses and is referred to only occasionally in this chapter (although see Section 1.5, where the relevance of the European Convention on Human Rights to the termination of residential tenancies is considered in the context of the Supreme Court's decision in *McDonald* v *McDonald* [2016] 3 WLR 45 (SC)).

Today, leasehold arrangements are still very important. In the last decade, increasing house prices and stricter criteria for **mortgage** finance have meant that many people, especially younger people, cannot afford to climb onto the so-called 'property ladder' of freehold ownership. The result has been a significant increase in the number of residential tenants occupying on short-term or periodic tenancies (see Section 7.4.2). In financial terms, the most significant use of leases is in the business world, for office blocks and factory units, for example. In most cases, when a person 'buys' a flat, they will be buying a long (often 99-year) lease of the flat, rather than its **freehold**. A long lease overcomes the problems associated with flying freeholds (that is, freehold estates that do not include the surface of the ground) and the enforcement of positive freehold **covenants** (see Chapter 12). However, long leases have their own problems. In particular, they are diminishing assets. Parliament has intervened (not particularly successfully so far) to give owners of long residential leases the right to extend the period of their leases or, in the case of houses, to buy the freehold (the Leasehold Reform Act 1967 as amended and Part II of the Leasehold Reform, Housing and Urban Development Act 1993). Long leaseholders of flats can also join together to acquire the freehold of their block by forming a 'right to enfranchise' company and following the procedure set out in Part I of the Leasehold Reform, Housing and Urban Development Act 1993. **Commonhold**, thought by many to be an attractive alternative to the use of the long lease, has made little headway since its introduction in 2002 (see Section 6.5).

Another problem with leases is that **lessors** tend to have significantly more power than their **tenants** or potential tenants. For example, it may be very important for a small business trading from rented premises to be able to renew its lease of those premises. Consequently, the lessor may feel able to demand a higher **rent** when the lease is due for renewal than they might have been able to charge to a new tenant. Parliament has intervened to protect such tenants with a complex set rules contained in Part II of the Landlord and Tenant Act 1954 and its accompanying regulations. Many residential tenants are also vulnerable to the interests of more powerful lessors. For much of the twentieth century, the policy of successive governments was to protect poor tenants by imposing rent control, security of **tenure** (allowing tenants to continue in occupation after the end of the original tenancy) and repairing obligations on landlords through a series of statutes, the last of which was the Rent Act 1977. However, in the 1980s this approach was abandoned in favour of stimulating the private rented sector. The Housing Act 1988 ended rent control and has, especially as amended, effectively removed the security previously enjoyed by private residential tenants. At the same time, public authorities became less able to provide adequate housing for those excluded from home ownership, and the responsibility in this area was transferred mainly to housing associations. These changes, together with a healthy economy, helped stimulate the so-called 'buy-to-let' market, with lenders eager to provide mortgages to support it. Such lending was quickly curtailed as a response to the financial crisis that hit the British economy and property market at the close of the first decade of the twenty-first century. In many cases, lessors fail to obtain the lender's consent to their leases, with the result that the tenant is at considerable risk of losing their home if the lessor defaults on their **mortgage** payments, even if the tenant has consistently paid the rent and observed the terms of the **tenancy**. The Mortgage Repossessions (Protection of Tenants etc) Act 2010 seeks to help such tenants by ensuring that they are allowed a reasonable amount of time to find alternative accommodation.

In 2006, the Law Commission published proposals (which included a draft Bill) to replace the present complicated statutory regime of residential tenancies with a much simpler system of occupation contracts based on a consumer protection approach, as in much of the rest of Europe (Law Com 297, 2006). The proposals applied to any agreement conferring the right to occupy premises as a home (clause 1(2)(a) of the draft Bill), termed 'occupation contracts'. Had the reforms been introduced, they would have removed the significance of the lease/licence distinction in the residential sector, a distinction that has taken up considerable judicial time (see, in particular, Section 7.5.1).

Despite all its faults, however, the lease remains an instrument of enormous flexibility. For example, leases:

- can control housing development, providing both long-term and short-term housing;
- can provide for the changing needs of businesses;
- provide a common and convenient means of holding agricultural land; and
- allow land to be used to provide an income and raise capital.

7.3 The vocabulary of leases

There are several words to describe a lease, including 'tenancy', 'letting', 'demise' and 'term of years absolute'. All these words have the same meaning, but lawyers tend to use 'tenancy' and 'letting' for a short period and 'lease' or 'demise' for a long one.

The word '*term*' can refer to one of the covenants or conditions set out in the lease, but it is also used to refer to the duration of the lease (as in 'term of years absolute').

▶ A lease is granted by a *lessor* (also referred to as *grantor* or *landlord*).
▶ The lessor's interest is referred to as the *reversion*.
▶ A lease is granted to a *tenant* (also referred to as *grantee* or *lessee*).
▶ An *assignment* occurs if the lessor or the lessee transfers the whole of their interest. The new landlord or tenant is referred to as the *assignee*.
▶ If a tenant grants a tenancy out of their own lease, this will be a *subtenancy* (also referred to as an *underlease* or *sublease*). In these circumstances the original tenant's lease is referred to as the *headlease* and the original tenant is the *mesne* (or intermediate) landlord. A sublease must terminate at least a day before the end of the term of the headlease.

One way of keeping track of the various relationships in cases, and when answering problem questions, is to represent the information in the form of a diagram, such as that in Figure 7.1. In this book, leases (including subleases) are always shown as vertical lines, and assignments as horizontal lines. Distinguishing the two types of transaction in this way helps to ensure that they are correctly identified, and that the correct set of rules (especially those in Chapter 8) are applied when analysing a case or problem question.

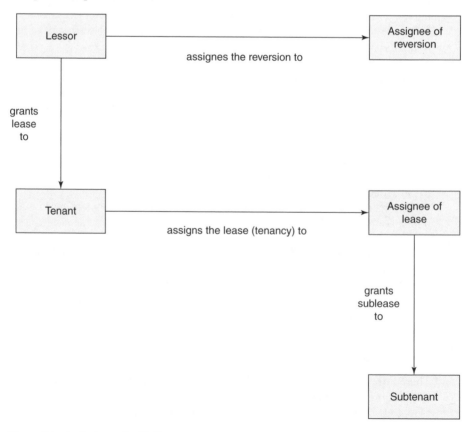

Figure 7.1 Assigning and subletting

7.4 Types of lease

There are several different types of lease. Although this chapter is mainly concerned with fixed term tenancies and periodic tenancies, it is important to be able to recognise other types of **tenancy** when they occur (as the case of *Mexfield Housing Co-operative Ltd v Berrisford* [2012] 1 AC 955 (SC), considered at Section 7.5.2, illustrates).

7.4.1 Fixed term tenancy

A lease granted for a specific period of time and which will terminate at the end of that period.

7.4.2 Periodic tenancy

A 'periodic tenancy' is a lease for a specific period that can be continually repeated until one side gives notice bringing it to an end. A weekly or monthly period is common for furnished accommodation, and a yearly period for agricultural tenancies. If a person uses land and regularly pays money to the owner, then, provided they also have **exclusive possession** (see Section 7.5.3), the common law implies a periodic tenancy unless the parties intended something else. The period of the tenancy is decided by the period by which **rent** is assessed, not necessarily by the period of payment (*Richardson v Langridge* (1811) 128 ER 27 (CP)). Thus, if the rent is '£1,000 per year, payable monthly', there is an implied legal yearly tenancy.

7.4.3 Tenancy at will

A tenancy at will is, in many ways, similar to a **licence**. Although the 'tenant' has exclusive possession of the land, either side can end the arrangement at any time, and it is not an **estate** in land. Tenancies at will can be created expressly or by implication, typically where the tenant has moved into possession, or is holding over at the end of the lease, while the terms of a new lease are being negotiated.

The circumstances giving rise to an implied tenancy at will can be very similar to those which create an implied periodic tenancy (see Section 7.4.2). The distinction is important because whereas periodic tenants have the protection of various statutory schemes, tenants at will do not. In many cases, the question of rent will be decisive. In *Banjo v Brent LBC* [2005] 1 WLR 2520 (CA), Mr Banjo originally occupied his house under a long lease and continued in occupation after the lease had expired. The Court of Appeal held that this was a tenancy at will and not an implied periodic tenancy because, as Chadwick LJ observed (at [18]):

> Mr Banjo paid no rent after the end of the contractual term of the long lease; and, so far as appears from the evidence, the Borough did not demand (or take any steps to enforce) payment of rent.

However, payment of rent is not conclusive, as according to Nicholls LJ in *Javad v Mohammed Aqil* [1991] 1 WLR 1007 (CA), at 1012:

> The law will imply, from what was agreed and all the surrounding circumstances, the terms the parties are to be taken to have intended to apply.

Erimus Housing Ltd v Barclays Wealth Trustees (Jersey) Ltd [2014] 2 P & CR 4 (CA) arose following protracted negotiations for a new tenancy after the original lease had expired in October 2009. The tenant had remained in occupation and paid rent. Although the terms of a new lease were eventually agreed, it was never completed and the tenant had indicated at several times that it intended to vacate the premises before the end of the term of the new lease. According to Patten LJ (at [23]):

> When a party holds over after the end of the term of a lease he does so, without more, as a tenant on sufferance until his possession is consented to by the landlord. With such consent he becomes at the very least a tenant at will ... The payment of rent gives rise to no presumption of a periodic tenancy. Rather, the parties' contractual intentions fall to be determined by looking objectively at all relevant circumstances.

Where the parties are negotiating the form of a new lease, as here, the usual inference will be that the parties did not intend to enter into any type of contractual arrangement, such as a periodic tenancy, that would be inconsistent with the ongoing negotiations.

7.4.4   Perpetually renewable leases

The perpetually renewable lease differs from the periodic tenancy (see Section 7.4.2) because the lease continues as long as the tenant chooses, with the lessor unable to give notice in any circumstances. This kind of arrangement was formerly common in agricultural lettings with absentee lessors, but is anomalous within the 1925 structure of land ownership. Since 1925, all new leases of this type are automatically converted into a lease for 2,000 years, with special rules for giving notice (see Schedule 15 of the LPA 1922). The courts now lean against interpreting a renewal clause as being perpetual, as in *Marjorie Burnett Ltd* v *Barclay* (1980) 258 EG 642 (Ch), where Nourse J held that a right to renew with a further right of renewal gave the tenant the right to renew twice, rather than perpetually.

7.4.5   Tenancy at sufferance

Tenancy at sufferance arises if a tenant remains in occupation ('holds over') after the lease has expired, without the lessor's agreement. The lessor can evict the tenant at any time, but if they accept **rent**, the tenant becomes a tenant at will or even a periodic tenant.

7.4.6   Leases for life or until marriage

Before 1926, there were two types of lease that could exist as legal estates: the **term of years absolute** and the lease for life or until marriage. By section 1 of the LPA 1925, only the first of these can now be legal, but because some people with legal leases for life or until marriage would have suddenly found themselves to be merely **equitable** lessees on 1st January 1926, section 149(6) of the LPA 1925 converted their interests into legal leases for 90 years, provided that **rent** is payable. Such a lease can be determined by one month's notice following death or marriage. The outcome in *Mexfield Housing Co-operative Ltd* v *Berrisford* (see Section 7.5.2(c)) means that section 149(6) is now of contemporary relevance and not just historical interest.

7.4.7   Lease of the reversion

Where a lessor creates a lease of their remaining interest, they are leasing the **reversion**. This is also called a 'concurrent lease'. The tenant of the reversion has the right to collect rent and enforce other covenants against the tenant of the lease. Note that a *lease of the reversion* is not the same as a *reversionary lease* (see Section 7.5.2(a)).

7.4.8   Tenancy by estoppel

If a person attempts to grant a lease that they could not grant because they had no **title**, they are estopped from subsequently denying their tenant's rights against them. This is part of the ordinary principle of **estoppel**. Such a tenancy is personal and does not create an estate in land. However, if the lessor subsequently gains the legal title, then the tenant is automatically 'clothed' with the legal lease (this is known as 'feeding the estoppel').

Feeding the estoppel

In *Bruton* v *London & Quadrant Housing Trust* [2000] 1 AC 406 (HL) (considered in detail in Section 7.5.3), the Trust expressly granted a **licence** to Mr Bruton. However, because the licence included all the ingredients characteristic of a tenancy, Mr Bruton was held to have a (contractual) lease, but not a legal estate. The question of a tenancy by estoppel did not arise in Bruton (per Lord Hoffmann, 415–16), but in *Kay* v *Lambeth LBC* [2006] AC 465 (HL) the House of Lords had to consider whether a 'Bruton-style' non-estate lease could be 'fed' so as to be binding on Lambeth LBC, which owned the **freehold** in the block of flats. The tenancy could not have been binding on the council when it was originally created, as the council did not grant it, and neither was it carved out of any estate granted by the council to the Trust. However, in 1995, after the grant of the tenancy to Mr Bruton, the council had granted the Trust a legal lease of the block of flats. This legal leasehold estate in the land was enough to 'feed the estoppel' implicit in the non-estate lease to Mr Bruton, converting Mr Bruton's tenancy into a legal estate. Unfortunately for Mr Bruton, however, his estate was subject to the terms of the 1995 lease. (The Trust could not give Mr Bruton a greater estate than they themselves owned.) In 1999, the council terminated the lease to the Trust, automatically determining any lesser estates dependent upon it, including those held by Mr Bruton and the other tenants of the flats. Consequently, the occupiers of the flats had no estate that they could enforce against the council, although they might have had an action in damages against the Trust if they could demonstrate that it was in breach of its obligations under the tenancies.

7.5   The essentials of a lease

It will often be of significant importance to the parties whether the relationship between them is an interest in the land or merely a contractual right to use the land. Normally, only a lease will be attached to the land so as to automatically bind any third party who acquires the **freehold reversion**. However, not all leases are legal **estates**, or even interests in land. In *Bruton* v *London & Quadrant Housing Trust* [2000] 1 AC 406 (HL), the House of Lords held that it was possible to create a purely contractual (or 'non-estate') lease that is not binding on third parties (see Section 7.5.3). Such contractual leases share this characteristic of **licences** while also affording the occupier of the land many of the statutory rights enjoyed by **tenants**. In practice, non-estate leases are very rare, and the lawyer's task is usually to determine whether a particular relationship is a lease or a mere licence. Licences are considered in detail in Chapter 9, and a number of more unusual types of lease have been explained at Section 7.4.

Perhaps the most well-known definition of a lease, to land lawyers, at least, is that provided by Lord Templeman in *Street* v *Mountford* [1985] AC 809 (HL) at 818:

> To constitute a tenancy the occupier must be granted *exclusive possession* for a *fixed or periodic term certain* in *consideration of a premium or periodical payments*. The grant may be express, or may be inferred where the owner accepts weekly or other periodical payments from the occupier. (Emphasis added.)

In much of his speech, Lord Templeman seems to use the term 'rent' to include both **premiums** and periodical payments. This is unfortunate as it might give the impression that payment of a **rent** is essential for the existence of a lease. This is not the case. Not only does section 205(1)(xvii) of the LPA 1925 define a **term of years absolute** as existing 'whether or not at a rent', but there is no requirement for consideration if the lease is created by a **deed** (*Ashburn Anstalt* v *WJ Arnold & Co* [1989] Ch 1 (CA)). In very long leases it is not uncommon for the rent to be a purely nominal sum, or even a peppercorn. A premium is an upfront capital sum paid by the tenant to the lessor: for example, the tenant of a long lease of a flat will usually pay a premium at the beginning of the lease, and a relatively nominal rent, unlike the substantial monthly rent that is usual with shorter residential tenancies.

7.5.1 Exclusive possession

7.5.1(a) The distinction between a lease and a licence

If a person occupying another's land does not have exclusive possession (the right to keep the owner out), they are not a tenant under a lease but only a licensee. The word 'licensee' describes anyone who has a permission to be on land. These 'non-interests-in-land' are considered in Chapter 9. A **licence** can be created by contract, with a regular payment of what looks like rent, in which case it may closely resemble a lease. However, licences are merely **personal rights**: they cannot usually be transferred to third parties and are unlikely to bind a buyer of the land.

The difference between a lease and a licence is 'notoriously difficult' (Bridge [1986] Conv 344), and there are hundreds of pages of judgments devoted to explaining the difference. Historically, the distinction was most important in the residential sector because of the rights given to many residential tenants by statute. For much of the twentieth century, statute law not only protected the occupation of private tenants, it also gave them the right to claim a fair **rent**. 'Mere licensees' enjoyed neither of these statutory protections, although certain terms are implied into licences (see Section 9.5.1). However, this difference is no longer of such importance. The Housing Act 1988 introduced the form of short-term residential **tenancy** known as the 'assured shorthold' tenancy with effect from 15th January 1989, and this and further reforms mean that private landlords can with a little care ensure that they receive a market rent without granting the tenant statutory security. The case law nevertheless remains relevant to commercial agreements, to any residential occupation agreements made before 15th January 1989, and to cases where an occupier must hold a lease in order to gain the benefit of a statute (as, for example, in *Bruton*).

7.5.1(b) Street v Mountford

The decision of the House of Lords in *Street* v *Mountford* [1985] AC 809 (HL) was a milestone in the case law on the lease/licence distinction. Mr Street (a solicitor) let Mrs Mountford live in a house that he owned in return for a weekly payment. In a written agreement, headed 'Licence', she accepted rules about visitors and heating, and eviction if the 'licence fee' was more than a week late. Mr Street reserved the right to enter the house to inspect it. Such agreements had formerly been assumed to be licences and the agreement between Mr Street and Mrs Mountford clearly stated that it was not intended to create a tenancy protected under the Rent Act 1977. Despite this, the House of Lords held that this was a weekly tenancy, thus allowing Mrs Mountford to claim the protection of the Act.

Lord Templeman was clear that an occupier of residential land must be either a tenant or a licensee, and (at 816) that:

> The tenant possessing exclusive possession is able to exercise the rights of an owner of land, which is in the real sense his land albeit temporarily and subject to certain restrictions. A tenant armed with exclusive possession can keep out strangers and keep out the landlord.

Consequentially, the normal test of a tenancy is the factual question of 'exclusive possession' rather than the expressed intention of the parties. As Lord Templeman explained at 818–19:

> The occupier is a lodger [licensee] if the landlord provides attendance or services which require the landlord or his servants to exercise unrestricted access to and use of the premises. … If on the other hand residential accommodation is granted for a term at a rent with exclusive possession, the landlord providing neither attendance nor services, the grant is a tenancy … The manufacture of a five-pronged implement for digging results in a fork even if the manufacturer, unfamiliar with the English language, insists he intended to make and has made a spade.

7.5.1(c) Exceptions to the rule

However, there are a limited number of situations where exclusive possession does not mean that the occupant is a tenant. In *Street* v *Mountford*, Lord Templeman explained (at 826–7):

> Sometimes it may appear from the surrounding circumstances that there was no intention to create legal relationships. Sometimes it may appear from the surrounding circumstances that the right to exclusive possession is referable to a legal relationship other than a tenancy. Legal relationships to which the grant of exclusive possession might be referable and which would or might negative the grant of an estate or interest in the land include occupancy under a contract for the sale of the land, occupancy pursuant to a contract of employment or occupancy referable to the holding of an office.

So, for example, in *Carroll* v *Manek* (2000) 79 P & CR 173 (Ch), a hotel manager who had accommodation on the premises was held not to be a tenant because, in the words of HH Judge Hicks QC (at [44]):

> Occupation by a service occupier of that kind is one of the classical examples of cases in which exclusive possession does not confer a tenancy.

The question of whether the circumstances negate the presumption of a tenancy is one of fact: the court must consider carefully the relationship between the parties and the intentions that should be attributed to them. In *Family Housing Association* v *Jones* [1990] 1 WLR 779 (CA), the court held that the intention to create a tenancy was not precluded where a housing association had provided temporary accommodation to a homeless person, pursuant to an arrangement with the local housing authority. In *Bruton* (see Sections 7.1 and 7.5.3) the House of Lords expressly adopted the reasoning of Slade LJ in *Jones* in holding that the case lay outside of the range exceptions to the principle in *Street* v *Mountford*, albeit with very little scrutiny. *Gray* v *Taylor* [1998]

1 WLR 1093 (CA) concerned a person who had been selected as an almsperson and given rooms in an almshouse run by a charity: it was held that she was a **beneficiary** under the trusts of the charity and that she occupied her rooms in that capacity and not as a tenant. Interestingly, *Family Housing Association* v *Jones* was cited in argument in *Gray*, but not referred to in any of the judgments. *Gray* v *Taylor* was recently applied in the recent case of *Watts* v *Stewart* [2017] 2 WLR 1107 (CA), where the evicted almsperson argued that her eviction would be a breach of her **human rights** under article 14 of the ECHR (discrimination) in conjunction with article 8 (the right to respect of her home). The Court of Appeal concluded that *Macdonald* v *Macdonald* [2017] AC 273 (SC) left the question as to when article 8 is engaged 'unclear on the authorities' ([75]), but decided that even if article 8 was engaged on the facts, it was doubtful that being an almsperson was a qualifying characteristic for the purposes of article 14 ([83]), and that even if it was, the difference of treatment as between the occupiers of almshouses and the occupiers of other forms of social housing was objectively justifiable ([87]).

7.5.1(d) Applying the rule in Street v Mountford

Subject to these exceptional circumstances, the principle in *Street* v *Mountford* has been held to apply to all types of occupation agreement, including shops and agricultural land. It soon became clear, however, that multiple occupation, as is common in rented flats, posed different problems. In *AG Securities* v *Vaughan* and *Antoniades* v *Villiers* [1990] 1 AC 417 (HL), the House of Lords held, in the first of this pair of cases heard together, that a group of four people who shared a flat could not be tenants, because they had independent agreements that did not confer a right of exclusive possession on any occupant. Each of the occupants had merely a right to share the flat with others. Further, because the four agreements had been made on different dates and with different terms and rents, they could not be construed as creating a **joint tenancy**, which was necessary if the occupiers were to share a legal estate in the land (see Sections 13.3 and 13.4). Consequently, in *AG Securities* v *Vaughan* the four occupants were merely licensees. In the case of *Antoniades* v *Villiers*, however, a 'licence agreement', which seemed to give the owner the right to sleep in the tiny flat with a cohabiting couple, was held to be a tenancy. The term looked as if it denied exclusive possession to the couple, but the House of Lords held that it was a pretence, inserted into the agreement merely in order to avoid giving Rent Act protection to the occupants. Consequently, the term had no effect.

Essentially, the question is whether the agreement itself gave exclusive possession to the tenant (or the tenants jointly) so that they had the right to keep the owner out. However, it is often impossible to decide what the agreement means, or whether a term in it is a pretence, without looking at the facts of the whole case. Thus, the House of Lords decided in *Westminster City Council* v *Clarke* [1992] 2 AC 288 (HL) that a person given temporary accommodation by a local council did not have a tenancy but only a licence. Lord Templeman held that this was 'a very special case' (at 302), quite different from private lettings, and that there was no exclusive possession because of the purpose of this agreement. A term that the occupant could be moved at any time to another room (thereby denying the occupant the degree of control characteristic of a tenant) was not a pretence, because the council needed it in order to fulfil its statutory duty to vulnerable people.

In *Bruton* v *London & Quadrant Housing Trust* [2000] 1 AC 406 (HL), the objectives of the housing trust were arguably very close to those of the council in *Clarke*. However, according to Lord Hoffmann (at 413):

the classification of the agreement as a lease does not depend upon any intention additional to that expressed in the choice of terms. It is simply a question of characterising the terms which the parties have agreed.

Consequently, despite the very clear wording of the licence agreement (see Section 7.1) and the fact that the Trust did not hold a legal **estate** in the land, the fact that the House of Lords was able to hold that Mr Bruton had exclusive possession of his flat meant that he was necessarily a tenant and not a mere licensee. Lord Hoffmann continued (at 413–14):

> There is nothing to suggest that he was to share possession with the trust, the council or anyone else. The trust did not retain such control over the premises as was inconsistent with Mr Bruton having exclusive possession, as was the case in *Westminster City Council v. Clarke* ... The only rights which it reserved were for itself and the council to enter at certain times and for limited purposes. As Lord Templeman said in *Street v. Mountford* ... such an express reservation "only serves to emphasise the fact that the grantee is entitled to exclusive possession and is a tenant".

The principle in *Street v Mountford* that the status of an agreement depends upon the substantive rights granted by it, and not the labels used within it, does not mean that the wording of the agreement is necessarily completely irrelevant. In *National Car Parks Ltd v The Trinity Development Co (Banbury) Ltd* [2002] 2 P & CR 18 (CA), Arden LJ observed (at [28]):

> the court must look to the substance and not to the form. But it may help, in determining what the substance was, to consider whether the parties expressed themselves in a particular way. ... It would in my judgment be a strong thing for the law to disregard totally the parties' choice of wording and to do so would be inconsistent with the general principle of freedom of contract and the principle that documents should be interpreted as a whole.

In *Clear Channel UK Ltd v Manchester City Council* [2005] EWCA Civ 1304, Clear Channel was given the right to erect large advertising signs within various plots of land owned by the council. In each case, the agreement identified the general site of the signs, without defining the specific land on which the signs were to be erected. The Court of Appeal held that for exclusive possession to exist the extent of the land concerned must be capable of precise definition. Although this was sufficient to decide the issue, Jonathan Parker LJ went on to say (at [29]):

> the fact remains that this was a contract negotiated between two substantial parties of equal bargaining power and with the benefit of full legal advice. Where the contract so negotiated contains not merely a label but a clause which sets out in unequivocal terms the parties' intention as to its legal effect, I would in any event have taken some persuading that its true effect was directly contrary to that expressed intention.

Both Arden LJ and Jonathan Parker LJ emphasised that they had no intention of undermining the principles of *Street v Mountford*. However, at least in the case of a commercial agreement, where both parties have equal expertise and bargaining power, an examination of the agreement as a whole would now seem to include considering the labels that the parties have chosen to use to describe their agreement.

7.5.2 A fixed beginning and a certain end

7.5.2(a) The general principles

The period of a lease (its term) can be anything from a few hours to thousands of years. The term does not need to start on the date of the document creating it; it can be set to start up to 21 years in the future (LPA 1925, s 149(3)): such a lease is called a **reversionary lease**. However, whenever the term begins, its maximum duration must be ascertainable at the outset. The terms of the lease may allow for it to end ('determine') earlier (see Section 7.7), but the maximum term granted must be certain. As Lord Greene MR explained in *Lace v Chantler* [1944] KB 368 (CA), at 370:

> A term created by a leasehold tenancy agreement must be expressed either with certainty and specifically or by reference to something which can, at the time when the lease takes effect, be looked at as a certain ascertainment of what the term was meant to be.

The present requirements for certainty of term were set out by the House of Lords in *Prudential Assurance Co Ltd v London Residuary Body* [1992] 2 AC 386 (HL) and summarised by Lord Neuberger MR in the Supreme Court case of *Mexfield Housing Co-operative Ltd v Berrisford* [2012] 1 AC 955 (SC) (at [33], with minor reformatting):

> (i)   an agreement for a term, whose maximum duration can be identified from the inception can give rise to a valid tenancy;
> (ii)   an agreement which gives rise to a periodic arrangement determinable by either party can also give rise to a valid tenancy;
> (iii)   an agreement could not give rise to a tenancy as a matter of law if it was for a term whose maximum duration was uncertain at the inception;
> (iv)   (a) a fetter on a right to serve notice to determine a periodic tenancy was ineffective if the fetter is to endure for an uncertain period, but (b) a fetter for a specified period could be valid.

Subparagraphs (i) and (iii) apply to fixed term tenancies; while (ii) and (iv) apply to periodic tenancies.

7.5.2(b) Fixed term tenancies

Prudential Assurance Co Ltd v London Residuary Body [1992] 2 AC 386 (HL) concerned an attempt by a London council to grant a lease of a piece of land until it was 'required by the council for the purposes of the widening of Walworth Road and the street paving works rendered necessary thereby'. Confirming previous authorities, including *Lace v Chantler*, the House of Lords held that there was insufficient certainty about the date of the end of the lease, and therefore it could not be a valid **term of years absolute**. It went on to hold that there was, instead, a lease 'from year to year' (a periodic legal tenancy) which the council's successor in **title** could end by giving six months' notice (as is usual under a yearly tenancy).

7.5.2(c) Periodic tenancies

Although a **periodic tenancy** is theoretically a lease for a specific term, in practice the term is continually renewed until one side gives notice bringing it to an end. As Baroness Hale noted in *Mexfield Housing Co-operative Ltd v Berrisford* [2012] 1 AC 955 (SC) (at [87]):

> Periodic tenancies obviously pose something of a puzzle if the law insists that the maximum term of any leasehold estate be certain. The rule was invented long before periodic tenancies were invented and it has always been a problem how the rule is to apply to them. In one sense the term is certain, as it comes to an end when the week, the month, the quarter or the year for which it has been granted comes to an end. But that is not the practical reality, as the law assumes a re-letting (or the extension of the term) at the end of each period, unless one or other of the parties gives notice to quit.

In *Mexfield*, the Supreme Court had to consider whether there was sufficient certainty of term for Ms Berrisford to have a periodic tenancy. The agreement was expressed to be from month to month, but it also provided that Mexfield could only terminate Ms Berrisford's occupancy in very limited circumstances. The Court of Appeal decided that there was no lease because the maximum term of the agreement was rendered uncertain by the limitations on Mexfield's right to terminate it. The Supreme Court agreed that Ms Berrisford's lease did not satisfy the certainty requirements for a periodic tenancy. However, the Court was persuaded of the existence of a common law rule (albeit a rather ancient and obscure one) that converts an attempt to grant a lease to an individual for an uncertain term into a lease for life. Such leases for life are, in turn, converted into leases for a fixed term of 90 years by section 149(6) of the Law of Property Act 1925 (see Section 7.4.6). Consequently, Ms Berrisford had been granted a 90-year lease.

This result seems to reflect the original intentions of the parties in *Mexfield* (Ms Berrisford's tenancy was the result of a **mortgage** rescue scheme set up by a bank to help people keep their homes when they fell into difficulty with their mortgage payments). However, as Baroness Hale noted (at [94]):

> ... our conclusions are in fact reflecting the intentions of the parties. But it is not difficult to imagine circumstances in which the same analysis would apply but be very far from the intentions of the parties. And that analysis is not available where the tenant is a company or corporation.

In the recent case of *Southward Housing Co-operative Ltd v Walker* [2016] Ch 443 (Ch), Hildyard J held that on the facts before him it was clear that the parties had never intended that the occupants would be legally entitled to stay in the premises for life. He went on to consider whether this meant that the rule in *Mexfield* would not apply. He acknowledged that the language of the judgments in *Mexfield* strongly suggests that the intention of the parties as to whether or not the rule applies is irrelevant. Ultimately, however, Hildyard J concluded (at [91]) that:

> the 'rule' does not depend for its application on the parties' intentions; but the judgments of the Supreme Court in the *Mexfield* case leave open the possibility that it may be disapplied where those intentions and fundamental aspects of their agreement would be confounded by it.

At [92] he added:

> I am fortified in this conclusion by the consideration that the origin of the 'rule' must have been intended to save agreements that would otherwise fail ... not to destroy the essence of their bargain and foist on them a long term relationship against their will and which one of them may not be able to terminate.

The problems with requiring certainty of term

Although well established in English law, the rule requiring certainty of term has attracted considerable judicial criticism. One concern is that it limits the contractual freedom of the parties for little apparent benefit. Another is that the recognition of periodic tenancies (that is, tenancies that are renewed indefinitely until one of the parties acts to terminate them) seems to be somewhat inconsistent with the insistence upon certainty. Lord Browne-Wilkinson concluded his speech in the *Prudential* case with the following words (at 396):

> This bizarre outcome results from the application of an ancient and technical rule of law. ... No one has produced any satisfactory rationale for the genesis of this rule. No one has been able to point to any useful purpose that it serves at the present day.

His comments were echoed by Lord Neuberger MR some 20 years later in *Mexfield*, while in the same case Baroness Hale remarked (at [88]) that:

> These rules have an Alice in Wonderland quality which makes it unsurprising that distinguished judges have sometimes had difficulty with them.

Kelvin Low, in his article 'Certainty of Terms and Leases: Curiouser and Curiouser' (2012) 75 MLR 401, has suggested that the judicial criticism of the rule is misplaced, at least in so far as that criticism is justified by reference to the way in which the rule interferes with the autonomy of the parties. As Low points out (at 403), however:

> it has long been recognised that contracting parties may not create property rights willy nilly as they fancy which thereafter bind their successors.

In *Mexfield*, Lord Neuberger set out six largely practical reasons why the Supreme Court could not simply jettison the certainty rule, including its antiquity, the fact that it is implicit in the definition of a term of years for the purposes of the LPA 1925, and because it was accepted, however reluctantly, by the House of Lords in the *Prudential* case ([35]–[37]). Low, however, suggests that we should be reluctant to tinker with the rule because it concerns a fundamental element of property law; the status of the *numerus clausus* (see Section 1.4.2). In *Bruton* (see Section 7.5.3), the House of Lords recognised that it is possible to create a lease that is not a legal estate. It might be argued that the certainty rule should, like the need for sufficient **title**, be treated as part of the requirements for a proprietary lease (by virtue of section 1(1)(b) of the LPA 1925), rather than an essential characteristic of a lease as such. However, a lease without the security of an estate is unlikely to be of long-term benefit, as Mr Bruton was ultimately to find.

7.5.3 Capable grantor and capable grantee

Prior to the case of *Bruton v London & Quadrant Housing Trust* [2000] 1 AC 406 (HL), it was generally thought that a lessor could only grant a lease if that lease were capable of existing as a legal **estate**. This required the lessor to own an estate in the land greater than the lease being granted (based on the principle of *nemo dat quod non habet*: no one can give something which they do not have). This requirement is not usually a problem, although it should be noted that:

- a minor (person under the age of 18) cannot hold a legal estate in land (LPA 1925, s 1(6));
- the law restricts the rights of those unable to deal with their own affairs because of mental illness or deterioration to create or transfer legal estates in land; and
- the power of corporate bodies to grant and accept leases will depend upon whether they are given the necessary powers by their memorandum and articles of association (in the case of a limited company) or by statute (in the case of local authorities and government-created agencies).

In *Bruton*, however, the House of Lords held that it was possible to create a purely contractual (or non-estate) lease. As Blackburne J (sitting in the Court of Appeal) explained in the case of *Islington LBC v Green* [2005] EWCA Civ 56 (at [10]):

> The relationship of landlord and tenant is not dependent on whether the lease or tenancy creates an estate or other proprietary interest which may be binding on third parties. Whether a lease creates a proprietary interest in turn will depend upon whether the landlord has an interest out of which he has granted it.

In *Bruton*, Mr Bruton had brought an action against the Trust, based on the covenants for repair that are implied into leases (but not **licences**) by section 11 of the Landlord and Tenant Act 1985 (the facts are set out in more detail in Section 7.1).

Having decided that the agreement satisfied all the other requirements for a lease (the main issue was whether **exclusive possession** had been granted; see Section 7.5.1), the House of Lords concluded that Mr Bruton had a tenancy of the flat even though he held no legal estate in the land. Consequently, section 11 applied to the arrangement between Mr Bruton and the Trust. While non-estate tenancies like Mr Bruton's may have significant implications for the original parties, their impact on third parties is much more limited, since they do not constitute proprietary interests (*Kay* v *Lambeth LBC* [2006] 2 AC 465 (HL), considered in Section 7.4.8).

7.5.4 Analysing an occupation agreement

When considering the status of a particular agreement it is important to systemati-cally consider all of the ingredients required for a lease. Although most cases and problem questions require greater attention to be given to some of them than others, all of the essentials for a lease must be demonstrated for there to be a valid legal ten-ancy. The diagram in Figure 7.2 suggests one way of approaching this type of ques-tion (including the place of the formalities referred to in the next section).

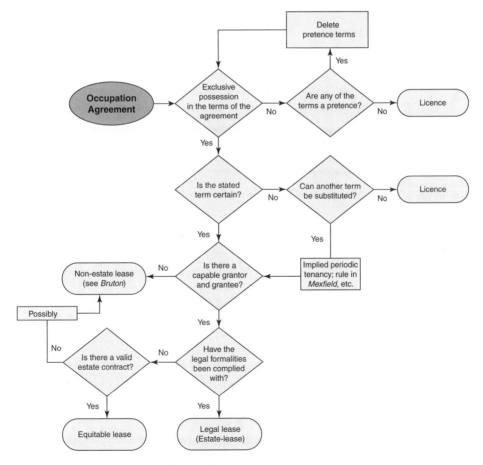

Figure 7.2 Analysing the status of occupation agreements

7.6   The creation of leases

7.6.1   Legal formalities

The rules for the creation of legal interests in land are examined in detail in Section 15.5. Briefly:

- no formalities are required to create a legal lease for a term not exceeding three years, provided that it takes effect in possession and is at the best **rent** reasonably obtainable (LPA 1925, ss 52 and 54(2));
- a **deed** is necessary to *create* any other legal lease; and
- a lease for a term exceeding seven years (and certain other types of lease) will only be legal **estates** if **registered** at the Land Registry (Land Registration Act (LRA) 2002, s 4(1) and s 27(2)(b); see Sections 4.4 and 15.5).

A deed is always required to *assign* a legal lease, even a lease falling within section 54(2) (*Crago* v *Julian* [1992] 1 WLR 372 (CA), see Section 15.5.1(c)). If there is no deed where one is needed (or the registered land procedure is not followed), then only an **equitable** interest will be created or transferred.

7.6.2   Equitable leases

Between the original parties, a valid contract for a lease is almost as good as a legal lease. In *Walsh* v *Lonsdale* (1882) LR 21 ChD 9 (CA), the parties had agreed a seven-year lease of a mill. Since the **tenant** had moved in and was paying a yearly **rent**, there was possibly also an implied legal periodic yearly tenancy. Jessel MR concluded (at 14–15):

> The tenant holds under an agreement for a lease. He holds therefore under the same terms in equity as if a lease had been granted, it being a case in which both parties admit that relief is capable of being given by specific performance.

The Judicature Acts of 1873 and 1875 (now the Senior Courts Act 1981, s 49(1)) required that where the rules of equity and the common law conflicted on the same matter, the **equitable** rules should prevail. The landlord of the mill was therefore able to enforce the 'rent in advance' term in the equitable seven-year lease against the tenant.

Walsh v Lonsdale was followed in *R* v *Tower Hamlets LBC, ex parte von Goetz* [1999] QB 1019 (CA). Miss von Goetz had a ten-year assured shorthold **tenancy** of a house. Although a written contract had been agreed (so the requirements of section 2 of the Law of Property (Miscellaneous Provisions) Act 1989 were satisfied), no **deed** had ever been executed. The council argued that this equitable lease could not attract a renovation grant under the Local Government and Housing Act 1989, since, in its view, such leases had to be legal. In rejecting the council's appeal, Mummery LJ stated (at 1023 and 1025) that Miss von Goetz had:

> for all practical purposes an interest as good as a legal interest … [and that] if she asked the grantors for a deed to perfect the legal title, there is no ground on which that could be refused.

Why an equitable lease is not as strong as a legal lease
As indicated above, the terms in a valid agreement for lease will normally prevail as between the original parties (for the requirements for a valid contract concerning land,

see Section 15.4). However, such a lease, while valid in equity, has a number of disadvantages when compared to a legal leasehold estate.

1. There is no guarantee that an equitable lease will be binding upon third parties. If the **title** to the land is **registered**, the equitable tenant's interest will almost certainly be **overriding** if the tenant is in actual occupation, otherwise it must be protected by entry of a **notice** on the **Title Register** (see Chapter 4). If title to the land is still **unregistered**, the equitable lease must be protected by registering a Class C(iv) **land charge** (see Section 5.4.2(c)).
2. A contract for lease can effectively be converted into a legal lease through the remedy of specific performance. However, because specific performance is an equitable remedy it is also a discretionary remedy and there will be circumstances in which the court will be unwilling to grant it. In particular, a successful claimant must come to equity 'with clean hands', willing and able to perform their side of the bargain.
3. If the agreement for lease pre-dates 1st January 1996, there is some doubt as to whether the burden of the **covenants** can pass on **assignment** (see Section 8.4.5).
4. Unlike a legal lease created by **deed**, a contract for lease is not a conveyance for the purposes of the LPA 1925. Consequently, the rights and privileges granted to the tenant will be limited to those set out in the contract and none will be incorporated by virtue of section 62 of the LPA 1925.

7.6.3 Statutory conditions

Generally, the parties to a lease are free to agree what terms they wish, although the common law will imply certain terms deemed characteristic of the relationship between **lessor** and **lessee**. Certain types of lease are also subject to terms implied by statute, such as the repairing obligations imposed on lessors of residential accommodation by section 11 of the Landlord and Tenant Act 1985. (See, for example, *Bruton* v *London & Quadrant Housing Trust* [2000] 1 AC 406 (HL) and Section 8.2.2.)

Part 4 of the Equality Act 2010, which came into force on 1st October 2010, prohibits owners of property discriminating on the grounds of disability, race, religion or belief, sex, sexual orientation or gender reassignment when choosing a tenant. The Act also requires lessors to make or allow reasonable adjustments to premises required to make it easier for people with disabilities to use them. The only common exceptions concern small houses or flats where the lessor lives on the premises and does not employ anyone to manage them. The 2010 Act simplifies and strengthens anti-discrimination law, which was previously contained in a number of pieces of legislation (including the Sex Discrimination Act 1975, the Race Relations Act 1976 and the Disability Discrimination Act 1995). Such discrimination is a tort, and the victim can take action for damages, an **injunction** and/or a declaration (Part 9 of the Equality Act 2010).

7.7 The ending (determination) of leases

Since all leases must be only for a limited period, sooner or later they must end ('determine'). This happens through:

- *forfeiture* (where the **lessor** repossesses the land following the **tenant's** breach of **covenant**; see Sections 8.6.1(c) and 8.6.2(a));
- *expiry* (when the period ends);

- *notice* (for example, a month's notice for monthly periodic tenancies, half a year's notice for yearly tenants, or as specified in the lease);
- *surrender* (where the tenant gives up the lease with the agreement of the lessor); there can be no unilateral surrender (*Barrett* v *Morgan* [2000] 2 AC 264 (HL));
- *frustration* (very rarely: for example, where there is some physical catastrophe; for discussion of the principles involved, see *National Carriers Ltd* v *Panalpina (Northern) Ltd* [1981] AC 675 (HL));
- *repudiatory breach* (rarely, but where the lessor is in fundamental breach of their obligations under the lease, it may be possible for the tenant to accept this breach and walk away from the lease; *Hussein* v *Mehlman* [1992] 2 EGLR 287 (CC) and Section 8.6.2(b)); or
- *merger* (where the tenant obtains the **freehold**). Certain tenants have the right under statute to extend their long lease or to buy their freehold, the main example being tenants of houses held on long leases at a low **rent**. When a number of his tenants exercised their rights under the Leasehold Reform Act 1967 to claim the freehold of their leases, the Duke of Westminster in *James* v *UK* (1986) 8 EHRR 123 argued unsuccessfully that his rights to his property under ECHR Article 1, Protocol 1 had been violated (see Section 1.4). The European Court of Human Rights found that the provisions of the 1967 Act, intended to provide a measure of protection for certain tenants against the diminishing value of their leases (see Section 7.2), were not disproportionate.

Summary

7.1 Leases sit at the boundary between contract law and property law. It is often important to determine whether a particular relationship is a lease or a licence.

7.2 Leases are common because of the flexibility they offer. They are socially and economically important.

7.3 Care must be taken to use the correct vocabulary when considering leases and any transactions involving them.

7.4 There are a number of types of lease. Care must be taken to identify a lease correctly as different rules apply to different types.

7.5 The main ingredients of a lease are:

- exclusive possession;
- a fixed beginning and a certain end; and
- a capable grantor and a capable grantee.

7.6 No formalities are required to create a lease not exceeding three years, provided it is at a market rent and takes effect in possession. Legal leases exceeding three years must be created by deed. Leases exceeding seven years will only be legal leases if completed by registration at the Land Registry. The terms of a lease are those agreed by the parties, together with any implied by statute.

7.7 There are a number of ways, in addition to expiry of the term, in which a lease may be determined (ended).

Exercises

 7.1 Complete the online quiz on the topics covered in this chapter on the companion website.

7.2 '[It] is common ground (a) that whether a contractual relationship governing the use and occupation of land creates a tenancy or a licence depends not on the label which the parties have applied to it but rather on their substantive rights and obligations under it; and (b) that for a tenancy to exist the occupier must have the right to exclusive possession of the land in question' (*Clear Channel UK Ltd* v *Manchester City Council* [2005] EWCA Civ 1304 (at [11]) (Parker LJ)). Discuss.

7.3 Pilbeam owns a house in London, which he converted into three one-bedroom flats some years ago. He granted Yasmin a lease of Flat 1 until she got married. The tenant of Flat 2 is Javed, who was told by Pilbeam that he could have a lease until his parents come over from Pakistan. Six months ago, Pilbeam rented Flat 3 to Brenda on a one-year 'licence agreement' in which Brenda agreed that Pilbeam could sleep there whenever he stayed in London. The three occupants all pay their rent monthly.

Advise Pilbeam whether Yasmin, Javed and Brenda have leases of their flats and, if so, what kinds of lease.

 You can find suggested answer plans to exercises 7.2 and 7.3 on the companion website.

Further reading

Bridge, '*Street* v. *Mountford* – No Hiding Place' [1986] Conv 344

Bright, 'The Uncertainty of Certainty in Leases' (2012) 128 LQR 337

Hinojosa, 'On Property, Leases, Licences, Horses and Carts: Revisiting *Bruton* v. *London & Quadrant Housing Trust*' (2005) 69 Conv 114

Low, 'Certainty of Terms and Leases: Curiouser and Curiouser' (2012) 75 MLR 401

Lower, 'The Bruton Tenancy' (2010) 74 Conv 38

Morgan, 'Leases: Property, Contract or More?' in Dixon (ed.), *Modern Studies in Property Law: Volume 5* (Hart 2009) 419

Chapter 8

Leasehold covenants

Key concepts

- **Covenant** – a promise made in a deed.
- **Forfeiture** – the right of a landlord to re-enter the land subject to a lease following a breach of covenant by the tenant.
- **New tenancy** – a tenancy granted on or after 1st January 1996 (see s 1(3) of the Landlord and Tenant (Covenants) Act 1995).
- **Privity of contract** – the relationship between the original landlord and the original tenant; this contractual relationship continues even if one or both of them has assigned the lease.
- **Privity of estate** – the relationship between the landlord for the time being and the tenant for the time being.

8.1 Introduction

The previous chapter examined the characteristics of different kinds of lease and how they can be created and ended. A properly drafted business lease or long residential lease will be lengthy and detailed and probably devoted mostly to the obligations of the **tenant**. On the other hand, some short leases, especially of residential tenancies, may not even be in writing, and any express agreement may have gone no further than to stipulate the amount of **rent** payable and the frequency with which the tenant should pay it. Even the simplest of leases, however, will contain many more terms than this, and it is fundamental that the parties should understand:

- their obligations under the lease;
- when assignees are bound by, or can enforce, these obligations; and
- the remedies which are available to either party in case of the other's breach.

It is the automatic transfer of both parties' rights and duties under the lease (the fact that the covenants 'run with the land') which makes leases so useful. Anyone who buys either the lease or the **reversion** takes the benefits and burdens of the covenants in the lease. 'Benefit' refers to the right to enforce the promise made in a covenant; the 'burden' is the duty to perform that promise. Thus, a person who buys the **freehold** and becomes the new landlord can sue for the rent; someone who buys the lease (that is, takes an assignment of the tenancy) can sue for repairs, and so on. This is also the main reason why almost all flats in England and Wales are sold by means of leases, rather than freehold. Only certain negative freehold covenants are enforceable against successors in **title** of the original covenantor (see Chapter 12). **Mortgage lenders** would be unlikely to lend money to buyers of flats or maisonettes if it were not possible to force the owners of the neighbouring flats to maintain their premises, thereby ensuring the continuing value of the lender's security. The Landlord and Tenant (Covenants) Act 1995 has revolutionised this area of the law for leases granted after 1995, but the old rules still apply to the thousands of leases (and any contracts for leases) made before that date.

It is probably the technicality of this area of law that is most off-putting, at least so far as the rules that determine liability after **assignment** are concerned. In most cases, however, it is relatively easy to reach a satisfactory result, provided that the relevant rules are applied systematically. The basic rules are set out in Sections 8.4 and 8.5. Before considering these rules, some of the most common and most important covenants will be examined.

8.2 Commonly found covenants

'Covenant' is the general name given to promises made in a **deed** (see Section 15.5.1). In this chapter, it is also used to refer to the obligations entered into by the parties to an oral lease (see Section 7.6.1). Covenants may be express (written or spoken) or implied (either by common law or by statute). The covenants commonly found in leases are listed below, before the most important of them are considered in more detail.

Common leasehold covenants
By the lessor

- not to derogate from their grant;
- to allow the **lessee** quiet enjoyment;
- to repair.

By the tenant

- to pay **rent** (sometimes also land taxes and/or a service charge);
- to repair;
- to permit the lessor to enter to inspect (or repair);
- to insure;
- not to alter the structure;
- not to assign or sublet without permission;
- to use the premises only for a specific purpose (such as a dwelling);
- not to deny the lessor's **title**.

8.2.1 Quiet enjoyment and non-derogation

Quiet enjoyment and non-derogation are the essence of the lease: if they are not expressed in the lease, they are implied by common law. The two promises are very closely connected. Whether the covenants have been breached is a question of fact.

8.2.1(a) Quiet enjoyment

'Quiet enjoyment' does not mean keeping quiet, but refers to the tenant's right to take possession as promised and to be able to enjoy all aspects of that possession without interference. The lessor promises not to interfere with the tenant's enjoyment of the land – that is, to allow the tenant to enjoy **exclusive possession** (see Section 7.5.1).

In *Browne* v *Flower* [1911] 1 Ch 219 (Ch), the tenants of a ground-floor flat complained that a new outside staircase, which ran alongside their bedroom windows, invaded their privacy. With regard to the covenant for quiet enjoyment, Parker J said, at 228:

> there must be some physical interference with the enjoyment of the demised premises and ... a mere interference with the comfort of a person using the demised premises by the creation of a personal annoyance such as might arise from noise, invasion of privacy, or otherwise is not enough.

The House of Lords considered the nature of the covenant for quiet enjoyment in *Southwark LBC v Tanner* [2001] 1 AC 1 (HL) (also known as *Southwark LBC v Mills*). The tenant in a local authority block of flats complained that, due to inadequate sound insulation, she could hear all the sounds made by her neighbours and that this was causing her tension and distress. Lord Hoffman said, at 10:

> The flat is not quiet and the tenant is not enjoying it. But the words cannot be read literally. ... The covenant for quiet enjoyment is ... a covenant that the tenant's lawful possession of the land will not be substantially interfered with by the acts of the lessor or those lawfully claiming under him.

When the flats were built in 1919, there had been no statutory requirement that they should be soundproofed. Each tenant had accepted the flat in the physical condition in which they had found it and subject to the rest of the building being used as flats. The House of Lords held that there had been no substantial interference with the tenant's possession (their ability to use the flat in an ordinary lawful way) and thus no breach of the landlord's covenant to allow them quiet enjoyment. In addition, both Lord Hoffmann and Lord Millett (who gave the substantial speeches in the case) expressed concern that the resource implications on the local authority would have been unsustainable had they found in favour of the tenants, since it would have cost over a billion pounds to bring all their premises up to modern building standards. Interestingly, Lord Hoffmann had not allowed himself to be influenced by similar factors (albeit affecting another type of social landlord) a year earlier when deciding *Bruton v London & Quadrant Housing Trust* [2000] 1 AC 406 (HL) (see Chapter 7).

8.2.1(b) Non-derogation

The lessor also promises not to take back what they have given. In *Browne v Flower*, Parker J held (at 226) that derogation from grant only occurs if property is rendered:

> unfit or materially less fit to be used for the particular purpose for which the demise was made.

As the rooms could still be used as bedrooms if the tenants drew the curtains, the tenants failed to establish a breach of covenant in regard to either quiet enjoyment or non-derogation of grant.

In *Harmer v Jumbil (Nigeria) Tin Areas Ltd* [1921] 1 Ch 200 (CA), land was leased expressly for the storage of explosives. The landlord then decided to build on his neighbouring land, which would have made this storage illegal. The tenant was able to prevent the landlord erecting the building as doing so would have amounted to a breach of his covenant not to derogate from his grant. In the more recent case of *Platt v London Underground Ltd* [2001] 2 EGLR 121 (Ch), London Underground was held to be in derogation from its grant of a lease of a kiosk located near the south exit to Goodge Street station. This particular exit was only opened to the public during the morning rush hour, thereby discouraging trade at the kiosk for a substantial part of the day. However, Mr Platt's victory was somewhat limited because he also had a lease of a second kiosk at the main exit to the station. Neuberger J held that London Underground were entitled to take into account any increased profits made at the second kiosk (resulting from the closure of the south exit) by way of set-off against any damages due to Mr Platt.

8.2.1(c) Further protection for residential tenants

In leases of residential accommodation, these common covenants are reinforced by section 1 of the Protection from Eviction Act 1977, amended by section 29 of the Housing Act 1988. The section allows a local authority to prosecute a lessor for the crime of harassment where they '[do] acts likely to interfere with the peace or comfort of the residential occupier' or refuse any facilities (such as the electricity supply) knowing or believing that this will discourage the occupier from enforcing their rights. This section protects residential licensees as well as tenants.

An example is provided by *Cardiff City Council* v *Destrick*, unreported, 14th April 1994. A landlord cut off the gas and electricity to a flat rented by a couple with a young baby. He was charged with the offence of doing an act with intent to cause the occupier to leave (Protection from Eviction Act 1977, s 1(3)), and also with doing an act which was likely to make the occupier leave (s 1(3A)), but was acquitted of both charges. He argued that he had had no intention to force them out (it was summer, not winter) and, further, that it was reasonable (under s 1(3B)) to act as he did because the tenants were behind with their payments. The magistrates agreed with him. On appeal, the court recognised that Parliament's intention was to protect residential tenants by ensuring that if a lessor wants an eviction, they must go to court and may not rely on self-help or 'indulge in harassment'. However, the court found that the magistrates' decision had not been so irrational that it should be overruled. This case may have opened a useful escape route for lessors; the reasonableness of the lessor's conduct will need to be assessed on the basis of the evidence in each individual case.

Section 27 of the Housing Act 1988 also creates a tort of unlawful eviction with the potential for substantial damages to be awarded against the landlord. *Tagro* v *Cafane* [1991] 1 WLR 378 (CA) is 'a cautionary tale for landlords who are minded unlawfully to evict their tenants by harassment or other means' (per Lord Donaldson MR, at 236). Mr Cafane harassed his tenant and eventually totally wrecked her room and possessions. Miss Tagro was awarded £31,000 damages, assessed by virtue of section 28 of the Act on the difference between the value of the premises with the tenant in occupation and their value with vacant possession. Since *Tagro* v *Cafane* the trend has been towards the award of much lower damages, perhaps reflecting a landlord's ability more easily to end tenants' possession lawfully under the assured shorthold regime.

8.2.2   Condition and repair

At common law, a furnished dwelling must be fit for habitation at the start of the lease; so, for example, in *Smith* v *Marrable* (1843) 152 ER 693 (Ex), a landlord was unable to recover **rent** from a tenant who had abandoned the demised house on finding it to be full of bugs. However, no such covenant is implied into leases of other kinds of property. The only statutory provision which requires the lessor of a dwelling to keep it fit for human habitation at the start and throughout the lease is section 8 of the Landlord and Tenant Act 1985. However, the section applies only to tenancies let at a very low rent and, since there are very few, if any, of these tenancies left, it has little impact today.

The covenant to repair the property is fundamental to the lease of a building or part of a building. Whether the burden of this covenant falls on the landlord or the tenant will depend on the kind of property and the length of the lease. If there is nothing expressed in the lease, under common law a periodic tenant with a year's term or less will normally be required to use the premises in a 'tenant-like manner'. This is a vague expression, but Lord Denning MR gave some helpful examples in *Warren v Keen* [1954] 1 QB 15 (CA), at 20. A weekly tenant must, for example, clean windows and unblock sinks:

> In short, he must do the little jobs about the place which a reasonable tenant would do. In addition, he must, of course, not damage the house ... [But] if the house falls into disrepair through fair wear and tear or lapse of time, or for any reason not caused by him, then the tenant is not liable to repair it.

Sections 11–14 Landlord and Tenant Act 1985 impose a duty on the lessor of any dwelling let for a term of less than seven years to keep:

▶ the structure and exterior of the dwelling-house in repair (s 11(1)(a)); and
▶ installations for the supply of water, gas and electricity and for sanitation and space and water heating in repair *and proper working order* (s 11(1)(b), (c)).

A covenant to repair (as in s 11(1)(a)) requires the covenantor to make good any damage to the physical condition of whatever must be repaired, but it does not require them to address inherent defects or design faults. Consequently, in *Quick v Taff Ely BC* [1986] QB 809 (CA), a council tenant was unable to rely on a covenant 'to keep in repair the structure and exterior of the dwelling-house' to insist that the council replaced windows that caused excessive condensation and made the premises unfit for human habitation. In contrast, a covenant to keep in 'proper working order' (as in s 11(1)(b) and (c)) is more extensive. According to Lord Phillips MR in *O'Connor v Old Etonian Housing Association Ltd* [2002] Ch 295 (CA), at [15]:

> An installation cannot be said to be in proper working order if, by reason of a defect in construction or design, it is incapable of working properly.

O'Connor concerned water pipes which had been working properly but failed to provide a proper supply when the water pressure dropped. The Court of Appeal held that the question of what amounted to 'proper working order' was dependent on the facts: in this case the Housing Association would be in breach of its covenant if the drop in pressure was foreseeable, unless the reason for it was temporary and external, such as a drought. The lessor's liability under sections 11–14 of the Landlord and Tenant Act 1985 is subject to their being given notice that remedial work is needed and having a reasonable opportunity to carry it out (*O'Brien v Robinson* [1973] AC 912 (HL)). Where the demised dwelling-house forms part of a larger building that is not wholly owned by the lessor, the lessor's section 11 covenants do not extend to those parts of the building in which they have no estate or interest (s 11(1A) of the Act, as interpreted by the Court of Appeal in *Niazi Services Ltd v Van der Loo* [2004] 1 WLR 1254).

8.2.3　Covenants not to assign or sublet

Theoretically, tenants have an unlimited right to assign or sublet. In practice, a tenant often covenants not to assign or sublet, since the lessor needs to be able to protect their **reversion** against unsuitable assignees or subtenants. This covenant may be 'absolute', in which case the lessor can prevent the tenant from assigning or subletting, however unreasonable this may be. If the covenant is 'qualified' (that is, the tenant has agreed not to assign or sublet without the landlord's consent), section 19(1) of the Landlord and Tenant Act 1927 provides that the consent cannot be unreasonably withheld, 'notwithstanding any provision to the contrary'. The Landlord and Tenant Act 1988 places the burden of proof on the lessor to show that the refusal of consent was reasonable (s 1). Section 22 of the Landlord and Tenant (Covenants) Act 1995 amended these rules for new commercial leases by inserting a new section 19(1A) into the 1927 Act. In the case of non-residential leases made after 1st January 1996, lessors and lessees can agree the circumstances under which consent to **assignment** may be given or refused. Where they have done so, the courts may not enquire into the reasonableness of any refusal of consent. This provision has had significant implications in the commercial sector, but it does not affect non-business or pre-1996 leases.

If the consent is withheld, the tenant is placed in a difficult position. They can take a chance that the refusal is unreasonable and assign or sublet regardless, but if they wrongly assign or sublet, they may lose their lease (see Section 8.6.2). If they are not sure whether the lessor is being reasonable, they can go to court for a declaration, but the delay may lose them the prospective assignee or subtenant.

By statute, it is unreasonable to refuse consent on the grounds of a person's sex, race or disability unless the lessor lives on the premises (Equality Act 2010, s 34). Otherwise, whether a refusal is reasonable is a question of fact in every case. As Lord Denning MR remarked in *Bickel* v *Duke of Westminster* [1977] QB 517 (CA), at 524:

> no one decision will be a binding precedent as a strict rule of law. The reasons given by the judges are to be treated as propositions of good sense – in relation to the particular case – rather than propositions of law applicable to all cases.

A useful test can be found in *International Drilling Fluids Ltd* v *Louisville Investments (Uxbridge) Ltd* [1986] Ch 513 (CA), where it was said by Balcombe LJ at 520, to be a question of whether the lessor's decision was one 'which might be reached by a reasonable [man or woman] in the circumstances', provided the refusal was connected to the lessor/lessee relationship. Reasonable refusals include the unsatisfactory references of the proposed tenant and the fact that a subletting would create a **tenancy** protected by statute.

In *Jaison Property Development Co Ltd* v *Roux Restaurants Ltd* (1997) 74 P & CR 357 (CA), Aldous LJ quoted with approval from the judgment of Warrington LJ in *Houlder Bros & Co Ltd* v *Gibbs* [1925] Ch 575 (CA), at 585:

> When you look at the authorities ... this, at any rate, is plain, that in the cases to which an objection to an assignment has been upheld as reasonable it has always had some reference either to the personality of the [proposed] tenant or to his proposed user of the property.

The Court of Appeal was faced with an interesting issue in *Olympia & York Canary Wharf Ltd* v *Oil Property Investments Ltd* (1995) 69 P & CR 43 (CA), where the lessor refused leave to an assignee of the lease who wanted to sell it to the original tenant. The reason for refusal was that the original tenant (but only the original tenant) had a **personal right** to end the lease (an event which would reduce the value of the lessor's interest by £6 million). The Court held that this was a reasonable ground to refuse consent to assignment.

In *Ashworth Frazer Ltd* v *Gloucester City Council* [2001] 1 WLR 2180 (HL), the House of Lords considered the status of a landlord's refusal to consent to an assignment where the landlord thought that the proposed assignee would probably be in breach of a user covenant in the lease. Approving the approach in *International Drilling Fluids Ltd*, Lord Rodger held (at [70]) that reasonable lessors:

> need not confine their consideration to what will necessarily happen ... they may have regard to what will probably happen.

8.2.4　The 'usual covenants'

The phrase 'usual covenants' is a technical expression that refers to a particular set of covenants implied into a lease if the lease states that the parties will be bound by the 'usual covenants', or if the lease is silent as to most matters (as is common in short periodic tenancies). These 'usual covenants' are also implied in a contract for a lease, unless the parties intend otherwise. The 'usual covenants' are listed below, although other covenants may be 'usual' in certain circumstances (for example, because of local or trade customs).

The 'usual covenants'
By the lessor

- quiet enjoyment and non-derogation from grant;
- right of re-entry for non-payment of rent.

By the tenant

- to pay **rent**;
- to pay land taxes;
- to repair (or to allow access to the lessor to repair).

8.3　Liability for leasehold covenants

The basis of the liability between the original parties to a lease is essentially contractual, since, as Lord Hoffman explains in *Scottish & Newcastle plc* v *Raguz* [2008] 1 WLR 2494 (HL), at [1],

> at common law a lease is a contract between landlord and tenant.

Since the sixteenth century, common law has also allowed covenants to be enforceable by, and against, the assignees of the original parties to the lease. However, the common law rules, modified by sections 141 and 142 of the Law of Property Act 1925, did nothing to affect the liability of the original parties. Consequently, again in the words of Lord Hoffman, *Scottish & Newcastle plc* v *Raguz*, [1]:

> A tenant who has covenanted to pay the rent during the term is liable to pay the rent during the term, whether or not he has assigned the leasehold estate to someone else.

By the end of the twentieth century there was considerable concern about the consequences of this situation for original tenants. Lessors could potentially recover unpaid **rent** from original tenants who had assigned the lease decades previously, while the original tenant had no right to take possession of the land, or limit liability accruing by determining the lease. In 1988, the Law Commission recommended that liability be limited to the lessor and lessee for the time being (Law Com no 174, 1988), but unsurprisingly, this was not popular with institutional landlords. The story of the negotiations and compromises between the lessor and lessee lobbies that led to a series of hurriedly drafted provisions being given statutory effect in the Landlord and Tenant (Covenants) Act 1995 is told by Martin Davey in 'Privity of Contract and Leases – Reform at Last' (1996) 59 MLR 78.

Section 1 of the Landlord and Tenant (Covenants) Act 1995 divides tenancies into two types:

- leases created after 31st December 1995 (known as 'new tenancies'); and
- other tenancies.

In the case of a new tenancy, the rules determining the liability of the original parties, as well as the transmission of the benefit and burden of covenants, are found in sections 3–16 of the Act (see Section 8.5). Tenancies granted before 1996 remain subject to the common law rules, albeit mitigated by sections 17–20 of the Act (which apply to both types of tenancy).

8.4   The transfer of rights and duties: pre-1996 leases

The enforceability of a covenant in a pre-1996 lease depends upon the rules of privity of contract and privity of estate:

Privity of contract	the original parties are liable to each other for the whole of the term of the lease, even after they have assigned their interest to a third party.
Privity of estate	the relationship between the landlord for the time being and the **tenant** for the time being. The covenants included in this relationship are regulated by common law and sections 141–2 of the Law of Property Act (LPA) 1925 (see Section 8.4.3).

8.4.1   The tenant's assignee

The rule, traditionally traced to *Spencer's Case* (1853) 77 ER 72 (QB), is that when a lease is assigned, the benefit and burden of any tenant's covenants will pass to the new tenant provided that:

- there is '**privity of estate**'; and
- the covenant 'touches and concerns' the land.

Privity of estate means that there is a current legal relationship of landlord and **tenant** between the parties. A sign of privity of estate is that one person pays **rent** to the other; there is no privity of estate, therefore, between a head **lessor** and a subtenant (see Figure 8.1).

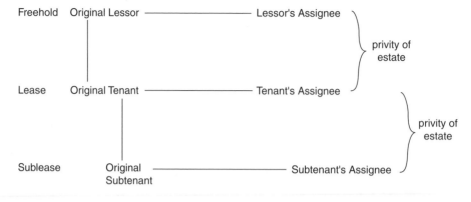

No privity of estate between Head lessor and Subtenant

Figure 8.1 Privity of estate

The phrase 'touches and concerns' originated in the sixteenth century and is used by the courts to decide whether promises ought, as a matter of public policy, to be attached to the land. Despite its importance to the law of covenants, it has proved notoriously difficult to provide a concise definition of the term. The basic question is whether the promise really affects the parties in their roles as lessor and tenant, or whether it affects them in their personal capacity. In *P & A Swift Investments* v *Combined English Stores Group plc* [1989] AC 632 (HL), Lord Oliver identified the following working test for whether the covenant touches and concerns the land (at 642, line breaks added):

(1) the covenant benefits only the reversioner [lessor] for time being, and if separated from the **reversion** ceases to be of benefit to the covenantee

(2) the covenant affects the nature, quality, mode of user or value of the land of the reversioner

(3) the covenant is not expressed to be personal, that is to say neither being given only to a specific reversioner nor in respect of the obligations only of a specific tenant

(4) the fact that a covenant is to pay a sum of money will not prevent it from touching and concerning the land so long as the three foregoing conditions are satisfied.

All the commonly found covenants considered in Section 8.2 touch and concern the land.

8.4.2 The lessor's assignee

Where the freehold **reversion** (or **headlease**) is transferred to a new owner by the **lessor**, the common law has been superseded by sections 141–2 of the LPA 1925.

LPA 1925, s 141   the lessor's assignee will be able to enforce the benefit of all the covenants which 'have reference to the subject matter of the lease'.

LPA 1925, s 142   the lessor's assignee will be bound by the burden of all covenants which 'have reference to the subject matter of the lease'.

The phrase 'have reference to the subject matter of the lease' means the same thing as 'touch and concern the land' (see Section 8.4.1).

8.4.3 The position of the original parties after assignment

As already indicated, the original lessor and lessee have promised to obey the covenants for the whole term of the lease. The doctrine of **privity of contract** means that they may continue to be liable to each other even after one or both of them have assigned their interest in the lease. The liability to be sued for unpaid **rent** and service charges can be a continuing worry for the original tenant of an expensive commercial lease, especially in times of recession. Although the original tenant and the original lessor can still be sued after they have assigned their interest, they generally cannot sue. This rule is based on the common law principle that a person cannot be sued by two parties for the same breach of covenant (*Re King* [1963] Ch 459 (CA)).

8.4.3(a) The basic position

Following assignment by the original tenant:

- the original tenant remains liable on the tenant's covenants and can be sued by the original landlord if the assignee (or any subsequent assignee) breaches those covenants;
- however, the original tenant can no longer sue for breach of the lessor's covenants.

Following assignment by the original lessor:

- the original lessor remains liable to the original tenant for breaches of covenant committed by any assignee of the **reversion**;
- however, the original lessor can no longer sue the tenant.

It is possible that the right to sue the original tenant passes automatically to the lessor's assignee under section 141 of the LPA 1925, without the need for express assignment. The editors of *Megarry & Wade: The Law of Real Property* (8th edn, Sweet & Maxwell 2012), at §§ 20–016 identify three cases where this interpretation of section 141 seems to have been assumed, but they concede that there is no reasoned authority to support it.

8.4.3(b) Release of the original tenant

There are a limited number of circumstances which will release the original tenant in whole or in part from liability for a breach of covenant by an assignee.

- In the absence of a contrary provision in the lease, the original tenant is not liable where a tenancy is extended beyond the end of its original term under the provisions of Part II of the Landlord and Tenant Act 1954 (*City of London Corporation* v *Fell* [1994] 1 AC 458 (HL)).
- An original tenant is not bound by later variations of the lease agreed between the lessor and an assignee unless the variations had been envisaged in the terms of the original lease (*Friends' Provident Life Office* v *British Railways Board* [1996] 1 All ER 336 (CA) and, now, section 18 of the Landlord and Tenant (Covenants) Act 1995). In the *Friends' Provident* case, the lessor and assignee had agreed a

substantial increase in rent together with changes in the user and **alienation** provisions. The original tenant was held to be liable for the payment of the original rent, only. However, where the original lease contains provisions for rent review, as is standard in longer commercial leases, the original tenant will, of course, be liable for any rent increase arising upon the review.

▷ Since 1st January 1996, an original tenant is not liable for any fixed charge (such as rent) unpaid by the current tenant unless the lessor notifies the original tenant within six months of the original payment falling due (see section 17 of the 1995 Act). If no section 17 notice is given, the original tenant escapes all liability for that debt. If the rent is in the course of being reviewed at the date of the section 17 notice, the landlord will have to serve a second notice covering any increase in the rent within six months of the new rent being determined (*Scottish & Newcastle plc* v *Raguz* [2008] 1 WLR 2494 (HL)).

8.4.3(c) *Remedies available to the original tenant*

If the original tenant is sued, the common law provides that they can claim an indemnity from the current tenant (*Moule* v *Garrett* (1871–72) LR 7 Ex 101 (ExCh)). If the present tenant is not worth suing (as is likely in such circumstances), the original tenant can choose to sue the person to whom they assigned their interest under the covenant implied into assignments of **unregistered** leases by section 77 of the LPA 1925 and transfers of **registered** leases by paragraph 20 of Schedule 12 of the Land Registration Act 2002. A well-advised tenant will normally seek an express indemnity from their assignee, rather than rely on section 77.

An original tenant who pays the sums due is now entitled to an 'overriding lease' by section 19 of the Landlord and Tenant (Covenants) Act 1995. This places them between the lessor and the current tenant, thus gaining some potential relief in exchange for their ongoing liability. They may, for example, take steps to terminate the lease and either occupy the premises or assign the overriding lease with vacant possession.

8.4.4 Subtenants and restrictive covenants

A head lessor does not have a relationship of **privity of contract** or **privity of estate** with any subtenant of the land. This can cause a significant problem to head lessors where their immediate tenant refuses to take action against a subtenant. However, a head lessor may be able to sue a subtenant for breach of a restrictive (negative) covenant under the rule in *Tulk* v *Moxhay* (1848) 41 ER 1143 (Ch) (see Chapter 12). Thus, in *Hemingway Securities Ltd* v *Dunraven Ltd* (1996) 71 P & CR 30 (Ch) a head landlord was able to prevent a subtenant from taking a **sublease** in breach of a covenant between the head landlord and its immediate tenant. In addition, there are two statutory provisions that may enable a head landlord to benefit from a term in the underlease, provided that the underlease makes appropriate provision for them to do so. Section 56 of the LPA 1925 allows covenants to be made with persons who are not party to the **deed** concerned, such as a head landlord. It is important, however, that the covenant is expressed as being *made with* the third party and not merely made for their benefit (as was the case in *Amsprop Trading Ltd* v *Harris Distribution Ltd* [1997] 1 WLR 1025 (Ch)). Alternatively, section 1 of the Contracts (Rights of Third Parties) Act 1999 allows a third party named in, or identifiable from, the contract to enforce a term in it if there is express provision for them to do so, or if the term purports to confer a benefit on them, and nothing in the contract rebuts this presumption.

8.4.5 Equitable leases made before 1996

There are different rules for **equitable** leases. In such cases, there is no **privity of estate**, since this depends on a *legal* relationship. Due to the wording of sections 141 and 142, the benefits and burdens of all covenants which touch and concern the land pass to any lessor, whether legal or equitable. As far as the equitable tenant is concerned, the benefit of covenants which touch and concern may pass, but it seems that the burden may not.

8.4.6 The pre-1996 rules in practice

Figure 8.2 summarises how the pre-1996 rules apply to a case where the leasehold **estate** and the **reversion** have both been assigned twice.

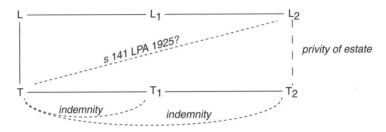

Figure 8.2 Applying the rules for pre-1996 leases

- There is mutual liability between L2 and T2 for all covenants that touch and concern the land (*Spencer's Case* (1583) and sections 141 and 142 of the LPA 1925).
- *If there had been no **assignments** by L and T2 was in breach:*
  - T would be liable for any breaches of covenant by T2 by virtue of privity of contract (subject to s 17 of the 1995 Act);
  - T would be entitled to seek an indemnity from T2 (the rule in *Moule v Garrett*) or T1 (LPA s 77 or any other indemnity covenant);
  - T would be entitled to an **overriding lease** (subject to s 19 of the 1995 Act) allowing T to take direct action against T2 to recover possession of the premises.
- However, the assignment of the reversion to L1 and L2 means that the current lessor (L2) has no **privity of contract** with T, unless it is transferred under section 141 of the LPA 1925 (see Section 8.4.3(a)).
- T2 has **privity of estate** with L2, but no privity of estate with L or L1. If L2 is in breach of contract, T2's only remedy is against L2.

8.5 The transfer of rights and duties: new tenancies

8.5.1 The tenant's assignee and the lessor's assignee

The Landlord and Tenant (Covenants) Act 1995 sets out new rules that regulate the transmission of the burden and benefit of covenants contained in leases granted on or after 1st January 1996. Sections 2 and 3 abolish the test of 'touch and concern' (see Section 8.4.1) and replace it by providing that for post-1995 leases all landlord covenants and **tenant** covenants pass automatically whenever the lease or **freehold** is assigned, unless they are specifically expressed to be 'personal'.

In *BHP Petroleum Great Britain Ltd v Chesterfield Properties Ltd* [2002] Ch 194 (CA), the question arose as to whether the original landlord or its assignee should be liable for carrying out remedial work on defects on the premises. Since the covenant was expressed to be a personal obligation on the part of the original landlord, the liability did not pass to the assignee, and the original landlord was held liable for the duration of the lease.

8.5.2 The original tenant after assignment

Section 5(2) of the 1995 Act provides that any tenant who assigns the whole of their lease:

- is released from the tenant covenants of the tenancy; and
- ceases to be entitled to the benefit of the landlord covenants of the tenancy, as from the assignment.

Any expressly personal covenant will continue to be binding on the original tenant throughout the term of the lease (*BHP v Chesterfield* at [61–2]).

In leases where the landlord's consent to an assignment of the lease is required, the landlord can insist that the assigning tenant guarantees that the assignee will perform the tenant covenants (s 16). If an **authorised guarantee agreement** (or AGA) is entered into, the assigning tenant will remain liable until their assignee transfers the lease to a further assignee with the consent of the landlord. A tenant cannot be required to guarantee a subsequent assignee under section 16. In *K/S Victoria Street v House of Fraser (Stores Management) Ltd* [2012] Ch 497 (CA) the Court of Appeal considered whether a landlord can insist that the tenant's guarantor acts as the guarantor of the tenant's assignee. The Court concluded that the clause in this particular lease fell foul of the anti-avoidance provisions in section 25 of the 1995 Act (see Section 8.5.6). However, according to Lord Neuberger (at [53]), there is no objection to achieving exactly the same outcome simply by requiring the guarantor to be party to a valid authorised guarantee agreement.

8.5.3 The original lessor after assignment

When a lessor assigns their **reversion**, they are not automatically released from their covenants under the lease. They may, however, apply to the tenant to release them (s 6). If the tenant refuses consent, the former lessor may ask the court to release them from the covenants (s 8). The court cannot, however, release the original lessor from their expressly personal covenants (*BHP v Chesterfield*). It is important that the tenant should have some say in whether the assigning landlord is released. An insolvent or reluctant lessor would be less likely to be able to perform their covenants, and in such circumstances the tenant would probably want the existing lessor to continue to be bound.

8.5.4 User covenants

Section 3(5) of the 1995 Act allows head lessors to enforce restrictive covenants directly against any person 'who is the owner or occupier of any demised premises to which the lease relates'. Thus, a head lessor can enforce a user covenant against a subtenant without the need to resort to the rule in *Tulk* v *Moxhay* or the Contracts (Rights of Third Parties) Act 1999 (see Section 8.4.4).

8.5.5 Equitable leases

The definition of 'tenancy' for the purposes of the 1995 Act expressly includes 'an agreement for a tenancy' (s 28(1)). Consequently, the rules for leases granted after 1995 apply to **equitable** leases in the same way that they apply to legal leases.

8.5.6 Anti-avoidance provisions

Section 25 of the Landlord and Tenant (Covenants) Act 1995 is a very broad provision intended to ensure that lessors in strong negotiating positions cannot force potential tenants to contract out of their rights under the Act. In the words of Patten LJ in *Tindall Cobham 1 Ltd* v *Adda Hotels* [2015] 1 P & CR 5 (CA) (at [45]):

> It is clear that s.25 was intended to provide a comprehensive anti-avoidance provision which, as Lord Nicholls said in *London Diocesan Fund* v *Phithwa [2005] 1 WLR 3956*, ought to be interpreted generously to ensure that the operation of the 1995 Act is not frustrated either directly or indirectly.

However, section 25 is not without its difficulties. For example, there are ways in which a lessor can effectively sidestep sections 6–8 of the 1995 Act if the tenant is not diligently advised. In *London Diocesan Fund* v *Phithwa* [2005] 1 WLR 3956 (HL), Avonridge Property Co Ltd had acquired the lease of seven shop units (of which the London Diocesan Fund was the landlord). Avonridge then sublet six of these units, charging substantial **premiums**, but only nominal rents. Avonridge covenanted with the subtenants that Avonridge would pay the **rent** due under the **headlease**, 'but not, in the case of Avonridge Property Co Ltd only, so as to be liable after the landlord has disposed of its interest in the Property'. Avonridge then assigned the headlease to Mr Phithwa, who promptly disappeared, leaving the rent due under the headlease unpaid. The London Diocesan Fund took action to forfeit the headlease on the basis of the unpaid rent (see Section 8.6.1(c)). The subtenants were granted relief from the **forfeiture** of the headlease on condition that they pay the rent arrears and take new leases of their individual units at market rents. The subtenants then sought to recover their losses from Avonridge on the grounds that Avonridge had not complied with sections 6–8 of the 1995 Act. The majority of the House of Lords held that section 6 was not relevant and that Avonridge was not, therefore, liable for the non-payment of rent by its assignee. Lord Nicholls explained (at [19]) that:

> Whatever its form, an agreed limitation of liability does not impinge upon the operation of the statutory provisions because … the statutory provisions are intended to operate to relieve tenants and landlords from a liability which would otherwise exist. They are not intended to impose a liability which otherwise would be absent. They are not intended to enlarge the liability either of a tenant or landlord.

This reasoning could be applied to almost all covenants made by landlords. Consequently, a careful draftsperson should be able to minimise the future exposure of an original lessor. Whether tenants accept such limitations will depend upon their relative bargaining power (and the quality of their legal team).

Section 24(2) of the 1995 Act provides that when a tenancy is assigned, any tenant's guarantor is released from liability to the same extent as the tenant itself. In *K/S Victoria Street* v *House of Fraser (Stores Management) Ltd* [2012] Ch 497 (CA), the Court of Appeal had to consider the relationship between section 24 and the anti-avoidance provisions in section 25. In particular, does section 24 preclude the tenant's guarantor also acting as grantor of the assignee? *House of Fraser* concerned a sale and lease back of a large department store in Wolverhampton. The structure of the transaction was somewhat complex, mainly for tax reasons. Immediately after purchasing the **freehold**, K/S granted a lease to one of the companies in the House of Fraser group (T1) with another company in the group (G) acting as guarantor. Clause 3.5(iii) of the lease provided that after three months, T1 would assign the lease to yet another House of Fraser company (T2) and that G would also guarantee T2's liabilities. The question before the court was whether clause 3.5(iii) of the lease frustrated the operation of section 24 because it would result in G not being released to the same extent as T1 from the covenants in the lease (s 24(2)). The Court of Appeal concluded that the provision requiring the original tenant's guarantor to guarantee the liability of the assignee was rendered void by section 25, even though it reflected a genuine agreement made for sound business reasons. As Lord Neuberger MR explained (at [21]):

> If it were otherwise, it would mean, for instance, that a landlord, when granting a tenancy, could require a guarantor of the tenant's liabilities, on every assignment of the tenancy, to guarantee the liability of each successive assignee. Such an obligation ('a renewal obligation') would plainly be wholly contrary to the purpose of section 24(2), as it would enable a well-advised landlord to ensure that any guarantor was in precisely the position in which it would have been before the 1995 Act came into force.

Section 24 after *House of Fraser*
When interpreting the provisions of a statute, the student, like the court, must consider the detailed provisions of the statute in question and seek to discern the intention of Parliament as expressed in the sections concerned. Arguably, this task is more difficult when the relevant provisions were prepared hurriedly, and without the usual expert scrutiny, as was the case for parts of the Landlord and Tenant (Covenants) Act 1995. In the years since *House of Fraser*, section 24 has come before the courts on a number of occasions.

In *Tindall Cobham 1 Ltd* v *Adda Hotels* [2015] 1 P & CR 5 (CA), the Court of Appeal considered the meaning of the words 'void to the extent that' in section 25, Patten LJ concluding (at [46]) that:

> Parliament did not intend to invalidate more of the relevant agreement than was necessary to safeguard the objectives of the Act in the context of the particular assignment under consideration.

In other words, the court, when applying section 25, must take a balanced approach to the transaction as a whole, neutralising the offending parts of the contract, but without changing the fundamental nature of the contract or rendering it unworkable (at least in so far as this is possible).

In *UK Leasing Brighton Ltd* v *Topland Neptune Ltd* [2015] 2 P & CR 2 (Ch), Morgan J felt able, albeit with some hesitation, to hold that an arrangement in which the guarantor reassumed liability after assignment did not fall foul of sections 24 and 25 of the 1995 Act. The facts concerned the reassignment of a tenancy to the original tenant (T1). When T1 had assigned the lease to T2 it had done so in breach of the terms of the lease. The result was that T2 was now the tenant, but that T1 and its guarantor (G) had not been released from their obligations under the lease (s 11 of the 1995 Act). All of the parties wanted to regularise the agreement, and the simplest way to do this was for T2 to reassign the lease to T1, with G executing a new guarantee. However, did this fall foul of sections 24 and 25? Applying what might be termed a sequential analysis, Morgan J held that it did not, explaining (at [32]) that:

> when the lease is assigned by T2 to T1, T1 is released from its original obligations by reason of s.11(2)(b) but becomes bound by the tenant covenants under s.3(2)(a). If G is released from its original obligations under its original guarantee but enters into a fresh guarantee in relation to the tenant covenants, then G is released to the same extent as T1 is released.

This reasoning did not appeal to Amanda Tipples QC (sitting as a deputy judge of the Chancery Division) in *EMI Group Ltd v O & H Q1 Ltd* [2016] 3 WLR 269 (Ch). This case concerned the validity of an attempt to assign the lease to the tenant's guarantor (the tenant company being in administration). The judge concluded that the purpose behind the 1995 Act is 'that a tenant or guarantor cannot, as the result of an assignment, re-assume the very same, *or essentially the same*, liabilities in respect of the tenancy' (at [81], emphasis added). It is not known how many leases have been assigned to guarantors since 1st January 1996. It is to be hoped that the Court of Appeal will soon have an opportunity to render their status more certain.

These cases form part of what Paul Clark has referred to, in his series of Practice and Precedent articles in the *Conveyancer and Property Lawyer*, as the 'GAGA Saga' (see, in particular, (2015) 79 Conv 191 and (2016) 80 Conv 174).

8.5.7 The post-1995 rules in practice

Using the rules contained in the 1995 Act to establish the rights and duties of the parties to a post-1995 lease requires a similar approach to that used with pre-1996 leases (see Section 8.4.6), except that greater attention needs to be paid to the circumstances of each **assignment** and the negotiations between the parties. The practical effect of many of the 1995 Act rules will depend on the relative negotiating strengths of the parties, especially after *London Diocesan Fund* v *Phithwa*, which will, in turn, be influenced by the state of the property market.

Figure 8.3 summarises how the rules in the 1995 Act apply to a case where the leasehold **estate** and the **reversion** under a post-1995 lease have both been assigned twice.

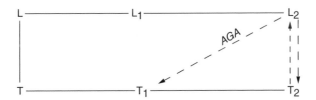

Figure 8.3 Applying the rules in the Landlord and Tenant (Covenants) Act 1995 to post-1995 leases

▶ The burden of the tenant's covenants and the benefit for the lessor's covenants passed to T1 and then to T2 by virtue of the respective assignments (s 3(2)).

▶ Assuming that the assignment to T1 was an authorised assignment (s 11), T was released from all its obligations except any that are expressly personal (section 5).

▶ Assuming that the assignment to T2 was an authorised assignment (s 11), T1 will be released from all its obligations under the lease.

▶ However, the lessor has insisted that T1 enter into an **authorised guarantee agreement** in respect of T2. This agreement must comply with section 16, and will not extend beyond any authorised assignment by T2. The lessor to give T1 notice of any fixed sums falling due within six months of the event.

▶ The burden of the lessor's covenants and the benefit for the tenant's covenants passed to L1 and then to L2 by virtue of the respective assignments (s 3(3)).

▶ However, neither L nor L1 would have been automatically released from their liabilities under the terms of the lease. Both L and L1 would need to obtain release from the tenant (ss 6 and 7) or by applying to the court (s 8).

8.6 Remedies for breach of covenant

The important question for a practical lawyer is always 'What remedy is available?' A lease is a contract, and, in general, contractual remedies are available. There are also remedies particular to leases. The rules are complicated, and only the briefest details of the main remedies are given here. For historical reasons, there are differences between the **lessor's** remedies for the **tenant's** breach of the covenant to pay **rent** and their remedies for the tenant's breach of other covenants. The circumstances in which a lessor can use **forfeiture** as a remedy depend upon whether the tenant's breach relates to a condition of the lease or a mere covenant. The differences between covenants and conditions are set out in Table 8.1.

Table 8.1 Conditions and covenants

Condition	The promise is called a 'condition', or is clearly intended to be a condition of the lease.	The lessor can automatically take possession of the land if the condition is broken (known as 'repossession', 're-entry' or 'forfeiture').
Mere covenant	Other promises contained in the lease.	The lessor can forfeit the lease or give 'notice to quit' only if there is a clause to that effect.

If the usual covenants are implied (see Section 8.2.4), then there will be a provision for forfeiture for non-payment of rent but not for breach of any other covenant.

It is also important to be aware of the doctrine of **waiver**. If a lessor accepts rent knowing of a breach of covenant or condition, they will be taken to have waived their right to take action for the breach. Any lessor who wants to enforce a forfeiture must avoid any action by which they indicate to the tenant that the lease will continue. However, there is no waiver if the lessor did not know of a breach when they indicated the continuance of the lease.

8.6.1　Non-payment of rent

The possible remedies are an action for recovery of rent, **distress** and **forfeiture**. The lessor can choose only one of these at a time.

8.6.1(a)　An action for recovery

An action can be brought for recovery of arrears of rent. Only the past six years of rent can be recovered (Limitation Act 1980, s 19).

8.6.1(b)　Taking control of the tenant's goods

Since 1066, a lessor has been able to enter the premises between sunrise and sunset and 'levy distress': they, or a certified bailiff, can take the tenant's belongings and sell them if the rent is not paid within five days.

In its Report No 194, 1991, the Law Commission concluded that distress for non-payment of rent is 'wrong in principle', and recommended its abolition. There were also concerns that levying distress may be in breach of the rights protected by the Human Rights Act 1998 as Lightman J explained in *Fuller* v *Happy Shopper Markets Ltd* [2001] 1 WLR 1681 (Ch) (at [27]):

> The ancient (and perhaps anachronistic) self-help remedy of distress involves a serious interference with the rights of the tenant under article 8 of the European Convention for the Protection of Human Rights and Fundamental Freedoms to respect for his privacy and home and under article 1 of the First Protocol to the Convention to the peaceful enjoyment of his possessions.

The common law right to levy distress for rent was abolished with effect from 6th April 2014, when Part 3 of the Tribunals, Courts and Enforcement Act 2007 (TCEA) came into force (s 71). A commercial lessor may now take advantage of the new statutory remedy of commercial rent arrears recovery (CRAR), provided that the lease is evidenced in writing (s 74). CRAR allows a lessor to recover rent arrears (but not arrears in respect of service charges or other payments (s 76(2)) by taking control of the tenant's goods. To ensure that the remedy is proportionate, a landlord cannot use CRAR until the arrears amount to least seven days' rent (s 77(3), (4) and Regulation 52 of the Taking Control of Goods Regulations).

8.6.1(c)　Forfeiture (the right of re-entry)

The right to re-enter makes it sound as if the lessor can just barge in, but, although they may physically re-enter commercial property, such re-entry must be peaceable and without the use of force, or they will commit an offence under section 6 of the Criminal Law Act 1977, as amended. The House of Lords in *Billson* v *Residential Apartments Ltd (No 1)* [1992] 1 AC 494 (HL) criticised the use of this self-help remedy, and it is usually safer for the lessor to go to court for an order for possession, particularly in the light of potential claims under the Human Rights Act 1998. Where the premises are residential, and the tenant is in occupation, under section 2 of the Protection from Eviction Act 1977 the lessor *must* apply to the court for a possession order before re-entering.

At common law, before the lessor may proceed to forfeit the lease for non-payment of rent, they must usually issue a formal demand for payment. However, most carefully drafted leases will contain a term permitting the lessor to forfeit the lease for non-payment of rent 'whether formally demanded or not'. If the lease contains such a term, or if the rent is six months or more in arrears, no formal demand is necessary before seeking to forfeit the lease.

Once the lessor has gone to court, the tenant might be able to claim 'relief' against forfeiture for non-payment of rent under section 212 of the Common Law Procedure Act 1852 (in the High Court) or section 138 of the County Courts Act 1984 (in the county court). This is exactly what it sounds like: very simply, if the tenant pays the arrears and costs, they may be reinstated. The rules here are intricate and somewhat illogical because of the interplay of equity, common law and statute.

8.6.2 Breach of other covenants

General remedies for breach of a tenant's covenant are forfeiture or damages or an **injunction**. Although a tenant cannot forfeit the lease when the lessor is in breach, a tenant might be able to use contract law to repudiate a tenancy where the lessor is in fundamental or repudiatory breach of a significant covenant (see Section 8.6.2(b)).

8.6.2(a) Forfeiture (the right of re-entry)

This remedy is only available to the lessor if it is included in the lease. If there is a forfeiture clause, the lessor must give notice to the tenant by section 146 of the LPA 1925. Section 146 notices do not apply in respect of non-payment of rent.

The section 146 notice must specify:

▶ the specific breach complained of;
▶ the remedy (if the breach is capable of remedy); and
▶ the compensation (if appropriate or required).

The purpose of the section 146 procedure is to give tenants an opportunity to remedy their breach, if this is possible, so that they do not lose their lease through forfeiture. It is, therefore, important to know which breaches can be remedied and which cannot.

The traditional view had been that the breach of a positive covenant could be remedied by the tenant simply performing whatever it was the lease required them to do, and some negative covenants could be remedied by ending the activity which was causing the breach, and promising to comply with the lease thereafter. The issue of remediability was examined in *Expert Clothing Service & Sales Ltd* v *Hillgate House Ltd* [1986] Ch 340 (CA). In this case, it had been agreed that the tenant should convert the premises, but, because of lack of money, the tenant had not even begun the work by the date by which the conversion should have been completed. Expert Clothing issued a section 146 notice, claiming that the breach was irremediable. The Court of Appeal stated that the purpose of section 146 was to give the tenant 'one last chance', and that whether a breach was capable of remedy depended, not on the nature of the breach, but rather on the nature of the harm caused to the lessor and whether financial compensation would be sufficient.

In *Savva* v *Hussein* (1997) 73 P & CR 150 (CA), the tenants were in minor breach of covenants not to put up signs or to alter the premises. On the question of whether such breaches were capable of remedy, Staughton LJ stated (at 154):

> it is a remedy if the mischief caused by the breach can be removed. In the case of a covenant not to make alterations without consent or not to display signs without consent, if there is a breach of that, the mischief can be removed by removing the signs or restoring the property to the state it was in before the alterations.

Akici v *LR Butlin Ltd* [2006] 1 WLR 201 (CA) concerned an alleged breach of covenant by the tenant by sharing possession of the premises. Neuberger LJ felt (at [65]) that there were very few breaches not capable of remedy:

> In principle I would have thought that the great majority of breaches of covenant should be capable of remedy, in the same way as repairing or most user covenant breaches. Even where stopping, or putting right, the breach may leave the lessors out of pocket for some reason, it does not seem to me that there is any problem in concluding that the breach is remediable.

The lessor is not disadvantaged in such circumstances, because the lessor is entitled to 'compensation in money ... for the breach' under section 146(1).

A wrongful subletting is irremediable, as is using the premises for immoral purposes in breach of covenant (*Rugby School (Governors)* v *Tannahill* [1935] 1 KB 87 (KB)). However, where the immoral activity is being carried out by a subtenant, the tenant's breach may be remediable, provided that the tenant acts immediately to evict the immoral subtenant (*Patel* v *K & J Restaurants Ltd* [2011] L & TR 6 (CA)).

If the tenant does not, or cannot, remedy the breach within a reasonable time, the lessor can go to court for a possession order. The tenant (or subtenant) can apply for relief under section 146(2) of the LPA 1925. In *Billson* v *Residential Apartments Ltd (No 1)* [1992] 1 AC 494 (HL) (see Section 8.6.1(c)), the House of Lords held that a tenant can apply for relief whether or not the lessor has actually re-entered the land, provided there is no final court order granting possession. Here the tenant was carrying out building work in breach of covenant, so the landlord served a section 146 notice and then re-entered by changing the locks. Since there was no court order granting possession at this stage (and the re-entry had been peaceable, so there had been no breach of the criminal law; see Section 8.6.1(c)), the House of Lords sent the case back to the trial court for a decision as to whether relief was to be granted.

Section 146(2) gives the court very wide discretion as to the granting of relief and upon the terms that can be imposed upon the tenant. The court must consider all of the circumstances of the case, including the conduct of the parties (*Hyman* v *Rose* [1912] AC 623 (HL)). In appropriate circumstances, relief may be granted in cases where the breach is considered irremediable, and even if the breach was a wilful and deliberate act by the tenant. The tenant's conduct is one of the most important factors to be considered. However, the court must also consider the value of vacant possession to the lessor. In some circumstances, such as those in the recent case of *Freifeld* v *West Kensington Court Ltd* [2016] 1 P & CR 5 (CA), the value of this 'windfall' to the lessor may be out of all proportion to the culpability of the tenant. On the facts of *Freifeld*, the court ordered that there be relief from forfeiture, provided that the lease was sold within a period of six months.

If the lease is forfeit, any **sublease** will also disappear, since its existence depends on the **headlease**. Therefore, section 146(4) of the LPA 1925 allows the subtenant to apply for relief; if they are successful, they step into the shoes of the tenant but cannot gain a term longer than their original sublease. **Mortgagees** of the leasehold interest can also apply for relief, remedy the breach and add the cost of doing so to the **mortgage** debt.

In an attempt to prevent abuse of the section 146 procedure by lessors, especially when attempting to forfeit the lease against leaseholders who are unable or unwilling to pay unreasonable service charges, sections 168 and 169 of the Commonhold and Leasehold Reform Act 2002 prevent most lessors of residential leases over 21 years from issuing a section 146 notice unless either the leaseholder has admitted the breach of covenant or the lessor has established the breach to the satisfaction of a leasehold valuation tribunal. If the breach consists of arrears of service charges, the lessor must also show that the charges are not excessive. Even if the tribunal is satisfied as to the breach, the leaseholder may not be served with the section 146 notice for a further 14 days.

8.6.2(b) Termination by repudiatory breach

It is a general rule of contract law that a contract may be terminated if one of the parties breaches its terms in such a way as to make it clear that they no longer intend to be bound by the contract. Some older cases cast doubt on whether this remedy applies to leases, but since the county court decision in *Hussein v Mehlman* [1992] 2 EGLR 287, the list of circumstances in which it has been granted has been growing steadily. In *Hussein,* a rented house was uninhabitable due to the lack of repair; the tenant not only won damages but also was entitled to end the lease because of the fundamental nature of the landlord's breach of covenant. Since *Hussein,* the Court of Appeal has, on a number of occasions, accepted that repudiation by a tenant can be appropriate, although in none of the cases is the Court of Appeal's decision dependent upon this. For example, in *Chartered Trust plc v Davies* (1998) 76 P & CR 396 (CA), the lessor allowed the occupier of a neighbouring unit to obstruct access to the defendant's unit. The Court of Appeal dealt with this as a case of derogation from grant, but Henry LJ concluded his judgment by noting, at 409:

> The trial judge found this to be a repudiation of the lease – a substantial interference with the tenant's business driving him to bankruptcy. That was a judgment he was entitled to come to on the evidence he heard.

This is a welcome extension of contractual principles. However, despite appearing to be similar to the lessor's remedy of forfeiture, it is, by its very nature, clearly limited to cases where the lessor has breached a fundamental term of the lease. It is not clear whether the remedy is also available for the lessor in the case of a tenant's repudiatory breach. It seems unlikely, since that would mean that an uncompromising lessor could avoid the statutory and common law protection available to tenants (see Section 8.6.2(a)). Without deciding this question, the Court of Appeal in *Reichman v Beveridge* [2007] 1 P & CR 20 (CA) held that there was no obligation on a lessor to minimise the tenant's liability under the lease by accepting the tenant's repudiatory breach of contract.

8.6.2(c) Damages, injunctions and specific performance

Damages and/or an injunction may be appropriate remedies for some breaches, and are available to both lessor and lessee. Specific performance was once thought to be available only to the tenant in cases of the lessor's breach of their repairing covenant; *Rainbow Estates v Tokenhold* [1999] Ch 64 (Ch) extended this remedy to the lessor 'in appropriate circumstances'. Such circumstances will be rare. In *Rainbow Estates,* the lease had no provision for the landlord to forfeit the lease for the tenant's breach or even to enter the premises to carry out the repairs himself. Specific performance will not usually be available if damages are an appropriate remedy, but here the property was a listed building in serious disrepair, and the condition of the premises was continuing to deteriorate; an award of damages would not have helped the landlord. The traditional reason for the courts' reluctance to order specific performance in these circumstances, that the order would need continuing supervision by the court, was not seen as presenting a difficulty if there was a clear definition of the work to be done.

The House of Lords took the orthodox approach to specific performance in *Co-operative Insurance Society Ltd v Argyll Stores (Holdings) Ltd* [1998] AC 1 (HL), in which it refused to make an order preventing Safeway from closing one of its stores, despite the company having contracted with its landlord, the owner of a shopping mall, to keep it open. Lord Hoffmann distinguished the performance of repairing obligations in a lease from the obligation to continue in a business relationship.

At present, tenants often have very serious problems in persuading their lessors to carry out repairs; one rationale for the introduction of **commonhold** has been the need to address the problems faced by tenants in rundown blocks of flats (see Section 6.5). Although tenants can seek the remedies discussed above, if they hold a comparatively insecure assured shorthold tenancy they may be reluctant to bring an action against their lessor, knowing that renewal or extension of their tenancy would probably be unlikely. An alternative remedy could be to pay for the repairs themselves and deduct the cost from the rent without becoming liable for non-payment (a 'right of set-off'; *Lee-Parker v Izzet (No 1)* [1971] 1 WLR 1688 (Ch)).

Instead of relying on contractual provisions within the lease (whether set out in the lease or implied by statute), sometimes the residential tenant's best solution is to get the local authority to take action. Part 1 of the Housing Act 2004 gives local authorities the power to take steps against the lessor to ensure that residential accommodation is brought up to a reasonable standard.

Summary

8.1 The rules relating to leasehold covenants are the product of the need to balance the demands of landlords, tenants and wider society. They are highly technical, but can be applied successfully provided that the issues are approached systematically.

8.2 Commonly found leasehold covenants include the lessor's covenants for quiet enjoyment and non-derogation from grant, covenants to repair and the tenant's covenant not to assign or sublet without consent.

8.3 The relevant rules for determining whether a party can enforce or is bound by a particular covenant depend upon whether the lease was granted before 1996 or after 1995.

8.4 If the lease was granted before 1996 (or pursuant to a contract made before 1996):

- ▶ its covenants automatically run with the land if there is privity of estate, and the covenant touches and concerns the land;

- ▶ the original tenant remains liable on all the covenants but may claim an indemnity from their assignee or the current tenant; and

- ▶ the original tenant is entitled to an overriding lease when they have paid money due by the current tenant.

8.5 Leases made after 1995 fall within the rules contained in the Landlord and Tenant (Covenants) Act 1995:

- ▶ all covenants run with land unless they are expressed to be personal;

- ▶ the original tenant ceases automatically to be liable for any breach after assigning the lease (but can be liable under an 'authorised guarantee agreement');

- ▶ the original lessor may remain liable, unless they obtain a release from the current tenant or from the court.

Summary cont'd

8.6 There are a number of remedies available to landlords and tenants in addition to the usual contractual remedies:

▶ Remedies for non-payment of rent are normally forfeiture, CRAR or an action for recovery.

▶ Remedies for breaches of other covenants by the tenant include forfeiture, damages and injunction.

▶ A tenant may have the right to repudiate the lease in certain circumstances.

▶ A tenant of residential property may be able to involve the local authority if the lessor is in breach of their repairing covenant.

Exercises

 8.1 Complete the online quiz on the topics covered in this chapter on the companion website.

8.2 Consider the advantages and disadvantages of using long leases to regulate the ownership of a number of residential flats making up a single building. How, if at all, do the changes introduced by the Commonhold and Leasehold Reform Act 2002 assist the lessor and the tenants in this situation?

8.3 Four years ago, Ronald granted a six-year lease of a house to Alan. Alan covenanted that he would pay the rent on time, would paint the exterior every three years and would not use the premises for illegal or immoral purposes. Ronald reserved the right to re-enter the premises for breach of any covenant.

The following year, Ronald sold his freehold reversion to Keegan. Two years ago, Alan assigned his lease to Jane.

Keegan has found out that Jane has been smoking cannabis in her house, that she has allowed her friend Sally to use it for prostitution (much to the annoyance of the next-door neighbour) and that she has not painted the house at all. She is five months in arrears with her rent. Four months ago, the roof began to leak badly whenever it rained, and the bedroom ceiling has collapsed as a result. Keegan has steadfastly refused to carry out any repairs, and Jane is obliged to live on the ground floor.

Jane wants to know what she can do about the state of the house and whether Keegan can evict her. Advise her.

 You can find suggested answer plans to exercises 8.2 and 8.3 on the companion website.

Further reading

Bridge, 'First Tenant's Liability in the Lords' (1994) 53 CLJ 28

Bridge, 'Former Tenants, Future Liabilities and the Privity of Contract Principle: The Landlord and Tenant (Covenants) Act 1995' (1996) 55 CLJ 313

Davey, 'Privity of Contract and Leases – Reform at Last' (1996) 59 MLR 78

Dixon, 'A Failure of Statutory Purpose or a Failure of Professional Advice?' (2006) 70 Conv 79

Chapter 9

Licences

Key concepts

▶ **Estoppel** – an equitable interest arising out of the claimant's detrimental reliance upon an expectation encouraged by the defendant.
▶ **Licence** – permission to enter onto land.

9.1 The case of the resident daughter-in-law

In 1936, Mr Errington senior bought 27 Milvain Avenue in Newcastle as a home for his son, who had recently married the defendant (Mary Errington). He paid £250 in cash (which he told Mary was a present) towards the house and borrowed the balance of £500 from a building society on the security of the house. The house was conveyed into the name of Mr Errington senior, and he also took the **mortgage** from the building society in his sole name. However, he handed the building society book to Mary, telling her not to part with it and that the house would belong to her and her husband when they had paid the last instalment on the mortgage.

When Mr Errington senior died some nine years later, legal **title** to the house passed to his widow (also called Mary Errington). The daughter-in-law continued to occupy the house and to pay the instalments of the mortgage. The mother then claimed possession of 27 Milvain Avenue.

The question before the Court of Appeal in *Errington v Errington & Woods* [1952] 1 KB 290 (CA) was, 'What is the result in law of these facts?' (Denning LJ at 295). The court's answer can be found at Section 9.5.3.

9.1.1 What legal or equitable interests may exist here?

The various legal and **equitable** interests that are recognised in land are introduced in Section 2.2. All three members of the Court of Appeal in *Errington* rejected the conclusion of the County Court judge that a special form of **lease** had been created. (The ingredients required for a lease are considered in Chapter 7.) If the case were to be decided today, it would almost certainly be treated as an interest arising by way of **proprietary estoppel** (see Chapter 18). However, the doctrine of estoppel was much less developed at the date of *Errington*, and the Court of Appeal felt that its only alternative was to hold that the daughter-in-law occupied the house as a licensee.

9.1.2 Are these rights binding on third parties?

One of the characteristics of the interests in land recognised by the law or at equity is that they are proprietary interests; that is, they are usually binding on third parties.

However, the younger Mary Errington did not have one of these interests. What protection, if any, should her licence give her against her mother-in-law's claim for possession of 27 Milvain Avenue?

It is important to recognise from the outset that there is no single correct answer to this question. The status of licences is just one example of a wider problem: how can one reconcile the need for certainty (reflected in the closed list of property interests, for example) with the flexibility to reflect the wishes of the parties and the needs of justice in a particular case? Other examples of this tension can be found throughout this book: see, for example, Sections 12.5, 14.5 and 14.6.

9.2 Types of licence

A person who has a licence to be on another's land has that person's permission to be there; in other words, a licence prevents someone from being a trespasser.

Licences cover a huge variety of activities. A fan at a football match is a licensee, as is a secretary working in an office, a customer in a shop, a paying guest in a hotel, and perhaps a cohabitee sharing their lover's house. Licences may last for a few minutes or for life and are found within both family and commercial settings. For example, a licence may be created deliberately or accidentally instead of a **lease** (see Chapter 7) or in place of an **easement** (such as a right of way) if the necessary formalities have not been complied with (see Chapter 10). It is hardly surprising that there are several types of licence and that the rights and remedies of licensees differ widely.

Licences can be divided into four main categories:

1. bare licences;
2. licences coupled with an interest in land;
3. contractual licences; and
4. licences by **estoppel**.

This chapter considers each type of licence in turn, and, in particular, the extent to which they might be interests in land or whether they are merely **personal rights**. The distinction is important, since **property rights** attach irrevocably to the land, are sold along with the land and, if protected in the appropriate way (see Chapters 4 and 5), will bind a purchaser of the burdened land and benefit the purchaser of any dominant land.

9.3 Bare licences

A bare licence arises when the landowner gives permission for another person to be on their land. This may be express, such as an invitation to a friend to come in and have a cup of coffee, or implied, such as for a postal worker delivering letters. Such licences are gratuitous (that is, given without consideration) and can lawfully be revoked whenever the landowner wishes. The licensee must then leave within a reasonable time, or they become a trespasser and may be physically removed. The licensee cannot transfer this kind of licence to another person. Neither will this type of licence bind someone who buys the land from the licensor.

9.4 Licences coupled with an interest in land

When a person owns a *profit à prendre* (a legal interest giving them the right to take something from another person's land; see Sections 10.2 and 10.10), they will be unable to exercise the right without a licence to go onto the land. So, for example, the owner of a profit of piscary (the right to take fish) automatically has a licence to cross the grantor's land in order to get to the river. This form of licence cannot be revoked and will continue for as long as the interest exists, binding third parties in the same way as the *profit*.

9.5 Contractual licences

9.5.1 Contractual rights

A contractual licence is created wherever a person has permission to be on another's land as part of a contract between them. Examples include the fan at the football match and the paying guest in the hotel. The rights of a contractual licensee depend upon the terms of the contract. In *Winter Garden Theatre (London) Ltd* v *Millennium Productions Ltd* [1946] 1 All ER 678 (CA), at 680, Lord Greene MR stated that:

> A licence created by a contract … creates a contractual right to do certain things which otherwise would be a trespass. It seems to me that, in considering the nature of such a licence and the mutual rights and obligations which arise under it, the first thing to do is to construe the contract according to ordinary principles.

It is often assumed that a contractual licence is worth less than a **lease**. This may be true with regard to the licensee's security if the land is sold, and, in general, licences do not attract the statutory protection afforded to leases. However, there are occasions when it is more beneficial to be a licensee than a **tenant** under a lease. For example, in *Wettern Electric Ltd* v *Welsh Development Agency* [1983] QB 796 (QB), a company held the licence of factory premises which were so badly constructed and became so unsafe that the licensee company had to leave. The licensee company successfully sued for breach of an implied term that the premises would be fit for their purpose. This term could not be implied into a contract for a lease, not being one of the 'usual covenants' (see Section 8.2.4). However, in a licence, the ordinary rules of contract law applied. Judge Newey QC explained (at 809):

> The sole purpose of the licence was to enable the plaintiffs to have accommodation in which to carry on and expand their business while their existing factory was being enlarged. If anyone had said to the plaintiffs and the defendants' directors and executives at the time when the licence was being granted: 'Will the premises be sound and suitable for the plaintiff's purposes?' they would assuredly have replied: 'Of course; there would be no point in the licence if that were not so.' The term was required to make the contract workable.

Contractual licences are common and are generally created expressly. However, in the 1970s, the Court of Appeal used the device of the implied contractual licence to solve certain types of family dispute, such as those in *Errington* v *Errington & Woods* [1952] 1 KB 290 (CA) and *Tanner* v *Tanner (No 1)* [1975] 1 WLR 1346 (CA). In *Tanner*, Miss MacDermott (who changed her name to Mrs Tanner) had moved from her Rent Act-protected **tenancy** into a house bought by Mr Tanner, to live there with their twin children. Mr Tanner then formed a relationship with another woman and tried to evict Mrs Tanner. The Court of Appeal held that Mrs Tanner had a contractual licence which could not be revoked until the twins reached the age of 18. However, since she had already been rehoused following the decision at first instance (which had gone against her) she was awarded £2,000 to compensate her for her loss. This contractual analysis, with the accompanying traditional contractual requirements of consideration and the intention to create a legal relationship, has proved highly problematic when applied to family and domestic arrangements. Today, such cases are usually argued on the basis of a **common intention constructive trust** (see Section 17.3) or an **estoppel** (see Chapter 18).

9.5.2 Revocability

There has been continuing debate on whether a contractual licence can be revoked by the licensor. In *Hurst* v *Picture Theatres Ltd* [1915] 1 KB 1 (CA), for example, a cinema customer was physically removed because the owner (wrongly) believed he had not paid for his ticket. The Court of Appeal decided that the licensor should not have turned the licensee out and that the licensee was entitled to damages for false imprisonment and breach of contract. The decision was based on the argument that the **equitable** remedies of specific performance of the contract and an **injunction** to prevent the breach would, in theory, have been available to the customer, who therefore was seen by equity as having a right to remain in the cinema. Consequently, he could not be a trespasser.

In the *Winter Garden Theatre* case [1946] 1 All ER 678 (CA) and [1948] AC 173 (HL), the theatre owner attempted to revoke a licence allowing a theatre company to produce plays and concerts in the theatre, although there was no provision in the contract for him to do this. The House of Lords stated that whether a contractual licence could be revoked depended entirely on the construction of the contract. In this case, the licence was not intended to last forever and could therefore be determined by the theatre owner on reasonable notice.

Verrall v *Great Yarmouth BC* [1981] QB 202 (CA) is a clear example of a case in which a contractual licence could not be revoked. Following a change in its political control, a local council tried to revoke a licence to use a hall for a two-day conference which it had previously granted to an extreme-right-wing political organisation. It was held that the council could not do so. Damages for breach of contract would not be a sufficient remedy, since no alternative venue was available, so the Court of Appeal unanimously held that the contract should be specifically enforced. Lord Denning MR said, at 216:

> An injunction can be obtained against the licensor to prevent [the licensee] being turned out. On principle it is the same if it happens before he enters. If he had a contractual right to enter, and the licensor refuses to let him come in, then he can come to the court and in a proper case get an order for specific performance to allow him to come in.

Where a person is occupying premises as their residence under a contractual licence they will enjoy additional rights by virtue of the Protection from Eviction Act 1977 (see also Section 8.2.1(c)). In most cases, the licensor will not be entitled to recover possession of the premises without either a court order or the licensee's consent, even if the licence has expired (s 3(2B)). If the licence is a periodic one, then the licensee will normally be entitled to four weeks' written notice before the licence can be determined (s 5(1A)).

9.5.3 Effect on buyers of land and other third parties

If it is correct that in some circumstances a licence cannot be revoked, then it is necessary to consider the effect of such a licence on a purchaser of the land from the licensor. Has an irrevocable licence now become an interest in the land to which it relates, thus binding third parties, or does the traditional view prevail, that a licence is merely a personal right?

King v *David Allen & Sons Billposting Ltd* [1916] 2 AC 54 (HL) is an example of the traditional approach. The licence in this case was to fix advertising posters to the licensor's wall. The licensor then granted a long **lease** of the building, a cinema, and the leaseholder prevented the licensee from fixing the posters. The House of Lords held that the licensor was liable to pay damages for breach of contract. Although the cinema leaseholder was not a party to the case, Lord Buckmaster LC several times referred to the licence as a purely personal right and not an interest in land. Consequently, the licence did not bind the cinema leaseholder.

However, in *Errington* v *Errington & Woods* [1952] 1 KB 290 (CA), the facts of which are set out in Section 9.1, the Court of Appeal held that an arrangement between a father and his daughter-in-law was a contractual licence that could not be revoked so long as one of the licensees kept to their side of the bargain, and that it would bind a purchaser who had **notice** of it. Lord Justice Denning explained at 296–8:

> The couple were licensees, having a permissive occupation short of a tenancy, but with a contractual right, or at any rate, an equitable right to remain as long as they paid the instalments, which would grow into a good equitable title to the house itself as soon as the mortgage was paid … contractual licences now have a force and validity of their own and cannot be revoked in breach of contract. Neither the licensor nor anyone who claims through him can disregard the contract except a purchaser for value without notice.

In later years, it was Lord Denning's view that equity would enforce a contractual licence against anyone who ought fairly to be bound by it. In *Binions* v *Evans* [1972] Ch 359 (CA) at 368, for example:

> Wherever the owner sells the land to a purchaser, and at the same time stipulates that he shall take it 'subject to' a contractual licence, I think it plain that a court of equity will impose on the purchaser a constructive trust in favour of the beneficiary. … It would be utterly inequitable that the purchaser should be able to turn out the beneficiary.

Binions v *Evans* concerned a contractual licence permitting a widow to remain in a cottage for the rest of her life which bound (under a **constructive trust**) buyers of **unregistered land** who had agreed to take the land subject to her rights.

The view of Denning LJ in *Errington*, that contractual licences can bind third parties, was discredited in *Ashburn Anstalt* v *WJ Arnold & Co* [1989] Ch 1 (CA). However, the Court of Appeal in *Ashburn Anstalt* approved Lord Denning's imposition of a constructive trust in the later case of *Binions* v *Evans*. In that case, the constructive trust was necessary to protect the licensee against unconscionable dealing by the new legal owners, who had expressly agreed to uphold her rights. Nevertheless, in *Ashburn Anstalt*, the court took a restrictive view on the use of constructive trusts in such situations, since (per Fox LJ at 25):

> The court will not impose a constructive trust unless it is satisfied that the conscience of the estate owner is affected. The mere fact that that land is expressed to be conveyed 'subject to' a contract does not necessarily imply that the grantee is to be under an obligation, not otherwise existing, to give effect to the provisions of the contract.

9.6 Licences by estoppel

9.6.1 Remedial licences

The circumstances in which detrimental reliance on an expectation encouraged by the legal owner will give rise to an equity (the doctrine of **proprietary estoppel**) are considered in Chapter 18. An interest arising by way of estoppel will be satisfied by a remedy designed to do minimum justice between the parties and compensate the claimant for the detriment they have suffered. This remedy may sometimes be the award of an **estate** in the land, as in *Pascoe* v *Turner* [1979] 1 WLR 431 (CA) (see Section 18.5). However, the award of a licence for the claimant to remain on the land is not uncommon. For example, in *Inwards* v *Baker* [1965] 2 QB 29 (CA), a son was encouraged to build a bungalow on his father's land by the father's promise that the son could remain on the land. The son built the bungalow, but when the father died his heirs claimed the land. The Court of Appeal held that, since the father would have been estopped from going back on his promise, and the heirs were in the same position as the father, the son's equity should be satisfied by the award of a licence to stay on the land. Similarly, in *Greasley* v *Cooke* [1980] 1 WLR 1306 (CA), a maid who had lived in the house for many years was awarded an irrevocable licence to continue to occupy it for as long as she wished (see Section 18.5).

9.6.2 Effect on buyers of land

It is evident that Lord Denning felt that **estoppel** rights were capable of binding a buyer of the land. In *Inwards* v *Baker*, for example, he said (at 37):

> any purchaser who took with notice would clearly be bound by the equity.

He followed this in *ER Ives Investment Ltd* v *High* [1967] 2 QB 379 (CA). While a block of flats was being built, it was discovered that the foundations trespassed onto Mr High's land. Mr High agreed, unfortunately not by **deed**, that the foundations could remain in return for him being allowed to drive over the developer's land. He then built a garage on his own land at the end of the drive. The block of flats then changed hands, and the new owners tried to prevent Mr High using the drive. Lord Denning held that since the earlier owner of the flats would have been estopped from denying Mr High a right to use the drive belonging to the flats, the successors in **title** to that earlier owner were also bound by that right.

In *Re Sharpe (a bankrupt)* [1980] 1 WLR 219 (Ch), a woman lent £12,000 to her nephew to buy a maisonette on the basis that they would live there together. He became bankrupt, and the **trustee in bankruptcy**, having contracted to sell the maisonette, sought a possession order against her. Although the case was decided on the basis that the woman had a contractual licence to remain in the property until the loan was repaid, Browne-Wilkinson J said (at 223):

> If the parties have proceeded on a common assumption that the plaintiff is to enjoy a right to reside in a particular property and in reliance on that assumption the plaintiff has expended money or otherwise acted to his detriment, the defendant will not be allowed to go back on that common assumption and the court will imply an irrevocable licence or trust which will give effect to that common assumption.

This licence was binding on the **trustee in bankruptcy**. Although the judge was not required to express a view on the position of the purchaser from the trustee, he thought that it was possible that the rights of a purchaser without express **notice** of the contract would have prevailed over those of the licensee.

In **unregistered land**, whether a licence by estoppel binds a purchaser will usually depend upon whether the purchaser had notice of the equity (as in *ER Ives Investments Ltd* v *High*). In **registered land**, section 116 of the Land Registration Act (LRA) 2002 provides that an equity by estoppel is capable of binding purchasers, provided, of course, that it is combined with actual occupation (Sch 1, para 2 and Sch 3, para 2 LRA 2002; see Section 4.6.2).

9.7 The status of licences

If one thing is clear about licences, it is that there is not one answer to the questions 'Are licences interests in land?' and 'Are they property?' Probably the best conclusion to be drawn from the brief summary in this chapter is that licences are not in themselves interests in land. However, licences combined with a recognised interest in land, usually an **estoppel**, will benefit from the proprietary character of that interest.

The twentieth-century story of licences is an excellent illustration of how the law changes in response to changing social and economic values and concerns. Not that long ago, a number of academics and judges believed that twentieth-century land law would soon develop the contractual licence into a new type of interest in land, in a process equivalent to the development of the **restrictive covenant** in the nineteenth century. For example, in 1984 Sir Robert Megarry could write at page 808 of the leading textbook, *Megarry and Wade*:

> The courts seem to be well on their way to creating a new and highly versatile interest in land which will rescue many informal and unbusinesslike transactions, particularly within families, from the penalties of disregarding legal forms. Old restraints are giving way to the demands of justice.

For some, such licences were symbols of a new form of property, a right to share, which would take its place beside the traditional private and exclusive **property rights**. However, a few years later the Court of Appeal reaffirmed that circumstances such as those in *Errington* v *Errington & Woods* [1952] 1 KB 290 (CA) could not give rise to an interest in land, Fox LJ making it clear in *Ashburn Anstalt* v *WJ Arnold & Co* [1989] Ch 1 (at 15) that:

> A mere contractual licence to occupy land is not binding on a purchaser of land even though he has notice of the licence.

To hold otherwise would be to ignore earlier binding decisions of the House of Lords (including *King* v *David Allen & Sons Billposting Ltd* [1916] 2 AC 54 (HL)). Consequently, section 34–019 of the 2012 edition of *Megarry and Wade* reads very differently from its predecessor. The 'old restraints', such as the need for certainty of conveyancing and its formal processes, appear to have reassumed their importance, albeit that the equity raised by a **proprietary estoppel** retains its proprietary character. The history of licences is an important reminder to the land lawyer that they must be prepared to look beneath the surface of the law when asked to comment on or to evaluate any particular rule.

Summary

9.1 Licences are a mechanism, like interests in land, that allow a person to enjoy rights over land. Historically, however, they have not been recognised as proprietary rights.

9.2 A licence is a permission to be on land; it may be a bare licence or one coupled with an interest in the land, such as a *profit à prendre*, or it may arise through contract or estoppel.

9.3 A bare licence can be revoked at any time.

9.4 A licence coupled with an interest in land will last as long as the interest in question.

9.5 Whether a contractual licence can be revoked depends on the terms of the contract.

9.6 An estoppel licence may be awarded by the court when a person acts to their detriment in reliance on a promise that they will gain an interest in land. Licences by estoppel and licences that give rise to a constructive trust may bind a buyer of land.

9.7 Despite attempts to raise contractual licences to proprietary status during the latter half of the twentieth century, it now seems to be accepted that licences cannot bind a third party unless they are combined with a recognised interest in land, such as a *profit à prendre*, constructive trust or estoppel.

Exercises

 9.1 Complete the online quiz on the topics covered in this chapter on the companion website.

9.2 Are licences property?

9.3 John and Linda are the registered proprietors of a large house. When they bought it 15 years ago, it was very rundown, and they did not have the time or money to renovate it by themselves. They therefore agreed with Hannah and Joshua (Linda's sister and brother-in-law) that they would move in and help with the work; they said Hannah and Joshua would be able to make their home there. Hannah won £15,000 in the lottery and lent it to John and Linda so they could pay for a new roof. Joshua gave up his job to work on the house and look after John and Linda's children. He has been in hospital since falling off a ladder while mending one of the chimneys last year.

John and Linda are now going to separate. They have transferred the land to Damien, who has been registered as proprietor. Advise Hannah and Joshua.

 You can find suggested answer plans to exercises 9.2 and 9.3 on the companion website.

Further reading

Anderson, 'Of Licences and Similar Mysteries' (1979) 42 MLR 203
Battersby, 'Contractual and Estoppel Licences as Proprietary Interests in Land' [1991] Conv 36
Dewar, 'Licences and Land Law: An Alternative View' (1986) 49 MLR 741
McFarlane, 'Identifying Property Rights: A Reply to Mr Watt' [2003] Conv 473

Chapter 10

Easements and profits

Key concepts

- ▶ **Dominant tenement** – the land which benefits from an easement or profit.
- ▶ **Easement** – a right to do something on land belonging to someone else.
- ▶ **Profit à prendre** – a right to take something from someone else's land.
- ▶ **Servient tenement** – the land over which an easement or profit is exercised.

10.1 The case of the middle cottage

Teign Valley Road runs north–south through Christow, a small village on the edge of Dartmoor. To the east side of the road is a terrace of cottages known as Teign Terrace. Figure 10.1 shows a simplified plan of the three cottages, Nos 1, 1A and 2, at the northern end of the terrace.

Each of the cottages has a small yard to the rear. The yard to the central cottage (No 1A) can only be reached by passing through the cottage itself or by a path through the garden and yard to No 1 (X–Y on Figure 10.1). Y marks the front gate onto the road, and X marks a gate in the wall dividing the rear yards of Nos 1 and 1A. Gate X was installed by Mr Tucker, the owner of No 1, in 1964 'as a means of facilitating friendly social visits by him to his neighbour at No 1A'. This use continued until Mr Tucker's death in 1969.

Miss Cutler purchased No 1A in May 1970. However, she wanted more room, so when No 1, the larger of the two cottages, came on the market a year later, she bought it. For a week in October 1971, Miss Cutler owned both cottages. No 1A was then conveyed to Miss Winning, and ultimately to Mr and Mrs Payne.

The gate in the wall seems to have been largely forgotten or ignored during the years after 1969. When Miss Cutler owned No 1A, she seems to have believed that she had a right to have coal delivered via the path and gate, and the particulars of sale of No 1A in 1979 referred to 'the side and rear access from adjoining property'. Mr and Mrs Leigh, who owned No 1A from 1979 to 1981, did not use the path or the gate, but their successors, Mr and Mrs Payne, did.

In 1989, Mr and Mrs Inwood purchased No 1 from Miss Cutler, and in December 1991 they obstructed gate X and refused to allow Mr and Mrs Payne to use the path from the road. Ultimately Mr and Mrs Payne sought the assistance of the courts, and in 1995 His Honour Judge Galpin, sitting in the Exeter County Court, decided that they had an easement of right of way over the disputed route. Mr and Mrs Inwood appealed. In *Payne v Inwood* (1997) 74 P & CR 42 (CA) it fell to the Court of Appeal to determine whether the rights claimed by Mr and Mrs Payne amounted to an easement (one of the legal interests capable of existing in land). The two questions that needed to be answered were:

1. Was the right being claimed *capable* of being an easement?
2. If so, had the requirements for the *creation* of a legal easement been met?

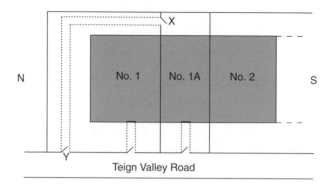

Figure 10.1 Teign Terrace

They are answered at Sections 10.5.5 and 10.7.8 respectively.

If the right was not capable of being an easement, it would be, at best, a **licence**. The significance of this is that, while an easement is a property right, attached to the land and passing automatically with it on **assignment**, a licence is a personal right rarely binding third parties and thus probably neither passing to a new owner of the land nor burdening a successor of the licensor (see Chapter 9).

10.2 Easements and profits in context

English law has long recognised easements and *profits à prendre* as property interests enjoyed over someone else's land.

▶ *Easements* are rights to do something on land belonging to someone else (for example, to use it to gain access to your land, as claimed by Mr and Mrs Payne).
▶ A *profit à prendre* is a right to take something from another's land (such as firewood or gravel).

In medieval times, profits were very nearly as important as the fee simple; the rules concerning them were settled centuries ago and have changed little. Easements are also ancient, but they only achieved their present form within the past couple of centuries, after the enclosures of commonly held rural land and the rapid growth of towns and cities. Easements are now much more important than profits, with at least 65% of registered freehold title being subject to one or more easements (Law Commission, *Easements, Covenants and Profits à Prendre* (Law Com CP No 186, 2008), para 1.3). New profits are rarely created these days, having largely been replaced by contractual **licences** (see Chapter 9).

Easements and profits (such as the right of way claimed by Mr and Mrs Payne) can add significantly to the value of the land that benefits from them. Indeed, it may be impossible to use any buildings on the land without them (the right to run and use gas and water pipes, drains and electric cables, for example). The essential problem for judges in this area of land law (which is hardly touched by the 1925 legislation) is to balance at least two conflicting demands. First, if it increases the value of land that benefits from it, it may also decrease the value of the other land over which it can be exercised. For example, the right claimed by the Paynes would have reduced their neighbours' privacy (the path ran through the gardens and past the kitchen windows of cottage No 1). Second, it is important that anyone being granted rights over land can rely upon those rights being secure, but it is equally important that such rights do not unduly burden the subject land, preventing the exercise of other valuable rights. As well as these tensions between the interests of private land-owners, and between them and the general public interest in the market in land, there is also the tension between private land ownership and public access to land. Most public rights of access to land are not easements, but creations of statute (most recently the Countryside and Rights of Way Act 2000) and largely fall outside the scope of this chapter (but see Section 10.12).

10.3 Dominant and servient tenements

Easements and *profits à prendre* have a vocabulary appropriate to their great age. Perhaps the most important aspect of the terminology to grasp is the distinction between the **dominant tenement** and the **servient tenement**:

▶ The land over which the right is exercised is *burdened* by the easement or profit; it is known as the *servient tenement*.
▶ An easement must benefit (*accommodate*) another piece of land. The land that benefits from the easement is known as the *dominant tenement*. A profit may, but does not have to, benefit a dominant tenement (see Section 10.10).

Two further points are worth stressing about these terms. First, they refer to land (strictly speaking **estates** in land), not to the owner for the time being. Second, the word 'tenement' does not imply that the land is necessarily subject to a **tenancy**: it is derived from the ancient doctrine of **tenure**, rather than the law of landlord and tenant. In fact, legal easements can be indefinite (**freehold**) or limited to a term of years (s 1(2)(a) of the LPA 1925).

10.4 Types of easement

This section contains a summary of some of the main types of easement. It is not offered as a comprehensive list, but as a way of getting a 'feel' for the topic and its blurred edges. Some students will, therefore, prefer to start with the systematic treatment of the four essential characteristics for an easement considered in Section 10.5.

Easements comprise a wide variety of types of right, some more common than others. Many of these types were first recognised before judicial adoption of the systematic approach which forms the basis of Section 10.5. As a result, some rights long recognised as easements do not fit at all comfortably within the now accepted norms. Neither are the categories of easement fixed. However, although it is generally agreed that any new easement must share the general character of already recognised easements, it is not always possible for judges to agree about whether or not a particular right does so (compare, for example, the majority judgment with the dissenting judgment of Lord Carnwath in *Regency Villas Title Ltd* v *Diamond Resorts (Europe) Ltd* [2018] 3 WLR 1603 (SC)).

10.4.1 Rights of way

Rights of way are, perhaps, the most commonly encountered easements. It is important not to confuse the rights enjoyable under such easements with public or permissive rights of way granted to the public in general.

An easement of way can be general. Alternatively, it may be restricted in some way; for example, it may exclude the use of vehicles or may only be exercisable at certain times of day. Many of the cases involving easements of way are concerned with the precise extent of the rights that have been acquired. For example, in *Donovan v Rana* [2014] 1 P & CR 23 (CA) an express right of way 'for all purposes connected with the use and enjoyment of the property but not for any other purpose' was held to include a right of access for workers to connect the property to mains services.

Once created, the route of the easement is usually fixed. In *Greenwich Healthcare NHS Trust v London & Quadrant Housing Trust* [1998] 1 WLR 1749 (Ch), Lightman J explained (at 1754) that:

> a servient owner has no right to alter the route of an easement of way unless such a right is an express or implied term of the grant of the easement or is subsequently conferred on him.

This is true even when, as in this case, the new route would improve access and safety for the people benefiting from the easement. However, that does not mean that the **dominant tenement** will be able to insist on using the original route. In *Greenwich Healthcare NHS Trust* Lightman J went on to hold that the circumstances of the case meant that an **injunction** to reinstate the original route was inappropriate and limited the remedy to the payment of damages.

10.4.2 Rights of light

English law does not recognise a general right to light, nor the right to enjoy a particular view (see Section 10.5.4(a)). However, a **dominant tenement** is entitled to enough light through a particular window or aperture to render occupation of a dwelling-house 'comfortable according to the ordinary notions of mankind' or to enable the dominant tenement holder to continue to beneficially carry on business from the premises (*Colls v Home & Colonial Stores Ltd* [1904] AC 179 (HL), a case is notable for being argued twice before the Appellate Committee of the House of Lords, and for the death of one of the Law Lords hearing the appeal before judgment was delivered).

It is easier to acquire a right of light than it is to acquire other types of easement under the Prescription Act 1832 (see Section 10.7.6), not least because there is no need to show that the use has been enjoyed as of right. However, the Rights of Light Act 1959 enables the owners of **servient tenements** to register a notice that prevents rights to light being acquired over their property arising by **prescription** without having to erect a physical obstruction. Rights of light are sufficiently significant to have been the subject of a Law Commission consultation in 2013, and the resulting report, *Rights to Light* (Law Com 356, 2014), is commended to students wishing to consider them in more detail.

10.4.3 Rights of water

The law recognises a wide variety of easements concerning the taking of water from, and the discharging of water onto (or through) neighbouring land. These include the right to water cattle at a pond, the right to receive water through a pipe, the right to discharge water (and other matter) through a pipe, and the right to discharge water onto the **servient tenement**. In *Atwood* v *Bovis Homes Ltd* [2001] Ch 379 (Ch) the defendant began building houses on land that had the benefit of a right of drainage onto land owned by the claimant. Mr Justice Neuberger held that the **dominant tenement** could continue to benefit from this easement as (on the facts) the new use of the land did not significantly increase the burden on the servient tenement.

10.4.4 Rights of support

All land has a natural right of support from neighbouring land (see Section 10.12.2), but this right does not extend to the support of any buildings on that land. However, it is possible to acquire an easement of support for buildings. Indeed, such easements may be very important. For example, semi-detached houses are usually mutually dependent for support. Once acquired, an easement of support continues, even if the use of the **dominant tenement** changes unless, as Wilmer LJ explained in *Ray* v *Fairway Motors (Barnstable) Ltd* (1969) 20 P & CR 261 (CA), at 266, the building on the dominant tenement:

> is so altered or reconstructed as to throw a substantially increased burden on the servient tenement to the prejudice of the owner thereof.

10.4.5 Rights of fencing

The right to require a neighbour to fence land and keep those fences in good repair can be very valuable, especially in rural communities. The possibility of such rights existing as easements was recognised by the Court of Appeal in *Crow* v *Wood* [1971] 1 QB 77 (CA). However, the right to have a fence or wall kept in repair is a very unusual type of easement ('spurious' is one of the words used to describe it in *Crow* v *Wood*) because it requires positive action and expense by the owner of the **servient tenement** (see Section 10.5.4(d)).

10.4.6 Rights of air

There is no natural right to the air that passes across neighbouring land. It is, however, possible to acquire an easement of air, provided that the passage of the air is confined to a defined channel, such as a ventilator in the wall of a building (as in *Cable* v *Bryant* [1908] 1 Ch 259 (Ch)). *Hunter* v *Canary Wharf Ltd* [1997] AC 655 (HL) concerned not a right to air, but the interference to television reception in London Docklands caused by the building of the Canary Wharf tower. The House of Lords refused to recognise the existence of an easement to receive television signals and the local residents' claim for compensation failed.

Negative easements
Most easements are positive, that is they give the owner of the **dominant tenement** the right to do something on someone else's land. Rights of support, air, light, and the receipt of water, however, give the dominant tenement holder the right to take or receive something from the servient land. Despite this anomaly, they have long been recognised as *negative* easements.

The courts are 'very wary' of creating new kinds of negative easement. For example, in *Phipps* v *Pears* [1965] 1 QB 76 (CA), a neighbour demolished a house which was built very close to that of the claimant, who claimed he had an easement of 'protection from the weather' with which the neighbour had interfered (in effect, a negative easement, preventing the neighbour from developing his land). In this case, Lord Denning MT, at 82, defined the difference between positive and negative easements:

> positive easements, such as a right of way, which give the owner of land a right himself to do something on or to his neighbour's land: and negative easements, such as a right of light, which gives him a right to stop his neighbour doing something on his (his neighbour's) own land.

Of course, a positive easement will, by definition, prevent servient owners doing things on their land which interfere with the exercise of that easement. The reluctance to recognise entirely negative rights as easements is understandable, at least for so long as legal easements can be acquired by long user (**prescription**, see Section 10.7.6), because a servient owner might not know that the easement was being acquired. The right claimed as an easement in *Phipps* v *Pears* was held not to be an easement of support and, indeed, was not an easement at all, because it would 'unduly restrict the enjoyment' of the servient land and prevent its development.

Restrictive covenants (see Chapter 12) may offer more appropriate solutions in situations like this, but the answer might also be found in the law of tort. In *Bradburn* v *Lindsay* [1983] 2 All ER 408 (Ch), Mr Bradburn, owner of one of a pair of semi-detached houses, was concerned that the dry rot in his neighbour's derelict house would spread to his own property. The house had to be demolished by the council, and Mr Bradburn claimed damages from his neighbour for loss of support and exposure of the side of his house to dry rot and decay. There was clearly an easement of support, but Mrs Lindsay was under no obligation to maintain it by keeping the wall in repair. Mr Bradburn therefore successfully relied on the torts of negligence and nuisance.

In its 2008 consultation on *Easements, Covenants and Profits à Prendre* (Law Com CP No 186), the Law Commission raised the possibility of abolishing negative easements, but this proposal was not among the recommendations made in the report that followed in 2011 (see paras 3.81 and 5.94–9 of Law Com 327, 2011). Nevertheless, the range of negative easements recognised at law is unlikely to be extended.

10.4.7   Other types of easement

Many other types of rights have been recognised as easements, some of which are referred to elsewhere in this chapter. They include:

- the right to store coal in a shed (*Wright* v *Macadam* [1949] 2 KB 744 (CA));
- the right to use a lavatory (*Miller* v *Emcer Products Ltd* [1956] Ch 304 (CA));
- the right to cause certain types of nuisance (such as noise, *Lawrence* v *Fen Tigers Ltd* [2014] AC 822 (SC)); and
- the right to use any sporting or recreational facilities on an adjoining estate (*Regency Villas Title Ltd* v *Diamond Resorts (Europe) Ltd* [2018] 3 WLR 1603).

As Lord St Leonards explained over 150 years ago in *Dyce* v *Hay* (1852) 1 Macq 305 (HL) at 312–13, the list of easements is not closed:

> The category of ... easements must alter and expand with the changes that take place in the circumstances of mankind.

However, neither is the list capable of infinite extension, as Lord Brougham LC made clear in the still earlier case of *Keppell* v *Bailey* (1834) 39 ER 1042 (Ch), at 1049:

> it must not therefore be supposed that incidents of a novel kind can be devised and attached to property at the fancy or caprice of any owner.

In *Regency Villas*, the majority of the Supreme Court was in no doubt that recognising the right to use facilities such as a heated swimming pool and an 18-hole golf course as an easement was 'breaking new ground by comparison with *In re Ellenborough Park*' ([75]). The two main justifications for this were:

- common law has always sought, so far as possible, to adapt 'to new types of property ownership and new ways of enjoying the use of land' ([76]); and
- the recognition of recreational easements in other common law jurisdictions ([77]).

While these two principles are almost certainly sound, it is not difficult to appreciate Lord Carnwath's doubts about their application to the type of rights ultimately recognised in *Regency Villas* ([96]), not least because even Lord Briggs, speaking for the majority, did not think the use of easements 'ideal' for achieving the objectives of timeshare ownership schemes (see [80]).

10.5 The nature of easements

It is generally recognised that for a right to be classified as an easement, it must comply with the four requirements listed by Geoffrey Cheshire in his *Modern Law of Real Property*. These four requirements were famously adopted by Evershed MR in the leading case of *Re Ellenborough Park* [1956] Ch 131 (CA) and affirmed by the Supreme Court some 60 years later in *Regency Villas Title Ltd* v *Diamond Resorts (Europe) Ltd* [2018] 3 WLR 1603. These four 'well-established conditions for the recognition of a right as an easement', to use the words of Lord Briggs at [35] in his judgment in *Regency Villas*, are (to adopt the format of the Official Transcript of the case):

(i)   There must be a dominant and a servient tenement;
(ii) The easement must accommodate the dominant tenement;
(iii) The dominant and servient owners must be different persons;
(iv) A right over land cannot amount to an easement, unless it is capable of forming the subject matter of a grant.

10.5.1 Dominant and servient tenements

There must be separate dominant and servient land. The need for there to be a **dominant tenement** means that an easement cannot exist *in gross*, there must be land to be benefited by the right. This requirement, which does not apply to **profits à prendre**, seems to have been adopted during the nineteenth century under the influence of Roman law in response to judicial concern to preserve certainty with respect to rights over land. As Peter Gibson LJ explains in *London and Blenheim Estates Ltd* [1994] 1 WLR 31 (CA), at 37:

> If one asks why the law should require that there should be a dominant tenement before there can be a grant, or a contract for the grant, of an easement sufficient to create an interest

in land binding successors in title to the servient land, the answer would appear to lie in the policy against encumbering land with burdens of uncertain extent.

In his article 'Easements in Gross' (1980) 96 LQR 557, Michael F Sturley argued that the authority for requiring a dominant tenement is very weak and that allowing easements to exist in gross would not unduly burden **titles**. He suggested that allowing easements which are not attached to benefiting land to exist, such as the right to land a helicopter on distant land, would actually encourage greater utilisation of land. However, this argument was rejected by the Law Commission in its report, *Making Land Law Work: Easements, Covenants and Profits à Prendre* (Law Com 327, 2011), para 2.24.

The existence of dominant and **servient tenements** was not an issue in the leading cases of *Re Ellenborough Park* and *Regency Villas*. Sometimes, however, this is not so obvious. In *Miller v Emcer Products Ltd* [1956] Ch 304 (CA), a **tenant** occupying the ground floor of premises claimed an easement to use the **landlord's** lavatory on the floor above. In that case, the dominant and servient tenements were not two plots of land, but the **freehold estate** and a **leasehold** estate in part of the same land. The tenant had the dominant tenement, and the landlord the servient.

The wording of section 1(2)(a) of the Law of Property Act 1925 makes it clear that a legal easement may exist for a period equivalent to either a freehold or a leasehold estate. Although there is no requirement that an easement for a **term of years absolute** is linked to the grant of a **lease**, the majority of such easements will have been granted by **lessors** to their tenants. Typically, this occurs where the lease is of a building with common parts, as was the case in *Miller v Emcer Products Ltd*. In the rather unusual circumstances of *Wall v Collins* [2007] Ch 390 (CA), the Court of Appeal had to consider what happened if the lease had come to a premature end by being merged into the freehold title. It held that such easements are not 'attached' to the leasehold interest out of which they are created and may, therefore, continue to exist for the remainder of the original term of the lease.

Is an easement attached or appurtenant?
In the first half of the twentieth century it was common for houses to be sold on long leases rather than freehold because this allowed developers to preserve the character of the estate that they had built. The two adjoining semi-detached houses at the centre of the dispute in *Wall v Collins* [2007] Ch 390 (CA) were 231 and 233 Leigh Road, Bolton; they had been built in 1911 and acquired by their original owners on 999-year leases. Mr Wall, the owner of 231, sought to enforce a right of way over land forming part of number 233 in order to reach his garage on land that his predecessors had acquired by **adverse possession** (see Chapter 16). The parties agreed that such an easement had been included with the original lease of number 231. However, in 1986, Mr Wall's predecessors in title had acquired the freehold as well as the leasehold interest in number 231, and when Mr Wall purchased the house in 1999 the leasehold title was closed by the Land Registry, the leasehold title having merged into the freehold. The 999-year lease had come to an end. The question was whether the end of the lease meant that the easement had also come to an end.

In *Making Land Law Work: Easements, Covenants and Profits à Prendre* (Law Com 327, 2011), para 3.242, the Law Commission noted that *Wall* v *Collins* raises the question of whether easements created in such circumstances are appurtenant to the lease, or attached to the land. The word 'land' in this context cannot mean the leasehold estate. Presumably, it must, therefore, refer to either the freehold estate, or even to the physical land. In its submission to the Law Commission's consultation, the Chancery Bar Association summed up the conflict between principle and pragmatism as follows (Law Com 327, 2011 at para 3.244):

> We agree that where an easement is attached to a leasehold estate, the easement should be automatically extinguished on termination of the estate. As a matter of principle that must be correct. Nevertheless, we note ... the potentially disastrous consequences which might ensue ... [for] the dominant owner who stands to lose his right through merger in these circumstances.

There are major issues of jurisprudence here. Is it more important that the law be consistent, or that it is perceived to be just? In *Wall* v *Collins* Lord Justice Carnwath concluded, at [18], that:

> As a matter of common sense, it is difficult to see why a lessee should be worse off, so far as concerns an easement annexed to the land, merely because he has acquired a larger interest in the [dominant tenement].

In contrast, the Law Commission, despite the representations of the Chancery Bar Association and others, concluded that the Court of Appeal's decision in *Wall* v *Collins* should be reversed by statute. Who is right? Land law students must decide for themselves.

10.5.2   Accommodating the dominant tenement

Just as in the pre-1996 law of **leases**, where the **covenant** must 'touch and concern' the land (see Section 8.4.1), the claimed easement must benefit the land itself and not merely the landowner. The Law Commission has summarised this requirement as follows (Law Com 327, 2011, at para 2.25):

> The requirement is that the right must be of some practical importance to the benefited land, rather than just to the right-holder as an individual: it must be 'reasonably neces- sary for the better enjoyment' of that land. The land can be 'accommodated and served' by being made more useful; for example, by an easement entitling its owner to walk across the neighbouring field to church, or from a right of eavesdrop onto the neighbour's garden. The requirement means that the two plots of land must be reasonably close to each other, even if not actually adjoining.

In *Regency Villas*, Lord Briggs, with whom a majority of the judges agreed, identi- fied four factors relevant to establishing that a right accommodates the **dominant tenement**.

1. *The right must be connected with the normal use of the dominant land* (Regency Villas *[40]*).
   It is not enough that the right is annexed to the dominant tenement, or that it increases the value of the dominant land. It must actually benefit the normal use of the dominant tenement.

2. *Normal use may be residential or business, actual or contemplated* (Regency Villas *[41]*).

Re Ellenborough Park, for example, concerned the rights of owners of houses situated around or close to Ellenborough Park in Weston-super-Mare to use the park as a leisure garden. Evershed MR, having decided that a garden is connected with the expected use of a house, continued (at 174):

> we can see no difference in principle between Ellenborough Park and a garden in the ordinary significance of that word.

The earlier case of *Moody* v *Steggles* (1879) 12 Ch D 261 (Ch) concerned the right to hang a pub sign on neighbouring land. Fry J held that the right was an easement because it was impossible to distinguish between the dominant tenement and the business carried on there (at 266). The decision in *Moody* v *Steggles* has often been contrasted with that in *Hill* v *Tupper* (1863) 159 ER 51 (Ex), where the court refused to recognise as an easement an exclusive right to hire out pleasure boats on the Basingstoke Canal from a narrow strip of land on its bank. However, in the opinion of the majority in *Regency Villas* (see [54–7]), *Hill* v *Tupper* was decided on the basis that the right granted was purely personal and, therefore, incapable of being annexed to land at all.

3. *The fact that the right involves the use of a chattel does not prevent it from being an easement* (Regency Villas *[42]*).

In the judgment of the Court of Appeal in *Regency Villas*, there was a sharp distinction between rights over land (which could be easements) and rights in respect of services, equipment or chattels situated on land (which could not): see, for example, [2017] Ch 516 (CA), [61]. The majority of the Supreme Court, however, had no such concerns about easements that included the use of gym equipment, or even a restaurant, at least not within the overall context in which the rights were created.

4. *The question is 'primarily one of fact'* (Regency Villas *[43]*).

In other words, the previous three factors must be considered within the specific context in which the rights concerned were created (see, also, Evershed MR in *Re Ellenborough Park* at 173).

One question that has concerned commentators since *Re Ellenborough Park* is whether a right amounting to 'mere recreation or amusement' can ever be an easement. The controversy can be traced back to the origins of easements in the Roman law doctrine of servitudes (see Evershed MR at 163), under which it was impossible to have a recreational right to wander over someone else's fields (a *ius spatiandi*). According to Lord Briggs in *Regency Villas* (at [44]), the correct question is not whether the right claimed relates to sport or recreation, but whether:

> the sporting or recreational right will be enjoyed for its own sake … rather than as a means to some end consisting directly of the beneficial use of the dominant tenement.

Lord Briggs went on to hold (at [57]) that there is no requirement that the right must be proportionately subordinate or ancillary to the use of the dominant tenement, provided that the question that the dominant tenement actually benefits from the right. In the words of Warren J in the earlier case of *Polo Woods Foundation* v *Shelton-Agar* [2010] 1 P & CR 12 (Ch), at [53]:

there is no test of real or appreciable benefit to the dominant tenement which has to be passed before a right claimed can be said to 'accommodate' it or to establish the necessary connection or nexus between the right and the dominant tenement …

It is generally recognised that there must be some physical proximity between the two tenements if the right is to accommodate the dominant one. In *Bailey* v *Stephens* (1862) 142 ER 1077 (CP), Byles J doubted that a right over an estate in Northumberland could be said to benefit an estate in Kent. However, the two plots do not need to be adjoining. As the Law Commission explains (Law Com 327, 2011 at 2.26):

it is difficult to say that a garden in Westminster benefits from an easement over land in Islington, 3.5 miles away, although not implausible to say that a house benefits from a right of drainage through a pipe that passes not only through the neighbour's land but also through a series of properties, some of them some distance away.

10.5.3 Different ownership or occupation

People cannot have rights against themselves. If both tenements come into the hands of one person, the easement is ended ('extinguished by unity of **seisin**'; see Section 10.9.2(b)). If what was formerly an easement, for example to cross one field to get into the next, continues to be used by the owner of both tenements it is not an easement, but a quasi-easement (see Sections 10.7.4 and 10.7.5).

10.5.4 Capable of being the subject of a grant

The exact significance of the requirement that an easement must be capable of being the subject of a grant is, 'at first sight, perhaps, not entirely clear' (Evershed MR in *Re Ellenborough Park* [1956] Ch 131 (CA), 164). Its origin lies in the fact that not all easements are created by **deed**; easements can also be acquired by prescription (that is, long use of the right being claimed: see Section 10.7.6). At its simplest, this fourth condition requires the right claimed to be capable of being a contract or licence which both the grantor and grantee are competent to create by deed. Consequently, both parties must be legal persons, and that grantor must have sufficient interest in the servient tenement under the principle of *nemo dat quod non habet* (no one can give something which they do not have). In *London & Blenheim Estates Ltd* v *Ladbroke Retail Parks Ltd* [1994] 1 WLR 31 (CA), the appellants had been granted an option to acquire land owned by the Leicestershire Co-operative Society Ltd together with an easement to park cars on other land owned by the Co-op. However, by the time the plaintiff exercised its option, the potentially servient land had been transferred to the defendant. The Court of Appeal rejected the appellant's claim that they had an easement over the defendant's land, holding that for an easement to be created, the dominant land must be in the possession of the grantee, and the grantor must own the servient land.

However, as Lord Briggs notes in *Regency Villas* [2018] 3 WLR 1603 (SC), [58], the requirement that the right must be capable of being the subject matter of a grant

has come to be a repository for a series of miscellaneous requirements which have been held to be essential characteristics of an easement.

The most important of these requirements will now be considered in turn.

10.5.4(a) Sufficiently definite

The nature and extent of the right must be capable of sufficiently accurate definition. For example, *Aldred's Case* (1610) 77 ER 816 (KB) confirms that the right to a good view cannot amount to an easement, because such a thing is too imprecise to describe (it is, however, possible to protect one's view by using a **restrictive covenant**: see *Davies* v *Dennis* [2009] EWCA Civ 1081). Recently, however, there have been signs that this requirement is to be applied with a certain degree of flexibility. In *Lawrence* v *Fen Tigers Ltd* [2014] AC 822 (SC), Lord Neuberger was prepared to recognise the possibility of an easement allowing noise to be made on the **dominant tenement**. Similarly, the majority in *Regency Villas Title Ltd* v *Diamond Resorts (Europe) Ltd* [2018] 3 WLR 1603 (SC) had no doubt that the grant of a right 'to use the swimming pool, golf course, squash courts, tennis courts, the ground and basement floor of the Broome Park Mansion House, gardens and other sporting or recreational facilities ... on the Transferor's adjoining estate' was sufficiently clear and precise (see [8] and [60]), despite also holding that the right extended to any additional or replacement facilities installed after the date of the grant ([26]).

10.5.4(b) Within the general nature of rights recognised as easements

To be capable of being an easement, the right concerned must fall within the general nature of the rights that are already recognised as easements. So, for example, the courts will not recognise a right that is 'purely precarious', that is 'liable to be taken away at the whim of the servient owner' as an easement (*Regency Villas*, [58]). It has frequently been said that a right of mere recreation and amusement cannot, by definition, be an easement, despite the fact that Evershed MR rejected this argument in *Re Ellenborough Park* (see 177–9). In Law Com No 327, 2011 at para 2.29, the Law Commission removed the reference to recreation, limiting the scope of the exclusion to 'a right merely for amusement'. However, the majority in the now leading case of *Regency Villas* rejected this rule completely. Consequently, as Lord Briggs explained at [59], if:

> the accommodation test is satisfied, then the fact that it may be a right to use recreational or sporting facilities does not ... disable it from being an easement ... Recreation, including sport, and the amusement which comes with it, does confer utility and benefit on those who undertake it.

10.5.4(c) No exclusive use

When Lord Evershed MR came to consider whether the rights claimed in *Re Ellenborough Park* were capable of forming the subject matter of a grant, he concluded (at 164) that they could not be easements:

> if and so far as effective, such rights would amount to rights of joint occupation or would substantially deprive the park owners of proprietorship or legal possession.

In other words, because an easement is an interest over someone else's land, any right that effectively transfers ownership of that land to the dominant tenement holder cannot be an easement.

In many cases the rights recognised as easements fall very short of depriving servient tenement holders of the effective ownership of their land; however, in other cases they significantly limit the ability of the servient tenement owner to enjoy that land.

In *Miller* v *Emcer Products Ltd* [1956] Ch 304 (CA), the tenant's right to use a lavatory could be an easement because the tenant would only have been using the lavatory some of the time. The right to store goods can, but will not necessarily be, an easement. In *Wright* v *Macadam* [1949] 2 KB 744 (CA), the right to store coal in a coal shed was held to amount to an easement. In contrast, Upjohn J decided in *Copeland* v *Greenhalf* [1952] Ch 488 (Ch) that the right to store and mend vehicles on a strip of land belonging to the claimant was not an easement. The fact that Upjohn J did not refer to the binding authority of *Wright* v *Macadam* has spawned various attempts to reconcile the two decisions. In reality, Upjohn J's decision in *Copeland* v *Greenhalf* rests at least as much on the vague character of the right being claimed (see Section 10.5.4(a)) as it does on the ouster of the landowner by the rights claimed (see Haley and McMurtry, 2007).

The question of whether the rights granted are too excessive should, according to Lord Briggs in *Regency Villas* at [64]:

> Be addressed by reference to what may be supposed to have been the ordinary questions of the parties, at the time of the grant, as to who, as between dominant and servient owners, was expected to undertake the management, control and maintenance of the servient tenement.

However, *Regency Villas* leaves unanswered the controversy about the standard by which excessive use is to be judged ([61]). The controversy itself is relatively straightforward, but many students are confused by it because of inconsistency in how one of the main terms in the debate is used. The relevant term is the 'ouster principle'. The term is used in two main ways and it is important, therefore, to discern how the term is being used in a particular context (or even the same context: see [61] of Lord Briggs' judgment in *Regency Villas*).

- In its narrow sense, the 'ouster principle' refers only to the 'reasonable use' test adopted by the Court of Appeal in *Batchelor* v *Marlow* [2003] 1 WLR 764 (CA). This, for example, is the usage adopted by the Law Commission in paragraphs 3.188–3.211 of *Making Land Law Work: Easements, Covenants and Profits à Prendre* (Law Com 327, 2011).
- In its wider sense, the 'ouster principle' simply refers to the rule that the rights over the servient tenement must not be excessive, rather than to the specific content of that rule. An example of this usage can be found towards the end of [61] in *Regency Villas*, where Lord Briggs distinguishes between two possible 'views' of what the 'ouster principle' comprises.

In *Batchelor* v *Marlow* [2003] 1 WLR 764 (CA), Mr and Mrs Marlow had parked vehicles on land owned by Mr Batchelor from 8.30 am to 6.00 pm, Monday to Friday, for many years. It was common ground in the Court of Appeal that the relevant test was that distilled by Judge Paul Baker QC in *London & Blenheim Estates Ltd* v *Ladbroke Retail Parks Ltd* [1992] 1 WLR 1278 (Ch), at 1288:

> The essential question is one of degree. If the right granted in relation to the area over which it is to be exercisable is such that it would leave the servient owner without any reasonable use of his land, whether for parking or anything else, it could not be an easement though it might be some larger or different grant.

The Court of Appeal held that the effect of the rights claimed by the Marlows would be to seriously curtail Mr Batchelor's ability to use his land for significant periods of each week. The fact that Mr Batchelor could sell the land (subject to the Marlows' rights) or park on the land himself or charge others for doing so outside business hours did not amount to 'reasonable use' of his land. Such ownership would, in the words of Tuckey LJ, be merely 'illusory'.

The 'reasonable use' test does not totally preclude easements to park, but it does restrict the circumstances in which a right to park can be an easement. For example, in *Hair* v *Gillman* (2000) 80 P & CR 108 (CA), the Court of Appeal had already held that permission to park a car anywhere 'on a forecourt which was capable of taking two or three other cars' (112) was an easement. Similarly, in the unreported case of *R Square Properties Ltd* v *Nissan Motor (GB) Ltd*, 13 March 2014 (Ch), Mr Stuart Isaacs QC, sitting as a deputy judge of the Chancery Division, distinguished *Batchelor* v *Marlow* in deciding that an exclusive right to use 80 parking spaces on an industrial estate could be an easement, because the owner of the car park had reserved specific rights to enter and use the land. The servient tenement owner's unsuccessful application for leave to appeal is reported at [2014] EWCA Civ 1769. However, it will not always be possible to distinguish *Batchelor* v *Marlow*.

The question in *Moncrieff* v *Jamieson* [2007] 1 WLR 2620 (HL) was whether an expressly granted right of way by vehicle also included an implied right to park on the servient land. The circumstances were somewhat unusual in that it was impossible to park on the dominant tenement due to the nature of the terrain (a Scottish cliffside). As a Scottish case, *Moncrieff* v *Jamieson* is not directly binding on English courts. However, Lord Scott, who believed there to be no difference between the two jurisdictions so far as the relevant issues were concerned, took the opportunity to criticise *Batchelor* v *Marlow*. Although Lord Scott was concerned that the 'reasonable use' test introduced too much uncertainty (by what standard is 'reasonableness' to be measured?), his main objection was that this test deprived landowners of the right to do with their land whatever they wished. He concluded at [59]:

> I would, for my part, reject the test that asks whether the servient owner is left with any reasonable use of his land, and substitute for it a test which asks whether the servient owner retains possession and, subject to the reasonable exercise of the right in question, control of the servient land.

This test is usually referred to as the 'possession and control' test.

Despite the weight of Lord Scott's observations in *Moncrieff* v *Jamieson*, it seems that *Batchelor* v *Marlow* remains the binding English authority. It has already been noted that the Supreme Court did not find it necessary to address the issue in *Regency Villas,* mainly because of the way in which the case had been pleaded ([61] and [62]). However, Lord Briggs did take the opportunity to stress that the right of the owner of a dominant tenement to 'step in' to maintain the servient land if its owner failed to do so cannot be used, in itself, to demonstrate that the rights granted are excessive ([64] and [65]).

Easements and exclusive possession
In a sense, the 'ouster principle' controversy is caused by the difficulty in finding the abstract concepts and the language needed to contain the range and flexibility the 'real world' requires when it comes to recognising and regulating privileges exercisable over another person's land. Peter Luther traces the problem, in part at least, to a change in

attitude to the role of **exclusive possession** (see 'Easements and exclusive possession' (1996) 16 *Legal Studies* 51).

Prior to the decision in *Street* v *Mountford* [1985] AC 809 (see Section 7.5.1), exclusive possession was understood as the practical ability to exclude others incident upon owning an estate. It was in this context that much of the law relating to easements and their extent developed. With *Street* v *Mountford*, however, exclusive possession was transformed into *the right* that characterised the legal estate, and distinguished it from a personal right (and, indeed, a non-estate interest in the land). Thus, the logical test for whether or not a right is too extensive to be an easement becomes whether it is inconsistent with the servient tenement owner's exclusive possession of their land, and there is no justification for adding further rules (see Haley and McMurtry, 'Identifying an Easement: Exclusive Use, *De Facto* Control and Judicial Constraints' (2007) 58 NILQ 405). In its report, *Making Land Law Work: Easements, Covenants and Profits à Prendre* (Law Com 327, 2011), para 3.028, the Law Commission also concluded:

> that while an easement must not grant exclusive possession, the ouster principle should be abolished. An easement that stops short of exclusive possession, even if it deprives the owner of much of the use of his land, or indeed of all reasonable use of it, is valid. The effect of this would be to reverse, for the future, the decision in *Batchelor* v *Marlow*, for example, and therefore to validate a potentially wide range of parking easements. In particular, easements that confer an 'exclusive right to park' would be clearly valid, provided that the servient owner can access the land (to however limited an extent).

There is little sign of the Law Commission's recommendation being introduced by statute.

10.5.4(d) Passivity

It is generally accepted that an easement should not require any positive action or expense by the owner of the servient tenement (the only significant exception being the 'spurious' easement of fencing considered at Section 10.4.5). This does not mean that an easement cannot be granted over a facility that is maintained by the servient tenement holder. It is usual in such circumstances for the servient tenement owner to be able to recover the costs of doing so from the dominant owners, as was the case in *Re Ellenborough Park* [1956] Ch 131 (CA). It is not essential, however, for the cost of maintenance to be borne by the users of the easement (*Regency Villas Title Ltd* v *Diamond Resorts (Europe) Ltd* [2018] 3 WLR 1603 (SC), [69]). What is more important is that it is possible for the dominant tenement owners to provide the facilities themselves if the servient owner fails to do so. It is the answer to this question that separates Lord Carnwath from the majority in *Regency Villas*. He was of the opinion, at [95], that:

> The intended enjoyment of the rights granted in this case, most obviously in the case of the golf course and swimming-pool, cannot be achieved without the active participation of the owner of those facilities in their provision, maintenance and management.

Despite the extensive nature of the rights granted, the majority accepted that sufficient 'meaningful use' could be made of them even if the servient tenement owner ceased completely to operate its land as a leisure complex, and that this was enough ([71]). As to whether this conclusion is justified on the facts, students must read both judgments and make up their own minds.

10.5.5 Applying the rules to *Payne* v *Inwood*

If Mr and Mrs Payne's right to use the path was an easement, it must meet the four requirements set out in *Re Ellenborough Park* and *Regency Villas*.

1. The **dominant tenement** is No 1A (the middle cottage owned by Mr and Mrs Payne). The **servient tenement** (the land over which the right is being claimed) is No 1 (owned by the Inwoods).
2. There seems to be little doubt that the right of way being claimed benefited No 1A. The only other access to the yard was through the house. Although the yard was not landlocked, most people would prefer to have an alternative route over which to bring goods (such as coal) destined for the yard.
3. Different people owned the two cottages at the date that the right was claimed. However, the cottages had been in common ownership for a brief period in 1971. Any easement that existed prior to the period of **co-ownership** would have been extinguished or converted to a **quasi-easement** (see Section 10.5.3).
4. Rights of access, such as that claimed by Mr and Mrs Payne, have long been recognised as an important category of easement. The right being claimed was capable of being the subject of a grant.

However, concluding that the right is capable of being an easement was not sufficient in itself to establish that Mr and Mrs Payne had an interest that was binding on their neighbour. They also had to demonstrate that the right of access had been acquired in such a way as to create a legal easement.

10.6 Legal and equitable easements

Easements (and profits) can be either legal or **equitable** (see Section 2.2). A legal easement must be:

- for one of the terms referred to in section 1(2)(a) of the LPA 1925;
- created by one of the methods considered in Section 10.7; and
- registered if it falls within the scope of section 27(2)(d) of the Land Registration Act (LRA) 2002.

The LPA 1925 provides that an easement can only be legal if it is to last indefinitely, like a fee simple, or for a period of time with a fixed beginning and end, like a **lease** (s 1(2)(a)). Consequently, if the right is granted for an indefinite but limited time, such as 'until I sell my house' or 'for your life', it cannot be a legal easement (see Section 7.5.2).

An easement or profit will be **equitable** if

- it fails to meet any of the requirements for legal status; or
- the grantor owns only an equitable **estate** in the land.

Whether an easement is legal or equitable has a fundamental bearing on whether a successor of the owner of the **dominant tenement** will be able to enforce it and, equally, whether it will be binding on a successor of the servient owner. In **unregistered land**, a legal interest binds the world, but equitable easements and profits need to be protected under the Land Charges Act 1972 (see Section 5.4). The rules in **registered land** are more complicated, not least because of the transition between the LRA 1925 and the LRA 2002 (see Section 4.6.3). It should be noted, however, that easements or profits created expressly since 13th October 2003 will only take effect at law once they have been entered in the Charges Register of the servient Registered Title (LRA 2002, s 27(2)(d)). All equitable easements must be protected by an entry on the relevant **Register of Title** (see Section 4.5).

10.7 Acquisition of legal easements

There are a number of ways of acquiring a legal easement.

▶ Express provision in a **deed**.
▶ Easements recognised as being included in a deed even though they are not expressly mentioned in it (through the common law doctrines of implication or section 62 of the LPA 1925).
▶ The doctrine known as 'prescription': long usage giving rise to a presumption that the easement was created by a (fictional) deed.

It is also possible for easements to be created by statute (examples include major gas pipelines and electricity cables). Figure 10.2 shows the various ways in which legal easements can be acquired.

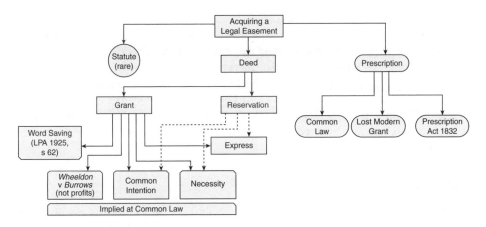

Figure 10.2 Acquisition of easements at law

Easements can be created by grant or by reservation.

▶ A *grant* of an easement is where the seller gives a right over a part of their land to a person buying another part of it.
▶ *Reservation* is where they keep back for themself a right over a part of their land which they are selling.

As can be seen in Figure 10.2, the distinction between *grant* and *reservation* is particularly important when it comes to applying the rules that allow easements to be acquired by implication. It is much more difficult to reserve an easement than it is to grant one, because the courts are generally unwilling to allow a person to claw back an interest in land that they have transferred to another (what is known as 'derogating' from their grant; see Section 8.2.1(b)).

There is a considerable body of law on the acquisition of easements. Judges tend not to use the categories consistently, so in practice they overlap (especially easements of necessity and intended easements). All of the methods grouped under 'Deed' in Figure 10.2 depend upon the intention of the parties to the transaction to which the deed relates. The best evidence of their intention is, of course, the express wording of the deed. Their intention to create an easement will, however, be inferred when the circumstances justify it (under the doctrines of necessity, common intention and the rule in *Wheeldon* v *Burrows* and the word-saving provisions of section 62 of the LPA 1925), provided, always, that there is no stronger evidence of contrary intention (*Nickerson* v *Barraclough* [1981] Ch 426 (CA)). This reflects the fact that much of the law on easements created by implication is based on the old principle of non-derogation from grant (see Section 8.2.1(b)). *Wong* v *Beaumont Property Trust Ltd* [1965] 1 QB 173 (CA) is a good example of this. A basement was let subject to the condition that it was to be used as a restaurant, but it could not be used for this purpose without a ventilation duct over the land retained by the **lessor**. Consequently, it must have been the common intention of the parties that the **lease** should include such an easement.

10.7.1 Express grant and reservation

Like so many cases, the case of *Payne* v *Inwood* (1997) 74 P & CR 42 (CA) (the facts are set out at Section 10.1) arose because insufficient attention was given to the importance of a particular right when land was sold. For a short period in 1971, Miss Cutler owned both No 1 and No 1A. If the **conveyance** of 1A had expressly included a right of way over the path marked 'X–Y' there would have been no doubt that Mr and Mrs Payne had the right to use the path in 1991. Since 13th October 2003 (the date that the LRA 2002 came into force), any express grant or reservation of a legal easement *must* both be made by **deed** *and* be entered on the **registered title** of the **servient tenement**.

10.7.2 Necessity

An easement of necessity arises where the right is essential for the use of the land granted or retained. As the Law Commission explained in *Making Land Law Work: Easements, Covenants and Profits à Prendre* (Law Com 327, 2011), para 3.208, this:

> is a question of whether the land can be used at all without the implied grant or reservation. Claims are only successful where the land is 'absolutely inaccessible or useless' without the easement. So, for example, land will have to be truly landlocked for an easement of necessity to be implied so as to create an access; it will not be implied merely because it makes it more convenient to use the land.

So, for example, in *Walby* v *Walby* [2012] EWHC 3089 (Ch) (a case concerning reservation of a right), Morgan J held that a right of drainage could not be acquired by necessity since ([49]):

> the absence of a drainage easement would not significantly affect the ability to use that land.

In the case of *Manjang* v *Drammeh* (1990) 61 P & CR 194 (PC), another reservation case, a person owned land situated between a river and a road. He sold the part of his land that adjoined the road, but failed to reserve for himself an easement to cross it in order to reach the rest of his land on the bank of the river. The Privy Council refused to imply an easement across the land he had sold, since it was possible for him to get to his retained land by boat, and occasionally in the past he had done so. The claimant in *Titchmarsh* v *Royston Water Co Ltd* (1899) 81 LT 673 (Ch) discovered too late that the land he had purchased was surrounded on three sides by the land of the vendor, and on the fourth side by a drop of 20 feet (about seven metres) down to a roadway. While the climb up the cutting was inconvenient, it was possible, and consequently it was held that there could be no easement of necessity over the vendor's land. The more recent case of *Adealon International Corp Proprietary Ltd* v *Merton LBC* [2007] 1 WLR 1898 (CA) also concerned land that was not entirely landlocked by the potential **servient tenement**. Lord Justice Carnwath, giving the main judgment in the Court of Appeal, explained at [16] that:

> The grantee's normal expectation is that access, if not otherwise available, will be allowed as an incident to the grant, and thus that it will be provided by the grantor over land within his control.

However, where it is the transferor that is claiming the easement (that is, where the claim involves reservation):

> the presumption is that any rights he requires over the land transferred will have been expressly reserved in the grant, and the burden lies on the grantor to establish an exception.

In *Adealon International Corp Proprietary Ltd* v *Merton LBC*, the claimant had expected, at the time of the transfer, to have access to the retained land from the land of a third party. This was held to be sufficient to negate any easement of necessity over the land that it had sold.

10.7.3 Common intention

According to Lord Parker in *Pwllbach Colliery Company Ltd* v *Woodman* [1915] AC 634 (HL), at 646–7:

> The law will readily imply the grant or reservation of such easements as may be necessary to give effect to the common intention of the parties to a grant of real property, with reference to the manner or purposes in and for which the land granted or some land retained by the grantor is to be used. ... But it is essential for this purpose that the parties should intend that the subject of the grant or the land retained by the grantor should be used in some definite and particular manner.

In the more recent case of *Donovan* v *Rana* [2014] 1 P & CR 23 (CA), Mrs Donovan sold a plot of land adjacent to her house in the residential suburb of Gravesend in Kent as a building plot. The purchaser covenanted 'to erect within one year from the date [of the transfer] upon the property, the dwelling house to the satisfaction of the Local Authority'. The transfer granted a specific right of way, but was silent as to other easements. Mr and Mrs Rana subsequently acquired the building plot and duly built their new house, which they named 'Shalimar'. During its construction, the contractors dug up land belonging to Mrs Donovan and her husband to connect 'Shalimar' to mains drainage, water, gas, electricity and telephone. They did so without the express permission of Mr and Mrs Donovan, who responded by bringing court proceedings. The Court of Appeal had no doubt that the parties must have intended that the building of a dwelling-house on the building plot 'to the satisfaction of the Local Authority' would include the connection to the mains utility services. Indeed, Vos LJ observed at [29] that:

> The suggestion that a dwelling-house in such an environment might sensibly be expected by the parties to be constructed without connections to the mains utilities just a few metres away ... is, if I may say so, a somewhat optimistic submission.

Both easements of common intention and easements of necessity are based upon implication and the doctrine of non-derogation from grant. However, while easements of necessity are normally restricted to the minimum rights needed to gain access to the land, easements derived from the parties' intended use of the land will extend as far as is necessary to achieve the parties' expressly intended purpose (*Donovan v Rana* at [33]). As with easements of necessity, it is possible to reserve an easement of common intention by implication, but the courts will not do so readily.

10.7.4 The rule in *Wheeldon v Burrows*

The rule in *Wheeldon v Burrows* (1879) LR 12 Ch D 31 (CA) states that when a landowner sells part of their land any **quasi-easements** previously exercised by the seller over the retained land may be converted into easements benefiting the land that has been sold. Quasi-easements are rights which would have been easements had the land concerned been in separate ownership. A concise explanation of the rule, including a diagram, can be found at paragraphs 3.19 and 3.20 of *Making Land Law Work: Easements, Covenants and Profits à Prendre* (Law Com 327, 2011).

The case of *Wheeldon v Burrows* concerned a site adjoining Stockbrook Street in Derby. All of the land originally belonged to Mr Allen, who built a workshop on it. The workshop eventually passed to Mr Burrows and the rest of the land to Mrs Wheeldon. Mrs Wheeldon erected hoardings on the edge of her land which prevented light reaching the windows of Mr Burrows' workshop. The question that the Court of Appeal had to decide was whether Mr Burrows' land had the benefit of an easement of light. In explaining why there was no easement of light on the facts of this case, Thesiger LJ stated what has become known as 'the rule in *Wheeldon v Burrows*. Unfortunately, he stated it twice, in slightly different forms.

The basic principle is that where a person sells part of their land which has the benefit of a *quasi-easement* the buyer will gain the benefit of the quasi-easement if at the time of the grant:

1. the seller was using the quasi-easement for the benefit of the land they were selling;
2. the use of the quasi-easement was 'continuous and apparent' (such as an obvious track, or a drain which could have been discovered on inspection); and/or
3. the quasi-easement was necessary for the reasonable enjoyment of the land sold.

It is not clear from his judgment whether Thesiger LJ meant conditions 2 and 3 to be cumulative or alternatives. In many cases, of course, if the quasi-easement (for example, a right of way) satisfies one test, it will also satisfy the other. The third condition does not require the easement to be 'essential' in the way that easements implied by necessity must be essential, but it does require that there can be no reasonable enjoyment of the land without the easement. Incidentally, the requirement that the right be 'continuous and apparent' would appear to preclude the rule in *Wheeldon* v *Burrows* being used to create profits as it is difficult to see how a profit can satisfy this part of the rule.

In *Millman* v *Ellis* [1996] 71 P & CR 158 (CA), the Court of Appeal held that Mr Millman had successfully proved an easement under the rule. He had bought a large house from Mr Ellis and also part of Mr Ellis' remaining land; he claimed the right to use the driveway which Mr Ellis had always used to get to the house and which was safer than using the main road. In *Wheeler* v *JJ Saunders Ltd* [1996] Ch 19 (CA), however, Mr Wheeler had bought part of a farm and claimed an easement to allow him to pass through a gap in a wall to get to a road. It was held that this access was not necessary for the reasonable enjoyment of the house because there was another equally suitable access route in the field.

For the rule in *Wheeldon* v *Burrows* to apply, the land must have been in common occupation immediately prior to the transfer. Common ownership (for example, by a common **landlord**) is not sufficient in itself (see *Kent* v *Kavanagh* [2007] Ch 1 (CA)). In *Chaffe* v *Kingsley* (2000) 79 P & CR 404 (CA), the Court of Appeal confirmed that the rule applies only to the creation of an easement by grant: it cannot be used to infer a reservation for the benefit of retained land.

10.7.5 Section 62 of the LPA 1925

Section 62 of the LPA 1925 was intended to be a 'word saving' provision to free conveyancers from having to list every last right that was included with the transfer of a parcel of land. However, as the Law Commission observed (Law Com 327, 2011, para 3.55), the wording of the section has been held to produce two further effects:

> First, on the conveyance to a tenant of the freehold in the land that was subject to the lease, any property rights which are annexed to the leasehold estate are 'upgraded'. By being written into the conveyance of the freehold, they become freehold easements or profits appurtenant to it. Second, other arrangements (to use a broad term) which are not easements or profits, but could be, are transformed by their incorporation into the conveyance into interests appurtenant to the estate sold.

Before considering these consequences of section 62 in more detail, two other features of it should also be noted.

- The wording of section 62 refers only to the granting of rights. Section 62 cannot, therefore, operate to reserve easements over the transferred land.
- The operation of Section 62 upon a transaction can be expressly excluded by the parties, and in practice often is.

Wright v *Macadam* [1949] 2 KB 744 (CA) (see Section 10.5.4(c)) illustrates the potential of section 62. Here, with her **landlord's** permission, a **tenant** was storing coal in a shed; then, when a new lease was granted to her (which is a **conveyance** for the purposes of section 62), her **licence** was converted into an easement. It was an 'advantage … appertaining to the land' and, when section 62 implied it into the **deed**, it grew from being a purely personal right into a legal easement that could not be revoked by the landlord.

Wright v *Macadam* was followed in *Hair* v *Gillman* (2000) 80 P & CR 108 (CA) (see Section 10.5.4(c)). In this case, the licence to park a car given to the tenant of land used as a nursery school was 'crystallised' into an easement under section 62 when she was granted the **freehold**. Chadwick LJ felt it to be a matter of regret that a property right binding the servient land could be created unintentionally. He repeated the comments of Tucker LJ in *Wright* v *Macadam* (at 755) that such decisions:

> may tend to discourage landlords from acts of kindness to their tenants. But there it is; that is the law.

The power of section 62 to convert rights into easements has always been somewhat controversial. Not only is it a trap for the unwary, but there has also been uncertainty about the circumstances in which it operates and how far it overlaps with the rule in *Wheeldon* v *Burrows*. It was for these reasons that in 2011 the Law Commission recommended that section 62 cease to operate to convert permissive rights into easements. Since then, however, some of the uncertainty as to the scope of section 62 seems to have been settled by the Court of Appeal's decision in *Wood* v *Waddington* [2015] 2 P & CR 11 (CA). According to Lewison LJ, who gave the only substantial judgment, section 62 operates:

1. in all cases where there had been diversity of occupation prior to the conveyance; *and*
2. in cases where the land had been in common occupation prior to the conveyance (unity of occupation cases) where the usage of the right claimed was 'continuous and apparent' at the time of the conveyance.

The application of section 62 to **quasi-easements** in unity of occupation cases had been doubted by a minority in the House of Lords in *Sovmots Investments Ltd* v *Secretary of State for the Environment* [1979] AC 144 (HL) and by the Court of Appeal in *Payne* v *Inwood*. However, the decision in *Wood* v *Waddington* reflects the views expressed in more recent cases such as *P & S Platt Ltd* v *Crouch* [2004] 1 P & CR 18 (CA) and *Alford* v *Hannaford* [2011] EWCA Civ 1099 (CA): quasi-easements can be converted into easements by section 62. It is not entirely clear why usage of the rights must be 'continuous and apparent' in unity of occupation cases but not in those where there is diversity of occupation. As Simon Gardner observes in his casenote on *Wood* v *Waddington*, Lewison LJ gives no explanation for this additional requirement, which is a concept imported from the rule in *Wheeldon* v *Burrows* (see Section 10.7.4). Section 62 itself makes no reference to any rights needing to be continuous and apparent; rather it includes all rights 'enjoyed with the land'. Whether a particular usage is continuous and apparent will depend upon the facts of the case.

Section 62 and the rule in *Wheeldon* v *Burrows* compared
One of the consequences of the line of cases ending in *Wood* v *Waddington* [2015] 2 P & CR 11 (CA) is that there is a considerable overlap between the circumstances in which the rule in *Wheeldon* v *Burrows* and the 'legal metamorphosis' of section 62 of the LPA 1925 (see Tee, 1998) will apply. However, the rules are not identical and the facts of a case (or problem question) will need to be analysed carefully to ensure that the correct result is reached using the correct rule. An example of such an analysis is illustrated in Figure 10.3.

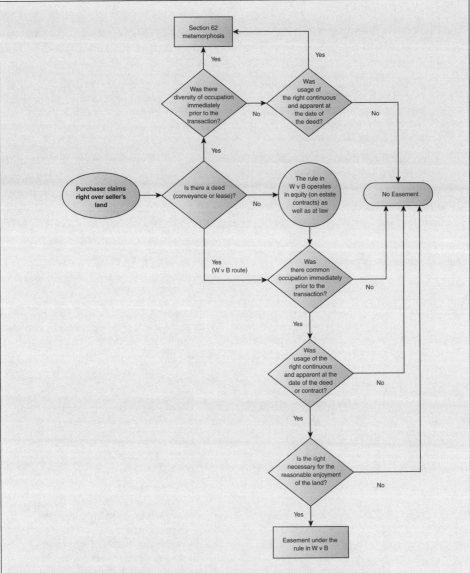

Figure 10.3   Section 62 and the rule in *Wheeldon* v *Burrows* in practice

The main points to note are:

- Section 62 requires a deed (conveyance, transfer, lease); it can only, therefore, create legal easements.
- The rule in *Wheeldon* v *Burrows* operates at law, but it can also operate on the transfer or creation of an **equitable** estate.
- Section 62 applies where there is diversity of occupation: the rule in *Wheeldon* v *Burrows* does not.
- Both the rule in *Wheeldon* v *Burrows* and Section 62 can apply where there is unity of occupation: in both cases the use of the right being claimed must be continuous and apparent.
- An easement can only be created under the rule in *Wheeldon* v *Burrows* if it is necessary for the reasonable enjoyment of the land. There is no equivalent requirement in section 62.

10.7.6 Prescription

The use for many years of a right which is capable of being an easement can create a legal easement by 'prescription'. The role of this doctrine was summarised by Elias LJ in *Dewan v Lewis* [2010] EWCA Civ 1382, at [33]:

> As Lord Hoffmann observed in the House of Lords in *R v Oxfordshire CC ex p Sunningwell PC* [2000] 1 AC 335, at 349 D, the purpose of rules of prescription is to 'prevent the disturbance of long established de facto enjoyment.' In English law, the fiction is that at some point a right was conferred on the owner of the dominant tenement. The right must relate to what has in fact been enjoyed.

There are three forms of prescription: common law, 'lost modern grant' and statutory prescription under the Prescription Act 1832. The requirements for each form of prescription are summarised in Table 10.1. A more detailed explanation of the present rules, which are obscure and complex, can be found in paragraphs 3.89 to 3.108 of *Making Land Law Work: Easements, Covenants and Profits à Prendre* (Law Com 327, 2011).

Table 10.1 Methods of Prescription

Method	Basis of Claim	Evidence required
Common law	The right has been enjoyed since time immemorial (which for common law purposes is usually considered to begin in 1189).	At least 20 years' use as of right at any time (continuously or discontinuously), provided that the right could have been exercised in 1189.
Lost modern grant	The right was granted in a deed, but that deed has now been lost.	Use as of right for any 20 years provided that the person presumed to have made the grant was legally competent to do so.
Prescription Act 1832	Statute law.	*Light:* continuous use without written permission for at least 20 years immediately prior to the proceedings. *Other easements:* • continuous use as of right for at least 20 years immediately prior to the proceedings; or • continuous use as of right for at least 40 years immediately prior to the proceedings, regardless of whether the freeholder was in possession of the land.

There are, however, certain conditions that are common to most rights recognised as easements by prescription. Firstly, any right claimed by prescription must usually be made by a **freeholder** against another freeholder; that is to say easements acquired by prescription will almost always be for the equivalent of a fee simple. It is fundamental to the doctrine of prescription that the **freehold** owner of the servient land knew (or was taken to have known) of the rights being exercised and was in a position to prevent them being exercised (*Llewellyn (Deceased) v Lorey* [2011] EWCA Civ 37). It seems, however, that section 2 of the Prescription Act 1832 allows an easement, other than one for light, to be acquired by 40 years of use, even where the servient land is not occupied by its freeholder (where it has been let to a tenant, for example). Secondly, the right must have been within the lawful power of the landowner to grant (*Bakewell Management Ltd* v *Brandwood* [2004] 2 AC 519 (HL)). Finally, with the exception of a right of light claimed under the Prescription Act 1832, the right claimed must also have been exercised 'as of right'. According to Lord Walker in *R (on the application of Lewis)* v *Redcar & Cleveland BC (No.2)* [2010] 2 AC 70, at [20]:

> The proposition that 'as of right' is sufficiently described by the tripartite test *nec vi, nec clam, nec precario* (not by force, nor stealth, nor the licence of the owner) is established by high authority.

10.7.6(a) Nec vi: *without force*

The right must have been exercised without violence or threat of violence, and without damage to property on the **servient tenement**. However, 'force' does not require physical violence. In the case of *Winterburn* v *Bennett* [2015] EWCA CA Civ 482, the owners of a car park had put up signs making it very clear that the customers for the claimants' fish and chip shop must not park there. The Court of Appeal held that the claimants could not rely on parking in deliberate defiance of the notices in order to establish an easement by prescription.

10.7.6(b) Nec clam: *openly*

As Romer LJ opined in *Union Lighterage Company* v *London Graving Dock Company* [1902] 2 Ch 557 (CA), at 570–1:

> Now, on principle, it appears to me that a prescriptive right to an easement over a man's land should only be acquired when the enjoyment has been open – that is to say, of such a character that an ordinary owner of the land, diligent in the protection of his interests, would have, or must be taken to have, a reasonable opportunity of becoming aware of that enjoyment.

10.7.6(c) Nec precario: *without permission*

As the Law Commission explains at para 3.92 of its 2011 report:

> the use cannot be by permission; use as of right is inconsistent with the permission of the servient owner since someone who has a right does not need permission. Permission may be express or may be inferred from 'overt and contemporaneous acts of the owner'.

However, if permission is to be inferred there must be some positive act by the owner of the servient land. As Lewison LJ observed in *London Tara Hotel Ltd* v *Kensington Close Hotel Ltd* [2012] 1 P & CR 13 (CA), at [86]:

> It is quite wrong to treat a land owner's silent acquiescence in persons using his land as having the same effect as permission communicated to those persons … Even encouragement of the activity by the land owner will not necessarily amount to an implied licence … But there must be some overt act (which may be a non-verbal communication) which is intended to be understood, and is understood, as permission to do something which would otherwise be an act of trespass.

In 1966, the Law Reform Committee recommended the simplification of prescription law (14th Report, Cmnd 3100); it also described the Prescription Act 1832 as 'one of the worst drafted Acts on the Statute Book' (at para 40). Despite this, no new statute was forthcoming. The Law Commission and the Land Registry subsequently proposed (in their 1998 consultation paper *Land Registration for the Twenty-First Century*, Law Com No 254, paras 10.79ff) that the sole method of acquiring an easement by prescription in **registered land** should be by the Prescription Act 1832. In its consultation paper on *Easements, Covenants and Profits à Prendre* (Law Com CP No 186, 2008), the Law Commission identified several concerns about the operation of prescription. In particular, at para 4.1.76:

1. Prescription allows the claimant to get something for nothing.
2. Prescription may penalise altruism. The claim may well originate from the servient owner's 'good neighbourly' attitude.
3. Prescription may sometimes operate disproportionately by giving the claimant a proprietary interest in the servient owner's land.

In its subsequent report, *Making Land Law Work: Easements, Covenants and Profits à Prendre* (Law Com 327, 2011) the Law Commission recommended that a new, single statutory method of prescription replace the three methods of prescription presently available. The government has given no indication of any plans to implement this reform.

10.7.7 Proprietary estoppel

Where a claimant has detrimentally relied on an expectation that an easement will be granted, the court may declare that the claimant is entitled to an easement if this is necessary to satisfy the **estoppel** (as, for example, in *Joyce v Epsom and Ewell BC* [2012] EWCA Civ 1398 where there was an unconscionable refusal of a right of way).

10.7.8 Applying these rules to *Payne v Inwood*

Three different possible methods of creation were pleaded during the course of *Payne v Inwood*. All three were ultimately rejected, and Mr and Mrs Payne failed to establish that No 1A had the benefit of an easement over No 1.

10.7.8(a) Section 62 LPA 1925

The main issue before the Court of Appeal was whether an easement was created by virtue of section 62 of the LPA 1925 when Miss Cutler sold the **freehold** to No 1A in 1971 (see Section 10.7.5). Roch LJ, who gave the only substantial judgment in the Court of Appeal, held that there were two reasons why no easement had been created by section 62:

1. There was no evidence that any **licence** or other right that could be turned into an easement had actually existed at the date of the 1971 conveyance (at 47).
2. There was no diversity of occupation of the two parcels of land immediately prior to the 1971 conveyance.

The second reason, which was *obiter dictum* (and based on the *dicta* in the *Sovmots Investments* case) is no longer good law (see Section 10.7.5 above). However, the lack of any right that could be turned into an easement means that the argument based on section 62 would still fail today.

10.7.8(b) The rule in Wheeldon v Burrows

The claim that an easement had been created in 1971 by virtue of the rule in *Wheeldon* v *Burrows* was rejected by the trial judge, and this decision was not appealed. At first sight, this might seem like a case in which the rule is likely to apply. The problem, however, is establishing that the right was 'necessary to the reasonable enjoyment' of No 1A. The right claimed by Mr and Mrs Payne is very similar to that unsuccessfully claimed by Mr Wheeler in the earlier case of *Wheeler* v *JJ Saunders*, where it was held that the access was not necessary for the reasonable enjoyment of the land (see Section 10.7.4).

10.7.8(c) Prescription

The claim that an easement had been created under the doctrine of lost modern grant (see Section 10.7.6(c)) was also rejected by the trial judge and not resurrected before the Court of Appeal. The 20-year period began to run when Miss Cutler sold No 1A in 1971; any easement or prescription period before that date was extinguished by Miss Cutler's common ownership of Nos 1 and 1A in 1971 (see Section 10.9.2(b)). In fact, it seems that the route of the path was not blocked until just over 20 years after the 1971 conveyance. Unfortunately, however, there was no evidence that the path had been used for at least the first half of that period.

10.8 Remedies for infringement of easements

The remedies available to the aggrieved owner of an easement are through the self-help remedy of **abatement** and by means of an action in the courts.

Abatement means that the owner of the easement can go onto the **servient tenement** and, for example, break a padlock on a gate if this is necessary. However, the courts are wary of abatement, and the dominant owner must choose the least mischievous method and refrain from causing unnecessary damage.

The owner of the easement may claim an **injunction** and/or damages and/or a declaration against the owner of the servient land. They can also take action against third parties who interfere with their right.

10.9 The ending of easements

Easements and profits may be ended by statute or through an act of the parties, either by release, through abandonment or through unity of **seisin**.

10.9.1 Statute

There is no statutory provision equivalent to section 84 of the LPA 1925 which allows the Lands Tribunal to discharge or modify a **restrictive covenant** (see Section 12.9.2). However, there are a number of statutes that allow easements and profits to be terminated. For example, under the Town and Country Planning Act 1990, local authorities may, in the course of development, end easements and profits. They can also be ended under the Commons Registration Act 1965.

In certain circumstances, the provisions of the LRA 2002 will effectively extinguish easements over **registered titles** (see Section 10.9.2(d)).

10.9.2 Act of the parties

10.9.2(a) Release

An easement or profit can be released explicitly by **deed**. An agreement to release without a deed may be enforceable in equity.

10.9.2(b) Unity of seisin

As stated at Section 10.5, a person cannot have an easement or profit against themself, so an easement ends if one person owns both tenements; of course, as indicated earlier, it might be resuscitated under section 62 of the LPA 1925 or under the rule in *Wheeldon* v *Burrows* (1879) LR 12 Ch D 31 (CA).

One situation that is worthy of special mention is where a **leasehold** interest is merged with the **freehold reversion**. This may occur when a **tenant** purchases the freehold to the land that they occupy. Many residential tenants with long **leases** of residential properties have a statutory right to purchase the **freehold title** to their homes under the Leasehold Reform Act 1967. One would expect that any easements granted by the tenant would be extinguished by merger of the lease with the freehold **estate**. However, in *Wall* v *Collins* [2007] Ch 390 (CA), the Court of Appeal held that such easements were not 'attached to' the leasehold estate and would continue to bind the land (including the freeholder) for the full term of the lease. The considerable problems with this reasoning are discussed at Section 10.5.1.

10.9.2(c) Abandonment

If the owner of the easement or profit abandons the right, they cannot later resurrect it. However, the benefit of an easement cannot be lost simply by non-use, even where the period of non-use is substantial (175 years in the case of *Benn* v *Hardinge* (1993) 66 P & CR 246 (CA)). For abandonment, there must also be a manifest intention to abandon, and this is very difficult for the servient owner to establish. As Lloyd LJ explained in *CDC2020 plc* v *George Ferreira* [2005] EWCA Civ 611, at [24], the owner of the **dominant tenement**:

> must make it clear that his intention is that neither he nor his successors in title should thereafter make any use of the right … abandonment is not to be lightly inferred because owners of property do not normally wish to divest themselves of property unless to do so is to their advantage, even if they have no present use for the property in question.

Intention to abandon an easement can be implied because of the circumstances, but rarely is. In the *CDC2020* case, the Court of Appeal refused to infer an intention to abandon a right of way, even when the garages to which it related had been demolished. Similarly, in the recent case of *Annetts* v *Adeleye* [2018] EWCA Civ 555 the sale of the dominant tenement to a new owner who covenanted to fence it off from the land over which it enjoyed a right of access did not amount to abandonment of the right of access.

Swan v *Sinclair* [1925] AC 227 (HL) provides an example of circumstances in which abandonment will be inferred. A number of adjoining houses and their gardens had been sold in 1871. Each garden included part of a strip of land to the rear of the houses that had been designated as the route of a right of way giving access to the back gardens. By the date of the action in 1923, several householders had built fences across the strip of land, and one had changed the level of the strip adjacent to his land by some six feet. The House of Lords was satisfied that any right of way over the strip of land had been abandoned by common consent of the various owners: the right had never been exercised, and no action had been taken to enforce it for over 50 years.

10.9.2(d) Non-use of easements over registered land

Unless protected by registration, a legal easement over **registered land** may be unenforceable against the new registered proprietor of the **servient tenement** (LRA 2002, s 29 and Sch 3, para 3). This statutory provision is entirely independent of the doctrine of abandonment, and its rules are considered in more detail at Section 4.6.3. The Law Commission has recommended that, in registered land, an easement created by implication or **prescription** should be deemed to have been abandoned if the dominant owner cannot show that it has been used within the previous 20 years *Land Registration for the Twenty-First Century* Law Com No 254, 1998, para 5.24).

10.10 Profits

10.10.1 The nature of profits

A profit is the right to take something from someone else's land. For example, there are profits of piscary (fish), turbary (turf), estovers (wood for firewood or other purposes) and pasture (the right to graze as many animals as can be supported through the winter months). Some of these profits are still economically very important to their owners.

The rules on profits are fairly similar to those on **easements**, except that profits can either:

▶ be *appurtenant* (that is, benefiting a **dominant tenement**); or
▶ exist *in gross* (without a dominant tenement).

Thus, a person can own a profit to graze a goat on someone else's meadow, even though they own no land which can benefit.

Where a profit is attached to land, it must accommodate the dominant tenement, just like an easement. In *Bailey* v *Stephens* (1862) 142 ER 1077 (CP), the owner of a field claimed a profit appurtenant to take wood from a neighbouring copse. It was held that this was not valid because it did not benefit the field. It might have been different if the alleged dominant tenement had been a house, and the wood had been used as firewood.

A profit may be 'sole', where only one person can take the thing, and the owner of the **servient tenement** is excluded from it. Alternatively, it can be shared with the servient owner and is then known as a profit 'in common'.

The owner of a profit automatically has a **licence** entitling them to enter the servient tenement in order to exercise their rights (see Section 9.4).

10.10.2 Creating profits

Profits can be acquired in most of the same ways as **easements** (see Section 10.7). However, because a profit cannot be 'continuous and apparent', *Wheeldon v Burrows*

(1879) LR 12 Ch D 31 (CA) probably cannot apply. In addition, the relevant periods under the Prescription Act 1832 are 30 and 60 years for profits, a little longer than those required for easements.

10.10.3 Remedies for the infringement of profits

The remedies for infringement of profits are the same as those for infringement of easements (see Section 10.8), save that a profit holder is also entitled to take action against third parties as well as the **servient tenement** holder if their actions interfere with their rights. For example, in *Nicholls v Ely Beet Sugar Factory (No 1)* [1931] 2 Ch 84 (Ch) the owner of a profit of piscary sought damages from the owner of a factory upstream which had polluted the river and killed the fish. The court held that the profit gave the claimant sufficient possession to bring the action and that the defendant could not require the claimant to first prove **title** to the profit.

10.10.4 Ending a profit

The rules for terminating a profit are the same as those for ending an easement (see Section 10.9).

10.11 Reform of the law of easements and profits

The Law Commission's report, *Making Land Law Work: Easements, Covenants and Profits à Prendre* (Law Com 327, 2011), which has already been referred to in this chapter, is well worth reading, not least for its accessible analysis of the present law. The Commission's main recommendations (of which there is little sign of implementation) are:

▶ the statutory reversal of *Wall v Collins* [2007] Ch 390 (CA) (see Section 10.5.1);
▶ the statutory abolition of the 'ouster principle' (see Section 10.5.4(c));
▶ that section 62 of the LPA 1925 no longer convert permissive rights into easements (see Section 10.7.5);
▶ a single statutory method of creation by implication be introduced (replacing the rules considered at Sections 10.7.2, 10.7.3, 10.7.4 and 10.7.5);
▶ the introduction of a single statutory method of **prescription** (replacing the methods considered in Section 10.7.6); and
▶ the abolition of prescription and implication as means of creating profits.

10.12 Rights over another's land other than easements and profits

This section lists a number of other interests in land which appear similar to easements or profits, but which are classified differently by lawyers.

10.12.1 Public rights

These are rights which can be used by anyone, such as the right to fish between high- and low-water marks. The most familiar are rights of way, which include roads as well as footpaths, but the 'right' to use a road is now more like a **licence**, since it can be denied at the discretion of a police officer (Public Order Act 1986). The Countryside and Rights of Way Act 2000 provides a limited statutory right of public access to open countryside (the 'right to roam') and is intended to bring about the modernisation of the public rights of way network.

10.12.2 Natural rights

These rights exist automatically and arise out of the nature of land. There is a right to water flowing naturally in a definite channel, but not to water which percolates through the land. All land has a natural right of support from neighbouring land, so you may not dig a large hole in your garden if your neighbour's land consequently collapses. In *Holbeck Hall Hotel Ltd* v *Scarborough BC* [2000] QB 836 (CA), the council-owned land between the sea cliffs and the hotel. Coastal erosion caused part of the hotel to disappear into the sea, and the rest of it had to be demolished. Its owners sued the council in the tort of nuisance. The Court of Appeal stated that a landowner could be liable for not acting to prevent the hazard, but only if it could reasonably be expected to know about it. In this case, the danger could not reasonably have been foreseen by the council, and it was therefore not just and reasonable to impose a liability on it.

There are no automatic rights to light and air, so if such rights are to exist they must amount to easements, unless the tort of nuisance can provide a remedy. The quick-growing bush *Cupressus leylandii* has deprived many landowners of natural light for their gardens and homes and has frequently given rise to heated and even violent disputes. The Anti-social Behaviour Act 2003, Part 8 (most of which came into force on 1st June 2005) provides local authorities with powers to intervene in such neighbourly disputes and to issue remedial notices in certain circumstances.

10.12.3 Customary rights

Sometimes a group of people, for example, the residents of a particular village, have a right which looks like an easement, but it is not because the group is not a legal person.

10.12.4 Town or village greens

Since 1970, it has been necessary to protect town or village greens by registration under the Commons Registration Act 1965. However, it is possible for land to become a new town or village green if it has been used as such by local inhabitants for a period of not less than 20 years. The Commons Act 2006, when fully implemented, will repeal the 1965 Act but preserves the requirement for registration and the acquisition of town or village green status by long user.

10.12.5 Licences

See Chapter 9.

10.12.6 Access to Neighbouring Land Act 1992

A particular difficulty can arise for a landowner whose premises are built right up to the boundary with the neighbouring land. In the past, if they did not have an easement to go onto their neighbour's land to repair or maintain their own property, and the neighbour refused to give them permission to do so, there was little they could do except watch their wall crumble away. Now, however, under the Access to Neighbouring Land Act 1992, in cases in which it is reasonably necessary to carry out work to preserve their land, and this work can really only be carried out from a neighbour's land to which they cannot otherwise gain access, a landowner may apply to the court for an order to allow them access to carry out the work. The court will not automatically make the order and may impose conditions on the applicant.

10.12.7 Party Walls Act 1996

Extensive rights are given under the Party Walls Act 1996 to landowners who want to go onto the neighbouring property in order to carry out repairs to the party wall, so landowners should use this Act rather than the more restrictive Access to Neighbouring Land Act if it is appropriate to do so. The adjoining owner must first be served with a notice in prescribed form; the person carrying out the works has the right to enter any land (and may break open doors to do so, if necessary, so long as a police officer is present); weatherproofing may need to be provided to protect the neighbouring property, and there may be a requirement to pay compensation for loss or damage caused to the adjoining owner. This Act would have been very helpful to Mr Bradburn in *Bradburn* v *Lindsay* [1983] 2 All ER 408 (Ch) (see *Negative Easements* at Section 10.4.6) and exists to prevent exactly that kind of mischief.

Summary

10.1 Easements and profits are property interests enjoyed over someone else's land. Easements are rights to do something on land belonging to someone else. There are two main stages in establishing whether a particular right is an easement or profit:

(a) is the right claimed capable of being an easement or profit; and, if it is,
(b) has an easement or profit actually been created?

10.2 Easements are rights to do something on land belonging to someone else. A *profit à prendre* is a right to take something from another's land (such as firewood or gravel).

10.3 The land that is subject to the burden of the easement is the 'servient tenement'. The 'dominant tenement' has the benefit of the easement rights.

10.4 Easements include a wide variety of interests over land.

10.5 To be an easement, a claim over another person's land must fulfil the four requirements of *Re Ellenborough Park* [1956] Ch 131 (CA); that is:

- there must be dominant and servient tenements;
- the right must accommodate the dominant tenement;
- the two tenements must be in different ownership or occupation; and
- the right must be capable of being the subject of a grant.

Summary cont'd

10.6 Easements are capable of being legal interests and equitable interests.

10.7 Legal easements may be acquired expressly or impliedly, by grant or reservation or by court order. They may also be acquired by prescription.

10.8 Remedies for infringement of an easement or profit are abatement or action.

10.9 Easements and profits may be ended by statute, release, abandonment or unity of seisin.

10.10 Profits are rights to take something from another person's land. The rules relating to profits are very similar to those relating to easements. The main differences are that profits may or may not be appurtenant and may be in common or sole.

10.11 The Law Commission has proposed significant changes to some of the rules governing covenants. Even if these proposals are not implemented, engaging with the reasoning behind them will lead to a deeper understanding of the issues surrounding easements.

10.12 Easements and profits must be distinguished from other claims, such as natural, customary or public rights, from statutory rights and from licences.

Exercises

 10.1 Complete the online quiz on the topics covered in this chapter on the companion website.

10.2 'The extension of easements to include the use of facilities such as tennis courts, swimming pools, gyms and golf courses is unjustifiable since such rights cannot benefit land and depend upon the active maintenance of chattels by the owner of the servient tenement.'

Critically discuss this evaluation of *Regency Villas Title Ltd* v *Diamond Resorts (Europe) Ltd* [2018] 3 WLR 1603 (SC).

10.3 Critically consider the Law Commission's proposal, in *Making Land Law Work: Easements, Covenants and Profits à Prendre* (Law Com 327, 2011), that there should be a single statutory method of creating easements by implication, with no distinction between grant and reservation.

10.4 In 1995, Megan sold half her farm to Jeff, but she continued to keep her tractors in a barn on the land she had sold to him. In 2005, she leased one of her remaining fields to Jeff, by deed, for 20 years, giving him permission to use a shortcut to the field across her land 'for as long as he needs to'; he had, in fact, already been using the field and shortcut for several weeks. Last year, Jeff agreed in writing with Megan that the children attending her nursery school could play on his smallest field.

Megan has just died, and her heir, Sam, wants to know whether any of these arrangements will affect him.

 You can find suggested answer plans to exercises 10.2, 10.3 and 10.4 on the companion website.

Further reading

Burns, 'Easements and Servitudes Created by Implied Grant, Implied Reservation or Prescription and Title-by-Registration Systems' in Dixon (ed.), *Modern Studies in Property Law: Volume 5* (Hart 2009)

Gardner, 'The grant of an easement under the Law of Property Act 1925 section 62' (2016) 132 LQR 192

Haley and McMurtry, 'Identifying an Easement: Exclusive Use, *De Facto* Control and Judicial Constraints' (2007) 58 NILQ 405

Law Commission, *Making Land Law Work: Easements, Covenants and Profits à Prendre* (Law Com 327, 2011)

Smith, 'Centre Point: Faulty Towers with Shaky Foundations' [1978] Conv 449

Sturley, 'Easements in Gross' (1980) 96 LQR 557

Tee, 'Metamorphoses and s.62 of the Law of Property Act 1925' [1998] Conv 115

Xu, 'Easement of Car Parking: The Ouster Principle is Out but Problems May Aggravate' (2012) 76 Conv 241

Chapter 11

Mortgages

Key concepts

▶ **Equity of redemption** – the rights of the mortgagor in the land subject to the mortgage; in particular, the right to recover the mortgaged land upon payment of moneys due.

▶ **Mortgage** – the transfer of property to secure the repayment of moneys lent by a debtor (the 'mortgagor') to their creditor (the 'mortgagee').

▶ **Mortgagee's powers** – the powers given to a mortgagee either expressly in the mortgage deed or, if not excluded by the deed, by Part III of the LPA 1925.

11.1 The case of the borrower's last chance

In early 1990, Mrs Norgan was in serious danger of losing her home, a period farm-house in Wiltshire which she shared with her husband and their five sons. By May of that year, the arrears of interest on her £90,000 mortgage amounted to over £7,000 and were set to double by the end of the year. The mortgage lender had lost patience and applied to the county court for an order allowing it to take possession of the mortgaged house and land.

The mortgage itself dated back to 1986. Mr Norgan, needing additional capital for his business, sold his half-share in the matrimonial home and its eight acres of land to his wife, making her the sole owner. She had financed the transaction by means of a building society loan of £90,000, to be repaid at the end of 22 years from the proceeds of various investments. In the meantime, Mrs Norgan would pay the interest that accrued on the outstanding capital by monthly instalments. The house and land were provided as security for the loan. In practice, the payments were met from the joint funds of Mr and Mrs Norgan, so when Mr Norgan ran into business difficulties, neither he nor his wife was able to keep up the payments due to the building society.

At the hearing in November 1990, the district judge made a possession order in favour of the building society, but suspended it for 28 days to allow Mrs Norgan to arrange to refinance the loan. The loan was not refinanced, and there followed a series of hearings in which the building society sought permission to enforce the possession order, and the Norgans sought to persuade the court to continue to suspend it. Mrs Norgan managed to obtain housing benefit that would cover future interest payments, but by September 1993 there were still considerable arrears outstanding, and a district judge refused to suspend the possession order any further. Mrs Norgan appealed, first to a judge of the county court and then to the Court of Appeal. By the time the matter reached the Court of Appeal in 1995, there was considerable dispute about the amount owing in arrears (in addition to the original £90,000 loan). The building society calculated the figure at £29,000, Mrs Norgan half that figure. The total value of the mortgaged land was said to be in the region of £225,000. The building society wanted to repossess the house, presumably to sell it with vacant possession at auction. If it were to do this, the building society would recover all the sums that were owing to it, and the balance of the proceeds of the sale would be returned to Mrs Norgan. Mrs Norgan, along with her family, wanted to continue to live in the family home.

The case of *Cheltenham & Gloucester Building Society* v *Norgan* [1996] 1 WLR 343 (CA) (which is considered in detail at Section 11.5.1(b)(ii)) was concerned with such questions as:

▶ Should Mrs Norgan be given any further time to pay off the arrears?
▶ If so, how long and on what conditions?
▶ How long should a lender be forced to wait before being allowed to enforce its security?

However, beneath these issues lie deeper tensions that illustrate how land simultaneously fulfils several functions, including shelter, security, and direct or indirect investment. The different demands of these various functions make it difficult to balance the competing interests when a dispute occurs:

▶ How can the courts recognise the commercial and contractual reality of mortgage agreements, while at the same time protecting the vulnerable?
▶ How should the law balance the interests of those living on the land with the commercial interests of lenders and the need for a buoyant property market, especially if there are beneficiaries (or, as was the case in *Norgan*, children) who were not parties to the mortgage?
▶ Should the law intervene to protect people who mortgage their land for the benefit of another? For example, the purpose of the transfer of the house and the mortgage in the *Norgan* case was to raise funds for Mr Norgan's business. Would the outcome have been different if, instead of transferring his share in the family home to his wife, Mr Norgan had simply persuaded her to agree to a joint mortgage of the house to guarantee his business overdraft?
▶ How can the interests of various lenders be balanced where there is more than one mortgage over the same interest in land, but insufficient equity to redeem them all?

11.2 Introducing mortgages

According to Lindley MR in *Santley* v *Wilde* [1899] 2 Ch 474 (CA) at 474, a mortgage is:

> a conveyance of land … as security for the payment of a debt or the discharge of some other obligation for which it is given.

To put it more succinctly, a mortgage is a transfer of land as security for a loan. Technically, a *mortgage* (which involves the transfer of a legal **estate** to the lender) should be distinguished from a *charge* (which gives the lender rights in the land but no estate). However, the terms are now widely treated as being interchangeable, not least because of the terminology of the LPA 1925 (see Section 11.3.1).

Mortgage relationships have existed since Anglo-Saxon times, but their form has changed a good deal since then, modified by equity and, more recently, by the intervention of Parliament. Many of the rules are relatively straightforward. However, the language and the concepts are not always quite as they might appear at first sight, resulting in a mismatch of expectation and theory that can be somewhat disconcerting. Consequently, it is essential to keep hold of the rules while exploring the theory. As far as the language is concerned, perhaps the easiest way to assimilate the technical terms is to try to explain them to your most tolerant friend.

11.2.1 Mortgagor and mortgagee

Contrary to the way most people talk, the mortgage is the interest in the land exchanged for the money, not the money being borrowed. When the letter arrives to say that a bank or a building society will lend the money to buy a house, the pedantic borrower should not say, 'They're giving me a mortgage!' but rather, 'They're letting me grant them a mortgage.' This is illustrated in Figure 11.1.

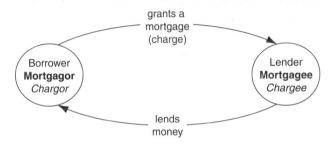

Figure 11.1 The mortgage relationship

11.2.2 Law and equity

Historically, a mortgage secured a legal debt repayable on a specific date. If the loan was repaid on this date (the legal date of redemption) the mortgaged land would be returned to the borrower. If not, the lender was entitled to keep the land as well as sue the debtor for the unpaid debt. In the seventeenth century, equity began to soften this harsh common law approach by allowing borrowers to recover their land after the legal date of redemption had passed. This right, known as the '**equity of redemption**', is the basis of modern mortgage lending and is considered in Section 11.4. It might be expected that the date of legal redemption would become irrelevant, but this is not so. The legal date of redemption (usually six months after the date of creation of the mortgage) continues to be the trigger for a number of the remedies available to the lender (see Section 11.5).

The equity of redemption is not linked to the legal or **equitable** status of the mortgage itself. It is possible to create a mortgage that only operates at equity (see Sections 11.3.2 and 11.6), but the equity of redemption is as essential to legal mortgages as it is to equitable ones.

11.2.3 The significance of mortgages today

It has already been noted how this area of land law illustrates the way in which land can simultaneously fulfil a variety of not necessarily consistent functions. The mortgage is the device by which most people become landowners: the bank or the building society lends money to buy land, which itself provides the security for the loan. Such mortgages are known as 'acquisition mortgages'. The landowner may then use the land to provide a home or to carry out their business activities. Many small businesses are financed by means of a mortgage on the home of the owner of the business; alternatively a mortgage may be granted to assist with a significant expense, which may or may not be directly linked to the land (such as an extension or a new car). One of the reasons for doing this is that the interest charges on mortgages are generally lower than on unsecured loans. For the lender, the land is an investment, security against a loan, through which it is making money for its investors. Most homeowners hope that their land is also an investment that will appreciate in value. Unfortunately, this is not always the case, as demonstrated by the slump in property values in the early 1990s, followed by another less than a decade into the twenty-first century. Some borrowers find that they end up owing more than their land is worth, in which case they are said to be in 'negative equity'.

11.3 Creating and ending mortgages

11.3.1 Creating legal mortgages

The LPA 1925 provided two methods by which a legal mortgage could be created:

- the grant of a long **lease** or, in the case of **leasehold estates**, a **sublease**, pursuant to sections 85 and 86 (a 'mortgage by **demise**'); and
- charge by way of legal mortgage pursuant to section 87 (a **legal charge**).

In practice, the first method is no longer used to create mortgages. The creation of a demise (or subdemise) is more complex than using the form of charge by way of legal mortgage, and, in any event, can only be used where the land concerned is **unregistered** (LRA 2002, s 23(1)(a)). However, as the Court of Appeal explained in *Regent Oil Co Ltd v J A Gregory (Hatch End) Ltd* [1966] Ch 402 (CA) the wording of section 87 of the LPA 1925 means that a charge by way of legal mortgage still operates by creating a demise. The **mortgagee** is granted a term of 3,000 years (in the case of a freehold) or the term of the lease, less one day, in the case of a leasehold (s 87(1)), and although the mortgagee does not acquire a legal estate, it is fully protected as if there were a lease.

A legal mortgage granted over a registered **title** must be completed by registration (LRA 2002, s 27(1), (2)(f)). The grant of a first legal mortgage over an unregistered freehold will trigger compulsory first registration of the land (LRA 2002, s 4(1)), regardless of what method is used to create it.

11.3.2 Creating equitable mortgages

It is important to know whether a mortgage is legal or **equitable** because, as well as the lesser security of equitable interests if the land is sold, the lender's remedies may be different.

An equitable mortgage can arise in a number of circumstances, including:

- Where the borrower has only an equitable interest in the land, such as a **beneficial interest** under a **trust** (see Chapters 13, 14 and 17). This equitable interest is mortgaged by assigning it in writing to the lender, who will promise to reassign it when the debt is repaid.

▶ Where there is a contract for a legal mortgage under section 2 of the Law of Property (Miscellaneous Provisions) Act 1989, or by **estoppel**. An equitable mortgage, therefore, will come into existence before its conversion into a legal mortgage through the execution of a **deed** (see Section 15.3).

Before the 1989 Act, an equitable mortgage could also be created by depositing the title deeds or land certificate to the land with the lender, in exchange for the loan. However, as this method is based on the doctrine of performance of an oral contract it is obsolete, as confirmed in *United Bank of Kuwait plc* v *Sahib* [1997] Ch 107 (CA) (see Section 15.4.5).

11.3.3 The discharge of mortgages

A mortgage is ended when the **lease**, **sublease** or **charge** is removed from the **title** to the property:

▶ In **registered land**, the mortgage can be discharged electronically or by sending a form to the Land Registry.
▶ Normally, in **unregistered land**, the borrower obtains a signed receipt on the mortgage document, and (in the case of a first charge) the title deeds are returned to the landowner.

11.4 The position of the borrower

Over the centuries, both policymakers and lawyers seem to have accepted that borrowers are vulnerable to exploitation by lenders. Lenders are almost always in the stronger negotiating position and, it is argued, have little interest in the relationship beyond personal profit. Consequently, the borrower has been given special rights to protection against oppression by a **mortgagee**, especially in relation to the terms of the contract. Many of these rights are creations of equity, while others have been introduced by statute. Those that relate directly to the borrower are dealt with in this section. Rights that arise when the lender's powers are exercised are examined in context in Section 11.5.

11.4.1 The equity of redemption

As mentioned in Section 11.2.2, mortgage agreements normally specify a contractual date for the repayment of the loan (the legal date of redemption), usually six months from the date of the loan. Where it is fair to do so, equity refuses to enforce this contractual date. Instead, the lender is required to accept the money even though the legal date of redemption has passed, thereby creating an **equitable** right to redeem. Few, if any, modern mortgages are created with the expectation that the loan will be repaid in full on the legal date of redemption. Instead, provision is made for the loan to be repaid over a much longer period, typically 25 years. The lender will usually only take action to enforce the **charge** earlier than this if the borrowers default on their repayments or breach the terms of the mortgage in some other way.

Historically, equity looks at the substance of an agreement and not at the name given to it. If the effect of an agreement is to create a loan on the security of land, equity will recognise the transaction as a mortgage and protect the borrower, following the maxim 'once a mortgage, always a mortgage'. The rules are summarised in the expression that there must be 'no clogs or fetters on the equity of redemption' and are explained below. However, it must be noted that some of the older cases reflect both a different financial world and one in which the House of Lords was bound to follow its own earlier decisions. Modern judges usually attempt to find a way around inconvenient precedents by, for example, applying general contractual doctrines such as duress and restraint of trade, rather than considering whether a term amounts, in mortgage law theory, to a 'clog'.

11.4.1(a) No irredeemability

Equity will not allow a lender to enforce a promise that prevents a borrower from ever redeeming the mortgage. For example, *Samuel* v *Jarrah Timber & Wood Paving Co Ltd* [1904] AC 323 (HL) concerned a mortgage of company stock (a debenture). In the mortgage deed, the borrower gave the lender an option to purchase; the lender could therefore choose to buy the stock from the borrower, thus preventing the borrower from redeeming the mortgage. The House of Lords declared the option void because it made the equitable right to redeem 'illusory'. The decision was made very reluctantly (in 1904, the House could not reverse its own decisions) as their Lordships believed that this arrangement, made by two large companies, was quite different from the kind of case for which the rule had been established. As Lord Macnaghten explained, at 327:

> The directors of a trading company in search of financial assistance are certainly in a very different position from that of an impecunious landowner in the toils of a crafty money-lender.

In *Jones* v *Morgan* [2002] 1 EGLR 125 (CA), the Court of Appeal struck out a term in a mortgage agreement that purported to give the lender a right to buy a half-share in the mortgaged land. In an ordinary contract, the term would have been valid, but since the term was contained within a mortgage agreement, the doctrine of clogs and fetters applied because, again, the Court found itself bound by precedent. However, the doctrine received considerable criticism from Lord Phillips MR, who said (at [86]):

> the doctrine of a clog on the equity of redemption is, so it seems to me, an appendix to our law which no longer serves a useful purpose and would be better excised.

If the option to purchase is a separate agreement from the mortgage, it can be enforced. In *Reeve* v *Lisle* [1902] AC 461 (HL), a mortgage of a ship was created and, some 12 days later, the mortgagor granted the lender an option to purchase it. The court did not see this as a clog, since the later agreement could be separated from the mortgage, and the option was held to be enforceable. Whether there is a separate agreement is not always easy to determine. For example, in *Jones* v *Morgan*, Pill LJ dissented from the majority judgment, holding that the right to buy the half-share was a separate agreement and that it was not, therefore, a clog on the equity of redemption. Less than two years after *Jones* v *Morgan*, the Court of Appeal had the opportunity of reviewing the law on the extent to which an option to purchase amounts to a clog on the equity of redemption in *Warnborough Ltd* v *Garmite Ltd* [2003] EWCA Civ 1544. Jonathan Parker LJ stated (at [73]) that:

the mere fact that, contemporaneously with the grant of a mortgage over his property, the mortgagor grants the mortgagee an option to purchase the property does no more than raise the question whether the rule against 'clogs' applies: it does not begin to answer that question ... the court has to look at the 'substance' of the transaction in question: in other words, to inquire as to the true nature of the bargain which the parties have made.

He went on to state that where the original seller of the property was also both mortgagee and the grantee of the option, as in the *Warnborough* case, there would be a strong likelihood that the transaction would be held to be one of sale and purchase rather than one of mortgage, and so the doctrine of clogs would not apply.

An agreement which postpones the equitable right to redeem so that it effectively becomes meaningless is likely to be void. This happened in *Fairclough* v *Swan Brewery Co Ltd* [1912] AC 565 (PC), where Mr Fairclough held a 17-year lease of a hotel. His landlord was the Swan Brewery, which lent him money on the security of his lease. The contractual date of redemption was fixed for a few weeks before the lease was due to expire. As the equitable right to redeem does not arise until the contractual date has passed, the mortgage was effectively irredeemable, and the promise was therefore held void. However, in *Knightsbridge Estates Trust Ltd* v *Byrne* [1939] Ch 441 (CA); [1945] AC 613 (HL), a case between two large companies, the contractual date for redemption of the mortgage (for £310,000) was set 40 years in the future. Given the reluctance of the courts to intervene when the parties are of equal bargaining power, and the fact that the land was **freehold**, both the Court of Appeal and the House of Lords held that the term was enforceable. This was, in the words of Sir Wilfred Greene MR in the Court of Appeal (at 455):

a commercial agreement between two important corporations, experienced in such matters, and has none of the features of an oppressive bargain.

11.4.1(b) Post-redemption conditions

Another of equity's concerns was the unfair advantage taken by a lender who sought to restrict the borrower's commercial activities, such as by requiring a shopkeeper mortgagor to buy wholesale goods only from the mortgagee. These kinds of agreement are known as '*solus* agreements' and are common between oil companies and filling stations, and between breweries and publicans. Equity declares void any terms in a mortgage agreement which would prevent the borrower from freely enjoying their land after they have repaid all the money. An example of this is *Noakes & Co Ltd* v *Rice* [1902] AC 24 (HL), where the owner of a 26-year lease of a pub mortgaged it to a brewery, promising he would buy liquor only from the lender for the whole term of the lease. The House of Lords held that the promise was ineffective and that the borrower would be free from the tie once he had repaid the loan. In *G&C Kreglinger* v *New Patagonia Meat & Cold Storage Co Ltd* [1914] AC 25 (HL), however, the House of Lords decided that a collateral promise that the borrower would sell his sheepskins to only the lender for five years, regardless of when the loan was repaid, was valid and not a clog on the equitable right to redeem. In that case, the mortgage agreement was a commercial arrangement on reasonable terms between two companies at arm's length, and, after redemption, the mortgagor would be able to enjoy the land in the same state as it had been before the mortgage. Nowadays, the courts tend to apply the contractual doctrine of restraint of trade to this kind of issue (see *Esso Petroleum Co Ltd* v *Harpers Garage (Stourport) Ltd* [1968] AC 269 (HL)).

11.4.1(c) Other oppressive terms

Equity developed rules against other clogs on the equity of redemption and declared void any other 'unconscionable or oppressive terms' in the mortgage. In *Multiservice Bookbinding Ltd* v *Marden* [1979] Ch 84 (Ch), the bookbinding company granted a mortgage as security for a loan of £36,000. The interest rate was linked to the Swiss franc, because the pound was very unstable. The fluctuation in the money markets meant that the borrower would have to pay £45,000 in interest. Browne-Wilkinson J held that this may have been unreasonable, but it was not oppressive or unconscionable. For a promise to be struck out, it must be shown that the objectionable terms were imposed 'in a morally reprehensible manner ... which affects [the mortgagee's] conscience' (at 110). This is another example of the court being reluctant to intervene in a commercial agreement between equals.

Many mortgage agreements permit the lender, at its discretion, to vary the interest rate payable by the borrower. The Court of Appeal in *Paragon Finance plc* v *Nash* [2002] 1 WLR 685 (CA) protected the borrower against the arbitrary exercise of this discretion by holding that such agreements contain an implied term that the interest rates 'would not be set dishonestly, for an improper purpose, capriciously or arbitrarily' (Dyson LJ at [36]). In a later case concerning the same lender (*Paragon Finance plc* v *Pender* [2005] 1 WLR 3412 (CA)), a differently constituted Court of Appeal decided that there was nothing in this implied term preventing a lender from increasing the interest rate above that of most of its competitors, provided that the decision to do so is a genuinely commercial one.

11.4.2 Statutory protection from unfair agreements

The vast majority of first mortgages of residential property (except for purchasers buying the property as an investment to let out) will fall within the provisions of the Financial Services and Markets Act 2000, which came into force on 31st October 2004. This Act imposes the Mortgage Conduct of Business (MCOB) rules upon mortgage lenders, a code of practice designed to promote transparency and preclude extortionate charges being imposed. The MCOB rules are regularly reviewed and updated, most recently in 2016 to accommodate the requirements of the European Mortgage Credit Directive. A lender in breach of the Code may find itself subject to disciplinary action by the Financial Conduct Authority, and the borrower may have an action for damages under section 150 of the Act. However, breaching the Code does not make the mortgage void or limit the **mortgagee's** remedies (Financial Services and Markets Act 2000, s 151(2)).

Until April 2008, most other mortgages granted by individuals fell within sections 137–40 of the Consumer Credit Act 1974, regulating extortionate credit bargains. **Mortgagors** could ask the courts to reopen a credit bargain if the payments were 'grossly exorbitant' or 'grossly contravene[d] ordinary principles of fair dealing'. Sections 137–40 have now been repealed and replaced by a new scheme allowing the court to intervene if it finds that the relationship between the creditor and the debtor arising out of a credit agreement is unfair to the debtor (Consumer Credit Act 2006, ss 19–22).

Like sections 137–40, the new scheme applies to agreements between an individual borrower (including an individual in the course of business) and anyone who lends money. It does not apply to first **legal charges** over residential land regulated under the Financial Services and Markets Act 2000 (see above), but will apply to many second mortgages. Many second mortgages are arranged for purposes such as home improvements or securing a business loan, but sometimes they are an act of desperation by a defaulting borrower, and here in particular the borrower needs protection.

Under section 140A of the Consumer Credit Act 1974 (as amended), the court may decide that the relationship is unfair to the debtor because of one or more of:

(a) any of the terms of the agreement or of any related agreement;
(b) the way in which the creditor has exercised or enforced any of their rights under the agreement or any related agreement; and
(c) any other thing done (or not done) by, or on behalf of, the creditor (either before or after the making of the agreement or any related agreement).

If satisfied that an agreement is unfair, the court has considerable powers to intervene on behalf of the borrower. It may, for example, alter the terms of the agreement or order repayment or the return of property (s 140B). However, the courts seem to be as unwilling to intervene in credit agreements under section 140A as they were to use their earlier powers under sections 137–40. This is possibly because the needier (and therefore weaker) the borrower, the more justified is the lender in imposing a high interest rate: the interest rate must, it is argued, reflect the degree of risk being taken by the lender. The counter-argument, that if the borrower defaults, the lender can realise the security of the land, appears to hold little attraction.

11.4.3 Section 91(2) LPA 1925

If the value of land falls below the interest and capital due under the mortgage (so-called negative equity), the borrower may be keen to sell the land to repay as much of the debt as possible in order to prevent the interest due on the loan from spiralling upwards. The lender may be equally keen to prevent a sale, preferring to **lease** out the land in the hope that it might increase in value at some point in the future. This situation arose in *Palk v Mortgage Services Funding plc* [1993] Ch 330 (CA), where the borrower had found a buyer for the land, but the price was about £50,000 less than the mortgage debt. The interest on the debt was accumulating at a rate of £43,000 a year, and the annual **rent** would not have been more than about £13,000. The mortgagee argued that it could prevent a sale if the price were less than the amount needed to repay the debt in full. Mrs Palk claimed, however, that under section 91 of the LPA 1925 the court had discretion to order a sale of mortgaged property. Section 91 of the LPA 1925 is the latest incarnation of a statutory provision dating back to the Chancery Amendment Act 1852, introduced, as Sir John Romilly MR explained in *Hurst v Hurst* (1852) 51 ER 822 (Ch), at 823:

> in order to avoid the great delay and expense which is occasioned by foreclosure and redemption in a case where there is a great number of successive mortgages.

The Court of Appeal held that section 91(2) gave the court unfettered discretion to order a sale if doing so was necessary in order to prevent 'manifest unfairness' to the borrower. In Mrs Palk's case, the court felt that it would be unjust not to order a sale as not only was the debt increasing at several times the rental value, but there was no reason why the lender should not acquire the **title** to the property in return for its market value if it was so confident that property values were going to increase.

11.4.4   Avoiding undue influence and misrepresentation

The question of the effect of undue influence or misrepresentation on the validity of a mortgage came to prominence with the increase in family home repossessions in the early 1990s, when interest rates were high and the value of property was falling. In a typical case of this type, a lender seeks to repossess a home because of arrears, and one of the joint borrowers then claims to have signed the mortgage **deed** or stood surety for the loan, because the other misled her (it is typically a male partner who is alleged to be at fault) or exploited the relationship of trust that existed between them. As Patten LJ observed in *Royal Bank of Scotland plc* v *Chandra* [2011] EWCA Civ 192 (CA) (at [32]), the defence may be based on:

- undue influence, where a relationship of trust and confidence has been abused in order to procure consent to a mortgage or guarantee; or
- misrepresentation, where consent has been procured not by the exercise of some form of pressure or domination but by the making of a false statement which the other person in the relationship of trust has relied upon.

In both situations, the question for the court is not whether one party acted towards the other unconscionably or in breach of **trust**, but whether the lending institution had notice of the undue influence or misrepresentation, or was in some other way responsible for it. If the lender did not take steps to ensure that the signature was properly obtained without any undue influence or misrepresentation, the mortgage will be void as far as the injured party is concerned.

The facts of two House of Lords cases are typical of the kinds of situation where a lender might be fixed with notice of the wrong committed against a borrower. In the first of the cases, *Barclays Bank plc* v *O'Brien* [1994] 1 AC 180 (HL), Mr O'Brien was the sole legal owner of the matrimonial home, but his wife held a **beneficial interest** in it. He told her he was borrowing £60,000 on a mortgage for three weeks to save his business, so she signed all the surety forms at the bank without reading any of them and without any independent advice. In fact, the loan was for £135,000. Within six months, the repayments were seriously in arrears, and the bank sought possession. Mrs O'Brien successfully argued that her agreement to the mortgage was the result of her husband's misrepresentation about the size of the loan being secured on the house, and that the bank had constructive notice of this, giving rise to her right to set the mortgage aside.

In the second case, *CIBC Mortgages* v *Pitt* [1994] 1 AC 200 (HL), the facts were fairly similar, but here Mrs Pitt, the wife, was a joint legal owner of the home. As joint legal owner she could be presumed, on the facts, to be benefiting financially from the mortgage loan. The lender was told that the money would be used to pay off an outstanding mortgage and to buy a second home, and therefore it was not put on notice to take steps to protect Mrs Pitt. In fact, the husband really wanted the money to play the stock market.

After a series of undue influence cases in the lower courts, the House of Lords reviewed this area of the law in what is now the leading case on undue influence: *Royal Bank of Scotland plc* v *Etridge (No 2)* [2002] 2 AC 773 (HL). The questions were:

- what are the requirements that need to be met to establish that undue influence has occurred?
- under what circumstances is a lender put on notice that there may have been undue influence?

▶ if the lender is on notice, what steps must it take to avoid any subsequent claim by the innocent joint borrower or surety?

The answers to the second and third questions will depend upon whether the transaction took place before or after the House of Lords' decision in *Etridge*, and are summarised in Table 11.1.

Table 11.1 *Royal Bank of Scotland plc v Etridge (No 2)* [2002] 2 AC 773 (HL)

	Pre-*Etridge* transactions	Post-*Etridge* transactions
The lender is placed on inquiry	In situations in which the surety trusted the debtor to deal with her financial affairs or where both were living together in a close emotional relationship.	In all cases in which the relationship between the debtor and the surety is non-commercial.
In such circumstances	'The bank will ordinarily be regarded as having discharged its obligations if a solicitor who was acting for the wife in the transaction gave the bank confirmation to the effect that he had brought home to the wife the risks she was running by standing as surety' (Lord Nicholls, *Etridge* at [80]).	'The furthest a bank can be expected to go is to take reasonable steps to satisfy itself that the wife has had brought home to her, in a meaningful way, the practical implications of the proposed transaction. This does not wholly eliminate the risk of undue influence or misrepresentation. But it does mean that a wife enters into a transaction with her eyes open so far as the basic elements of the transaction are concerned' (Lord Nicholls, *Etridge* at [54]).
	Additional steps may be required, especially where the lender was aware that the guarantor's circumstances made her particularly vulnerable to exploitation (see, for example, *National Westminster Bank plc v Amin* [2002] UKHL 9, Lord Scott at [24]).	The bank will be considered to have taken these reasonable steps if: • it tells the wife or other person in a non-commercial relationship to the debtor that it requires her to consult a solicitor of her choice (who may be the family solicitor, but who must be acting for her); • it provides the necessary financial information to allow the solicitor properly to advise the borrower (if the debtor will not allow such confidential information to be passed on, the transaction will not be able to proceed); and • it obtains written confirmation from the solicitor that the documents and the practical implications of the arrangement (that is, that she risks losing her home if the mortgage payments are not met) have been explained to the borrower. If the bank has reason to believe that the wife is not acting of her own free will, it must inform the solicitor of this.

The case of *Hewett v First Plus Financial Group plc* [2010] 2 P & CR 22 (CA) demonstrates the consequences of a lender still failing to take these relatively simple steps. At the time that he asked his wife to sign the mortgage, not only had Mr Hewett failed to disclose to her that he was having an extra-marital affair, but he had taken great pains to stress his commitment to his family. On the facts of the case, the Court of Appeal held that this amounted to undue influence. The lender conceded that it had failed to take the steps outlined in *Etridge* necessary to protect it from being affected by Mr Hewett's conduct. Consequently, it could not enforce its **legal charge** against what was now Mrs Hewett's home. However, the lender could still enforce the debt against Mr Hewett, and was entitled to ask the court to make an order charging Mr Hewett's **beneficial interest** in the land by way of security (this is known as a charging order). This meant that Mrs Hewett's home (although not her share in it) was still at risk because the lender could seek an order for the sale of the land under section 14 of the Trusts of Land and Appointment of Trustees Act 1996 (see Section 14.5).

This complex area of mortgage law indicates the policy tensions which can arise in land law and how the courts deal with them. It is important that lenders are able to lend money on the security of property without being concerned that their security will be lost, but at the same time it is just as important that the rights of more vulnerable owners are protected (see also, for example, *Williams & Glyn's Bank Ltd v Boland* [1981] AC 487 (HL), *City of London Building Society v Flegg* [1988] AC 54 (HL), considered at Section 4.6.2).

11.5 The position of the legal lender

The **mortgagee** has remedies to enforce the payment of the money due to it, together with certain other rights. Some of these rights (such as the right to take possession) are characteristic of all mortgages. Others may be granted by the terms of the mortgage deed or implied under the provisions of Part III of the LPA 1925.

The legal mortgagee's most important rights are to:

1. take possession of the property;
2. sell the property;
3. appoint a receiver;
4. **foreclose**;
5. sue on the personal covenant;
6. consolidate;
7. hold the title deeds if the land is still **unregistered**; and
8. exercise rights in connection with a series of mortgages (**tacking**: see Section 11.7.1).

The lender does not have to choose only one of these remedies; it can pursue several of them, either at the same time or sequentially. Figure 11.2 illustrates how the most important of them can be applied when advising the parties after the borrower has breached the terms of the mortgage. All of these remedies date from a time when mortgages were not commonly used for home buying. Over the years, they have been adjusted by statute in an attempt to protect the security of home buyers, although there are still some gaps, many of which arise because of the basic right of the mortgagee to take possession of the land.

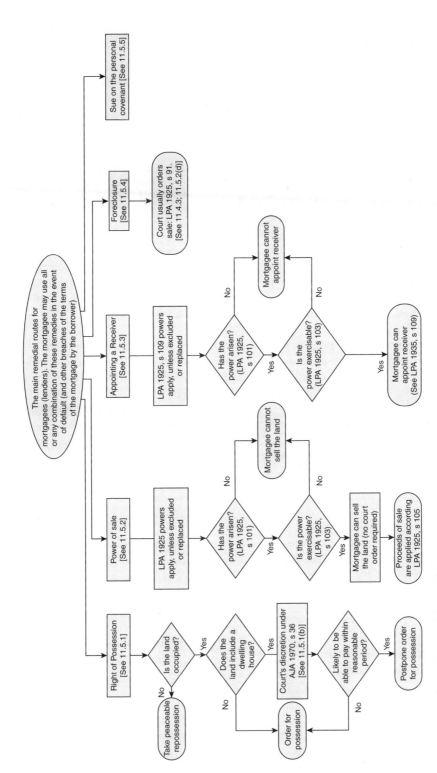

Figure 11.2   The main remedial routes for mortgagees

11.5.1 Taking possession

11.5.1(a) The general rules

Historically, a mortgagee had an **estate** in the land. Even today, when mortgages are almost invariably created by 'charge by deed expressed to be by way of legal mortgage', the mortgagee is treated as if it has a **lease** (see *Regent Oil Co Ltd* v *J A Gregory (Hatch End) Ltd* [1966] Ch 402 (CA) and Section 11.3.1). One of the consequences of this, as Harman J explained in *Four-Maids Ltd* v *Dudley Marshall (Properties) Ltd* [1957] Ch 317 (Ch) at 320, a lender has the right to:

> go into possession before the ink is dry on the mortgage unless there is something in the contract, express or by implication, whereby he has contracted himself out of that right.

It might seem extraordinary that the lender has the right to move in as soon as the mortgage deed is signed, but it was once common for the mortgagee to take possession of the land at the beginning of the mortgage and to take the produce of the land in the days before it was usual (or even permissible) to charge interest on loans. The modern lender will not usually wish to take possession unless the borrower fails to pay the instalments due under the terms of the loan. Even then, the lender will want to sell the property rather than move in and occupy the property itself. By far the most common reason for seeking possession, therefore, is to gain vacant possession of the property in readiness for selling it.

Although a court order is not strictly necessary before taking possession, a lender will usually seek the authorisation of the court unless it is sure that the premises are unoccupied (as they were in *Ropaigealach* v *Barclays Bank plc* [2000] QB 263 (CA), for example). Section 6 of the Criminal Law Act 1977 makes it an offence to use or threaten violence to gain entry into premises and a court order is the safest way to ensure that no offence is inadvertently committed. At common law, as Russell J explained in *Birmingham Citizens Permanent Building Society* v *Caunt* [1962] Ch 883 (Ch), at 91:

> the court has no jurisdiction to decline the order or to adjourn the hearing whether on terms of keeping up payments or paying arrears, if the mortgagee cannot be persuaded to agree to this course.

However, the common law position has been modified by statute where the mortgaged property includes a dwelling-house. In such circumstances, section 36 of the Administration of Justice Act 1970 (as amended by s 8 of the Administration of Justice Act 1973) gives the court the discretion to postpone an order giving the lender possession if the borrower 'is likely to be able within a reasonable period to pay any sums due under the mortgage.'

11.5.1(b) Relief under section 36 of the Administration of Justice Act 1970

In order to succeed under section 36, the borrowers must first establish that the section applies to their circumstances, and then persuade the court to exercise its discretion in their favour.

11.5.1(b)(i) The court's jurisdiction Borrowers can only apply for relief pursuant to section 36 if:

- the mortgaged land includes a dwelling-house; and
- the **mortgagee** has brought an action for possession; and
- any order for possession has not yet been put into effect (*Deutsche Bank Suisse SA* v *Khan* [2013] EWCA Civ 1149 (CA)).

Ropaigealach v *Barclays Bank plc* [2000] QB 263 (CA) is a relatively rare example of a lender not obtaining a court order before going into possession. In this case, the borrowers had moved elsewhere, and the house subject to the mortgage was standing empty. The Court of Appeal concluded, albeit reluctantly, that the borrowers were not entitled to section 36 relief in such circumstances. To allow relief in these circumstances would effectively prevent a mortgagee from taking possession without first obtaining a court order, which went beyond what Parliament had enacted in section 36. It has been suggested that this result contravenes the borrower's rights under Articles 6 and 8 and Article 1, Protocol 1 of the European Convention on Human Rights (ECHR) (see Rook, 2001, 199), although this line of argument was subsequently rejected by Briggs J in *Horsham Properties Group Ltd* v *Clark* [2009] 1 WLR 1255 (Ch). In *Horsham Properties*, very unusually, the lender exercised its power of sale without first obtaining possession. Ownership of the land passed to Horsham, who then sought possession of the land from the borrowers. The borrowers' claim for relief under section 36 was refused because section 36 only applies where possession is being sought by the *mortgagee*. This is a convenient way of avoiding the court's discretion to postpone possession orders under section 36 of the Administration of Justice Act 1970, but not one that will be pursued by major lenders. Immediately after *Horsham*, the Council of Mortgage Lenders voluntarily issued guidance to its members directing them not to exploit the decision.

11.5.1(b)(ii) The court's discretion   A number of cases have focused on the circumstances in which it is appropriate for the court to exercise its section 36 discretion. Perhaps the most important case is that of *Cheltenham & Gloucester Building Society* v *Norgan* [1996] 1 WLR 343 (CA), the facts of which are set out at Section 11.1. The main question before the Court of Appeal was what amounted to a reasonable period for the purposes of its section 36 discretion. In the years before *Norgan*, a period of two years had become fairly established in judgments as the normal standard. The Court of Appeal held that 'a reasonable period' was not limited to any particular length of time. In *Norgan*, the mortgage term was to end 13 years from the time of the claim for a possession order, and the Court held that this could be a reasonable period within 'the logic and spirit of the Act' (at 353). However, given the significant dispute about the size of the arrears, the Court felt that it could only comment on the principle of the matter. The case was effectively referred back to a lower court to decide whether it could reschedule the debt over the whole repayment period. In theory, such a rescheduling from the outset of the **mortgagor's** difficulties should avoid the continuing struggle and repeated orders and delays in repossession proceedings that characterised the proceedings in *Norgan*.

The judgments in *Norgan* also contain some useful guidance as to how the court should exercise its discretion under section 36. The underlying principle seems to be that the lender's security must not be put at risk by allowing the postponement of the possession order. Consequently:

- borrowers should produce detailed explanations, that do not depend upon hopes and speculations, of how the arrears and future payments falling due under the mortgage will be met;
- the value of the property must exceed the value of the moneys due (in *Cheltenham & Gloucester plc* v *Krausz* [1997] 1 WLR 1558 (CA) the Court of Appeal refused to postpone a possession order so that the borrowers could sell the property where

there was negative equity and no evidence of any other funds being available to meet the shortfall); and

- the court should be cautious about granting a further postponement if the borrower fails to comply with the original terms under which the grant of the possession was delayed.

11.5.2 Sale

11.5.2(a) The power of sale

Although the **mortgagee** has no power of sale at common law, a statutory power of sale is provided by the LPA 1925. All mortgages that satisfy the conditions set out in section 101 of the LPA 1925 benefit from this statutory power of sale, except in so far as it is modified or excluded by the terms of the mortgage. This was the case, for example, in *Ropaigealach v Barclays Bank plc* [2000] QB 263 (CA), where different conditions were substituted for those set out in the LPA 1925.

Two sets of conditions need to be satisfied before a lender can exercise its power of sale under the LPA 1925. The power must have *arisen* under section 101, and it must have become *exercisable* by virtue of at least one of the conditions in section 103 having been satisfied.

Section 101: The power of sale arises if:

- the mortgage is made by **deed** (s 101(1)); and
- the deed contains no provisions excluding the statutory power (s 101(4)); and
- the contractual date for redeeming the mortgage has passed (that is, the mortgage money has become due; s 101(1)(i)).

In most domestic mortgages, the contractual date of redemption is usually set six months after the creation of the mortgage.

Section 103: The power of sale becomes exercisable if:

- the default continues three months after a notice requiring payment is served; or
- interest is two months in default; or
- the borrower has broken another term of the mortgage.

Under the provisions of the LPA 1925, the lender is entitled to sell the whole of the borrower's interest in the land as soon as one of the conditions in section 103 has been fulfilled (LPA 1925, ss 88–9). No court order is required to authorise a sale pursuant to the powers in the LPA 1925, although in most cases the lender will first obtain a court order granting possession. A sale under section 101 overreaches the interest of the borrower in a similar way to the **overreaching** of **beneficial interests** when the proceeds are paid to two **trustees** (see Section 14.6.1). Thus, in *Horsham* v *Clark* (see Section 11.5.1(b)), the purchaser of the house was able to obtain possession from the borrowers who were still living there at the time of its sale. Any interest that the borrowers had in the land had been transferred to the proceeds of sale paid to the lender. The Ministry of Justice, in its response to the decision in *Horsham* v *Clark* (Consultation Paper CP55/09 *Mortgages: Power of Sale and Residential Property*), suggested that the law should be changed so that mortgagees of owner-occupied residential properties would need the approval of the court before exercising their power of sale (through the existing procedure for a possession order or by a new form of order approving sale). However, no steps have been taken to implement these proposals, which were, in any event, somewhat limited: they would not, for example, apply to mortgages over a dwelling-house securing a business debt.

The exercise of the power of sale against the family home can have distressing effects on the family, but attempts to invoke ECHR Article 8 (the right to respect for a person's private and family life and home) have not been successful thus far. According to Lord Scott in *Harrow LBC* v *Qazi* [2004] 1 AC 983 (HL) at [135], the Article cannot be used 'to diminish the contractual and proprietary rights of the mortgagee under the mortgage' (see also *Horsham* v *Clark*, [23–42]).

11.5.2(b) The lender's duty to the borrower

Although the lender may choose when to sell and does not have to wait for an upturn in the market, when it does sell it is under a duty to the borrower to take reasonable care to get the best price reasonably obtainable 'on the day'.

In a Privy Council case from Hong Kong, *China & South Seas Bank* v *Tan* [1990] 1 AC 536 (PC), there was a mortgage loan of $HK30 million on the security of shares. Mr Tan, as surety for the mortgage, undertook to repay all the moneys owed by the debtor. When the repayment became due, the shares were worth enough to repay the debt, but by the time the mortgagee decided to exercise his power of sale, the shares were worthless. Mr Tan argued that the mortgagee owed him a duty of care to sell as soon as possible, but this was rejected by the Privy Council. As Lord Templeman explained, at 545:

> If the creditor chose to exercise his power of sale over the mortgaged security he must sell for the current market value but the creditor must decide in his own interest if and when he should sell. The creditor does not become a trustee of the mortgaged securities.

In another case from Hong Kong, *Tse Kwong Lam* v *Wong Chit Sen* [1983] 1 WLR 1349 (PC), Tse had granted a mortgage to Wong in 1963 on a large development in Hong Kong. Three years later, he was in arrears, and the land was sold at auction to the only bidder, a company owned by the lender and his wife and children. The ownership of the company was not, in itself, the issue; rather, according to Lord Templeman (at 1359), the lender could not show that:

> he protected the interests of the borrower taking expert advice as to the method of sale, as to the steps which ought reasonably to be taken to make the sale a success and as to the amount of the reserve [minimum price].

The normal remedy in such a case is for the sale to be set aside, but here the Privy Council did not do so, because the borrower had been 'guilty of inexcusable delay' having not pursued the matter for many years. He won the alternative remedy of damages, the difference between the price which was obtained and the price which should have been obtained.

Cuckmere Brick Ltd v *Mutual Finance Ltd* [1971] Ch 949 (CA) is an example of where a lender was negligent when exercising its power of sale. In this case, the lender failed to advertise to prospective purchasers the full extent of the planning permission which attached to the property. The price paid for the land was almost certainly lower than what would have been obtained had the value of the planning permission been taken into account. The Court of Appeal held that the mortgagee had failed to meet the duty that it owed to the **mortgagor** to take reasonable care to obtain a proper price. As a result, the lender was liable to the mortgagor for any shortfall between the price obtained by the lender and the true value of the land.

11.5.2(c) The proceeds of sale

Once the land is sold, the lender is under a duty to account to the borrower. It must also take care to protect the interests of others. The lender must apply the proceeds in the order set out in section 105 of the LPA 1925, which is:

- any prior mortgages, unless the property was sold subject to them;
- the expenses of the sale;
- the capital and interest due under the mortgage;
- any second or subsequent mortgages; and
- the borrower.

Although the lender is not a **trustee** of its power of sale, it is, by virtue of section 105, a trustee of the proceeds of sale and must act in good faith.

A buyer from a mortgagee must check that a power of sale exists, but need not make sure that it has actually become exercisable (LPA 1925, s 104(2)). However, if the buyer knows of, or suspects, any improper or irregular use of the mortgagee's powers, they would be wise to ensure that the mortgagee has taken reasonable care (otherwise they might lose the land and have to be content with a remedy in damages against the mortgagee).

11.5.2(d) The general power to order sale

In addition to the power given mortgagees by section 101 of the LPA 1925, courts have the general power to order sale at the instance of any 'person interested' by virtue of section 91 of the LPA 1925. The court's general power to order sale may be employed as an alternative to foreclosure (see Section 11.5.4) and can also be used at the request of the borrower (see Section 11.4.3). Occasionally, as in *Target Home Loans Ltd v Clothier* [1994] 1 All ER 439 (CA), the courts will postpone a possession order to allow the borrower, rather than the lender, to sell the property, since the borrower is likely to get a higher price. However, following the Court of Appeal decision in *Cheltenham & Gloucester plc v Krausz* [1997] 1 WLR 1558 (CA), it is unlikely that the courts will take this line in cases where the value of the property is less than the balance owed ('negative equity').

11.5.3 Appointing a receiver

A lender can appoint a receiver to manage the land in the same circumstances in which it has the power of sale (LPA 1925, ss 101, 109(1)). This can be very convenient in a commercial mortgage, for example, if the land is let to **tenants**, and the mortgagee wants the rents to pay off interest which is due. The advantage of appointing a receiver rather than going into possession is that a mortgagee in possession is personally liable to the borrower for any loss, but a receiver must pay for their own mistakes. This is because, by section 109 of the LPA 1925, the receiver is deemed to be the agent of the mortgagor (the borrower), rather than the mortgagee who appointed them. The receiver's primary objective is to create a situation whereby the secured debt can be paid off (*Medforth v Blake* [2000] Ch 86 (CA)). In *Silven Properties v Royal Bank of Scotland plc* [2004] 1 WLR 997 (CA), the Court of Appeal confirmed that the receiver's duty to manage the property does not require them to go so far as to making improvements to the land in order to increase its value. Neither is a receiver obliged to run any business that the borrower was operating from the premises, but if they do they must try to carry it on profitably and with due diligence (*Medforth* v *Blake*).

11.5.4 Foreclosure

Once the legal date of redemption has passed, a foreclosure order is theoretically available from the court. However, these **equitable** orders are rarely, if ever, sought today. A foreclosure order transfers legal and equitable **title** in the land to the lender, free from all the borrower's rights in the land (including the right to redeem the mortgage). An order is only granted if the court is certain that the borrower will never be able to repay, but even when an order has been granted, the court has the power to reopen the foreclosure (as in *Campbell* v *Holyland* (1877–78) LR 7 Ch D 166 (Ch)). Any application for a foreclosure order today will now almost certainly result in the court making an order for sale pursuant to its powers under section 91 of the LPA 1925 (see Sections 11.4.3 and 11.5.2(d)).

11.5.5 Suing on the personal covenant

If the amount realised on the sale of the mortgaged land is insufficient to cover the amount owed to the lender, the borrower remains personally liable to the lender for the shortfall, and the lender may sue them for the outstanding sum. During the recession of the 1990s, many borrowers left their homes and handed over the keys to lenders in the expectation that this would bring their indebtedness to an end. However, when, due to falling house prices, the proceeds of sale were insufficient to meet the mortgage arrears, the unfortunate borrowers found themselves being sued for the balance.

The right to sue on the personal covenant to repay the mortgage debt must be exercised within 'twelve years from the date on which the right to receive the money accrued' (Limitation Act 1980, s 20). Initially, this date is the contractual date of redemption set by the mortgage, but the 12-year period recommences each time any payment of capital or interest is made or written acknowledgement of liability is given by the mortgagor (Limitation Act 1980, ss 29, 30). The limitation period for interest due under the mortgage (as opposed to the capital debt) is six years from the date that the interest fell due (Limitation Act 1980, s 20(5)).

In *West Bromwich Building Society* v *Wilkinson* [2005] 1 WLR 2303 (HL) the lender obtained an order for possession of the borrowers' home in 1989, selling it a year later and leaving a shortfall of nearly £24,000. Only in 2002 did the lender begin proceedings for nearly £47,000, which was the initial shortfall and the interest on it since 1990. The lender argued that section 20 did not apply, and that even if it did, the limitation period did not start running until after the land had been sold, when the total shortfall would be known. The House of Lords rejected both arguments. Section 20 applies to all actions derived from a mortgage, even if the lender has sold the land concerned. The effect of the wording of the mortgage in this case, combined with sections 101 and 103 of the LPA 1925, was that the whole of the mortgage advance fell due as soon as the borrowers had defaulted, and the lender made demand for payment. Consequently, the 12 years began to run in 1989, with the result that the action was statute barred.

The borrower's personal liability can have very serious consequences, not only for the borrower, but also for anyone else occupying the mortgaged land. In *Alliance & Leicester plc* v *Slayford* (2001) 33 HLR 66 (CA), a lender had been unable to get an order for possession against a borrower due to the wife of the borrower having a very small equitable interest in the house that was not subject to the mortgage. The lender decided to sue on the borrower's personal covenant to repay, which would have had the eventual effect of making the borrower bankrupt. The **trustee in bankruptcy** could then apply for sale of the house under section 14 of the Trusts of Land and Appointment of Trustees Act 1996 and would almost certainly succeed (see Section 14.5.4). Although the lender would lose its priority over the bankrupt borrower's unsecured creditors, at least by these means it would get some of its money back. The wife, however, would lose her home, despite the mortgage having earlier been declared void against her. In somewhat forthright language, the trial judge stated that the mortgagee's tactic amounted to an abuse of the process of the court. The Court of Appeal had little difficulty in finding for the mortgagee: it was not an abuse for it to employ any or all of the legal remedies available to it.

11.5.6 Consolidation

In rare cases, where the mortgagee has lent money on mortgages granted by the same borrower over different pieces of land, it has a right to consolidate them. This means that it may join the various mortgages together and refuse to allow the borrower to redeem one of the mortgages without redeeming any others. Consolidation can be useful if one piece of land is not sufficient security for the debt. The right arises when the power is contained in the mortgage itself, and is exercisable only when the contractual date for redemption has passed.

11.5.7 Holding the title documents

The first legal mortgagee of **unregistered land** is entitled to hold the **deeds**, which are returned to the borrower on redemption. This is a very effective way of ensuring that the land is not sold without the lender's knowledge, as any attempt to sell the legal estate will require the seller to produce the title deeds. Of course, the title deeds will not be available to any second or subsequent mortgagee, which must protect its interest by registering a Class C(i) land charge under the Land Charges Act 1972 (see Section 5.4.2(a)). All first legal mortgages created after March 1998 will trigger the first registration of the land (see Section 4.6).

If the title is registered, any **charge** must be protected (and in the case of a **legal charge**, completed) by entry on the register (see Section 4.5). Prior to 13th October 2003, the Land Registry issued a charge certificate to the mortgagee each time a new mortgage was registered. Charge certificates have not been issued since the LRA 2002 came into force, although the registration of a new **legal charge** will prompt the issue of a new 'title information document'.

11.6 The position of the equitable lender

Both **equitable** mortgagees and equitable chargees can sue on the borrower's personal promise to pay, but apart from this their rights differ.

11.6.1 The equitable mortgagee

Unless an **equitable** mortgage has been made by **deed**, there is no automatic power to sell or appoint a receiver (LPA 1925, s 101). However, the mortgagee can obtain a court order for sale using section 91 of the LPA 1925. If there is a deed, the equitable lender generally has the same remedies as a legal lender, but it must be careful to draft the document to give it the right to sell the legal **estate**. It is not clear whether it has an automatic right to go into possession.

11.6.2 The equitable chargee

The rights of 'a mere equitable chargee' are fewer than those of other lenders. This kind of lender has only the remedy of sale or appointment of a receiver, both by order of the court.

11.7 Priority of mortgages

11.7.1 The general rules

The rules about priority in mortgages come into play when there are several mortgages of one piece of land. If the borrower defaults, and the land is not worth enough to pay back all the debts, then one or more of the lenders may lose money. The priority rules determine which of the lenders is to be unlucky. There have been few cases in the past hundred years on priorities, and basic rules are stated very briefly here.

There are also special rules about the situation where several mortgages exist on one piece of land and a **mortgagee** owns two or more of them. In these circumstances, the mortgagee may be allowed to 'tack'. It is convenient to illustrate this with a fictional example. Suppose Oliver purchased his flat with the help of a mortgage from Ceele Bank plc. A few years later, he granted a second mortgage to Klayton Finance Ltd to secure a loan to his business. Finally, when Ceele Bank lent Oliver yet more money this loan was also secured (by a third mortgage) on the flat. If Ceele Bank decides to enforce its charges, it may tack its mortgages; that is, it may jump over Klayton's second mortgage by attaching the third mortgage to the first. (Compare consolidation of mortgages at Section 11.5.6.)

11.7.2 Mortgages of a legal interest in registered land

In **registered** land, the general rule is that, once a mortgage or charge has been protected on the Register, it will defeat all later mortgages as well as earlier mortgages which have not been protected by registration. Thus, the first mortgage entered on the Register ranks first, and the remainder rank according to the date of their registration (LRA 2002, s 48).

11.7.3 Mortgages of a legal interest in unregistered land

The rules relating to the priority of mortgages in **unregistered land** are now mainly of historic interest since all new first mortgages of **freeholds** and long leases since 1998 will have triggered first registration of the land (see Section 4.6). Mortgages in unregistered land must be protected either by the deposit of **title** deeds or by registration as a **land charge** (see Section 5.4.2). Where a mortgage has to be registered as a C(i) land charge (legal mortgage) or a C(iii) land charge (equitable mortgage of a legal **estate**), its priority is ranked according to the date of registration, not the date of its creation. Subject to fraud or negligence, the general rules are that:

▷ any legal mortgage accompanied by the deposit of title deeds takes priority over all mortgages except an earlier mortgage which was properly registered on the Land Charges Register; and
▷ any mortgage without deposit of title deeds is subject to:
 – any earlier mortgage with deposit of deeds; and
 – any other mortgage which was properly registered on the Land Charges Register.

11.7.4 Mortgages of an equitable interest in any land

In the rare case where the interest mortgaged is an **equitable** interest under a **trust**, the mortgages rank according to the order in which notice of the mortgage was received by the **trustees**, regardless of whether the title is registered or unregistered (LPA 1925, s 137).

11.8 Conclusion

The law of mortgages demonstrates the tensions that exist between the various approaches to ownership of land, especially where the same land is being used as a home and as security for a loan. The case of *Royal Bank of Scotland plc v Etridge (No 2)* (see Section 11.4.4) is an example of how the courts have decided where to draw the line between commercial expediency and the need to protect the vulnerable. Institutional lenders will be alerted more frequently than before to the possibility that undue influence may have taken place, but it will not be difficult for them to discharge their obligations. The use of the mortgage of family property remains such an important source of capital for small businesses that any shift in the balance towards the further protection of co-owners would limit that source of financial provision. Equally, if the restrictions on lenders are eased too much, the consequences will be unacceptable for vulnerable and emotionally involved occupiers who have been persuaded by their partners in financial difficulties to agree to a risky mortgage loan.

The law of mortgages also illustrates very clearly the difference between legal rules and what really happens: in every part of this area of law, theory and practice diverge. There is no reason why the rules need to be so complex. The anachronistic theoretical foundations and the miscellaneous protections offered by a random combination of common law and equitable and statutory rules could easily be replaced by new interests in land that simply provide security for the loan, as proposed by the Law Commission in 1991 (Law Com No 204). The fact that Parliament has not acted upon the Law Commission's proposals suggests, however, that behind the façade of unchanging concepts and rules, the law and those who use it have proved flexible enough to provide an adequate response to social and economic change. Problems may arise, especially when the economic climate is particularly harsh, but to date it has proved possible to adjust the existing system rather than replace it. Much of this adjustment is achieved voluntarily through UK Finance (a new trade organisation created in July 2017 incorporating, among others, the Council of Mortgage Lenders; see www.cml.org.uk/home) with the occasional direct intervention by Parliament (as, for example, with the Mortgage Repossessions (Protection of Tenants etc) Act 2010).

Summary

11.1 Mortgages are very important to the ownership and utilisation of land. However, the different demands made of land (and of these various functions – e.g. shelter, security, direct or indirect investment) make it difficult to balance competing interests when a dispute occurs.

11.2 Lawyers today use the word 'mortgage':

▶ to describe the relationship between a landowner and a money-lender (the landowner creates a charge over the land in favour of the lender); and

▶ to refer to the interest granted as security (the charge).

11.3 Legal mortgages are made by deed and must usually be completed by registration. Equitable mortgages may be of a legal or equitable interest. Legal interests may be mortgaged equitably by a contract to grant a legal mortgage or by equitable charge. Equitable interests can also be mortgaged by conveyance and reconveyance.

11.4 The borrower's rights include:

▶ the right to redeem the mortgage (the equitable right of redemption);

▶ the equitable right not to have the equitable right to redeem restricted; and

▶ equitable rights (reinforced by statute) not to have to suffer unconscionable or oppressive terms.

The lender must take care to avoid being fixed with the undue influence or the misrepresentation of a mortgagee over a surety where there is a non-commercial relationship between the two.

11.5 The legal lender has a number of remedies available. The most important are:

▶ the right to take possession of property (mortgagors of residential premises are given limited protection by statute); and

▶ the power of sale.

11.6 Equitable mortgagees and chargees may have fewer rights than legal lenders.

11.7 Where there is a succession of mortgages, the rules of priority (which differ depending on the type of land and the type of mortgage) are applied to decide in what order the lenders should have their money repaid.

Exercises

 11.1 Complete the online quiz on the topics covered in this chapter on the companion website.

11.2 Critically discuss the extent to which the law protects a mortgagor from being unjustifiably dispossessed of their home by a mortgagee, and consider whether these safeguards are adequate in modern economic conditions.

11.3 Clayton owns a freehold shop with a flat above, where he lives with Emily, who has an equitable share in the land. For some years, he has run a business selling computer games from the shop. A couple of years ago, a rival company set up nearby and took away most of Clayton's trade. Last year, in order to clear his previous mortgage and his other debts and to provide a financial restructuring of the business, he borrowed £150,000 on mortgage from Sharks Ltd, who gave him documents for Emily to sign. Emily signed them but she did so without reading them when Clayton told her that they were 'just something about my will'. The interest rate was set at 5 per cent above the bank rate.

The restructuring has not worked out, and in the past six months Clayton has been unable to make any repayment. There is little or no equity in the property. Advise Emily.

 You can find suggested answer plans to exercises 11.2 and 11.3 on the companion website.

Further reading

Brown, 'The Consumer Credit Act 2006: Real Additional Mortgagor Protection?' (2007) 71 Conv 316

McMurtry, 'Mortgage Default and Repossession: Procedure and Policy in the Post-*Norgan* Era' (2007) 58 NILQ 194

Rook, *Property Law and Human Rights* (Blackstone Press 2001)

Thompson, 'The Cumulative Range of a Mortgagee's Remedies' [2002] Conv 53

Chapter 12

Covenants in freehold land

- ▶ **Benefit** – the right to enforce a covenant.
- ▶ **Burden** – the obligation to perform a covenant.
- ▶ **Restrictive covenant** – a negative covenant; one that requires the covenantee to refrain from certain actions.

12.1 The case of the disputed roof

In 1960, Mr Garland decided to divide Walford House, in the Somerset village of Combwich, into two separate dwellings. As the building was roughly L-shaped, it was relatively easily divided between the leg (which became Walford Cottage) and the larger foot (which continued to be known as Walford House). However, the structure of the building meant that the roof of Walford House also covered one end of Walford Cottage.

In August 1960, Mr Garland conveyed Walford Cottage to its new owners, and in the years that followed, both the cottage and the house changed hands several times. By 1984, Mr and Mrs Rhone owned the cottage, and Mrs Barnard owned the house. Unfortunately, Mrs Barnard seems not to have paid too much attention to the part of her roof that protected the cottage, and by the beginning of 1984 Mr and Mrs Rhone were complaining of leaks into one of their bedrooms. Although Mrs Barnard arranged for some repairs to be carried out, the Rhones were not satisfied. Eventually, after being refused access to the roof to carry out further repairs, Mr and Mrs Rhone commenced court proceedings. Not long afterwards, Mrs Barnard died, and responsibility for defending the claim fell to the executor of her will, Mrs Stephens.

In support of their claim, Mr and Mrs Rhone pointed to clause 3 of the original conveyance of Walford Cottage in 1960:

> 3. The vendor [Mr Garland] hereby covenants for himself and his successors in title owner or occupiers for the time being of the property known as Walford House aforesaid to maintain to the reasonable satisfaction of the purchasers and their successors in title such part of the roof of Walford House aforesaid as lies above the property conveyed in wind and water tight condition.

This clause contains a formal promise by Mr Garland that, if effective, gives the owners of Walford Cottage the right to force the owner of Walford House to repair the relevant section of the roof and to recover damages if it is not properly maintained. This type of promise is quite different from an **easement** (considered in Chapter 10).

Easements allow landowner A to use land belonging to landowner B. Covenants enable landowner A directly to control what landowner B does on B's land. In many ways, Mr Garland's promise is similar to the sort of covenant that might be found in a lease, but for the fact that both the house and the cottage are **freehold** land. Like leasehold covenants, freehold covenants arise out of a contract. However, unlike leasehold covenants, neither **privity of estate** nor the Landlord and Tenant (Covenants) Act 1995 (see Chapter 8) are relevant to the relationship between successors to separate freehold titles.

In order to find an answer to a question concerning freehold covenants, it is necessary to establish the relationships of the claimant and the defendant to the promise which has been, or may be, broken. This can be conveniently done using a simple diagram, as in Figure 12.1. The vertical line represents the promise, with the covenantor (the person who made the promise) at the top and the covenantee (the person benefiting from the promise) at the bottom. Any transfer of either of the parcels of land is shown by a horizontal line. In most cases, it will be easy to identify the original parties to the covenant, as they will be named in the documentation.

In *Rhone v Stephens* [1994] 2 AC 310 (HL), Mr Garland is the covenantor (he made the promise), and the original purchaser of the cottage is the covenantee. The key relationships in the case are summarised in Figure 12.1. Whether the Rhones could use the promise made by Mr Garland to force Mrs Stephens to carry out the work to the roof depended upon the answers to two questions:

1. Had the burden of the covenant passed to Mrs Stephens?
2. Had the benefit of the covenant passed to Mr and Mrs Rhone?

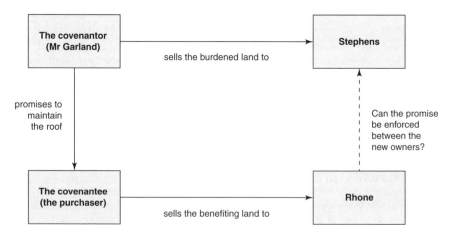

Figure 12.1 *Rhone v Stephens* [1994] 2 AC 310 (HL)

In order to find the answers to these questions, the rules of law and equity considered in Sections 12.3–12.5 must be applied in turn. A 'map' of these sections is provided in Figure 12.2. How these rules might be applied to answering a problem question is shown in Figure 12.4, later in this chapter.

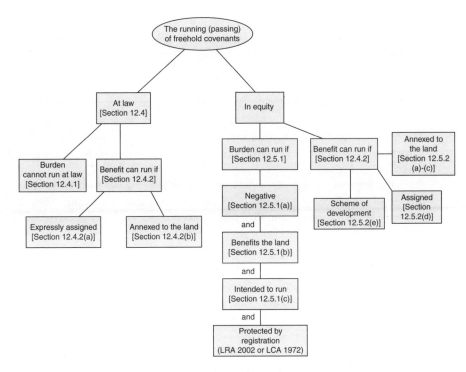

Figure 12.2 The passing of freehold covenants at law and in equity

12.2 A brief history of freehold covenants

It has long been possible for the *benefit* of a contract (such as a freehold covenant) to be transferred to a third party. There is also a long-established rule that the burden of a freehold covenant cannot be attached to land so as to bind buyers of that land. This is often referred to as the rule in *Austerberry* v *Oldham Corp*, after the decision of the Court of Appeal in that case ((1885) LR 29 Ch D 750 (CA)). Despite its long pedigree, this rule has a number of disadvantages, something which the courts of equity had begun to address even before the decision in *Austerberry* itself. By the end of the nineteenth century, it was accepted that the *burden* of a freehold covenant could be attached to land (affecting anyone who owned the land), provided that the terms of the covenant were 'restrictive'. Restrictive covenants are promises that prevent the owner from doing something. Even today, the burden of restrictive covenants can only pass in **equity**. Consequently, they must be protected by registration (see Sections 4.5.1 and 5.4.2(d)), and the remedies for the breach of such covenants are discretionary (see Section 1.3.2(b)).

During the nineteenth century, the courts were concerned with finding a balance between protecting third-party interests in land and encouraging land development, themes which also run through the law of **leases** and **easements**. Perhaps inevitably, therefore, the courts adopted the established policy test of whether the covenant 'touches and concerns' or 'accommodates' the land concerned (see leasehold covenants in Section 8.4.1 and easements in Section 10.5.2). *Tulk* v *Moxhay* (1848) 41 ER 1143 (Ch) is an early case in which a court enforced a covenant on freehold land against a successor to the original covenantor. Mr Tulk sold freehold land in Leicester Square in London, and the buyer promised, on behalf of himself and his successors in **title**, to:

> keep and maintain the said parcel of ground and square garden, and the iron railing around the same in its [present] form and in sufficient and proper repair, as a square garden and pleasure ground, in an open state, uncovered with any buildings, in a neat and ornamental order.

The land changed hands several times, and a later owner decided to build on the garden, although he had known about the covenant before he bought the land and had paid less because of it. In a dramatic decision, the Court of Chancery allowed Mr Tulk, the original covenantee to whom the promise had been made, to enforce the burden of the covenant against a successor of the original covenantor. The decision was based on the doctrine of **notice** and the inequitable consequences that would follow if (in the words of Lord Cottenham at 778):

> the original purchaser should be able to sell the property the next day for a greater price, in consideration of the assignee being allowed to escape from the liability which he had himself undertaken.

In succeeding decisions, equity came to provide a cheap and effective planning law nearly a hundred years before the State seriously took on the control of land use. Many urban areas have their present shape and character because of covenants imposed by careful developers. Nowadays the public restrictions on the use of land (for example, planning law and building regulations) are normally of greater significance, but covenants are still imposed and enforced because they allow for more detailed and individual control than public planning law can provide. According to the Law Commission's Consultation Paper 186, 2008, some 79 per cent of **registered** freehold titles are subject to restrictive covenants. However, although covenants are still among the main legal strategies used to control the use of land, the underlying rules are unnecessarily complex and anachronistic. The LPA 1925 contained a statutory scheme for modifying and discharging obsolete covenants (see Section 12.9.2), together with a number of word-saving provisions. The benefits of some of the latter have been considerable, due to benevolent interpretation by the courts (s 78, for example; see Section 12.5.2(a)). However, it is still necessary to track the benefit and the burden using two different sets of rules, and the burden of a positive covenant cannot run under either set. Land lawyers have responded, as they so often do, by making the best of the rules that are available, not least by developing a number of indirect methods of enforcing positive covenants (see Section 12.6). Inevitably, such methods tend to add a further level of complexity and more possible pitfalls for the unwary.

Reform of covenants in freehold land has been considered several times since 1925. In 1984, the Law Commission proposed a new and simple law to govern the running of benefit and burden at law of both restrictive and positive covenants through the creation of two new legal interests in land, 'Neighbour Obligations' and 'Development Obligations' ((1984) Law Com No 127). This proposal was supplemented in 1991 by the recommendation that a restrictive covenant cease to be enforceable after 80 years unless the owner of the benefit could show it was not obsolete ((1991) Law Com No 201). The Law Commission's most recent proposals can be found in *Making Land Law Work: Easements, Covenants and Profits à Prendre* (Law Com 327, 2011). They will be reviewed in the final section of this chapter.

12.3   The running of covenants: the basic rules

The basic pattern for determining whether a **freehold** covenant can be enforced is relatively straightforward, provided one remembers four things:

1. there are two independent sets of rules: *legal* and *equitable*;
2. each set of rules is divided into subsets of rules for the passing of the benefit and the burden, respectively;
3. the legal and equitable rules relating to passing the benefit are similar, but not identical; and
4. the burden can only pass in equity.

The sets of rules are largely the result of case law, and different authors tend to classify the contents of each set slightly differently. The statement of the rules that follows seeks to be as simple and accurate as possible. The rules are summarised in Table 12.1.

Table 12.1   Summary of the rules relating to the running of freehold covenants

	Benefit	Burden

At law (see Section 12.4)	1. It is expressly assigned (LPA 1925, s 136); or
	2. (a) it benefits the land; and
	   (b) the covenantee had a legal estate in the benefiting land; and
	   (c) the claimant has a legal estate in the benefiting land; and
	   (d) it was intended to run.
		Not usually possible.

In equity (see Section 12.5)	1. It benefits the land; and
	2. (a) LPA 1925, s 78 applies; or
	   (b) it was expressly or impliedly annexed to the benefiting land; or
	   (c) it was assigned to the claimant.
		Under the rule in *Tulk* v *Moxhay* (1848) 41 ER 1143 (Ch):
		1. it is restrictive; and
		2. it benefited land owned by the covenantee and now owned by the claimant or part of a scheme of development; and
		3. it was intended to run (LPA 1925, s 79); and
		4. it is protected by registration; and
		5. there is no reason to deny the claimant an equitable remedy.

12.4   The running of covenants at law

12.4.1   The running of the burden at law

As indicated in Section 12.2, the common law did not (and still does not) allow the burden of a **freehold** covenant to be attached to land so as to bind buyers. In *Austerberry* v *Oldham Corp* (1885) LR 29 Ch D 750 (CA), the Court of Appeal applied the contractual doctrine that only a party to an agreement can be burdened by it. Over a hundred years later, Lord Templeman had no hesitation in accepting the rule in his speech in *Rhone* v *Stephens* [1994] 2 AC 310 (HL) at 316–17:

> At common law a person cannot be made liable upon a contract unless he was a party to it ... As between persons interested in land other than as landlord and tenant, the benefit of a covenant may run with the land at law but not the burden.

Despite the apparent certainty of this rule, conveyancers have, with the cooperation of the courts, devised a number of indirect methods of enforcing positive covenants. The main examples are briefly explained in Section 12.6.

12.4.2 The running of the benefit at law

In answering the question 'Can the claimant sue at law?' (or 'Has the benefit passed to the claimant at law?'), two separate rules must be examined. The first provides for the express transfer of the benefit of the contract, and the second for the automatic running (implied transfer) of the benefit when the land is sold.

12.4.2(a) Express assignment

Anyone can expressly transfer the benefit of any contract to which they are a party, provided that the covenant is not a purely personal one. Under section 136 of the LPA 1925, the benefit of a promise relating to the use of land can be sold and will be enforceable at law by the buyer, provided that the **assignment** is in writing and express notice in writing has been given to the covenantor.

12.4.2(b) Running with the land

If there has been no express assignment of the benefit of a covenant, the law allows the benefit to pass automatically with the benefited land if:

1. the covenant benefits the land; and
2. the covenantee had a legal **estate** in the land when the promise was made; and
3. the claimant now has a legal estate in that land; and
4. the benefit was intended to pass.

For the covenant to benefit the land, it must be shown that the promise affects the land itself rather than its owner; that is to say, it must 'touch and concern' the land (see the discussion of *P & A Swift Investments* v *Combined English Stores Group plc* [1989] AC 632 (HL) in Section 8.4.1). There is some question about whether it is essential for the original parties to the covenant to have intended that its benefit should pass, as this intention is not included in the requirements set out by the House of Lords in *P & A Swift Investments*. Practically, however, the question is unlikely to be significant because of section 78 of the LPA 1925. This section provides that the benefit of a promise which 'relates to' (that is, touches and concerns) land is deemed to be made not only with the covenantee but also with all their successors in **title**. Section 78 means that anyone who owns a legal estate in land automatically has the benefit of any covenant made after 1925 which touches and concerns that land (see, also, Section 12.5.2(a)).

The importance of section 78 can be seen in the case of *Smith* v *River Douglas Catchment Board* [1949] 2 KB 500 (CA). In 1938, the Board promised Ellen Smith that it would maintain the banks of the Eller Brook adjoining her land in Lancashire. She sold the land to John Smith (the first claimant), and he leased it to Snipes Hall Farm Ltd. When the river flooded the land because of the Board's failure to carry out proper maintenance, John Smith and the tenant company tried to recover their losses from the Board, arguing that the benefit of the covenant had automatically passed to them when they acquired the land. It was held that:

1. the covenant did benefit their land;
2. it had been made with a legal owner of the land;
3. the present claimants were both legal owners; and
4. the benefit of the covenant had been intended to run by virtue of section 78 of the LPA 1925.

Both claimants could therefore claim damages for the Board's breach of covenant. The Farm, as **tenant**, succeeded because section 78 enables any legal owner (freeholder or leaseholder) to enjoy the benefit of a covenant relating to the land.

12.4.3 Applying the legal rules to *Rhone v Stephens*

To enforce the covenant at law, Mr and Mrs Rhone must demonstrate that they have the benefit of the covenant and that Mrs Stephens is subject to the burden. There is little doubt that the Rhones have the benefit of covenant, as the promise made by the original covenantor satisfies the requirements set out in *Smith v River Douglas Catchment Board*. However, Mrs Stephens cannot be subject to the burden of the covenant at law because of the rule in *Austerberry v Oldham Corp* (see Section 12.4.1).

12.5 The running of covenants in equity

12.5.1 The running of the burden in equity

In *Tulk v Moxhay* (1848) 41 ER 1143 (Ch) (the facts of which are set out in Section 12.2), Cottenham LC granted the claimant an **injunction** allowing him to enforce a covenant against the successor in **title** of the original covenantor. This appeared to be a straightforward decision. Lord Cottenham said, at 1145, that if the court had failed to enforce the promise:

> it would [have been] impossible for an owner of land to sell part of it without incurring the risk of rendering what he retains worthless.

This is true, although it was, and still is, possible for a landowner to maintain control over the land being sold by granting a long **lease** (with the appropriate covenants) instead of parting with the **freehold**. The leasehold covenants would be enforceable against subsequent assignees of the lease.

The decision in *Tulk v Moxhay* turned on the question of **notice** (see Section 5.2.2). If the purchaser of the affected land was found to have had notice of the burden of the covenant, then equity required that they be bound by it. This potentially opened the way to allowing the burden of all sorts of covenants, as well as other kinds of non-property obligations, to bind successors in title. However, later in the nineteenth century, judges seem to have thought that the now depressed land market required restrictions on land use to be kept to a minimum in order to encourage purchasers. This may also explain why the effect of *Tulk v Moxhay* came to be limited by increasingly complex and technical requirements.

Today, the burden of a covenant runs in equity if:

1. it is restrictive; and
2. it benefits land once owned by the covenantee and now owned by the claimant or is part of a scheme of development (see Section 12.5.2(e)); and
3. it was intended to run with the land.

Further, because this is merely an **equitable** interest:

4. the notice or registration rules must be complied with (these rules are set out in Chapters 4 and 5); and
5. the claimant must have 'clean hands' (that is, the claimant must act fairly; see Section 1.3.2(b)).

12.5.1(a) The covenant must be restrictive

Only the burden of 'covenants restricting the mode of using the land' can be enforced under the rule in *Tulk* v *Moxhay* (*Haywood* v *The Brunswick Permanent Benefit Building Society* (1881) 8 QBD 403). Whether a covenant is 'restrictive' depends on its substance, not its form. For example, a covenant to maintain the land uncovered with buildings, although positive in terms of the words used, is negative in substance because the covenantor can comply by doing nothing (that is, without spending money). However, a covenant not to allow a building to fall into disrepair is a positive covenant, because it requires the covenantor to meet the expense of any necessary repairs.

The rule that equity will enforce the burden of only restrictive covenants was restated by the House of Lords in *Rhone* v *Stephens* [1994] 2 AC 310 (HL), the facts of which are set out in Section 12.1. Lord Templeman reviewed all the authorities and concluded that the rule of restrictive covenants is a rule of property: an owner of land cannot exercise a right which has never been transferred to them. However, as he explained, at 69, equity follows the law, and:

> cannot compel an owner to comply with a positive covenant entered into by his predecessors in title without flatly contradicting the common law rule that a person cannot be made liable upon a contract unless he was a party to it. Enforcement of a positive covenant lies in contract; a positive covenant compels an owner to exercise his rights. Enforcement of a negative covenant lies in property; a negative covenant deprives the owner of a right over property.

He also believed that any judicial alteration of the rule now would cause chaos for landowners.

12.5.1(b) The covenant must benefit the claimant's land

The claimant's land (the land once owned by the covenantee) must be identifiable and either benefited ('accommodated') by the covenant or part of a scheme of development (see Section 12.5.2(e)). The point here is that equity will only enforce a restrictive covenant if its purpose is to protect the value and amenity of the covenantee's neighbouring land. So, for example, a covenant confining the use of the site to a broadcasting centre for the BBC was held not to bind the land in the case of *Cosmichome Ltd* v *Southampton City Council* [2013] 1 WLR 2436 (Ch), as it was impossible to demonstrate how the covenantee's land benefited from it. The person trying to enforce the covenant need not own a legal **estate** in the land and need not have bought the whole of the covenantee's land, so long as the part they own is capable of benefiting from the promise. In *London CC v Allen* [1914] 3 KB 642 (CA), Mr Allen promised the council that he would not build on a strip of land needed for the continuation of a road. The burdened land was ultimately conveyed to Mr Allen's wife, and Mrs Allen proceeded to build on it. It was held, with great regret, that the claimant authority could not enforce the covenant because it had sold the benefiting land. Local authorities and certain other bodies, such as the National Trust, are now statutorily exempt from this rule.

In *Dano Ltd v Earl Cadogan* [2004] 1 P & CR 13 (CA), the sixth Earl Cadogan had conveyed land in 1929 to a local authority, which covenanted with him on behalf of itself and its successors that the land would be used for no other purpose than the housing of the working classes 'so long as such adjoining or neighbouring property or any part thereof forms part of the Cadogan Settled Estate in Chelsea but not further or otherwise'. In the 1960s the Cadogan family rearranged its affairs, and the Settled Estate came to an end. Later, Dano Ltd acquired the land from the local authority and, wishing to build private houses on part of the site, sought a declaration that the covenant was unenforceable. Although the neighbouring land was still in the Cadogan family, it no longer formed part of the 'Cadogan Settled Estate in Chelsea', and the Court of Appeal held that this meant that there was no longer any land capable of benefiting from the covenant.

12.5.1(c) The parties must intend the covenant to run

This intention will usually be expressed in the document containing the covenant, but if not it may be implied by section 79 of the LPA 1925. Section 79 does not apply if the covenant was made before 1926, nor if the person making the covenant indicates that section 79 is not intended to apply to the transaction. Usually, such intention will be clearly stated in the wording of the covenant. However, the courts can construe the document as a whole in order to determine the intention of the original parties, as the Court of Appeal did when deciding that the site of Oxford United's new stadium and conference centre was not subject to a covenant prohibiting its use or the sale of alcohol (*Morrells of Oxford Ltd v Oxford United FC Ltd* [2001] Ch 459 (CA)). In *Roadside Group Ltd v Zara Commercial Ltd* [2010] EWHC 1950 (Ch), the question was whether a user covenant in a lease was binding on a subtenant as the successor in title of the **tenant** by virtue of section 79 so as to make the tenant directly liable for the subtenant's breach of covenant. Kitchin J concluded that the difference in wording between the user covenant and the other covenants in the lease indicated that the parties had intended to limit the scope of the user covenant and that to read the words of section 79 into the user covenant would be inconsistent with that intention. The landlord could, however, take proceedings directly against the subtenant (see Section 8.4.4).

12.5.2 The running of the benefit in equity

Equity also developed its own rules about the running of the benefit of a covenant, based on the legal rules:

- the covenant must touch and concern the land of the covenantee; and
- the benefit of the covenant must have passed to the claimant.

There are three ways in which the benefit of the covenant may pass to the claimant:

1. by annexation (statutory, express or implied); or
2. by **assignment**; or
3. under a scheme of development.

12.5.2(a) Section 78 annexation

For the benefit of a covenant to be annexed to the land it is necessary to establish that this was the intention of the original parties. Traditionally this was dependent upon how the court construed the document containing the covenant. However, the decision of the Court of Appeal in *Federated Homes Ltd* v *Mill Lodge Properties Ltd* [1980] 1 WLR 594 (CA) means that almost all covenants made since 1925 are deemed to be annexed to the land by section 78 of the LPA 1925.

The facts of the *Federated Homes* case were relatively simple and are shown diagrammatically in Figure 12.3. M Ltd owned a large estate, which was divided into three plots: blue, green and red. They sold the blue land to Mill Lodge Properties, who promised, for the benefit of the green and red land, that they would not build more than 300 houses on it. Both the green and the red land then came into the hands of Federated Homes. There was an unbroken chain of express assignments of the benefit of Mill Lodge's promise with the green land, but not with the red. Assignment of benefit is discussed in Section 12.5.2(d).

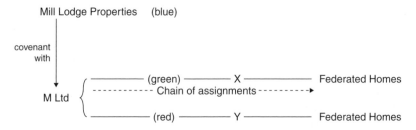

Figure 12.3 *Federated Homes Ltd* v *Mill Lodge Properties Ltd* [1980] 1 WLR 594 (CA)

Federated Homes successfully claimed an injunction for breach of the covenant when Mill Lodge began building 32 houses more than the covenant permitted. The defendant's arguments centred on technical details of the planning permission, but this was decided in the claimant's favour. It then became clear that, as owners of the *green* land with an unbroken chain of express assignments, Federated Homes had the benefit of the covenant and could enforce it against Mill Lodge. However, the judge at first instance went further and said that, under section 62 of the LPA 1925 (by which a conveyance of land transfers all rights which benefit it), Federated Homes could also enforce the covenant as owners of the *red* land.

The Court of Appeal agreed with the judge on the planning issue and the green land, but took a different view on the red land. Rather than section 62, they chose to use section 78 of the LPA 1925 to pass the benefit of the covenant to the claimants. Until then, it had been thought that section 78 was merely a word-saving provision, but Brightman LJ rejected this interpretation because, as he said at 604, it seemed to him to 'fly in the face of the wording of the section'.

The widest interpretation of *Federated Homes* is that the benefit of any covenant made since 1925 automatically runs in equity if it touches and concerns the land. This represents the radical obliteration of a century of case law about the annexation or assignment of freehold covenants. Annexation and assignment cases (briefly outlined in Sections 12.5.2(b), (c) and (d)) had been lovingly analysed by generations of conveyancers, academics and students. Although the Court of Appeal's decision surprised many commentators, *Federated Homes* has not been challenged, but the courts have had to address two questions not answered in the original case:

1. Is it necessary to identify the land benefiting from the covenant?
2. Can the parties displace the effect of section 78 by expressing a contrary intention?

Both of these questions were considered by the Court of Appeal in *Crest Nicholson Residential (South) Ltd v McAllister* [2004] 1 WLR 2409 (CA). Chadwick LJ answered the first question by confirming that the requirement for express annexation (set out in *Marquess of Zetland v Driver* [1939] Ch 1 (CA)) also applied to section 78 cases; that is, the land which is intended to be benefited by the covenant must be sufficiently defined so as to be easily ascertainable.

The second question was answered at first instance in *Roake v Chadha* [1984] 1 WLR 40 (Ch). In that case, there was a 50-year-old covenant not to build more than one house per plot on land in a London suburb, and a further clause in the conveyance that the benefit of the covenant would not pass unless it was expressly assigned. All the land changed hands, without an express assignment of the benefit of the covenant, and a later owner of the burdened land wanted to build another house in his garden. Judge Paul Baker QC held that there was nothing in the *Federated Homes* decision that prevented the parties to the covenant preventing it being annexed to the land by section 78 if that was their intention, saying, at 46:

> The true position as I see it is that even where a covenant is deemed to be made with successors in title as s.78 requires, one still has to construe the covenant as a whole to see whether the benefit of the covenant is annexed.

The effect of expressing contrary intention was contentious because, unlike sections 62 and 79 of the LPA 1925, there is no provision in section 78 allowing the parties to negate its effect by expressing their wish to do so. In the *Crest Nicholson* case, Chadwick LJ confirmed the decision in *Roake v Chadha*. He explained that the wording of section 78 means there is no need for it to include the words 'unless a contrary intention is expressed', because (at [43]):

> The qualification 'subject to contrary intention' is implicit in the definition of 'successors in title' which appears in section 78(1); that is the effect of the words 'the land of the covenantee intended to be benefited'. If the terms in which the covenant is imposed show ... [that the parties did not intend the benefit of the covenant to be annexed to the land] then the owners and occupiers of the land sold off in those circumstances are not 'owners and occupiers for the time being of the land of the covenantee intended to be benefited'; and so are not 'successors in title' of the original covenantee for the purposes of section 78(1).

The same argument does not apply to section 79, because of the specific meaning given to 'successors in title' in section 79(2).

Thus, the effect of *Federated Homes* is to annex the benefit of the covenant to each and every part of the land unless the parties have expressed their intention that this should not be the case and provided that the covenant was made after 1925 (*Seymour Road (Southampton) Ltd v Williams* [2010] EWHC 111 (Ch)).

12.5.2(b) Express annexation

In cases where section 78 does not apply, it is necessary to fall back on the old concepts of annexation and assignment created in nineteenth-century cases. When considering whether the benefit of a covenant falling outside section 78 has been annexed to the land, the situation is the reverse of that when section 78 of the LPA 1925 applies. For the benefit of such a covenant to be annexed it must be possible to establish that this was the positive intention of the parties from the text of the covenant in the original **deed** of grant. The best evidence for this is the use of express words to this effect, similar to those used in *Rogers* v *Hosegood* [1900] 2 Ch 388 (CA). In 1869, the Duke of Bedford had bought a plot of land in Kensington and had promised not to build more than one house on it. The deed stated that this was:

> with intent that the covenants might so far as possible bind the premises ... and might enure to the benefit of the [sellers] ... their heirs and assigns and others claiming under them to all or any of their land adjoining or near to the said premises.

The Duke's land passed to Hosegood, who decided to build a large block of flats on it. Rogers, an owner of adjoining land, wanted to prevent the development. The burden of the covenant had clearly passed to Hosegood, so the question was whether the benefit had passed to Rogers. It was held that the benefit had been annexed to his land by the words of the deed, so anyone who subsequently owned that land could enforce the covenant.

12.5.2(c) Implied annexation

If the original document lacks the kind of wording used in the covenant in *Rogers* v *Hosegood* (see Section 12.5.2(b)), it may be possible for the successor to the covenantee to show that annexation can be implied by considering the wording of the original document in the context of all the surrounding circumstances; see *Marten* v *Flight Refuelling Ltd (No 1)* [1962] Ch 115 (Ch).

12.5.2(d) Assignment

If there is no annexation, the benefit may still have been passed by a chain of assignments such as existed for the benefit of the green land in *Federated Homes* (see Section 12.5.2(a)). If there is no complete express chain, there may be an implied assignment of the benefit. For this to happen, the covenant must have been intended to benefit the land of the original covenantee, and the successor who is attempting to enforce the covenant must have had the benefit expressly assigned to them. In *Newton Abbot Cooperative Society* v *Williamson & Treadgold Ltd* [1952] Ch 286 (Ch), a covenant preventing the use of a shop as an ironmongery was not expressed to be for the benefit of the land belonging to the covenantee. The judge, however, was able to look at the surrounding circumstances and found (at 297) that the covenantee (who herself ran an ironmongery and understandably did not want competition):

> took the covenant restrictive of the user of the defendants' premises for the benefit of her own business of ironmonger and of her property ... where at all material times she was carrying on that business.

When the covenantee died, her heir received the land and the benefit of the covenant, which he could then assign expressly to his successor, who could enforce it.

12.5.2(e) Schemes of development

A final method by which successors in title of the original covenantee might enforce covenants is through what is known as a 'scheme of development'. A scheme of development (or 'building scheme') is another creation of equity and provides a useful method for the modern developer to create and preserve new estates. If the conditions for a scheme are fulfilled, then the burdens (provided the covenants have been protected by registration) and the benefits of restrictive covenants which touch and concern the land run automatically to all owners covered by the scheme, thus greatly simplifying the question of whether one owner can stop another breaching a covenant. In the recent case of *Birdlip Ltd* v *Hunter* [2017] 1 P & CR 1 (CA), Lewison LJ summarised the typical characteristics of such a scheme at [20].

1. It applies to a defined area.
2. Owners of properties within that area have purchased their properties from a common owner.
3. Each of the properties is burdened by covenants which were intended to be mutually enforceable as between the several owners.
4. The limits of that defined area are known to each of the purchasers.
5. The common owner is themself bound by the scheme, which crystallises on the occasion of the first sale of a plot within the defined area, with the consequence that they are not entitled to dispose of plots within that area otherwise than on the terms of the scheme.
6. The effect of the scheme will bind future purchasers of land falling within the area, potentially forever.

The first known scheme was created in 1767 and upheld in 1866. A large number were created in the nineteenth century and upheld by the courts, but after 1889 the number of successful schemes began to fall. Strict rules were laid down in the judgment in *Elliston* v *Reacher* [1908] 2 Ch 374 (Ch), and later judges treated them as if they were part of a statute. According to *Elliston* v *Reacher*:

- there had to be one seller; and
- the plots must have been laid out in advance; and
- mutual restrictions must have been established for the mutual benefit of the plots; and
- the purchasers of the plots must have known about the intended mutual enforceability.

Between 1908 and the 1960s, only two schemes were successfully enforced in reported cases, but then the climate appears to have changed again, and the rules in *Elliston* v *Reacher* relaxed. In *Re Dolphin's Conveyance* [1970] Ch 654 (Ch), there was no common vendor, nor were the plots laid out in advance. However, the local authority in Birmingham was prevented from developing the site because it was held that a building scheme had been created and that the proposed development would have been in breach of covenant. Stamp J said that the rules set out in *Elliston* v *Reacher* were only part of a wider rule, and that a scheme arose because of the existence of 'the common interest and the common intention actually expressed in the conveyances themselves' (at 664). The approach taken by Stamp J in *Dolphin's Conveyance* has stood the test of nearly half a century, and was most recently restated by Lewison LJ in *Birdlip Ltd* v *Hunter*, at [21]:

> There are two prerequisites of a scheme of mutual covenants namely: (1) the identification of the land to which the scheme relates, and (2) an acceptance by each purchaser of part of the lands from the common vendor that the benefit of the covenants into which he has entered will enure to the vendor and to others deriving title from him and that he correspondingly will enjoy the benefit of covenants entered into by other purchasers of part of the land:

In other words, there must be:

- mutually binding covenants
- applying within a clearly defined and commonly understood area.

The question of whether the covenants are sufficiently mutual is concerned with both the content of the covenants (whether they are all in broadly the same terms) and the awareness of the original covenantors that they were part of a building scheme. In the case of *Small* v *Oliver & Saunders (Developments) Ltd* [2006] 3 EGLR 141 (Ch), the company had started to build a second house on land forming part of the garden of an existing house that it owned. This house was part of an impressive 'estate' built around a central golf course between 1922 and 1950, and both the house and its garden were subject to a covenant to use the land only as a private residence. Mr Small, who owned a house nearby, argued that the company was in breach of this covenant because it was using one part of the garden to gain access to the other part, where it was building the new house. The judge rejected the claim that there was a building scheme, because Mr Smith was unable to demonstrate that the various people who had originally purchased the houses on the estate had been aware of the reciprocal nature of the obligations contained in the covenants concerned. Mr Smith was, however, able to establish that the benefit of the covenant had been annexed to the land that he himself owned (not that this enabled him to prevent the construction of the new house; see Section 12.8).

With older developments, there are often problems in finding sufficient numbers of the original documents, and often the original owners are beyond recall as well. In cases where common interest and intention cannot be shown from the covenants, it seems that the courts will apply the rules in *Elliston* v *Reacher* as in *Emile Elias & Co Ltd* v *Pine Groves Ltd* [1993] 1 WLR 305 (PC), where the Privy Council emphasised the necessity for a 'common code of covenants' (at 309 and 311).

In *Stocks* v *Whitgift Homes* [2001] EWCA Civ 1732, a large residential estate of some 440 acres had been developed in the 1920s and 1930s. Some of the estate was clearly intended to be within a building scheme, but there was a good deal of uncertainty about the rest. In finding that no building scheme existed, even among owners of the properties situated within the area originally intended to be part of the scheme, Judge LJ stated, at [110], that:

> the authorities show that [a] number of characteristics must be established. Among them is certainty: otherwise, in relation to each plot of land said to fall within the scheme, the question will continually arise: does it or does it not so fall? More precisely, is it, or is it not subject to mutually enforceable benefits and obligations, and, if enforceable, by and against the owners of which plots? This essential requirement of certainty makes obvious practical sense.

12.5.3   Applying the equitable rules to *Rhone* v *Stephens*

The diagram in Figure 12.4 and a return to the facts of *Rhone* v *Stephens* (see Section 12.1) might help make the application of all these rules clearer. The question was whether Mr and Mrs Rhone had the benefit, and Mrs Stephens the burden, of the promise made by Mr Garland. There was, of course, no building scheme.

A glance at the summary of the rules relating to the benefit and the burden (see Table 12.1) shows that the strictest requirement relates to the running of the burden. This is, therefore, always the place to start in a problem of this kind, since otherwise you may go to all the trouble of tracing the benefit, only to find that the burden cannot run in any event.

To decide whether the burden has passed with the land, it is necessary to apply the **equitable** rules in *Tulk* v *Moxhay*, since the burden cannot run at law. It will already be apparent from Section 12.5.1(a) that in this case the covenant is positive in substance. Consequently, the burden cannot run in equity. This is despite the fact that the other rules in *Tulk* v *Moxhay* are almost certainly satisfied: the covenant did benefit the land of the covenantee (the original purchaser of the cottage), and there is no evidence of contrary intention to negate the section 79 of the LPA 1925 assumption that it was intended to run.

On the facts of *Rhone* v *Stephens*, it is, therefore, unnecessary to test whether the benefit has passed with the land to Mr and Mrs Rhone. It is important to note, however, that when testing whether the benefit has passed, it is not permissible to mix legal and equitable rules. *Burden and benefit must run in the same medium* (that is, both must run at law, or both must run in equity). In practice, this means that if the burdened land has changed hands, requiring equitable principles to be applied to the burden, then the equitable rules must also be used for the benefit.

12.6   Indirect methods of enforcing positive covenants

There are many circumstances where a covenantee may wish the burden of a positive covenant to bind the successor in **title** of the original covenantor and where the court's refusal to permit this will cause significant inconvenience (as in *Rhone* v *Stephens* [1994] 2 AC 310 (HL)). It is not surprising, therefore, that lawyers have devised a number of methods of effectively enforcing positive covenants, although each has its own limitations.

12.6.1   A chain of indemnity

If the original covenantor, and each of their successors in title, obtains an indemnity covenant from the next purchaser, the continuing liability of the original covenantor can be offset by a claim against the landowner in breach of the covenant. It is essential, however, that the 'chain' of indemnity covenants be complete.

12.6.2   Pure 'benefit and burden'

The burden of a positive covenant may bind a successor who wishes to assert the benefit of a covenanted obligation, provided that there is reciprocity between the benefit and burden. The classic illustration of this principle is *Halsall* v *Brizell* [1957] Ch 169 (Ch),

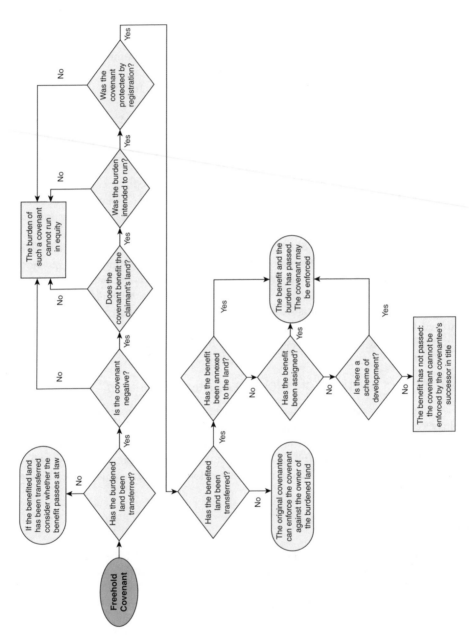

Figure 12.4 Applying the equitable rules to freehold covenants

in which Upjohn J held that the purchaser of a house on a residential estate could not enjoy the benefit of use of a private road without performing a freehold covenant to maintain it. However, unlike the doctrine of restrictive covenants (which creates an interest in the servient land), benefit and burden 'gives the third party nothing more than a personal right to enforce the covenant in equity against the registered proprietor' (per Patten LJ, *Goodman* v *Elwood* [2014] 2 WLR 967 (CA), [35]).

12.6.3   Rights of re-entry (see LPA 1925, s 1(2)(e))

The performance of a positive covenant can be attached to a right of re-entry that becomes exercisable if the covenant is breached. The right of re-entry, but not the covenant itself, would, if annexed to a **rentcharge**, run with the burdened land.

12.6.4   Leases

Since there is no prohibition on the transfer of a positive leasehold covenant, the landowner may prefer to grant a lease of the relevant part of their land (with appropriate covenants) rather than sell the **freehold**.

12.6.5   Commonhold

Under Part 1 of the Commonhold and Leasehold Reform Act 2002, it is possible for a development to be registered at the Land Registry by the freehold owner as a 'freehold estate in commonhold land'. The property is divided into 'units', each held by the unit owner on a freehold basis, with each freeholder owing obligations to the others through the medium of a Commonhold Association. Commonhold is examined in more detail in Section 6.5.

12.7   Section 56 LPA 1925 and the Contracts (Rights of Third Parties) Act 1999

Section 56 of the LPA 1925 may be relevant whenever the person claiming the benefit (or their predecessor in **title**) owned land nearby at the time the covenant was made. In a sense, it is a legal extension of **privity of contract** and provides that:

> A person may take ... the benefit of any ... covenant ... over or respecting land ... although he may not be named as a party to the conveyance or other instrument.

This is a way of giving the benefit of a covenant to someone other than those who are named in the deed, provided the covenant purports to be made with that person. The section applies if the person alleged to have the benefit of the covenant was identifiable in the covenant agreement and existed at the date of the covenant. The reason for these rules is that it would be unfair if the covenantor were effectively making their promise to everyone in the neighbourhood; they need to be able to identify, on the day they made the promise, the landowners who might be able to take action against them.

The rules were established in *Re Ecclesiastical Commissioners for England's Conveyance* [1936] Ch 430 (Ch). In that case, the court had to decide whether a large house near to Hampstead Heath in London was subject to a restrictive covenant.

The issue was whether neighbouring landowners had the right to enforce it, and this depended on whether the original landowners who had owned the neighbouring land at the time of the covenant could enforce it through section 56. A clause in the **conveyance** stated that the original covenantor made the promise, 'also as a separate covenant with … owners for the time being of land adjoining or adjacent to the said land hereby conveyed'. This was held to be enough for section 56 to apply. The neighbours were identifiable from the agreement and were in existence at its date. Their successors in title were able to claim the benefit from them by the usual rules for the running of the benefit, and thus were able to enforce the covenant.

For covenants made after 11th May 2000, the Contracts (Rights of Third Parties) Act 1999 can also be used in this situation. Under section 1 of the Act, a person who is not a party to the contract may enforce it if it purports to confer or expressly confers a benefit on them, so long as the contract identifies them by name, as a member of a class or as answering a particular description, even though they were not in existence when the contract was entered into. From its wording, it seems that operation of the Act is wider than section 56, since it will allow a landowner to enforce the benefit of a covenant even though it is not purported to be made with them and even though they might not have been identifiable when the covenant was created. However, there are unlikely to be a significant number of cases involving covenants using the 1999 Act as the provisions of section 56 of the LPA 1925 will usually be sufficient.

12.8 Remedies for breach of covenant

The **equitable** nature of restrictive covenants means that the burden of the covenant will need to be registered if it is to be enforced against a successor in **title** of the original covenantor. The detailed rules are examined in Chapters 4 and 5. Another implication of the rule that the burden of a restrictive covenant runs only in equity is that only equitable remedies are available to the courts when remedying any breach. In principle, therefore, a remedy will only be available if the wrong committed can be solved by an **injunction**. Further, all equitable remedies are given at the discretion of the court and can be refused if, for example, the claimant has unnecessarily delayed bringing their action or has otherwise acted improperly.

Although the usual remedy for the breach of a restrictive covenant will be a permanent injunction, the court has the power to award damages instead (but not in a case where an injunction could not be granted). The circumstances in which damages may properly be awarded in lieu of an injunction were summarised by A.L. Smith LJ in *Shelfer* v *City of London Electric Lighting Co (No 1)* [1895] 1 Ch 287 (CA), 322–3. Damages may be given in substitution for an injunction:

1. if the injury to the claimant's legal right is small, and
2. is one which is capable of being estimated in money, and
3. is one which can be adequately compensated by a small money payment, and
4. the case is one in which it would be oppressive to the defendant to grant an injunction.

For example, in *Small* v *Oliver & Saunders (Developments) Ltd* [2006] 3 EGLR 141 (Ch) (see Section 12.5.2(e)), the court took the view that it would be disproportionate to grant an injunction that would effectively prevent the defendant company from completing a nearly finished house. The claimant was awarded £3,270 as damages in lieu of an injunction.

The original covenantor will always be liable in contract law (unless a contrary intention is expressed in the contract), but the remedy against them can only be damages once they have parted with ownership of the burdened land.

12.9 Discharge and modification

Covenants are automatically ended ('discharged') in two ways: by the common law, and under statute. Statute also allows covenants to be modified. The power to discharge or modify covenants is important, because the very existence of the power encourages people to agree to waive covenants. Many cases do not go to litigation; it is often a question of the developer 'buying off' the covenants.

12.9.1 Common law

First, if the same person owns the burdened and benefiting lands, the covenant cannot be enforced: a person does not have rights against themself. However, if the covenant is part of a building scheme, life after death is possible: the covenants revive if the plots come into separate ownership again later.

Second, if the covenant has been abandoned, the courts will not enforce it. This was argued in *Chatsworth Estates* v *Fewell* [1931] 1 Ch 224 (Ch). In this case, there was a covenant on a house in a seaside resort restricting its use to that of a private dwelling. Thirty years later, the then owner started taking paying guests. The claimants warned him of the breach and asked whether he wished to apply to have the covenant modified or discharged under section 84 of the LPA 1925 (see Section 12.9.2), but he did nothing. When taken to court for the breach, he argued that the claimants had waived breaches by others in the neighbourhood and had therefore abandoned the benefit. The claimants won their **injunction** to end the breach. Abandonment is a question of fact in every case; here the essential residential character of the area remained, and the claimants could not be expected to conduct inquisitorial examinations into their neighbours' lives in order to see how they were using the land.

In *Shaw* v *Applegate* [1977] 1 WLR 970 (CA), a café owner in another resort was allowed to keep his amusement arcade, contrary to the covenant, because of the claimant's delay in enforcing it. On the facts, the delay had not meant that the claimants had acquiesced in the breach, which would have made the covenant unenforceable, but an injunction (an **equitable** remedy: see Section 12.8) was refused on the grounds that the café owner had been lulled into a false sense of security because of the delay, and damages were awarded instead.

12.9.2 Statute

Several statutes authorise the discharge of a covenant; one well-known example is section 237 of the Town and Country Planning Act 1971, which allows a local authority to carry out a development against a covenant, provided it pays compensation. The most important provision, however, is section 84 of the LPA 1925, as amended by section 28 of the LPA 1969.

A statutory power to end **freehold** covenants was deemed necessary in 1925 because restrictions on land use could enclose 'individual premises and often whole streets and neighbourhoods in a legal straitjacket' (Polden, 1986, p. 195). There was no discussion of section 84 in Parliament, although it allows the State to destroy private property (the right to enforce the covenant), sometimes without compensation. The question is now whether section 84 is in breach of Article 1, Protocol 1 of the European Convention on Human Rights. This issue has been tested before the European Commission of Human Rights in *S v UK* (1984) (Application No 10741/84). The applicant failed to prove her case well-founded on its facts, but it seems unlikely that any other application, even on different facts, would succeed because of the doctrine of proportionality and the public interest element: 'ensuring the most efficient use of the land for the benefit of the community' (see Dawson, 1986, 126).

Applications under section 84 are made to the Lands Tribunal, a body which spends much of its time determining land valuations for the purposes of rating and compulsory purchase. In June 2009, the Lands Tribunal joined the new two-tier tribunal system established by the Tribunals, Courts and Enforcement Act 2007 when it became the Lands Chamber of the Upper Tribunal. However, for the time being, at least, it is still referred to as the Lands Tribunal. Appeal on a point of law can be made to the Court of Appeal. The Lands Tribunal has the power to modify or discharge any restrictive covenant and some covenants in long **leases**. There is provision for compensation to be paid in certain cases.

Under section 84, a covenant may be discharged or modified if:

- it should be deemed obsolete due to changes in the character of the property or neighbourhood; or
- it impedes some reasonable use of the land, provided money is sufficient compensation and either (a) 'it provides no practical benefits of substantial value or advantage' or (b) it is contrary to the public interest; or
- the parties agree, expressly or impliedly, 'by their acts or omissions'; or
- it will not injure anyone entitled to the benefit.

The Tribunal must have regard to any planning permissions or local plans, but these are not decisive. There are innumerable cases on section 84, and each turns on its own facts. Two examples are briefly considered here.

Re Bass Ltd's Application (1973) 26 P & CR 156 (Lands Tribunal) concerned an application to use land, restricted to housing, as a lorry park. The owner of the burdened land already had planning permission, and the objectors to the covenant's discharge (the owners of the benefit) already suffered from serious traffic noise. The adjudicator found, from a visit to the site, that, although living close to heavy lorries was far from pleasant, the restrictive covenant still conferred a substantial advantage on the objectors in preventing any increase in the number of lorries, and the application therefore failed. This case contains a helpful list of the questions which must be asked in an application under section 84.

In *Re University of Westminster* [1998] 3 All ER 1014 (CA), the university applied to have discharged or modified covenants restricting the use of one of its properties to particular educational purposes. The Court of Appeal upheld the Lands Tribunal's determination: the covenants could be modified to permit the use of the property for the wider educational purposes the university proposed, but they would not be discharged entirely. The parties who had the benefit of the covenants had not objected to the proposal for discharge. However, the Lands Tribunal was not satisfied that they realised the possible effect of discharging them: the university, and any subsequent owner, would be able to use the property for any purpose. On this basis, the Lands Tribunal found that they had not therefore agreed to the discharge of the covenants, as required by section 84(1)(b). Nor was the Lands Tribunal convinced that some reasonable use of the property would be impeded by a failure to allow discharge.

It can be seen, even from this brief review, that the Upper Tribunal has a challenging role. Many different interests are involved in these cases: developers, nearby landowners intent on preserving the status quo, 'expert' planners, the general policy that contracts be respected, the wider public interest in land use and the views of particular political parties (such as the Conservative government's policy of reducing planning restrictions during the 1980s and 1990s). These difficult issues are part of the background of all planning law, private and public.

12.10 Proposals for reform

In its report *Making Land Law Work: Easements, Covenants and Profits à Prendre* (Law Com 327, 2011), the Law Commission identified several major defects in the law governing covenants (see para 5.4).

- It is difficult to identify who has the benefit of a restrictive covenant, for two reasons:
  - (a) there is no requirement that the instrument creating the covenant should describe the benefited land with sufficient clarity to enable its identification without extrinsic evidence; and
  - (b) the benefit of a restrictive covenant, being an **equitable** interest, cannot be registered as an appurtenant interest on the **Register of Title** to the dominant land.
- There are differing and complicated rules for the running of the benefit and burden of restrictive covenants.
- The contractual liability between the original parties to a covenant persists despite changes in the ownership of the land; when the land is sold, the original covenantor remains liable.
- Whereas the benefit of a positive covenant can run at law, the burden of a positive covenant does not run so as to bind successors in title.

The Law Commission responded by recommending the creation of the 'land obligation', a new type of legal interest in land to be added to those listed in section 1(2) of the Law of Property Act 1925. Land obligations would differ from freehold covenants in that:

- they could be positive as well as negative;
- both the benefit and burden would be capable of registration; and
- the original parties to the land obligation would not be liable for breaches of it occurring after they parted with the land (compare the rules on **leasehold** covenants introduced by the Landlord and Tenant (Covenants) Act 1995, considered at Section 8.4).

Only time will tell whether these proposals will fare any better than earlier proposals for reforming the law of covenants.

Summary

12.1 Covenants are interests that enable a landowner to directly control what another landowner does on their own land.

12.2 Many of the rules relating to enforcing covenants were developed by equity in the nineteenth century. Many people consider these rules to be anachronistic and unnecessarily complicated.

12.3 There are separate sets of rules to pass the benefit of a covenant at law and to pass both the benefit and the burden of a covenant in equity (see Table 12.1 in Section 12.3).

12.4 It is possible for the benefit of a covenant to run at law by express or implied assignment. However, it is not possible for the burden of a covenant to run at law.

12.5 It is possible for the burden of a covenant to run in equity if the conditions derived from *Tulk* v *Moxhay* (1848) 41 ER 1143 (Ch) are complied with, including the requirement that the covenant is negative in effect. The burden of positive covenants cannot run in equity. The rules for the passing of the benefit in equity are distinct from those at law and must be met in their own right.

12.6 Various indirect methods have been developed to enable positive covenants to be enforced against successors in title to the original parties.

12.7 Section 56 LPA 1925 allows a person not named in a deed to be a party to it if they were referred to in the deed and identifiable at that time. The Contracts (Rights of Third Parties) Act 1999 is wider and potentially more helpful.

12.8 Only the equitable remedies are available for breach of a restrictive covenant. The usual remedy will be an injunction, but the court has the power to award damages in lieu of an injunction or to decline to give any remedy where it feels this would be justified on the facts of the case.

12.9 Covenants (except those in building schemes) may be ended at common law if the benefiting and burdened land come into the same hands or if the benefit is abandoned. Section 84 LPA 1925 provides machinery for the discharge or modification of restrictive covenants which have outlived their useful life; each case is decided on its own facts.

12.10 In response to the problems caused by complexity of the rules relating to freehold covenants, the Law Commission has recommended the introduction of a new type of legal interest: the 'land obligation'.

Exercises

 12.1 Complete the online quiz on the topics covered in this chapter on the companion website.

12.2 'The law relating to the enforcement of restrictive covenants consists of a complicated mixture of common law, equity and statutory provisions, which makes it difficult to know whether freehold covenants remain enforceable after a transfer of the burdened land or the benefited land to new owners.'

Discuss this statement.

12.3 In 1950, Karen sold part of her large garden in the Chequers Estate to Barry, who built 'The Palace' on it. In 1965, she sold another part of her garden to Phil, who

Exercises (continued)

promised her that he would not build more than one house on the land and that he would erect and maintain a fence around the land. The promise was stated to be made 'also with owners for the time being of adjoining land, formerly part of the Chequers Estate'.

In 1990, a council estate was built in the fields neighbouring the estate. Karen died, and her executors sold her remaining land to Yehudi. Rita has bought Phil's land and plans to build a block of flats with an open, unfenced garden.

Who can enforce the covenants, and whom do they bind? What remedies are available to the parties?

You can find suggested answer plans to exercises 12.2 and 12.3 on the companion website.

Further reading

Dawson, 'Restrictive Covenants and Human Rights' [1986] Conv 124

Gravells, 'Enforcement of Positive Covenants Affecting Freehold Land' (1994) 110 LQR 346

Howell, 'The Annexation of the Benefit of Covenants to Land' [2004] 68 Conv 507

Law Commission, *Making Land Law Work: Easements, Covenants and Profits à Prendre* (Law Com 327, 2011)

Martin, 'Remedies for Breach of Restrictive Covenants' [1996] Conv 329

Polden, 'Private Estate Planning and the Public Interest' (1986) 49 MLR 195

Part IV

Sharing interests in land

Chapter 13

Concurrent co-ownership

Key concepts

- **Joint tenancy** – a form of co-ownership in which all the co-owners own the whole legal or beneficial title to the land.
- **Severance** – the conversion of a joint tenancy into a tenancy in common.
- **Tenancy in common** – a form of co-ownership in which the beneficial title is divided between the co-owners in separate shares.
- **Trust** – an equitable doctrine dividing the legal ownership from the beneficial ownership.

13.1 Co-ownership of land

There are many ways of dividing ownership of land. Indeed, many of the preceding chapters of this book have been concerned with how the different rights enjoyable over a single parcel of land can be shared among a number of people. Examples include the relationships between a **tenant** (entitled to possession) and a **lessor** (entitled to the **rent**) and between an owner of land and their neighbour who is allowed to use a path over it (an **easement**). In none of these cases do the various parties share all the rights that accompany the *ownership* of land (or, more strictly, ownership of a particular legal **estate** in the land). The rights are divided up between the freeholder and those with lesser interests in the land.

There are many reasons, however, why people may wish to share ownership of a single legal estate, or, to put it less technically, to be co-owners of the land. The examples in Table 13.1 are taken from cases considered either in this chapter or elsewhere in this book. Shared ownership, especially of the family home, is now so commonplace that it is easy to overlook the serious theoretical and practical issues that arise from it:

- *How can the policy that land should be capable of being bought and sold without undue delay or expense be balanced with the need to provide sufficient protection for all the co-owners of the land?*

This question is addressed briefly in Section 13.2 and in more detail in Section 14.6.

- *What happens if the relationship between the co-owners breaks down? What are the rules for resolving disputes?*

The most important rules are now contained in Part I of the Trusts of Land and Appointment of Trustees Act (TOLATA) 1996 (see Sections 14.4 and 14.5).

- *What should a co-owner of land actually 'own'? To put it another way, when a co-owner dies, what (if anything) will pass to their heirs?*

Table 13.1 Possible uses of co-ownership

Purpose of co-ownership:	Example cases:
To provide a family home	*Williams & Glyn's Bank Ltd* v *Boland* [1981] AC 487 (HL) *City of London Building Society* v *Flegg* [1988] AC 54 (HL) *Stack* v *Dowden* [2007] 2 AC 432 (HL)
To provide a home while studying at university	*AG Securities* v *Vaughan* [1990] 1 AC 417 (HL)
To divide up an inheritance	*Barclay* v *Barclay* [1970] 2 QB 677 (CA)
To provide premises for a business partnership	*Rodway* v *Landy* [2001] Ch 703 (CA)
To act as an investment	*Laskar* v *Laskar* [2008] 1 WLR 2695 (CA)

There are two main possibilities:

1. Each co-owner owns a share of the land, which they are free to dispose of as they wish.
2. The land is not divided between the co-owners. They do not have separable shares, but they together have a single interest in the whole of the land. One consequence of such a doctrine of co-ownership is that no co-owner has a 'share' with which they can deal (or which they can leave to their heirs).

This question forms the subject matter of Sections 13.3–13.6.

There is no single right answer to these questions. The most appropriate answer will depend upon the reason the co-owners are sharing the land and on wider social and economic values. For example, land law has tended to be led by the needs of large landowners and investors. The result is that land law, to put it rather crudely, generally seeks to achieve 'justice through certainty'. However, modern developments in this area of law are largely the result of the growth in land ownership by ordinary families. If a family breaks up, those involved will need to resolve the ownership of the family property. The effects of this can be far-reaching, since, as well as providing the family home, which is perhaps the real and symbolic focus of family life, the land may be the most valuable financial asset owned by any family member. Family law tends to be more interested in 'justice in the individual case'. Where the demands of certainty and individual justice diverge, there is bound to be some tension, and, possibly, confusion.

13.2 The trust as the basis of co-ownership

English law attempts to balance the apparently competing objectives of co-owners by imposing a **trust** whenever two or more people own land concurrently (see ss 34 and 36 of the LPA 1925). Since 1st January 1997, such trusts are trusts of land as defined by section 1(1) TOLATA 1996. The history of trusts of land and the detailed rules regulating them are considered in the next chapter.

In the simplest form of a trust, a **trustee** (or trustees) holds (hold) the legal **title** for the benefit of a **beneficiary** or beneficiaries (see Figure 13.1 and Section 2.2.3(a)). However, in many trusts of land, trustees are also beneficiaries. This is particularly common where a couple are the legal owners of the family home: they will hold it on trust for themselves as beneficial co-owners.

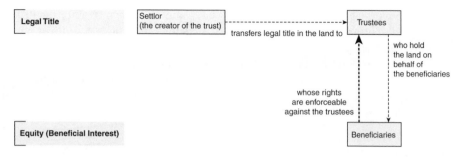

Figure 13.1   A simple trust

The detailed rules that regulate the relationships between the various parties concerned with a **trust of land** are contained in Part I of TOLATA 1996 and form the subject matter of Chapter 14.

13.3   Joint tenancy and tenancy in common

Since 1925, there have been two forms of concurrent co-ownership in England and Wales: joint tenancy and tenancy in common. A joint tenancy can exist at law or in equity (that is, as a **beneficial interest**), but a tenancy in common can only exist in equity. It is not possible to hold the legal **estate** as tenants in common. The key statutory provisions are sections 1(6), 34 and 36 of the LPA 1925.

13.3.1   Joint tenancy

Sir William Blackstone described the joint tenancy as a 'thorough and intimate union' (*Blackstone's Commentaries*, ii, 182). The basic principle is that, as far as outsiders are concerned, the owners are regarded as one person. They are united in every way possible, through 'the four unities': possession, interest, **title** and time (easily remembered by the acronym PITT).

A joint tenancy requires *the four unities*

▶ Possession: all the joint tenants are entitled to possess the whole of the land.
▶ Interest: they each hold an identical interest (**freehold, leasehold**).
▶ Title: their interest was obtained by the same document.
▶ Time: their interest vested in them at the same time.

In *AG Securities* v *Vaughan* [1990] 1 AC 417 (HL) (see also Section 7.5.1(d)), a claim that there was a joint tenancy of a **lease** of a student flat failed because the claimants had arrived at different times. Indeed, on the facts of the case, Lord Oliver found that none of the four unities was present, not even that of possession.

The basis of joint tenancy is that the joint tenants together own the whole **title** to the land rather than each having a share in the land. Consequently, and very importantly, joint tenants enjoy the 'right of survivorship' (*ius accrescendi*). Joint tenants are treated as if they were all one person, and if one dies it is as if they had never existed.

The survivor(s) still own the whole of the land, and there is nothing for the heirs of the dead joint tenant to inherit. It follows, therefore, that the last survivor among joint tenants will own the whole land absolutely.

The risk involved in the right of survivorship may seem unfair, but it is a convenient vehicle for legal ownership because of its simplicity. Since 1925, all co-owned legal **estates** are held as a joint tenancy, even if the **beneficial interest** is shared between the same co-owners as tenants in common (LPA 1925, ss 1(6), 34(1), 36(2)).

13.3.2 Tenancy in common

Tenancy in common is often referred to as 'undivided shares'. That is, although the land is held in separate shares, it has not been physically partitioned between the co-owners.

> A tenancy in common:
>
> ▶ requires only the unity of possession (although all three of the other unities may also be present); and
> ▶ does not give rise to any right of survivorship.

When a tenant in common dies, they can leave their share to anyone they please. This is the main reason why tenancy in common is no longer possible at law (LPA 1925, ss 1(6), 34(1), 36(2)). If legal tenancies in common were permitted, a purchaser would have to investigate the individual **titles** of each tenant in common, adding considerably to the time and expense of conveyancing. With a joint tenancy, there is only one title to investigate. As far as a buyer of land is concerned, the **beneficial interests** shared in equity are 'behind a curtain'. They can overreach all these interests (whether joint tenancy or tenancy in common) by complying with the requirements of sections 2 and 27 of the LPA 1925 (see Section 14.6.1).

13.4 Creating a joint tenancy or tenancy in common

13.4.1 At law

A joint tenancy at law arises whenever a legal interest in land is shared concurrently; that is, whenever land is conveyed into the names of two or more people (LPA 1925, ss 34(2) and 36(1)). There can be no more than four legal joint tenants (Trustee Act 1925, s 34(2)). If **title** to land is conveyed to more than four people, the first four named on the **deed** who are willing, at least 18 years old, and mentally competent will be the legal joint tenants (the **trustees**). The remainder will be beneficial owners only. There is no restriction on the number of joint tenants in equity.

Any attempt to create a legal **tenancy in common** will vest the legal title in the purchasers (or the first four of them named in the **conveyance** if there are more than four) as joint tenants, holding the land on **trust** for all of the purchasers as tenants in common (LPA 1925, s 34(2)).

13.4.2 In equity

In equity, there may be either a joint tenancy or a tenancy in common, or even a combination of the two.

The starting point in determining whether a person is a beneficial joint tenant or a beneficial tenant in common is the document through which **title** to the land was acquired. As Slade LJ explains in *Goodman* v *Gallant* [1986] Fam 106 (CA), 110–11:

> If ... the relevant conveyance contains an express declaration of trust which comprehensively declares the beneficial interests in the property or its proceeds of sale, ... the declaration contained in the document speaks for itself.

Consequently, if (as in *Pankhania* v *Chandegra* [2013] 1 P & CR 16 (CA)) the transfer to the parties includes an express declaration that they hold the beneficial interest as tenants in common, this declaration will be conclusive, unless it can be set aside because of fraud or mistake. Words that show that the owners intended that they should have *shares* in the beneficial interest in the land will also give rise to a tenancy in common. Such **'words of severance'** include 'equally', 'in equal shares', 'amongst' and 'share and share alike' (as, for example, in *Barclay* v *Barclay* [1970] 2 QB 677 (CA), where land was left 'equally' under an express trust in a will to the testator's five children).

In the absence of an express declaration and any words of severance, the presumption is that 'equity follows the law' and the beneficial interest be held as joint tenants (*Stack* v *Dowden* [2007] 2 AC 432 (HL), [33], [54] and [109]). Despite this principle, equity has historically inclined against the unpredictability of the right of survivorship. According to the Pricy Council cases of *Malayan Credit Ltd* v *Jack Chia-MPH Ltd* [1986] AC 549 (PC), equity *presumes* a tenancy in common where the co-owners:

1. make unequal contributions to the purchase price, provided that the property was not purchased by a cohabiting couple (*Stack* v *Dowden*, which is considered in more detail in Section 17.3);
2. are business partners; or
3. are lending money on a **mortgage**.

13.5 Severing a joint tenancy

Severance is the conversion of an **equitable** joint tenancy into a tenancy in common. It may occur because of the wishes of one or more of the joint tenants, or by operation of law if certain circumstances occur.

When a joint tenant severs their **beneficial interest**:

▶ they become a tenant in common in equity with an equal share of the value of the property whenever it comes to be sold;
▶ the right of survivorship will cease to apply to them, which means that:
  – their beneficial interest will pass to their heirs on their death; and
  – their beneficial interest in the property will not increase automatically on the death of any of the other tenants.

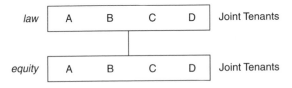

Figure 13.2 Legal joint tenants holding for themselves as beneficial joint tenants

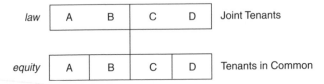

Figure 13.3 Legal joint tenants holding for themselves as beneficial tenants in common

When analysing problems concerning co-ownership, it can be helpful to show the various interests diagrammatically, using a single box to show a joint tenancy (see Figure 13.2) and a series of joined boxes for a tenancy in common (see Figure 13.3). In what follows, it must always be remembered that a legal joint tenancy cannot be severed (LPA 1925, s 36(2)). This means that any severance of the beneficial interests will not automatically affect the legal **title**. Indeed, whenever dealing with a series of events affecting co-owned land, it is important to track separately the consequences for the legal title and the beneficial interests.

Methods of severance

▷ The three methods of severing a joint tenancy of personal property listed by Page-Wood V-C in *Williams* v *Hensman* (1861) 70 ER 862 (QB) (LPA 1925, s 36(2)):

1. by 'an act of one of the parties interested operating on [their] own share';
2. by mutual agreement;
3. by a 'course of dealing' ('mutual conduct') which shows a common intention to sever.

▷ By notice in writing of immediate severance (created by LPA 1925, s 36(2)).
▷ Where a joint tenant kills another joint tenant (if the right of survivorship operated in such circumstances, the killer would be 'profiting from their own wrong').

Anything which creates a distinction between equitable joint tenants amounts to a severance. Whether severance has taken place always depends on the evidence, and the facts of a case or question may need to be examined in some detail. Frequently, the trigger for any dispute will be the death of one co-owner, and the question will be whether there was any severance of the equitable joint tenancy some time before the death.

13.5.1 Acting on a share

If a joint tenant assigns their share during their lifetime, the assignee will take it as a tenant in common with any remaining joint tenants (see, for example, the old case of *Partriche* v *Powlet* (1740) 26 ER 430 (Ch)). The following acts are also sufficient to sever a joint tenancy:

- granting a **mortgage** or **charge** (or even a **lease**) over the beneficial share;
- the vesting of a joint tenant's interest in a **trustee in bankruptcy** upon the joint tenant being declared bankrupt (*In Re Dennis (A Bankrupt)* [1993] Ch 72 (Ch));
- a fraudulent attempt to mortgage or convey the whole legal **estate** by a joint tenant (*First National Securities Ltd* v *Hegerty* [1985] QB 850 (CA) and *Ahmed* v *Kendrick* (1988) 55 P & CR 120 (CA)).

However, leaving the interest to a third party by will does not sever the joint tenancy (*Gould* v *Kemp* (1834) 2 My & K 304, 39 ER 959 (Ch)). The right of survivorship means that a joint tenant has no interest to leave by will, provided that at least one other joint tenant survives them.

13.5.2 Mutual agreement

Severance by mutual agreement requires the agreement of *all* of the joint tenants. However, the agreement does not need to be in a particular form, nor, it seems, in writing. In the words of Sir John Pennycuick in the case of *Burgess* v *Rawnsley* [1975] Ch 429 (CA) at 446:

> The significance of an agreement is not that it binds the parties; but that it serves as an indication of a common intention to sever.

It is essential, however, that the agreement relates to the severance of the joint tenancy. For example, in the unreported case *Marshall* v *Marshall*, 2 October 1998 (Lexis Citation 3054) (CA), Mrs Marshall died shortly after the decree absolute was issued in the divorce proceedings between herself and Mr Marshall. It had already been agreed that the matrimonial home would be sold, but there had been no express agreement as to how any proceeds of sale would be divided. The Court of Appeal refused to infer an agreement to sever solely from the agreement to put the house on the market, with the result that the **title** passed to Mr Marshall by survivorship. However, where there is evidence that the joint tenants placed the land on the market *having agreed that the proceeds were to be divided equally between them*, this will be enough to establish that severance has occurred, as in the subsequent case of *Davis* v *Smith* [2012] 1 FLR 1177 (CA).

13.5.3 Course of dealings

Severance by course of dealings differs from that by mutual agreement in that severance will be inferred from the conduct of the parties: there is no need for a meeting of minds between the joint tenants. In *Burgess* v *Rawnsley*, the Court of Appeal considered the possibility of a course of dealings as well as mutual agreement (see Section 13.5.2). Mr Honick and Mrs Rawnsley met at a religious rally. After a few months of friendship, they bought the house in which Mr Honick lived, as joint tenants at law and in equity. Mr Honick thought they were going to get married. However, Mrs Rawnsley merely intended to live in the upper flat. After a year or so, they discovered each other's error and agreed orally that Mr Honick should buy Mrs Rawnsley's share. However, they did not finally agree a price, and nothing more was done before Mr Honick died three years later. Mrs Rawnsley claimed the whole house by right of survivorship. As to a course of dealing between Mr Honick and Mrs Rawnsley, Lord Denning MR said, at 439:

> It is sufficient if there is a course of dealing in which one party makes clear to the other that he desires that their shares should no longer be held jointly but be held in common ... it is sufficient if both parties enter on a course of dealing which evinces an intention by both of them that their shares shall henceforth be held in common and not jointly.

The 'course of dealing' argument failed in *Greenfield* v *Greenfield* (1979) 38 P & CR 570 (Ch). Two brothers owned a house as joint tenants at law and in equity. When each married, they converted the house into two maisonettes, sharing the garden and some bills. When the elder brother died, his widow claimed that the division of the house showed an intention to sever the beneficial joint tenancy and that she had inherited her husband's tenancy in common. Fox J held (at 578):

> The onus of establishing severance must be on the plaintiff ... It seems to me that on the facts, the plaintiff comes nowhere near discharging that onus. Neither side made clear any intention of ending the joint tenancy. The defendant had no intention of ending it and never thought that he or [his brother] Ernest had ended it.

13.5.4   Written notice

Although, according to Sir John Pennycuick, *Burgess* v *Rawnsley* [1975] Ch 429 at 448,

> The policy of the law as it stands today, having regard particularly to section 36(2), is to facilitate severance at the instance of either party

neither a unilateral unstated intention to sever nor verbal notice by one party to another has ever been sufficient to sever a joint tenancy. However, section 36(2) of the LPA 1925 provides that notice in writing of the desire to sever by one joint tenant to all the others is sufficient to sever the joint tenancy. No agreement from the other joint tenants is required. Nor is it necessary to give the notice in any particular form, provided that it is worded in such a way as to make it clear that an immediate severance is being sought. However, expressing a wish to sever the joint tenancy in the future will not be sufficient (*Re Draper's Conveyance* [1969] 1 Ch 486 (Ch) and *Harris* v *Goddard* [1983] 1 WLR 1203 (CA)).

Severance by written notice is a unilateral act. It is not necessary for the other joint tenants to read the notice, provided that the notice has been properly served upon them. In *Kinch* v *Bullard* [1999] 1 WLR 423 (Ch), a wife suffering from a terminal illness was intending to divorce her husband. They were beneficial joint tenants of the matrimonial home, and, since she no longer wanted the right of survivorship to operate, she instructed her solicitors to send him a notice severing the joint tenancy. The solicitors sent the letter by first-class post. However, the husband suffered a serious heart attack before it was delivered. The wife, realising she would lose half the house if her husband died with the joint tenancy having been severed, destroyed the letter as soon as it arrived. Her husband died a week or so later and never learned about the letter. The wife died the following year, and the husband's executors brought an action claiming that the joint tenancy had been severed by the written notice and that they were therefore entitled to the husband's half-share in the property. The case turned upon whether the notice of severance had been properly served. By section 196 of the LPA 1925, a notice is properly served 'if it is left at the last known place of abode or business in the United Kingdom of the ... person to be served'. In this case, the court held that service occurred (and the notice became effective) when the letter fell through the letterbox onto the mat. The joint tenancy had already been severed, and the wife's right of survivorship lost, by the time she picked up the letter and destroyed it.

13.5.5 Homicide

The principle that a person should not benefit from their own crime (the forfeiture rule) means that, in most cases, a joint tenant will not be allowed to enjoy the benefits of survivorship if they criminally cause the death of another joint tenant. However, as Vinelott J noted in the case of *Re K* [1985] Ch 85 (Ch) at 100:

> There is curiously no reported case on the point in England but it has been held in other jurisdictions where the law was similar to English law before 1925 that where one of two joint tenants murders the other while the entire interest vests in the survivor the law imports a constructive trust of an undivided one-half share for the benefit of the next of kin of the deceased other than the offender ... Under English law since 1925 the result is more simply reached by treating the beneficial interest as vesting in the deceased and the survivor as tenants in common.

If there are only two joint tenants, the result will be the same whether it is reached by severance or by imposing a **constructive trust**. The killer-survivor will hold the legal **estate** on **trust** for themselves and the estate of their victim as equitable tenants in common in equal shares. However, where there are more than two joint tenants at the outset, the choice between automatic severance and the imposition of a constructive trust may be important as the latter allows the court more flexibility in allocating the beneficial entitlement.

Section 2 of the Forfeiture Act 1982 gives the court the power to modify the effect of this rule in cases other than murder where the justice of the case require[s] it. The Court of Appeal exercised this power (albeit by a majority) in the tragic case of *Dunbar* v *Plant* [1998] Ch 412 (CA). Miss Plant and Mr Dunbar attempted to kill themselves following a suicide pact. Miss Plant failed, but Mr Dunbar succeeded. Although the forfeiture rule applies in cases of aiding and abetting a suicide such as this, it was held that, under the particular circumstances of the case, the couple's joint tenancy of their house had not been severed. Consequently, Miss Plant was entitled to the whole of the **beneficial interest** in the proceeds of sale. The house had already been sold.

13.5.6 Applying the rules

Problem questions on severance (such as Exercise 13.3) require a step-by-step analysis of what happens to the legal and equitable ownership. This is, perhaps, most easily done initially with the help of diagrams.

Let us imagine that a group of five people, whom we shall call Annie, Belinda, Charlie, Dee and Ellen, buy a house as joint tenants in equity, each contributing equally to the purchase price. As they are all over 18 years old, the first four become the legal owners as joint tenants holding on trust for all five. Certain events now take place, each of which may affect the legal ownership or sever the **equitable** joint tenancy. A description of each event and an analysis of its effect are set out in Figures 13.4–13.7.

A systematic approach to applying the rules relating to severance to the facts of a case is illustrated in Figure 13.8. This kind of problem question often ends by stating that some of the surviving co-owners now want to sell, and others want to remain in the property. If so, any answer must continue by considering sections 14 and 15 of TOLATA and the relevant case law (Section 14.5).

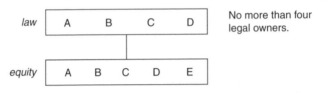

Figure 13.4 At the start

Figure 13.5 Annie dies

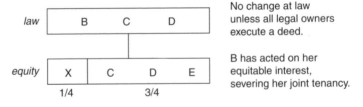

Figure 13.6 Belinda sells her share to Xena

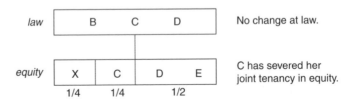

Figure 13.7 Charlie gives written notice of severance to Dee and Ellen

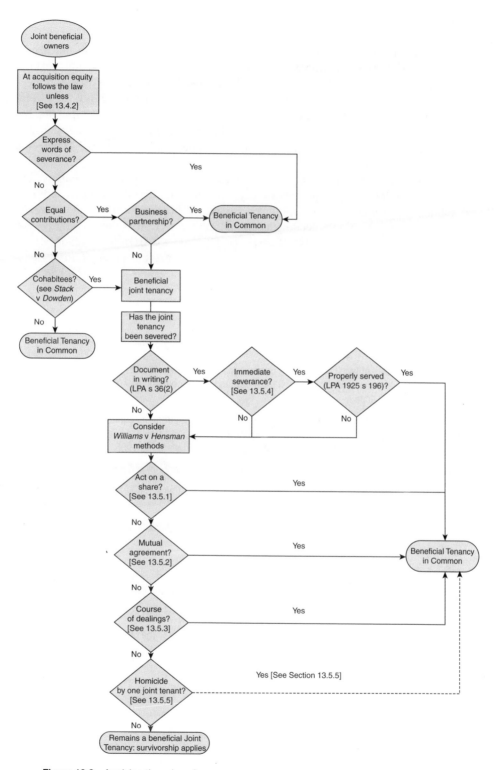

Figure 13.8 Applying the rules of severance

13.6 Is co-ownership 'fit for purpose'?

The rules about severance of an **equitable** joint tenancy, on which so much may depend, are sometimes uncertain and can result in expensive litigation and injustice. The written notice procedure introduced by section 36(2) of the LPA 1925 addresses many, but not all, of the potential problems, and the procedure is not itself completely free from uncertainty. From time to time, the case is made for simplifying the law. It has even been suggested that the equitable joint tenancy should be abolished in order to avoid potentially troublesome and expensive litigation (see Thompson, 1987a, b; Prichard, 1987).

In fact, the doctrines of joint tenancy and tenancy in common work quite well in practice, provided that co-owners are clear as to their motives and properly advised about the two alternatives before they complete the purchase of the land. However, problems can arise if title documents are not drafted as well as they should be. For example, the dispute in *Stack v Dowden* [2007] 2 AC 432 (HL) (see Sections 13.4.2 and 17.3) would have been avoided if the Land Registry's standard form of transfer (Form 19(JP) as then prescribed by the Land Registration Rules 1925) had been worded differently (see Baroness Hale at [50]).

Summary

13.1 Co-ownership of land is common in England and Wales. However, different people co-own land for different reasons. The legal rules have to try to accommodate and balance the resulting tensions.

13.2 The trust divides the legal title to land (held by the trustees) from the equitable (or 'beneficial') ownership of the land. In England and Wales, all co-owned land is held on trust regulated under the Trusts of Land and Appointment of Trustees Act 1996.

13.3 There are two types of co-ownership: joint tenancy and tenancy in common.

1. Joint tenants share the unities of possession, interest, title and time, and take the risk of the right of survivorship.

2. Tenants in common have 'undivided shares' in the land; the only unity that is essential is the unity of possession.

13.4 Legal title to land may only be shared under a joint tenancy. Equitable co-owners may be joint tenants or tenants in common, depending on whether there have been words of severance, or on the general circumstances of the creation of the trust.

13.5 Equitable joint tenants can sever their tenancy and become tenants in common.

13.6 Co-ownership works relatively well in practice, provided that all the parties are properly advised. However, the rules relating to the severance of a beneficial joint tenancy can sometimes cause confusion and even injustice.

Exercises

 13.1 Complete the online quiz on the topics covered in this chapter on the companion website.

13.2 'It is easy to understand a desire to make severance as flexible as possible. On the other hand, this can lead to considerable uncertainty as to property rights' (Smith, *Property Law, Cases and Materials*, 4th edn, Longman 2009, 367).

Critically discuss this statement.

13.3 Uri, Neil and Val work independently as freelance engineers. Three years ago, they purchased the registered freehold of Techno House, intending to use it as a base for their respective businesses as well as their home together.

A couple of months ago, there was a serious disagreement between Neil and the others. Uri and Val refused to speak to Neil, but left him a note demanding that he leave the house immediately. The note concluded by inviting Neil to 'consider his position in relation to our partnership'. Neil went to stay with his brother, Buzz, and made a will leaving all of his property to Buzz.

Last month, Neil wrote to Uri and Val, saying that he was willing to divide his share in the house between Uri and Val if they each paid him £60,000 in return. On receipt of the letter, Uri told Val that he was willing to agree to Neil's proposal, but Val said that she would never do so. However, Val then wrote to Neil offering to pay £120,000 for Neil's share in Techno House. Neil phoned Val to say that he would come round immediately to 'finalise the deal'. When Uri found out, he was very angry. He stormed out of the house, straight into the path of Neil's car. Uri died in the resulting accident.

Were Uri, Neil and Val originally beneficial joint tenants or tenants in common? Assuming that they were originally beneficial joint tenants, what interests, if any, do Neil, Val and Buzz hold in Techno House following Uri's death?

 You can find suggested answer plans to exercises 13.2 and 13.3 on the companion website.

Further reading

Conway, 'Joint Tenancies, Negotiations and Consensual Severance' (2009) 73 Conv 67

Cooke, 'Community of Property, Joint Ownership and the Family Home' in Dixon and Griffith (eds), *Contemporary Perspectives on Property, Equity and Trusts Law* (Oxford University Press 2007) 39

Prichard, 'Beneficial Joint Tenancies: A Riposte' [1987] Conv 273

Tee, 'Severance Revisited' [1995] Conv 104

Thompson (a), 'Beneficial Joint Tenancies: A Case for Abolition?' [1987] Conv 29

Thompson (b), 'Beneficial Joint Tenancies: A Reply to Professor Prichard' [1987] Conv 275

Chapter 14

Trusts of land

Key concepts

- **Overreaching** – transferring the beneficial interest from the land that was subject to the trust to the proceeds of sale (or mortgage) of the land.
- **Section 15 factors** – the factors listed in section 15 (especially, but not exclusively, those in s 15(1)) of the Trusts of Land and Appointment of Trustees Act 1996 to be taken into account when the court considers a dispute between co-owners.
- **Trust** – an equitable doctrine dividing the legal ownership from the beneficial ownership.

14.1 A brief history of trusts of land

The general policy of English law is to ensure, so far as is practicable, that land should be capable of being bought and sold without undue delay or expense. At the same time, it is important that land can be shared by more than one owner with some measure of security, in order to satisfy the different needs and ambitions of landowners (such as those set out in Table 13.1). As readers of Chapters 2 and 13 will already appreciate, those responsible for the reforms of 1925 chose the **trust** as the mechanism by which to balance these two sets of demands. All trusts including land are now regulated under the Trusts of Land and Appointment of Trustees Act (TOLATA) 1996, and most of this chapter is devoted to the rules contained in Part I of that Act. However, some knowledge of the earlier law is necessary. Much of the old law of trusts remains in place beneath TOLATA 1996, and some of the pre-1996 rules will almost certainly be encountered when reading earlier cases that remain relevant today.

The 1925 legislation recognised two main motives behind the **co-ownership** of land, and provided two very different schemes of statutory trusts to facilitate them:

1. preventing the fragmentation of the great aristocratic estates; and
2. investment, usually for the purpose of generating income.

The first of these objectives was accommodated by the strict **settlement**, regulated by the Settled Land Act 1925. Settlements under this act are now obsolete and lie outside the scope of this book. All other co-owned land was assumed to have been acquired for investment purposes and was deemed to be held subject to a statutory **trust for sale** under the LPA 1925. Consequently, as the statutory trust for sale applied to all co-owned land not subject to a strict settlement, it applied not only to land which was genuinely held for investment purposes, but also to land held for commercial purposes (for example, by a partnership of solicitors) and family land (for example, where the co-owned land was the family home).

The trust for sale was never really appropriate for commercial or family property. As the name suggests, it placed the **trustees** under an immediate and binding duty to sell the land, albeit with a power to postpone sale in order to receive the rental income. One of the consequences of this was that if the trustees disagreed about the future of the land (including a home or business premises), the default position was that it would be sold, even if a majority of the trustees did not want this. A further problem was the doctrine of conversion, which arises out of the principle that 'equity looks on that as done which ought to be done'. Even though the land had not yet been sold, equity treated it as though it had been *converted* into money. Consequently, the **beneficiaries** behind a trust for sale did not have an interest in land, but merely an interest in the proceeds of sale.

As the twentieth century progressed, land was, with increasing frequency, bought by co-owners for owner-occupation rather than income generation. In the minds of most such co-owners, the land was purchased to provide a home, not an income; and sale was merely a possibility at some time in the future, not the main purpose of acquiring the land. In response, the courts mitigated the doctrine of conversion by treating **beneficial interests** as interests in the land itself in certain circumstances. For example, in *Bull* v *Bull* [1955] 1 QB 234 (CA) (see Section 2.2.3(a)), the court held that Mrs Bull's beneficial interest included a right to occupy the house she shared with her son; and in *Williams & Glyn's Bank Ltd* v *Boland* [1981] AC 487 (HL), the House of Lords held that a *beneficial interest* in land held on a trust for sale was an interest capable of being protected by occupation of the land for the purposes of **registered title** (see Section 4.6.2). The courts also used the discretion granted to them by section 30 of the LPA 1925 to balance the duty to sell against the purposes for which the land had been acquired, producing a long line of case law.

In the end, and despite the valiant efforts of the courts, the machinery of the trust for sale and its accompanying doctrine of conversion were simply too far removed from the reality of land ownership by the closing years of the twentieth century. In 1989, the Law Commission observed (Law Com No 181, 1989), iv:

> We consider that the present dual system of trusts for sale and strict settlements is unnecessarily complex, ill-suited to the conditions of modern property ownership, and liable to give rise to unforeseen conveyancing complications.

The result was the Trusts of Land and Appointment of Trustees Act (TOLATA) 1996, the main provisions of which are summarised in Table 14.1. TOLATA replaced the trust for sale (and the strict settlement) with the new 'trust of land'. Since 1st January 1997, almost all trusts containing land are trusts of land. The only exceptions are strict settlements that existed when the Act came into force, and land held on trust by the colleges at Oxford, Cambridge and Durham Universities, and the public schools of Winchester and Eton (TOLATA, s 1(3)).

Table 14.1 The main provisions of Part I of the Trusts of Land and Appointment of Trustees Act 1996

Section 1	Any 'trust of property which consists of or includes land' is a *trust of land* (apart from the very limited exceptions in s 1(3)).
Section 2	No new strict settlements can be created after 31st December 1996.
Section 3	The doctrine of conversion does not apply to trusts of land. [Note, however, that this does not affect the doctrine of overreaching (LPA 1925, ss 2, 27; see Section 14.6.1).]
Section 4	If a new trust of land is *expressly created* as a trust for sale, the trustees will be allowed to postpone sale indefinitely. [Such a trust for sale is only appropriate if the main purpose of creating the trust involves the sale of the land.]

(Continues)

Table 14.1 *(Continued)*

Section 5	Trusts for sale are no longer implied by statute. Sections 34–6 LPA 1925 are amended so that such trusts are now trusts of land.
Sections 6–9A	TOLATA gives the trustees various powers that they need to deal with the land. (See Section 14.3.)
Section 11	The trustees have a duty to consult with the beneficiaries before making decisions about the land, even if such a provision is not expressly included in the terms of a trust. (See Section 14.4.2.)
Section 12	Beneficiaries have a right to occupy the land, subject to certain exceptions and provisos. [This replaces the common law right recognised in *Bull* v *Bull* [1955] 1 QB 234 (CA)).] (See Section 14.4.1.)
Section 13	Powers for the trustees to deal with any dispute where two or more beneficiaries wish to exercise their section 12 rights. (See Section 14.4.1.)
Sections 14–15	The statutory scheme for dealing with disputes between people with an interest in trust land. [This completely replaces section 30 of the LPA 1925.] (See Section 14.5.)
Section 16	Protection for buyers of trust land that is not yet registered. (See Section 14.6.3.)

14.2 Creating a trust of land

A trust of land may be created expressly, by statute or by implication.

Express trusts	An express trust of land must be evidenced in writing and signed by the person creating it in order for it to be enforceable by the **beneficiaries** (LPA 1925, s 53(1)(b)). It must declare the nature of the beneficial ownership and the terms of the trust.
Statutory trusts	In the absence of an express trust, whenever a legal **estate** in land is conveyed to two or more people, a statutory trust of land will be imposed (LPA 1925, ss 34–6).
Implied trusts	It is also possible for a person to gain a beneficial share in land in circumstances in which there is no express or statutory trust. In certain circumstances, equity will find that the land is co-owned because of the conduct of the relevant parties. These trusts are known as **resulting** and **constructive trusts** (see Chapter 17).

14.3 The powers and duties of trustees

The trustees of a trust of land hold the legal **title** to the land. If the trust is created expressly, the trustees are usually appointed in the trust deed. In the case of statutory and **implied trusts**, the trustees will be the persons who hold the legal title to the land. If there is no trustee (for example, if land is conveyed to a child who by s 1(6) of the LPA 1925 cannot own land), the court can appoint trustees. Part II of TOLATA (ss 19–21) gives **beneficiaries** a measure of control over their trustees, in that they can require the appointment of a new trustee or the retirement of a current trustee, unless the settlor has expressly specified that the beneficiaries should not have this power.

The rights and duties of trustees of land are subject to the general law of trusts, the rules contained in TOLATA and the particular provisions (if any) of the trust in question (TOLATA, s 8). The powers of trustees of charitable, ecclesiastical and public trusts continue to be regulated in special ways that lie outside the scope of this book. It should be borne in mind that the powers and duties contained in TOLATA are designed to equip trustees of land in a wide range of contexts and that not all of them will be relevant to a couple who co-own their own home. Indeed, the trustees and beneficiaries of a family home are often (but not always) the same people, and in such cases the distinction between the two roles is unlikely to be of practical significance unless they find themselves in dispute about the ownership or use of their land.

14.3.1 Sale, mortgage and lease

Section 6(1) of TOLATA provides that the **trustees** 'have all the powers of an absolute owner': thus, they may sell, **mortgage, lease** or otherwise deal with the land. It is possible for these powers to be restricted by the terms of the **trust** (s 8(1)), although it is not possible to exclude the trustees' statutory power to postpone sale (s 4). Section 6(3) of TOLATA expressly gives trustees the power (subject to the terms of the trust) to buy land with trust money as an investment or for occupation by a **beneficiary** or 'for any other reason'. In exercising these powers, the trustees must 'have regard to the rights of the beneficiaries' (s 6(5)). Section 13 gives the trustees the power to 'exclude or restrict' the entitlement of any of the beneficiaries to occupy the land. This power is considered alongside the statutory right to occupy in Section 14.4.1.

14.3.2 Transfer of legal title to beneficiaries absolutely entitled

Where the **beneficiaries** are of full age and capacity, the role of **trustees** may be limited or unnecessary. Consequently, section 6(2) restates the old rule that if such beneficiaries 'are absolutely entitled to the land', the trustees can convey the land to them.

14.3.3 Partition

Subject to the terms of the **trust**, the **trustees** may also have the power to physically divide up ('partition') the land between the **beneficiaries**, provide that they are tenants in common, absolutely entitled, and they all consent (s 7).

14.3.4 Delegation

The **trustees** may (subject to the terms of the **trust**) delegate their powers to **beneficiaries** of full age who are entitled to an interest in possession in the land (s 9). This allows beneficiaries in occupation to carry on the routine management of the land themselves.

14.3.5 Limitations on the trustees' powers

The **trustees** must exercise their powers with due regard for the rights of the **beneficiaries** (s 6(5)), the general rules of equity (s 6(6)) and the provisions of the instrument creating the **trust** (s 8(1)). A trust instrument may require the trustees to obtain consent from some specified person or persons before exercising their powers, and this limitation is given statutory recognition in section 8(2) (see, also, Section 14.6.3). For example, if a spouse dies and leaves their property to their children, it could be a term of the trust that the property can only be sold with the consent of the surviving spouse, who might well also have the right to live there, thus ensuring that the property remains unsold, at least for a time. Any requirement to obtain consent from a specified person must be distinguished from the section 11 duty requiring the trustees to consult (but not necessarily to obtain the consent of) the beneficiaries before exercising any of their functions, so far as it is practicable to do so (see Section 14.4.2). Trustees of land are also subject to the general duty of care to 'exercise such care and skill as is reasonable in the circumstances', imposed on all trustees by section 1(1) of the Trustee Act 2000.

14.4   The rights of beneficiaries

As well as the powers and duties of **trustees** of trusts of land, Part I of TOLATA also sets out the rights that will generally be enjoyed by the **beneficiaries** of such trusts. The rights contained in TOLATA are an attempt to respond to the difficult questions that conveyancers and the courts have puzzled over in previous centuries. One particular source of uncertainty has been the rights of each of the co-owners to use the land. For example, can a co-owner bring a friend or relative to stay on the property for a long time, regardless of the views of the other co-owners? And what happens if one of the co-owners is absent from the property for a long time: should they still have to pay towards its upkeep or should they be compensated for the benefit they are not enjoying from the land, and does it matter whether they left voluntarily or because of a disagreement with the other co-owners? These are complex questions, so it will not be surprising if the relevant provisions of TOLATA also seem more complex than might be wished.

14.4.1   Occupation

The statutory **trust for sale** under the LPA 1925 posed a conceptual problem for land lawyers, since the interests of the **beneficiaries** were in the proceeds of sale rather than in the land itself (see Section 14.1). Despite this, the courts, albeit slowly, came to recognise that beneficiaries might have a right to live on the land, although they could not completely ignore the doctrine of conversion. Section 3 of TOLATA abolished the doctrine of conversion in respect of almost all **trusts of land**, even where the trust is expressly created as a trust for sale and section 12 provides a new, statutory right for beneficiaries to occupy the trust land.

14.4.1(a) The right to occupy

Section 12 of TOLATA states that a beneficiary is entitled to live in the house if:

▶ the purposes of the trust include making the land available for their occupation … or
▶ the land is held by the **trustees** to be so available

provided that the land is not 'unavailable or unsuitable for occupation by [them]'.

In *Chan* v *Leung* [2003] 1 FLR 23 (CA), the Court of Appeal had to decide whether a large house in Surrey was suitable for occupation solely by Miss Leung, a university student. Jonathan Parker LJ stated, at [101], that:

> 'suitability' for this purpose must involve a consideration not only of the general nature and physical characteristics of the particular property but also a consideration of the personal characteristics, circumstances and requirements of the particular beneficiary.

Despite its size and the expense of its maintenance, the judge did not consider the house unsuitable for Miss Leung, especially as she would only wish to occupy it until the end of her studies. Even if this had not been the case, she had previously been living there with her partner, and the judge 'would have taken some persuading' that it was unsuitable for her simply because he had left.

14.4.1(b) Restrictions on the right to occupy

Section 13 of TOLATA gives the trustees certain responsibilities where two or more beneficiaries are entitled to occupy the land. Section 13(1) gives the trustees the power to exclude one or more, *but not all*, of the beneficiaries from the land. When exercising this power, the trustees:

- must not act 'unreasonably' (s 13(2));
- may impose 'reasonable conditions' on an occupying beneficiary (s 13(3));
- must take into account the intentions of the creator of the trust, the purposes of the trust and the circumstances and wishes of the beneficiaries (s 13(4)); and
- must not use their powers to prevent anyone already in occupation (whether or not they are a beneficiary of the trust) from continuing in occupation, or in an attempt to induce them to leave (s 13(7)).

Examples of 'reasonable conditions' might include paying expenses relating to the land or paying compensation to a beneficiary who has been reasonably excluded from occupation (ss 13(5), 13(6)). ·

Many cases concern land occupied as a family home. *Rodway* v *Landy* [2001] Ch 703 (CA), however, provides an example of the type of difficulties that may arise in a different context. In this case, two doctors in partnership had bought a property together from which to run their practice. They fell out, and one of them sought an order for the property to be sold to her under section 14 of TOLATA (see Section 14.5). The other asked the court to order that, since they were both trustees as well as beneficiaries, they use their powers under section 13 to divide the property in two, allowing one partner exclusive occupation of one part of the property, and the other partner exclusive occupation of the other part. The Court of Appeal decided that if the building lent itself to division in this way, the trustees were entitled under section 13 to exclude the beneficiaries' entitlement to occupy all of the building. The Court also held that, under section 13(3), the trustees could require the beneficiaries to contribute to the cost of adapting the building. Here, of course, the trustees and the beneficiaries were the same people, but it was important to keep the two roles and their functions separate in order to properly deal with the case.

14.4.2 To be consulted

Section 11(1) of TOLATA provides that when exercising any of their functions relating to the land, the **trustees** must:

(a) so far as practicable, consult the beneficiaries of full age and beneficially entitled to an interest in possession in the land, and

(b) so far as consistent with the general interest of the trust, give effect to the wishes of those beneficiaries, or (in case of dispute) of the majority (according to the value of their combined interests).

There are, however, certain exceptions. The **beneficiaries'** right to be consulted may be excluded by the terms of the trust (s 11(2)(a)) and will not normally apply to an express trust created before 1997 (s 11(2)(b)). Neither do the trustees need to consult the beneficiaries if they want to transfer the **title** to all of the beneficiaries under section 6(2) (s 11(2)(c)); section 6(2) is considered in Section 14.3.2.

At first sight, the section 11 right to be consulted seems to transfer considerable power to the beneficiaries. In fact, this is not the case, as even the wishes of a majority of the beneficiaries may be ignored if they are inconsistent with the 'general interest of the trust' (s 11(1)(b)). The right of consultation will, in any event, be meaningless in those cases where the people who are the beneficiaries are also the trustees.

14.5 Disputes concerning co-owned land

14.5.1 The powers of the court

If the land is sold or mortgaged in breach of **trust** because the provisions for consultation and the gaining of consents have not been observed, aggrieved **beneficiaries** can, in theory, sue their **trustees**. However, in most cases it is more appropriate to try to resolve any disputes using the mechanism contained in section 14 of TOLATA. The main exception is when a civil partnership or marriage breaks down; in such cases, any co-owned land is normally dealt with by way of a property adjustment order under the Civil Partnership Act 2004 or the Matrimonial Causes Act 1973.

Section 14(1) allows any person who is a trustee of land or who has an interest in land that is subject to a trust to apply to the court. Potential applicants include, therefore:

- a trustee;
- a beneficiary;
- a secured creditor (**mortgagee**);
- purchasers of the land who find themselves subject to the interests of a beneficiary whose rights were not overreached; and
- the **trustee in bankruptcy** of a beneficiary.

Section 14(2) gives the court the power to make an order:

(a) relating to the exercise by the trustees of any of their functions ... or

(b) declaring the nature or extent of a person's interest in property subject to the trust.

Many applications under section 14 ultimately come down to the question of whether the land should be sold. However, the court may be required to determine other matters, including a dispute over the allocation of the right to occupy (*Rodway* v *Landy* [2001] Ch 703 (CA), considered in Section 14.4.1(b)). The court's power under section 14 is extensive, but it is not unlimited, as the case of *Bagum* v *Hafiz* [2016] Ch 241 (CA) illustrates. A house was purchased by Mrs Bagum and her two sons (Mr Hafiz and Mr Hai) to provide a home for them and their families. Following a disagreement, Mr Hai and his family moved elsewhere and Mrs Bagum sought a court order requiring Mr Hai to sell his interest in the house to Mr Hafiz. The Court of Appeal had no doubt that such an order lay outside its powers under section 14(2). As Briggs LJ explained at [18] (emphasis added):

> the direct disposal of a *beneficiary's interest*, whether on sale to another beneficiary or otherwise is, quite simply, not a function of trustees of land.

However, in so far as the order requested relates to the exercise of the trustees' functions, he went on to say, at [23]:

> the clear object and effect of sections 14 and 15 is to confer on the court a substantially wider discretion, exercised on the basis of wider considerations, than might be enjoyed by the trustees themselves, acting without either the consent of their beneficiaries or an order of the court.

The court could, therefore, order the trustees to allow Mr Hafiz to purchase the house within a limited period and at a price determined by the court and that the house should be sold on the open market if Mr Hafiz chose not to buy it under these conditions.

The extent to which the court is constrained by the provisions of TOLATA has also arisen in the context of whether an absent co-owner should be compensated by the beneficiary in occupation of the land. According to Lady Hale (*Stack* v *Dowden* [2007] 2 AC 432 (HL), [94]):

> These statutory powers replaced the old doctrines of equitable accounting under which a beneficiary who remained in occupation might be required to pay an occupation rent to a beneficiary who was excluded from the property.

However, the 'old doctrines of equitable accounting' may still be relevant to cases that fall outside the scope of sections 12 and 13 of TOLATA. For example, in both *French* v *Barcham* [2009] 1 WLR 1124 (Ch) and *Davis* v *Jackson* [2017] 1 WLR 4005 (Ch) the High Court considered whether the trustee in bankruptcy of one co-owner was entitled to 'occupation **rent**' from the other co-owner. Blackbourne J and Snowden J respectively concluded *Stack* v *Dowden* could be distinguished where the circumstances lay beyond the scope of TOLATA (a trustee in bankruptcy is not 'beneficially entitled to an interest in possession' for the purposes of sections 12 and 13 of TOLATA). It should be noted, however, that they did not agree as to whether the general equitable rules usually entitled a trustee in bankruptcy to recover 'occupation rent' from a co-owner.

14.5.2   Factors to be considered

Section 15 lists several matters to which the court is to have regard when determining an application under Section 14. The relevant factors vary according to the circumstances, the most significant difference being where the application is made by a trustee in bankruptcy of one of the co-owners. The factors relevant to the most common types of application are summarised in Table 14.2.

Table 14.2　Main factors to be taken into account on an application under section 14 of the Trusts of Land and Appointment of Trustees Act 1996

	Sale by trustee, beneficiary, or secured creditor	Sale by a trustee in bankruptcy	Concerning the right to occupy
Main TOLATA factors	The section 15(1) factors	Section 335A of the Insolvency Act 1986 (TOLATA, s 15(4))	The section 15(1) factors or the factors referred to in section 13(8) if section 13(7) is engaged
Other TOLATA factors	The circumstances and wishes of the majority (according to value) of the beneficiaries of full age (s 15(3))		The circumstances and wishes of beneficiaries with a right to occupy under s 12 (s 15(2))

Section 6 of the Human Rights Act 1998 requires the court to take account of any rights under Article 1 of the First Protocol and Article 8 of the European Convention on Human Rights when exercising its powers pursuant to section 14. However, as Arnold J explained in *National Westminster Bank plc* v *Rushmer* [2010] 2 FLR 362 (Ch), [50]:

> it will ordinarily be sufficient for this purpose for the court to give due consideration to the factors specified in section 15 of TOLATA … I would not rule out the possibility that there may be circumstances in which it is necessary for the court explicitly to consider whether an order for sale is a proportionate interference with the Article 8 rights of those affected, but I do not consider that this will always be necessary.

When considering an application under section 14 of TOLATA, it is important to apply the whole of section 15, and not just the factors in section 15(1), although they will often require most attention. For example, in *Avis* v *Turner* [2008] Ch 218 (CA), a trustee in bankruptcy case, the court considered the implications of section 15(3) of TOLATA, Chadwick LJ concluding at [35] that it was open to the court to override the need for the consent of any particular person. It must not be forgotten, either, that the court may also have regard to factors not listed in section 15. The judgment of Birss J in *Parkes* v *Wilkes* [2017] 4 WLR 123 (Ch) offers a helpful example of how to deal with this type of question. After considering whether he has the power to make the order requested, he works systematically through the relevant section 15 factors (in that case ss 15(1)(a) and (b)), before considering whether there are any broader factors that need to be taken into account.

14.5.3　The section 15(1) factors

Section 15(1) lists four factors to which the court is to have regard in all cases except for applications by a **trustee in bankruptcy**. This list is not exhaustive, nor does the section give any indication of how the factors are to be weighted should they conflict in a particular case: that is a matter for the court to determine, and examples are referred to below.

Prior to TOLATA, the court's discretion to make an order concerning co-owned land was exercised under section 30 of the LPA 1925. The discretion under section 30 of the LPA 1925 was more limited than under section 15 of TOLATA because of the presumption in favour of a sale (see Section 14.1). Only if the underlying purpose of the **trust** was still achievable could the court block the **trustees'** duty of sale. The principles developed under section 30 of the LPA 1925 were highly nuanced by the time TOLATA came into force at the beginning of 1997. Section 15(1) of TOLATA seems to have been intended to place them on a statutory footing, free from the presumption in favour of a sale. Consequently, many of the cases decided under section 30 of the LPA 1925 continue to inform the courts' deliberations.

It has already been noted at Section 14.5.2 that section 15 effectively gives the court considerably more discretion than the trustees, who must comply with the general rules of equity (s 6(6)) which focus on protecting the **beneficiaries** as a class. In his judgment in *Bagum* v *Hafiz* [2016] Ch 241 (CA), at [23], Briggs LJ offered the following specific examples of the wider factors that the court, but not the trustees, are to have regard to:

> section 15(1)(c) requires the court to consider the welfare of a minor in occupation of the trust property as his home, whether or not that minor is a beneficiary of the trust. Section 15(1)(d) requires the court to have regard to the interests of secured creditors (rather than merely to respect their strict legal rights). As I have illustrated, section 15(1)(a) may bring into play the intention of the person who created the trust that benefits be conferred on particular beneficiaries.

Each of the section 15(1) factors is now considered in turn.

14.5.3(a) The intention of the person or persons (if any) who created the trust

This factor is most likely to be referred to where the trust was created expressly and the intention of the settlor is discernible from the document creating the trust. For example, in *Barclay* v *Barclay* [1970] 2 QB 677 (CA), the trust was created by a will in which the testator directed his bungalow be sold by his executor and the proceeds divided between certain persons. In the absence of a formal declaration of trust, it may be very difficult to establish the intentions of the settlor. Where there is more than one settlor there is every possibility that each of them will have slightly different intentions, in so far as those intentions are formulated at all. In *White* v *White* [2004] 2 FLR 321 (CA), Arden LJ was of the opinion, at [22], that:

> Where more than one person created the trust, the intention for the purposes of section 15(1)(a) must, as I see it, be the intention of all the persons who created the trust and be an intention which they had in common.

14.5.3(b) The purposes for which the property subject to the trust is held

In *Re Buchanan-Wollaston's Conveyance* [1939] Ch 738 (CA) the four owners of a plot of land entered into a mutual deed of covenant under which they agreed that any transaction involving the land required them to act unanimously. Despite the presumption in favour of a sale under the old law, the Court of Appeal refused to allow the claimant to rely on equity to escape from a contract that he had entered into freely. Conversely, in *Jones* v *Challenger* [1961] 1 QB 176 (CA) a house had been bought by a husband and wife as a matrimonial home, but the marriage had broken down, and the wife had left. There were no children, and the Court of Appeal held that the house should be sold because, as Devlin LJ explained, at 183:

> with the end of the marriage, [the] purpose [of the trust] was dissolved and the primacy of the duty to sell was restored.

In *Bank of Ireland Home Mortgages Ltd* v *Bell* [2001] 2 FLR 809 (CA) the Court of Appeal agreed with the district judge, who had concluded that the purpose of using the house as a family home ceased, if not as soon as the husband left (never to return), then certainly by the time the bank began possession proceedings a year and a half later.

There seems to be a considerable overlap between the first two factors listed in section 15(1), and the courts often consider the two factors together (as, for example, in *Holman* v *Howes* [2005] EWHC 2824 (Ch) at [64]; this part of the judgment was not challenged when the case reached the Court of Appeal). The second factor (s 15(1)(b)) is probably a little wider, and allows for the fact that the purpose of the trust may have evolved over time. In *First National Bank plc* v *Achampong* [2003] EWCA Civ 487, at [65], Blackburne J tentatively distinguished the original intention that the house provide a *matrimonial* home for the couple from its later purpose as a *family* home for them *and their children*. In *White* v *White*, Arden LJ accepted, at [24], that the purpose established at the outset of the trust could change, but only if both parties agreed to the change. She also accepted that purposes could be formulated informally, but emphasised that the purposes engaged by section 15(1)(b) are the purposes for which the property is actually held, rather than the wishes or expectations of one or more of the relevant parties.

14.5.3(c) The welfare of any minor who occupies or might reasonably be expected to occupy any land subject to the trust as their home

In the cases decided under section 30 of the LPA 1925, the courts distinguished between homes purchased merely to provide accommodation for the owners (as in *Jones* v *Challenger*) and those intended to provide a home for the co-owners and their children. In *Re Evers' Trust* [1980] 1 WLR 1327 (CA), an unmarried couple with three children had bought a house. The man left and applied for an order for sale in order to take out the money he had contributed towards the purchase price. Ormrod LJ found that the underlying purpose of the trust was to provide a family home and, since that purpose still subsisted, albeit without the man, declined at that time to make the order.

Section 15(1)(c) now requires the interests of any children who occupy (or who might be expected to occupy) the trust land as their home to be considered separately from the purpose of the trust. Although there has been relatively little judicial consideration of section 15(1)(c), it does seem clear that the mere presence of children (or grandchildren) living on the land will not be sufficient to make the factor relevant. The court must be provided specific evidence as to how the children's welfare will be adversely affected by any proposed order (Blackburne J, *First National Bank* v *Achampong* (CA), at [65]).

14.5.3(d) The interests of any secured creditor of any beneficiary

Under section 30 of the LPA 1925, when the party seeking an order for sale was a creditor, the courts applied the principles based on bankruptcy cases (see Section 14.5.4). The result was that, unless there were exceptional circumstances, the interests of a secured creditor would take precedence over the wishes of the beneficiaries (*Lloyds Bank plc* v *Byrne* [1993] 1 FLR 369 (CA)).

Under section 15(1), the interests of any secured creditor are only one consideration among several in section 15 to be taken into account by the court. In *Mortgage Corp Ltd* v *Shaire* [2001] Ch 743 (Ch), a case in which a secured creditor brought an action under section 14 for possession of the trust property following **mortgage** arrears, Neuberger J held that there was nothing to indicate that the interests of a secured creditor should take precedence over the other factors listed in section 15(1). The court was clear that section 15 was intended to enable the courts to exercise a wider discretion than formerly in favour of families as against secured creditors. With regard to previous authorities, he stated, at 761:

> there are obvious dangers in relying on authorities which proceeded on the basis that the court's discretion was more fettered than it now is. I think it would be wrong to throw over all the earlier cases without paying them any regard. However, they are to be treated with caution, in the light of the change in the law, and in many cases they are unlikely to be of great, let alone decisive, assistance.

Despite *Mortgage Corp Ltd* v *Shaire*, the Court of Appeal subsequently returned to the previous orthodoxy of *Lloyds Bank plc* v *Byrne*. In *Bank of Ireland Home Mortgages Ltd* v *Bell* [2001] 2 FLR 809 (CA), Peter Gibson LJ explained that although section 15 had increased the scope of the discretion available to the court, at [31]:

> a powerful consideration is and ought to be whether the creditor is receiving proper recompense for being kept out of his money, repayment of which is overdue.

In this case, there was no equity in Mrs Bell's property, the debt was continuing to increase, and her son was almost 18 (minimising the relevance of s 15(1)(c)). The court found little difficulty in ordering sale. In *First National Bank* v *Achampong* the Court of Appeal adopted the reasoning in *Bell*, despite the presence of infant grandchildren. In the words of Blackburne J, at [65]:

> Prominent among the considerations which lead to that conclusion is that, unless an order for sale is made, the bank will be kept waiting indefinitely for any payment out of what is, for all practical purposes, its own share of the property.

Despite the unfortunate consequences for the occupiers, there is a certain logic behind the decisions in *Bank of Ireland* v *Bell* and *First National Bank* v *Achampong*, since it is open to a creditor to initiate bankruptcy proceedings, then have the case heard under section 335A of the Insolvency Act 1986 and thus avoid the section 15(1) factors entirely (see Section 14.5.4).

14.5.4 Bankruptcy: section 335A of the Insolvency Act 1986

Section 15(4) of TOLATA provides that where the section 14 application is made by the **trustee in bankruptcy** of one of the parties the case is considered not under section 15(1–3), but under section 335A of the Insolvency Act 1986.

The court must make such an order 'as it thinks just and reasonable', having regard to:

- the interests of the bankrupt's creditors; and
- all the circumstances of the case except for the needs of the bankrupt.

Where the trustee in bankruptcy's application relates to a dwelling-house that has been the home of the bankrupt or the bankrupt's spouse or civil partner (or former spouse or former civil partner), the court will also have to take into account:

- the extent to which the spouse or partner contributed towards the bankruptcy;
- the needs and resources of the spouse or partner; and
- the needs of any children.

However, by section 335A(3), once a year has passed since the bankruptcy was declared, the court:

> shall assume, unless the circumstances of the case are exceptional, that the interests of the bankrupt's creditors outweigh all other considerations.

From time to time, the High Court is asked to consider whether the exercise of the rights contained in section 335A is compatible with the right to respect of the home and family life under Article 8 of the European Convention on Human Rights. The Court has repeatedly found the section compliant. In *Ford* v *Alexander* [2012] EWHC 266 (Ch), Peter Smith J opined, at [49]:

> the requirements in sub section (2) [of s 335A] and the change of emphasis in sub paragraph (3) do not infringe Article 8(2). They provide a necessary balance as between the rights of creditors and the respect for privacy and the home of the debtor. That balance serves the legitimate aim of protecting the rights and freedoms of others. I am therefore of the opinion that the requirements of section 335A satisfy the test of being necessary in a democratic society and are thus proportionate.

The reference to exceptional circumstances in section 335A(3) gave statutory effect to a principle originally developed by the courts. In *Re Citro (Domenico) (a bankrupt)* [1991] Ch 142 (CA), a case heard under the section 30 (LPA 1925) jurisprudence, the Court of Appeal considered the nature of exceptional circumstances. The disruption of losing a home and changing schools is 'not uncommon', and therefore not exceptional. Nourse LJ described this as 'the melancholy consequences of debt and improvidence with which every civilised society has been familiar' (at 157).

Before *Citro*, only in *Re Holliday* [1981] Ch 405 (CA) had the court postponed sale in a bankruptcy case. In *Holliday*, the spouse had made himself bankrupt, the creditors were not pressing for repayment, there were young children, and the wife would have been unable to find accommodation elsewhere in the area with her share of the proceeds of sale. As if that were not enough, the bankrupt had left his wife for another woman. Asking the question 'In all the circumstances of the case, whose voice in equity ought to prevail?', a different Court of Appeal from that in *Citro* felt able to postpone sale for five years.

Under the Insolvency Act 1986, if the court finds that there are exceptional circumstances it may postpone sale or refuse it entirely. It appears that the courts are prepared to offer a measure of protection to the family home in cases where the health of a member of the family who is suffering from a serious or terminal illness would be further prejudiced by a forced removal from their home. For example, in *Re Raval* [1998] 2 FLR 718 (Ch), an order for sale against a paranoid schizophrenic was postponed for a year to allow suitable accommodation to be found for her. In *Claughton* v *Charalambous* [1999] 1 FLR 740 (Ch), the bankrupt's spouse had severe medical problems, and the house they shared had been specially adapted for her. Jonathan Parker J found that these circumstances were exceptional and confirmed the decision of the county court to suspend the order for sale indefinitely. He seems to have been influenced by the fact that the creditors were unlikely to receive anything from the sale of the property, as its value was less than the costs that would be deducted by the trustee in bankruptcy. However, the likelihood that a bankrupt's creditors will be repaid in full if the sale of the family home is delayed does not amount to exceptional circumstances (see *Donohoe* v *Ingram* [2006] EWHC 282 (Ch)).

In *Barca* v *Mears* [2004] EWHC 2170 (Ch), the defendant raised the question of whether the narrow approach to 'exceptional circumstances' in *Citro* was consistent with the rights protected under Article 8 of the European Convention on Human

Rights. Although Mr Nicholas Strauss QC (sitting as a deputy judge of the High Court) had no difficulty in deciding that there were no exceptional circumstances in that case, he expressed some concern about the test as formulated by Nourse LJ, because (at [40]):

> This approach leads to the conclusion that, however disastrous the consequences may be to family life, if they are of the *usual kind* then they cannot be relied on under section 335A; they will qualify as 'exceptional' only if they are of an unusual kind, for example where a terminal illness is involved.

14.6 Protection for buyers of trust land

One of the main aims of land law reform in the twentieth century (and, indeed, the twenty-first) has been to ensure that land is freely and conveniently marketable. **Beneficial interests** are potential traps for buyers and **mortgagees** because such interests are not necessarily readily apparent from either the **title** documentation or an inspection of the property itself. The danger of these traps is minimised by a number of important statutory rules. However, although these rules offer increased protection to the buyer or mortgagee, they can only do so by reducing the security of the **beneficiaries**.

14.6.1 Overreaching

A buyer (including a **mortgagee**) of land subject to a **trust** 'shall not be concerned with the trusts' provided that they have satisfied the conditions in sections 2 and 27 of the LPA 1925. If the conditions are satisfied, the rights of the **beneficiaries** are automatically 'overreached'. They are detached from the land and attached to the purchase price (or **mortgage** advance), which is now in the hands of the **trustees**. If the conditions are not met, any **beneficial interests** will not be overreached and will be binding on the purchaser. In the recent case of *Mortgage Express* v *Lambert* [2017] Ch 93 (CA), the Court of Appeal held that rights arising out of an equity (in that case the right to set aside an unconscionable bargain) are also capable of being overreached, at least if there is the potential to trace the interest into the proceeds of sale.

To satisfy the section 2 and 27 conditions, the purchaser must:

▸ acquire (or take a mortgage over) a legal **estate**; and
▸ pay the purchase price (or mortgage advance) to at least two trustees or a trust corporation.

'Legal estate' in this context means one of the two estates in land, rather than the extended meaning given to it by section 205(1)(x) of the LPA 1925 (*Baker* v *Craggs* [2018] 3 WLR 401 (CA)). There are a limited number of public officials who can act as trust corporations, but most are companies set up by banks or a law firms to administer trusts and act as executors under wills. To be recognised as a trust corporation, a company must comply with the rule made under section 4(3) of the Public Trustee Act 1906. It also seems that the trustees must be acting in good faith for overreaching to occur. In *HSBC Bank plc* v *Dyche* [2010] 2 P & CR 4 (Ch), the transfer of a house that was a dishonest breach of trust was held not to have overreached the beneficiary's interest, even though the purchase price had been paid to two trustees.

Overreaching beneficiaries' interests simply by paying two trustees is very convenient for buyers. In theory, the beneficiaries are happy too because they are entitled to their share of the proceeds in the safe hands of their trustees. Two trustees are less likely to run off with the cash than a single trustee, but this is not unknown. For example, in the case of *City of London Building Society* v *Flegg* [1988] AC 54 (HL) Mr and Mrs Maxwell-Brown held the land on trust for themselves and Mr and Mrs Flegg. Without the knowledge of Mr and Mrs Flegg, the Maxwell-Browns (the trustees) granted a mortgage of the land to the City of London Building Society. When the Maxwell-Browns failed to keep up the mortgage payments, the question arose as to whether the **beneficial interests** claimed by Mr and Mrs Flegg were binding on the building society. The House of Lords held that the Fleggs' beneficial interests had been overreached when the mortgage advance was paid to two trustees (Mr and Mrs Maxwell-Brown). Consequently, Mr and Mrs Flegg had no beneficial interest in the land: all that they could do was to try to recover their share of the mortgage advance from the Maxwell-Browns. However, the result would have been very different if the mortgage advance had been paid only to a single trustee, as in the earlier case of *Williams & Glyn's Bank Ltd* v *Boland* [1981] AC 487 (HL). In *Boland*, the beneficial interest (belonging to Mrs Boland) was not overreached and was binding on the land in the hands of the bank. (See also the **unregistered land** case of *Kingsnorth Finance Co Ltd* v *Tizard* [1986] 1 WLR 783 (Ch), discussed in Chapter 5.)

The decision in the case of *State Bank of India* v *Sood* [1997] Ch 276 (CA), while making sound commercial sense, further prejudices the position of beneficiaries. In breach of trust, two trustees mortgaged a house which they held on trust for themselves and five other beneficiaries. The mortgage secured past indebtedness and future borrowing, and no capital money was paid to the trustees. In a somewhat strained interpretation of section 2 of the LPA 1925, the Court of Appeal held that this was a transaction which enabled the bank to overreach the **equitable** rights of the beneficiaries despite the fact that no money was paid to the two trustees. The overreaching took effect on the execution of the **charge**, and at that time the interests of the beneficiaries became attached to the **equity of redemption**. This decision is consistent with the policy of encouraging free alienability of land and conforms to lending practice, but it removes the protection for beneficiaries, whose interest is transferred to the capital money paid to the trustees. Peter Gibson LJ stated, at 290:

> Much though I value the principle of overreaching as having aided the simplification of conveyancing, I cannot pretend that I regard the resulting position in the present case as entirely satisfactory. The safeguard for beneficiaries under the existing legislation is largely limited to having two trustees or a trust corporation where capital money falls to be received. But that is no safeguard at all, as this case has shown, when no capital money is received on and contemporaneously with the conveyance.

In fact, overreaching is only convenient for beneficiaries if they agree that the money is as good as the land. The Law Commission has recommended (Law Com No 188, 1989, para 4.3) that the consent of beneficiaries in occupation should be obtained before overreaching can take place (as is common practice where there is only one trustee), but this recommendation has not been taken up.

14.6.2 Did a beneficial joint tenancy remain intact?

If a buyer is acquiring land formerly owned by joint tenants that is vested in a single surviving tenant, there is always a risk that the beneficial **joint tenancy** was severed prior to the death of one of the joint tenants (see Section 13.5). If **severance** occurred, there may be a number of **beneficial interests** in the land, and these will not be overreached unless a second **trustee** is appointed.

Section 1 of the Law of Property (Joint Tenants) Act 1964 addresses this problem if **title** to the land were still unregistered at the date of the transfer. In such cases, the buyer of **unregistered land** is entitled to presume that the joint tenancy remained unsevered provided that:

- the **conveyance** states that the seller is solely and beneficially entitled to the land;
- no note or memorandum signed by the joint tenants or one of them has been made on the title deeds recording that the joint tenancy was severed; and
- none of the joint tenants has been adjudged bankrupt. This can easily be discovered by a bankruptcy search in the Land Charges Register.

There is no similar rule for **registered title**.

14.6.3 Did the trustees obtain the necessary consents?

Where the terms of the **trust** make any sale subject to the consent of more than two people, section 10 of TOLATA provides that the purchaser only has to be sure that two have actually consented.

If **title** to the land was still unregistered at the date of the transfer, the buyer has even greater protection under section 16 of TOLATA:

- they do not need to concern themself with whether the **trustees** are acting in the interests of the **beneficiaries** or whether the beneficiaries have been consulted (s 16(1)); and
- they will still get good title to the land, even if the **disposition** is in breach of trust, so long as they do not have actual **notice** of that breach (s 16(2)).

As with the 1964 Act, the protection in section 16 is not extended to purchasers of **registered land**. This prompted some academic discussion as to whether **overreaching** occurs when a disposition of registered land is in breach of trust (see Ferris and Battersby [1998] Conv 168). However, in *HSBC Bank plc* v *Dyche* [2010] 2 P & CR 4 (Ch), the High Court confirmed that the interests of beneficiaries are not overreached by such a disposition.

14.7 Conclusion

The Trusts of Land and Appointment of Trustees Act 1996 provides a coherent conceptual foundation for **trusts** of land. Although not without its own difficulties, it has extended and clarified the roles of **trustees** and **beneficiaries** in relation especially to partition, consultation, rights of occupation and delegation, and it gives beneficiaries limited powers in respect of the appointment of trustees.

Some problems remain, not least for family members when a co-owner faces section 14 proceedings from a secured creditor or a **trustee in bankruptcy**. Although section 15 of TOLATA and the Insolvency Act 1986 were designed to provide a compromise between the needs of the family and the wishes of the creditors to get at their money, recent cases indicate that in most cases the court will order the home to be sold. Perhaps this is inevitable given TOLATA's heritage. The rules of equity have historically focused on the financial entitlement of individual parties, rather than the purpose of any **co-ownership** venture or the relationship between the parties (see Cooke, 2007). This is also reflected in equity's preference for **tenancy in common** over **joint tenancy** and its willingness to recognise **severance** (see Sections 13.4 and 13.5), although there is some evidence that this may be changing, at least in so far as family property is concerned (see *Stack* v *Dowden* [2007] 2 AC 432 (HL)). This can be contrasted with the 'community of property' enjoyed in several European states and the 'homestead legislation' of New Zealand and parts of North America, which are based on very different priorities from those implicit, if not actually embedded, in TOLATA (see Omar, 2006).

Summary

14.1 Trusts containing land are now 'trusts of land' and are regulated by the Trusts of Land and Appointment of Trustees Act (TOLATA) 1996. However, it is important to know something of the rules prior to TOLATA as aspects of pre-TOLATA cases may still be relevant.

14.2 Trusts of land may be created expressly, by statute or by implication.

14.3 The trustees are the persons who hold the legal title to the land. Their duties are contained in TOLATA and the Trustee Act 2000. Subject to the terms of the trust, trustees of land have the powers of an absolute owner of land together with power to transfer the land to adult beneficiaries absolutely entitled, to partition the land and to delegate their powers to beneficiaries.

14.4 Beneficiaries usually have the right to occupy the land, subject to rules to accommodate competing claims. They also have the right to be consulted by the trustees.

14.5 Under a trust of land, any trustee or beneficiary can go to court for an order of sale or otherwise. The court may make such order as it thinks fit, but where a party is bankrupt the land will probably be sold after a year, unless the circumstances are 'exceptional'.

14.6 When buying land subject to a trust, it is important to pay the price to two or more trustees or a trust corporation to ensure that any beneficial interests are overreached (that is, transferred from the land to the proceeds of sale).

Exercises

 14.1 Complete the online quiz on the topics covered in this chapter on the companion website.

14.2 Critically consider whether section 15 of the Trusts of Land and Appointment of Trustees Act 1996 has enabled the courts adequately to balance the interests of the various parties who may be interested in a dispute concerning co-owned land.

14.3 Five friends, Denise, Michael, Florence, Jacob and Ben, who had just graduated and found jobs, bought a house, intending to share it while they established themselves in their new careers. They each contributed £10,000 to the deposit and were equally liable for the mortgage repayments.

Denise decided to leave her job and sail round the world, so she sold her share of the house to her friend Amanda, who has now taken over her mortgage liability.

Florence and Michael became lovers and had a baby. Since the house is large, they want to divide it into two maisonettes, keeping the smaller one for themselves. The others want to keep it as it is.

Ben's business investments have failed, and he thinks he might be made bankrupt.

Discuss the rights of all the parties, and explain what might now happen to the land.

 You can find suggested answer plans to exercises 14.2 and 14.3 on the companion website.

Further reading

Baker, 'The Judicial Approach to "Exceptional Circumstances" In Bankruptcy: The Impact of the Human Rights Act 1998' (2010) 74 Conv 352

Bright, 'Occupation Rents and the Trusts of Land and Appointment of Trustees Act 1996: From Property to Welfare?' (2009) 73 Conv 378

Brown, 'Insolvency and the Matrimonial Home: The Sins of Our Fathers: *In re Citro (a Bankrupt)*' (1992) 55 MLR 284

Cooke, 'Community of Property, Joint Ownership and the Family Home' in Dixon and Griffith (eds), *Contemporary Perspectives on Property, Equity and Trusts Law* (Oxford University Press 2007) 39

Dixon, 'Trusts of Land, Bankruptcy and Human Rights' (2005) 69 Conv 161

Ferris and Battersby, 'The Impact of the Trusts of Land and Appointment of Trustees Act 1996 on Purchasers of Registered Land' [1998] Conv 168

Omar, 'Security over Co-owned Property and the Creditor's Paramount Status in Recovery Proceedings' (2006) 70 Conv 157

Pascoe, 'Section 15 of the Trusts of Land and Appointment of Trustees Act 1996: A Change in the Law?' [2000] Conv 315

Pascoe, 'Right to Occupy under a Trust of Land: Muddled Legislative Logic?' (2006) 70 Conv 54

Part V

Acquiring interests in land

Chapter 15

Land contracts and other formalities

Key concepts

- **Completion** – the creation or transfer of a legal estate or interest pursuant to a contract to do so.
- **Disposition** – the creation or transfer of an interest.
- **Estate contract** – a contract for the creation or sale of an interest in land.
- **Exchange** – the exchange of copies of the contract (one usually signed by the seller, the other by the buyer) in order to create a binding contract.

15.1 A typical domestic sale

Most, although not all, land transactions in England and Wales consist of two main stages:

- a contract to create or transfer the interest in land; and
- the actual transfer or creation of that interest.

The most common transaction concerning land is almost certainly the sale and purchase of a **freehold title** containing a house and garden, combined, in most cases, with the simultaneous grant of a **mortgage** in favour of a lender who has provided a considerable proportion of the purchase moneys. This is the type of transaction considered in this section by way of an illustration of a 'typical' land transaction. However, in recent years, the impact of the economic climate on earnings, and upon the lending policies of major banks and building societies, has meant that many potential buyers, especially first-time buyers, cannot afford to purchase a home outright. Some may be able to buy a share in a house with friends or family (see Chapters 13 and 14 for the rules regulating co-ownership); others may purchase a share in the **freehold** title and pay **rent** (usually to a social landlord) on the other share under a shared ownership scheme. Many, however, will find that they have little alternative but to rent their homes, often paying rent to a private landlord who has been able to purchase property with the aid of a so-called buy-to-let mortgage.

The process of acquiring a house is summarised in Table 15.1. It begins when the sellers advertise the house for sale. Traditionally, prospective buyers would have begun their search for a suitable property by looking at the cards in the windows of estate agents; today, they are more likely to use the internet. They will see one or more houses they like and arrange to visit them, before making an offer to purchase the house they want, at a price acceptable to the sellers. Once the buyers' offer has been accepted, the sale is said to be agreed '**subject to contract**'. Neither party is legally bound to honour this type of agreement; both are free to withdraw without giving any reason for doing so. At this point the

Table 15.1 The main stages in the purchase of a house

Time	Facts	Law	Section
	Advertising the house for sale. Buyer makes an offer.		
About 8 weeks	Negotiation of price, fittings, etc. Survey and finance arranged. Draft contract prepared by seller. Buyer checks the details of the property and makes searches and enquiries of the seller and others (such as the Local Authority to check planning, access, etc.). Contract agreed by buyer and seller.	None of these steps has any legal or equitable implications: there is no contract.	15.1
	Contracts signed by both parties are exchanged; the buyer pays a deposit to the seller.	Binding contract. Equitable title passes to the buyer.	15.4 15.3
Usually between 2 and 4 weeks	Pre-completion searches of title. Deeds of conveyance and mortgage are prepared. The lender releases the mortgage moneys.		15.5.1
	Completion by execution of the deeds and payment of the balance of the purchase price to the seller.		
Within 2 months	The transfer and mortgage are sent to the Land Registry for registration.		15.5.2
	The Land Registry completes registration and issues an official copy of the Register of Title.	Legal title is vested in the buyer.	

transaction usually passes into the hands of solicitors or qualified conveyancers, who will undertake the necessary enquiries and ensure that the required formalities are complied with. The buyers will want to know exactly what is included in the sale and to be sure that both the structure of the house and its title are in order. They will also need to arrange any mortgage finance that is needed, and the lender will also want to satisfy itself that the property is worth the value placed on it. It is the buyers' responsibility to carry out all the checks, searches and enquiries that they and their solicitor or licensed conveyancer feel are necessary. While the enquiries are being made, the lawyers will agree the terms of the formal contract for the sale and purchase of the house. In some cases, most of the terms of the contract will be the result of substantive negotiation, but most residential transactions incorporate a set of standard conditions published by the Law Society of England and Wales (presently the Standard Conditions of Sale (5th edn)). If the transaction includes a new lease the terms of that lease will also need to be negotiated.

This period of pre-contractual enquiries and negotiation is a time of great uncertainty for the buyers and sellers alike. Neither side can be sure of completing the sale. The buyers might fail to get the loan they need to finance the purchase, or they might decide that the house is too expensive. The sellers might receive a higher offer from another prospective buyer or might decide to withdraw the house from the market. Each side would like the other to be bound as soon as possible, but is wary of committing itself too soon. The proposed transaction will only become legally binding between the parties when they exchange signed copies of the contract (see Section 15.4). The buyer will usually be required to pay a deposit when contracts are exchanged.

Reaching the exchange of contracts is a major achievement for anyone involved in buying or selling a house. However, exchange of contracts is not the end of the process, as it does not transfer legal title to the buyers. Traditionally, the contract will set a date some two to four weeks in the future for the transfer of the legal title to the land in return for the payment of the balance of the purchase price. This period allows final checks to be made on the sellers' entitlement to sell the land; deeds of conveyance and mortgage are prepared and executed, and the mortgage advance is transferred to the buyers' lawyers in readiness. Once everything is in place, the transfer of the legal title can be completed. This long-planned-for day can be somewhat frantic, not least because there will often be a chain of completions that need to be coordinated; the buyers are probably selling a house, too, and the sellers will need somewhere to move to before the buyers arrive with all their belongings.

However, even a successful completion day, with the keys released and the various parties installed in their new homes, does not mean that the legal title has actually been transferred. The buyers' lawyers must arrange for the transfer of legal title to be registered; legal ownership is only vested in the buyers when the transfer has been recorded at the Land Registry.

15.2 Formalities when buying and selling interests in land

What are formalities and why do we need them?
In 'Taking Formalities Seriously' in Bright and Dewar (eds), *Land Law Themes and Perspectives* (Oxford University Press 1998), Patricia Critchley identifies three distinguishing characteristics of a formality:

- it is usually something additional or external to the transaction as such;
- it is a requirement if the transaction is to be effective; and
- there will be consequences if the requirement is not complied with.

Such formalities are not unique to land law, but they have been an important feature of it for centuries. One of the reasons for this is the intangible nature of many, if not all, interests in land. Unlike most **chattels**, it is not possible to physically hand over interests in land. One of the main purposes of insisting upon certain formalities when it comes to creating or transferring interests in land is that they provide evidence of what has been done: in other words, it is possible for third parties, as well as the parties to the transaction, to be sure of the legal situation. Such certainty is important if land is to be capable of being transferred freely and conveniently. Formalities bring additional benefits. The need to write and sign a formal document encourages the parties to think carefully about the transaction, and to be clear in their own minds about what they have agreed; it may also protect them from pressure to do something that they do not wish to do. However, formalities are not without their costs.

The costs may be financial: the need to instruct a lawyer or conveyancer (or learn the law for oneself); there will also be land registration fees to be paid. Another potential cost is that of justice if formalities are insisted upon too strictly. English law has long recognised that there will be circumstances in which justice requires interests to be recognised in the absence of the usual formalities. Examples include the doctrines of **prescription** (see Chapter 10), **constructive trusts** (see Chapter 17) and **proprietary estoppel** (see Chapter 18). Perhaps the doctrine of **adverse possession** (see Chapter 16) might also fall within this category. The Land Registration Act 2002 has, arguably, blurred the distinctions between formality and substance when it comes to creating and transferring legal interests in land, although even here the Register is not necessarily the last word (see Sections 4.9 and 4.10).

This chapter focuses on:

- the rules about the creation and enforcement of contracts for the sale of land, *because* unless these rules are observed, there will not be a binding contract between the parties; and
- the rules about deeds and registration, *because* failure to comply with these rules may mean that the buyer does not get the legal interest that they have paid for, but a much less secure equitable interest.

Other aspects of the process of buying and selling land will be referred to, but their details belong to courses on conveyancing rather than the study of land law. For practical purposes, 'land law' refers to the substantive law, whereas 'conveyancing' is concerned with procedural requirements. However, the dividing line is rather blurred (see, for example, the question of whether the LRA 2002 is substantive law or merely a set of conveyancing rules, referred to in Sections 4.6.2(a) and 4.10). The term 'conveyancing' is derived from 'conveyance', a word used to describe both the transfer of the property and the document (technically a **deed** of grant) which brings the transfer about. The term 'conveyance' is not necessarily restricted to the transfer of **freehold** land, but can also refer to the granting of mortgages and leases (LPA 1925, s 205(1)(ii)).

The Electronic Communications Act 2000 and Part 8 of the LRA 2002 provided the statutory framework for discarding the printed page in favour of electronic conveyancing. The original intention was that all stages of conveyancing, including signing and exchanging contracts, should be capable of being completed electronically. However, progress has been a lot slower than originally expected (see Section 4.2.1) and the majority of conveyancing looks likely to require the use of paper for the immediate future.

The main formality requirements, together with some important exceptions, are summarised in Table 15.2. As in all areas of land law, the rules on which this chapter focuses are affected by other rules. The most important are those about **registered** and **unregistered** land. However, legal **title** can also be obtained by long use, and equitable title by means of a **trust**. This is just one example of how it is impossible to divide land law into a series of completely self-contained units of study.

Table 15.2 A summary of formalities relating to dealings with land

Type of interest	Basic rule	Significant exceptions
Creation or transfer of a legal estate and legal interest	• Deed (LPA 1925, s 52) followed by registration under LRA 2002 (note that all legal interests in land are 'estates in land' for the purposes of LPA 1925, s 52 (see LPA 1925, s 1(4))); or • A limited number of transactions may be completed electronically	• Short leases (LPA 1925, s 52(2)(d); LRA 2002, ss 4(2) and 27(2)(b)) • Adverse possession (see Chapter 16) • The doctrine of prescription (see Section 10.7.6)
A contract for the sale or other disposition of an interest in the land (see Section 15.3)	• Writing satisfying Law of Property (Miscellaneous Provisions) Act 1989, s 2	• Short leases, public auctions, certain financial arrangements, and resulting implied and constructive trusts (Law of Property (Miscellaneous Provisions) Act 1989, s 2(5); see Section 15.4.2(c)) • Contracts subject to rectification (see Section 15.4.3(d))
Creation of a trust of land	• Evidenced in writing (LPA 1925, 53(1)(b))	• Statutory trusts of land on co-ownership (see Section 14.2) • Resulting implied and constructive trusts (LPA 1925, s 53(2); see Chapter 17)
Creation of other types of equitable interest in land	• Writing (LPA 1925, s 53(1)(a))	• Resulting implied and constructive trusts (LPA 1925, s 53(2); see Chapter 17) • Proprietary estoppel (see Chapter 18)
Transfer of equitable interests	• Writing (LPA 1925, s 53(1)(c))	• Resulting implied and constructive trusts (LPA 1925, s 53(2); see Chapter 17)

15.3 Contracts and the transfer of the equitable interest

The outline of a land transaction in Section 15.1, while typical, is not universal. There is no strict requirement to enter into a contract to transfer the land in advance of the transfer itself. For example, many leases, including most short residential leases and some longer business leases, will be granted without first exchanging contracts. It might be wondered why conveyancers normally proceed via exchange of contracts rather than simply proceeding directly to the transfer of the legal interest. The reason is that a considerable number of things need to be done, at considerable expense, to facilitate completion. Today, the main task is to organise the release of funds from the lender. Historically, however, investigating **title** was a much slower and riskier process than it is today. Buyers did not want to go to the expense of conducting the necessary examinations until they had some assurance that the seller would actually sell them the land. The parties to a sale of land could (and still can) usually feel secure once contracts had been exchanged, because the rules of equity provide that contracts relating to the disposition of interests in land are specifically enforceable. This remedy is available because 'equity regards as done that which ought to be done', although the **equitable** nature of the remedy also means that it is discretionary and will only be ordered if the claimant has behaved properly.

The availability of specific performance means that the sellers become, effectively, **trustees** of the equitable right of the buyers to become the legal owners when the contract is completed. As Jessel MR explained in the case of *Lysaght* v *Edwards* (1875–76) LR 2 ChD 499 (Ch), at 505–6:

> What is the effect of the contract? It appears to me that the effect of a contract for sale has been settled for more than two centuries. ... What is that doctrine? It is that the moment you have a valid contract for sale the vendor becomes in equity a trustee for the purchaser of the estate sold, and the beneficial ownership passes to the purchaser, the vendor having a right to the purchase-money, a **charge** or lien on the estate for the security of that purchase-money, and a right to retain possession of the estate until the purchase-money is paid.

The case of *Walsh* v *Lonsdale* (1882) LR 21 ChD 9 (CA) (see also Section 7.6.2) provides an example of the rule that an equitable interest in land is created as soon as there is a contract. Lonsdale entered into a contract to grant a seven-year lease of a mill to Walsh, but the parties never completed the deed necessary for transfer of the lease, the legal **estate**. Jessel MR concluded (at 14–15):

> The tenant holds under an agreement for a lease. He holds therefore under the same terms in equity as if a lease had been granted, it being a case in which both parties admit that relief is capable of being given by specific performance.

A written contract for the sale of land is, therefore, an equitable interest in land (called an **'estate contract'**). Walsh had a seven-year equitable lease, and one might have expected him to be delighted with this result. Unfortunately for him, it meant that he had to observe all the terms of the lease, including payment of **rent** in advance, so he owed Lonsdale £1,005.

The **trust** relationship that is created between the buyers and the sellers allows the sellers to retain some rights to enjoy the land. They can remain in possession of the land and exclude the buyers. However, the sellers must take care to keep the land in the same condition as it was when contracts were exchanged. The passing of the **beneficial interest** in the land to the buyers means that they must observe any obligations attached to that beneficial interest (which is why Walsh had to pay the rent due to Lonsdale). The burden of the risk of damage to the property is also transferred to the buyers at exchange of contracts. This means that they must pay the whole of the purchase price, even if the house has been completely destroyed between exchange of contracts and the completion of the legal transfer of the land. This rule can cause significant complications (particularly with respect to the insuring of the property between exchange and completion), so it is usual for the contract to reverse it by expressly providing that the sellers will retain the risk until completion.

An estate contract is an equitable interest, and will, therefore, need to be protected if it is to be binding on third parties. If title to the land is **registered**, then a **notice** must be entered on the Title Register of the estate concerned (see Section 4.5.1). If the land is not yet registered, the contract should be protected by registering a C(iv) land charge in the Land Charges Register (see Section 5.4.2(c)).

15.4 Creating a valid land contract

This section concerns the requirements that must be met for a contract concerning a **disposition** of an interest in land to be valid. All of the statutory references in this section are to the Law of Property (Miscellaneous Provisions) Act 1989 ('the 1989 Act') unless otherwise indicated.

In order to establish whether a particular agreement meets the requirements of section 2 of the 1989 Act, the provisions of each sub-section need to be systematically applied to the facts. The details of the relevant rules are considered in Sections 15.4.2 and 15.4.3. Figure 15.1 illustrates how they can be used to access the status of an agreement in a problem-style question.

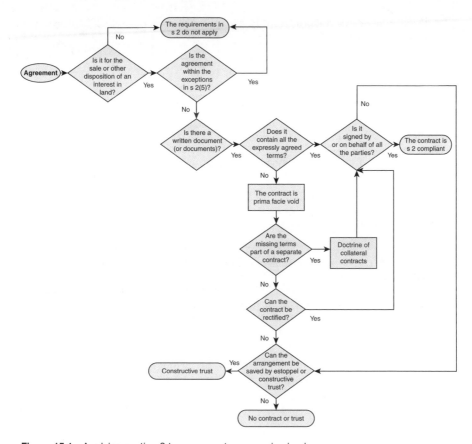

Figure 15.1 Applying section 2 to agreements concerning land

15.4.1 The history of land contract formalities

From the late seventeenth century until 1989, the rule was that a contract for the sale of an interest in land was not enforceable until there was some evidence of it either by writing or by part performance of the agreement. Over time, the legal rules about what would constitute written evidence and what counted as part performance of the contract became detailed and confusing. As a result, a completely new set of rules was introduced in section 2 of the Law of Property (Miscellaneous Provisions) Act 1989. These rules apply to all agreements for the sale of any interest in land made after 26th September 1989.

Section 2(1) of the 1989 Act states:

> A contract for the sale or other disposition of an interest in land can only be made in writing and only by incorporating all the terms which the parties have expressly agreed in one document or, where contracts are exchanged, in each.

Section 2(3) of the 1989 Act requires the document or documents to be signed by or on behalf of each of the parties to the contract.

Consequently, if an agreement falls within the scope of section 2, for a valid contract:

- there must be one document (or two identical documents, which is probably more usual);
- this document (or both of the identical documents) must contain all the terms that the parties have expressly agreed; and
- the document must have been signed by (or on behalf of) both the buyer and the seller (or, in the case of identical documents, signed and exchanged).

Although section 2 provides a welcome element of certainty compared to its immediate predecessor (s 40 of the Law of Property Act 1925), judges initially seemed reluctant to find that an unwritten agreement was not a contract merely because of section 2. Now, however, the courts are ready to insist upon compliance with all the formal requirements of section 2, even though this might be to the advantage of the less scrupulous litigant. As Biggs J said in *North Eastern Properties Ltd* v *Coleman* [2010] 1 WLR 2715 (CA), at [43]:

> the reported cases in which the courts have sought to interpret and apply section 2(1) of the 1989 Act demonstrate that, because of the rigorous discipline which it imposes upon parties to land contracts, it does indeed enable persons who have genuinely contracted to do just that. It enables parties to land contracts who have changed their minds to look around for expressly agreed terms which have not found their way into the final form of land contract which they signed, for the precise purpose of avoiding their obligations, on the ground that the lack of discipline of their counterparty, or even their own lack of discipline, has rendered the contract void.

One of the results of this strict application of the section 2 rules is that the courts have had to pay careful attention to the non-contractual remedies that may be available where there is a void land contract (see Section 15.4.5).

It is unlikely that the 1989 Act will be the final word on land contract formalities, especially given the present tendency towards greater digitisation. In the meantime, however, the use of technology must be 1989 Act compliant (see Section 15.4.3(a)).

15.4.2 The scope of section 2 of the 1989 Act

15.4.2(a) 'A contract' (s 2(1))

The requirements of section 2 are additional to the normal common law rules for the existence of a contract. Consequently, the normal prerequisites of a valid contract must be present, including offer, acceptance and consideration and the intention to create a legally binding relationship. Negotiations for the sale and purchase of land frequently include agreements that are expressed to be made '**subject to contract**'. Such an agreement is not an enforceable contract, but, as Sachs J explained in *Goding* v *Frazer* [1967] 1 WLR 286 (QB), at [293]:

> a transaction in which each side hopes the other will act like a gentleman and neither intends so to act if it is against his material interests.

Prior to the 1989 Act, it was usual for all pre-contractual negotiations concerning land to be headed 'subject to contract'. This was to prevent an oral agreement accidentally becoming enforceable under the provisions of section 40 of the LPA 1925. Although it is no longer possible to create a valid oral contract, 'subject to contract' remains in common use during negotiations and it may have significant consequences for the availability of alternative remedies if section 2 has not been complied with (see Section 15.4.5).

15.4.2(b) 'For the sale or other disposition of an interest in land' (s 2(1))

For the purposes of the 1989 Act section 2(6) (as amended by s 25(2) Trusts of Land and Appointment of Trustees Act 1996) defines an 'interest in land' as:

> any estate, interest or charge in or over land.

What is needed for a contract to be a 'contract for the sale or other disposition' of such an interest was considered by Arden LJ, in the case of *Joyce* v *Rigolli* [2004] EWCA Civ 79. She concluded at [31] that:

> for a contract to be one 'for' selling or disposing of land, it must have been part of the parties' purposes … in entering into such a contract, that the contract should achieve a sale or other disposition of land.

In that case, it was held that a boundary agreement did not fall within the scope of section 2 because the primary purpose of the agreement was to demarcate the boundary, albeit that this involved some land being exchanged.

Section 2 only applies to contracts that provide for the disposition to take place in the future: it does not apply once the disposition is complete. After reviewing the authorities, Henderson LJ, *Rollerteam Ltd* v *Riley* [2017] Ch 109 (CA), concluded at [38] that:

> section 2 of the 1989 Act applies only to executory contracts for the future sale or other disposition of an interest in land, and does not apply to a contract which itself effects such a disposition.

In *Helden* v *Strathmore Ltd* [2011] Bus LR 1592 (CA), one of the cases to which Henderson LJ referred, the claimant had sought to set aside a registered **legal charge** because it attempted to incorporate terms by reference to a document that had never existed. Lord Neuberger MR had no doubt (at [27]), that:

> a contract to transfer a freehold or a lease in the future, a contract to grant a lease in the future, or a contract for a mortgage in the future, are all within the reach of the section, provided of course the ultimate subject matter is land. However, an actual transfer, conveyance or assignment, an actual lease, or an actual mortgage are not within the scope of section 2 at all.

However, completion of the land element of an agreement that does not comply with section 2 will not rescue any non-land terms that formed part of the agreement (see *Keay* v *Morris Homes (West Midlands) Ltd* [2012] 1 WLR 2855 (CA)).

A disposition of land has been held to include:

- the grant of an option to buy land (*Spiro* v *Glencrown Properties* [1991] Ch 537 (Ch));
- the surrender of a lease (*Commission for New Towns* v *Cooper (GB) Ltd* [1995] Ch 259 (CA)); a contract to create a **mortgage** (*United Bank of Kuwait plc* v *Sahib* [1997] Ch 107 (CA)); and
- the variation of the terms to an existing contract (*McCausland* v *Duncan Lawrie Ltd* [1997] 1 WLR 38 (CA): see Section 15.4.3(b)).

However, section 2 has been held not to apply to:

- the exercise of an option to purchase land: the grant of the option is the contract, the exercise of it a unilateral act (see *Spiro* v *Glencrown Properties* at 541);
- an agreement by the seller not to consider any offers for the land from any other parties for a specific period (a 'lock-out agreement') (*Pitt* v *PHH Asset Management Ltd* [1994] 1 WLR 327 (CA));
- the grant of a right of first refusal (or 'pre-emption') if the landowner decides to sell a particular piece of land. However, any exercise of the right of pre-emption must satisfy section 2 for it to create a valid contract (see *Bircham & Co Nominees (2) Ltd* v *Worrell Holdings Ltd* (2001) 82 P & CR 34 (CA));
- an agreement about the priority of two mortgages (*Scottish & Newcastle plc* v *Lancashire Mortgage Corp Ltd* [2007] EWCA Civ 684 (CA)); or
- a boundary agreement (*Joyce* v *Rigolli*; *Yeates* v *Line* [2013] Ch 363 (Ch)).

15.4.2(c) Statutory exceptions (s 2(5))

The following types of contract do not have to satisfy the section 2 formalities because of section 2(5):

1. contracts to grant leases of three years or less which take effect in possession and are at the market **rent** (see LPA 1925, s 54(2) and Section 15.5.1(c));
2. contracts made in a public auction (where the agreement is made in public, with the auctioneer acting for both parties); and
3. contracts regulated under the Financial Services and Markets Act 2000, except for regulated mortgage contracts, regulated home reversion plans and regulated purchase plans. This exception governs investments such as shares, which may include interests in land.

Section 2(5) also provides that section 2 has no effect 'on the creation or operation of resulting, implied or **constructive trusts**'. This allows the courts to mitigate the consequences of the strict requirements of section 2 in some cases by recognising a constructive trust (see Chapter 17). Section 2(5) is silent as to any possible role for **proprietary estoppel** (see Chapter 18). The availability of **equitable** remedies when section 2 has not been complied with is considered in Section 15.4.5.

15.4.3 The written document

Morgan J set out a step-by-step approach to applying section 2(1) to a specific situation in his 'thoughtful judgment' in *Oun* v *Ahmad* [2008] EWHC 545 (Ch) (it was

The *Oun* v *Ahmad* approach

28. Section 2(1) requires the [signed] written document to incorporate all the terms which the parties have expressly agreed.

29. The first matter to be explored is a question of fact: What were all the terms which the parties had expressly agreed?

30. Once one has found all the terms which the parties have expressly agreed, then one can examine the written document to see if it incorporates all those terms or omits any.

31. If, on examination of the written document, it is found that it does not incorporate all the terms that the parties have expressly agreed, then prima facie there is no binding contract at all. ... There cannot be a binding contract for only those terms which have been incorporated, because they are not the complete set of terms which were expressly agreed.

32. The prima facie position may be displaced in two cases, in particular.

33. The first particular case is where there are two separate contracts and not one composite contract ...

34. The second particular case is where the written document, which does not incorporate all of the terms expressly agreed, can be rectified to include in the written document all of the terms expressly agreed.

praised as such by Lord Neuberger MR, *Helden* v *Strathmore Ltd* [2011] Bus LR 1592 (CA), [29]).

15.4.3(a) 'Signed' (s 2(3))

The written document must be signed by the parties or on their behalf (s 2(3)). Prior to the 1989 Act, the rules about what constitutes a signature were somewhat complex and would have surprised most non-lawyers. Fortunately, the Court of Appeal has held that these rules do not apply to contracts made under the 1989 Act. In the case of *Firstpost Homes* v *Johnson* [1995] 1 WLR 1567 (CA) (at 1576), Peter Gibson LJ refused to:

> encumber the new Act with so much ancient baggage, particularly when it does not leave the word 'signed' with a meaning which the ordinary man would understand it to have.

In *Firstpost Homes*, Peter Gibson LJ referred, with approval, to *Goodman* v *J Eban Ltd* [1954] 1 QB 550 (CA), in which Denning LJ said, at 561:

> In modern English usage, when a document is required to be 'signed' by someone, that means that he must write his name with his own hand on it.

However, although there is not, as yet, any decided authority that addresses this as part of its ratio, it now seems to be widely accepted that a signature does not require pen and ink. In *Electronic Execution of Documents* (Law Com Consultation No 237, 2018), the Law Commission expresses the provisional view at para 7.6 that:

> the combination of EU law, statute and case law means that, under the current law, an electronic signature is capable of meeting a statutory requirement for a signature if an authenticating intention can be demonstrated.

This is also the view of the Law Society Company Law Committee and the City of London Law Society Company Law and Financial Law Committees (2016), and was accepted, without criticism, by the Court of Appeal in *Golden Ocean Group Ltd* v *Salgaocar Mining Industries Pvt Ltd* [2012] 1 WLR 3674 (CA). It is reported that the first exchange of contracts using digital signatures took place in April 2017 (see Fouzder, 2017).

Section 2 allows a valid contract to be signed by the parties themselves, or by someone else on their behalf. In the unreported case of *Grunhut* v *Ramdas* (27 June 2002), the signature appeared to be that of the relevant party, but was actually a forgery. It was held, however, that even though the party did not sign it herself, the contract was still valid because (on the facts) she had authorised someone else to sign it on her behalf. This was not, however, the case in *Marlbray Ltd* v *Laditi* [2016] 1 WLR 5147 (CA), where Marlbray Ltd agreed to grant a lease of flat in central London to Dr Laditi and his wife at a considerable **premium**. Although the contract named both Dr and Mrs Laditi as purchasers, it was entered into without Mrs Laditi's consent and the only purchaser's signature on the contract was that of Dr Laditi. When he was unable to complete the contract because of difficulty in obtaining a mortgage, Dr Laditi sought to argue that the contract was void because it had not been signed by all of the parties to it. It is, perhaps, unsurprising that the Court of Appeal was not sympathetic to Dr Laditi's claim. As Gloster LJ explained, at [78]:

> It would make a mockery of the policy of [section 2] if the first respondent could rely on technical arguments, such as those presented to the court on this appeal, to escape from his several contractual obligations, in circumstances where the failure to obtain his wife's authority to sign the contract was entirely his.

The court held that there was a valid contract between Marlbray and Dr Laditi: there was a document incorporating all the terms of the agreement; this document had been signed by Dr Laditi; consequently, the requirements of section 2(3) were satisfied.

Where the contract is to incorporate terms from another document, it is important that both parties sign the primary document. In *Firstpost Homes* v *Johnson*, Mrs Johnson agreed orally to sell some farmland to the claimant. The buyer drafted a letter which had his name typed on it as addressee and contained the terms of the contract to sell the land 'shown on the enclosed plan'. He signed the plan but not the letter, and sent both documents to Mrs Johnson, who signed and dated them both. She then died. When the buyer sought to enforce the agreement, Mrs Johnson's personal representatives claimed there was no contract because section 2 was not satisfied. On appeal, it was held that the two documents could not be joined as one, since the plan (the only document signed by both parties) did not incorporate the letter. Enclosing the letter in the same envelope as the plan was insufficient to combine the two documents. In fact, as it was the letter which expressly incorporated the plan, it was the letter which should have been signed by both parties. The buyer's typed name on the letter did not amount to his signature.

15.4.3(b) 'Incorporating all the terms which the parties have expressly agreed' (s 2(1))

To satisfy section 2, all the expressly agreed terms of the agreement *must* be written in a single document (or duplicates for exchange) *or* incorporated into that document by reference to some other document (s 2(2)). Any variation of the terms must also satisfy section 2, as Morritt LJ explained in *McCausland* v *Duncan Lawrie Ltd* [1997] 1 WLR 38 (CA), at [40]:

> The choice lies between permitting a variation, however fundamental, to be made without any formality at all and requiring it to satisfy section 2. In my view, it is evident that Parliament intended the latter. There would be little point in requiring that the original contract comply with section 2 if it might be varied wholly informally.

Section 2(2) allows the terms to be incorporated into a document either by being set out in it or by reference to some other document. In *Courtney* v *Corp Ltd* [2006] EWCA Civ 518 (CA), a finance company's contract letter expressly incorporated its standard terms and conditions, which were contained in a separate document. The claimant did not read these conditions before signing the contract letter, and subsequently claimed that the contract was invalid. The Court of Appeal held that the express incorporation of the standard conditions was sufficient to satisfy section 2: there was no need for Mr Courtney to have seen or read them.

Where a formal contract is drafted in two parts, all the terms must be recorded identically in each part. This is the most usual way of preparing contracts for the sale of land. The seller signs one copy, and the purchaser signs the other. The contract comes into being when the two copies are exchanged and any deposit paid. It seems that if the two parts of the contract are not identical records of the terms, the formalities of section 2 are not satisfied.

Before section 2 came into force, it was possible to create a valid contract through the exchange of correspondence. The Law Commission proposed that creation of contracts by correspondence should continue (Law Com No 164, 1987, para 4.15). However, section 2 as enacted was significantly different from the bill proposed by the Law Commission. In *Hooper* v *Sherman* [1994] NPC 153 (CA), the Court of Appeal held, by a majority, that the exchange of two informal letters between the parties, each containing the terms and signed by the senders' solicitors, could amount to an 'exchange of contracts'. Morritt LJ dissented, however, on the ground that, although these letters would have been enough for section 40 of the LPA 1925, they were not sufficient for the clear terms of the new law. Shortly afterwards, in *Commission for New Towns* v *Cooper (GB) Ltd* [1995] Ch 259 (CA), a differently constituted Court of Appeal decided that it was not bound by *Hooper* v *Sherman* for procedural reasons and then went on to agree with Morritt LJ. In *Cooper*, the parties were in dispute as to the terms of payment for building work as part of a complex arrangement of various land agreements. They reached an agreement, subject to the approval of the claimant's directors, the terms of which were included in an exchange of faxes. One side claimed that this amounted to an 'exchange of contracts' for section 2, but the Court of Appeal unanimously held that it did not, because 'exchange of contracts' in section 2(1) refers to the exchanging of identical documents as part of a formal process indicating the intention to enter a contract. As Evans LJ explained at 295:

> In my judgment, when there has been a prior oral agreement, there is only an 'exchange of contracts' within section 2 when documents are exchanged which set out or incorporate all of the terms which have been agreed and when, crucially, those documents are intended, by virtue of their exchange, to bring about a contract to which section 2 applies.

Thus, it is not sufficient under section 2 for the documentation signed by the parties to confirm a prior oral agreement: the documents must, on proper construction, create the contract itself.

15.4.3(c) Composite contracts

Failure to include all of the expressly agreed terms in the written document may not prove fatal if any missing terms do not relate to the land *and* those terms are separable from the terms relating to the land. The Law Commission, in Law Com No 164, 1987, suggested that unincorporated terms could be valid if they fell within the doctrine of 'collateral contracts' (that is, contracts 'on the side'). Initially, the courts seemed receptive to this approach, as in *Record* v *Bell* [1991] 1 WLR 853 (Ch). In this case, an additional term was agreed after the two copies of the contract had been signed. The seller promised that there were no unforeseen burdens affecting the **title** to the land **registered** at the Land Registry. The buyer subsequently wished to withdraw from the contract and argued that the extra term meant that section 2(2) of the 1989 Act had not been complied with and that the contract was, therefore, void. Judge Paul Baker QC rejected this argument. He held that there were two contracts: (1) one for the sale of the land, and (2) the agreement to complete this sale in consideration of the seller's extra promise. He went on to hold that the second contract was collateral to the first and did not relate to a disposition of an interest in land. Consequently, neither agreement failed for non-compliance with section 2. The first contained all of its terms in writing, and the second agreement did not need to be in writing as it was not a contract for the disposition of land.

The courts have subsequently taken a stricter line in respect of collateral contracts. In *Godden* v *Merthyr Tydfil Housing Association* (1997) 74 P & CR D1 (CA), the Court of Appeal stressed that the existence of a collateral contract was a question of fact based on the commercial reality of the agreement. The relevant test is whether the completion of the land contract is conditional upon the completion of the other terms (see *North Eastern Properties Ltd* v *Coleman* (at [54]), quoted below). The court cannot artificially divide what is in reality a single agreement. As Briggs J, sitting in the Court of Appeal, explained in the case of *North Eastern Properties Ltd* v *Coleman* [2010] 1 WLR 2715 (CA), at [54]:

(i) Nothing in section 2 of the 1989 Act is designed to prevent parties to a composite transaction which includes a land contract from structuring their bargain so that the land contract is genuinely separated from the rest of the transaction in the sense that its performance is not made conditional upon the performance of some other expressly agreed part of the bargain. Thus ... parties may agree to the sale and purchase both of a house and of its curtains and carpets in a single composite transaction. Nonetheless it is open to them to agree either (a) that completion of the purchase of the house is dependent upon the sale of the carpets and curtains or (b) that it is not. They are free to separate the terms of a transaction of type (b) into two separate documents (one for the house and the other for the carpets and curtains) without falling foul of section 2 ...

(ii) By contrast, the parties to a composite transaction are not free to separate into a separate document expressly agreed terms, for example as to the sale of chattels or the provision of services, if upon the true construction of the whole of the agreement, performance of the land sale is conditional upon the chattel sale or service provision.

15.4.3(d) Rectification

The possibility of saving a seemingly invalid contract through the equitable remedy of **rectification** (that is, the courts' power to correct an error in a document) is expressly recognised by section 2(4) of the 1989 Act. Rectification will render valid an otherwise void contract and section 2(4) gives the court the power to specify the date upon which the contract became legally effective.

In *Wright* v *Robert Leonard Developments Ltd* [1994] EGCS 69 (CA), contracts were exchanged for the sale of a show flat, but the exchanged contracts failed to refer to the expressly agreed term that the furnishings would be included in the sale. Although the furnishings were not **fixtures** and were not, therefore, land within the meaning of section 2(1), the Court of Appeal held that on the facts the agreement about the furnishings could not be separated from the rest of the transaction (see Section 15.4.3(c)). However, the Court agreed that the document could be rectified to include the missing term. Once the missing term was inserted, the contract satisfied section 2.

'Rectification is about setting the record straight' (per Morgan J, *Oun* v *Ahmad* [2008] EWHC 545 (Ch) at [46]). It is a discretionary remedy which allows the court to correct a mistake in the way in which the terms of the agreement have been recorded in writing. It is not a vehicle for varying or clarifying the terms of the agreement. Peter Gibson LJ summarised the basic requirements to justify rectification in the case of *Swainland Builders Ltd* v *Freehold Properties Ltd* [2002] 2 EGLR 71 (CA) (at [33]):

1. the parties had a common continuing intention … in respect of a particular matter in the instrument to be rectified;
2. there was an outward expression of accord;
3. the intention continued at the time of the execution of the instrument sought to be rectified;
4. by mistake, the instrument did not reflect that common intention.

In *Sargeant* v *Reece* [2008] 1 P & CR DG8 (Ch), Deputy Judge Edward Bartley Jones QC reviewed the Court of Appeal cases on the doctrine of rectification and particularly the burden of proof falling on the claimant. He concluded that the claimant does not need to be able to prove the exact form of words that should have been used in the written document, provided that they can establish the substance of the missing term or terms in sufficient detail. The amount and type of evidence needed to do this will depend upon the quality of the document concerned, but will need to be sufficiently convincing to outweigh the evidence of the written contract itself. In *Thomas Bates & Son Ltd* v *Wyndham's (Lingerie) Ltd* [1981] 1 WLR 505 (CA) (at [521]), Brightman LJ explained:

> It is not, I think, the standard of proof which is high, so differing from the normal civil standard, but the evidential requirement needed to counteract the inherent probability that the written instrument truly represents the parties' intention because it is a document signed by the parties.

15.4.4 Remedies for breach of contract

If there is a valid contract, then the buyer or the seller will usually be entitled to specific performance if the other party defaults (damages rarely, if ever, being a sufficient remedy given the unique nature of each parcel of land). However, specific performance is an equitable remedy available at the discretion of the court and it may be denied because of the claimant's conduct ('he who comes to equity must come with clean hands'). In *Wilkie* v *Redsell* [2003] EWCA Civ 926, the Court of Appeal refused to grant a rogue specific performance of his contract to buy land, since, first, there was no evidence that he would be able to pay the purchase price to complete his side of the bargain and, second, he had 'abused the facilities of the court in relation to the very matter in respect of which he [sought] relief' (at [34]) and so did not have clean hands. Even if a person is entitled to specific performance, the court may award damages if it would be fairer to do so, as would be the case where the land had already been sold to a third party.

Under the Law Society's Standard Conditions of Sale, if the buyer refuses to complete, the seller may retain the deposit (a powerful incentive for the buyer), subject always to the courts' statutory discretion to order the return of the deposit pursuant to section 49(2) of the LPA 1925. Other remedies for the buyer include suing for the restitution of a lost deposit or for misrepresentation. In *McMeekin* v *Long* (2003) 29 EG 120 (QB), the buyers of a house were awarded £67,000 damages for fraudulent misrepresentation when the sellers deliberately failed to disclose a dispute with their neighbours.

15.4.5 Remedies where there is no valid contract

The requirements of section 2 of the 1989 Act cause no problems in the vast majority of transactions concerning land. The need to satisfy the provisions of section 2 means that the parties can be certain both as to whether they have entered into a binding contract and about the terms of that contract. However, as Chadwick LJ observed in *Bircham & Co Nominees (2) Ltd* v *Worrell Holdings Ltd* (2001) 82 P & CR 34 (CA), [15]:

> There are obvious difficulties in the way of a claimant who seeks specific performance of an agreement which, by reason of the provisions enacted in section 2 of the 1989 Act, has no contractual effect.

Consequently, if a party spends money or other resources in reliance upon an agreement that has yet to satisfy section 2, they do so at their own risk. Without a valid contract, they cannot force the other party to honour the agreement. Biggs J, sitting in the Court of Appeal in the case of *North Eastern Properties Ltd* v *Coleman* [2010] 1 WLR 2715 (CA), observed (at [43]) that:

> [Section 2] enables parties to land contracts who have changed their minds to look around for expressly agreed terms which have not found their way into the final form of land contract which they signed, for the precise purpose of avoiding their obligations, on the ground that the lack of discipline of their counterparty, or even their own lack of discipline, has rendered the contract void.

Equity has long recognised that there are circumstances in which it would be unfair not to provide a remedy to a claimant who has acted to their detriment as a result of the other person's actions simply because of the absence of the signed document.

Prior to section 2, a contract relating to land was merely unenforceable if the formality requirements had not been complied with. The contract was still valid, and evidence that the claimant had performed a part of (or had done some other act showing the existence of) the unwritten contract, and that the defendant knew of this, would render the contract enforceable in equity through the doctrine of 'part performance'. Although the 1989 Act does not expressly abolish part performance, the Court of Appeal has now confirmed that it is not compatible with the jurisprudence of section 2 (see, for example, *United Bank of Kuwait plc* v *Sahib* [1997] Ch 107 (CA) and *Yaxley* v *Gotts* [2000] Ch 162 (CA)).

The Law Commission expected the role played by part performance to be taken by **proprietary estoppel**, although it did not anticipate frequent resort to equity. As the Commission explained in Law Com No 164, 1987, para 4.13:

> In putting forward the present recommendation we rely greatly on the principle, recognised even by equity, that 'certainty is the father of right and the mother of justice'.

Proprietary estoppel is considered in more detail in Chapter 18, but was conveniently summarised by Edward Nugee QC, sitting as a High Court judge, in the case of *Re Basham (decd)* [1986] 1 WLR 1498 (Ch), at 1503, as meaning that:

> where one person, A, has acted to his detriment on the faith of a belief, which was known to or encouraged by another person, B, that he either has or is going to be given a right over B's property, B cannot insist on his strict legal rights if to do so would be inconsistent with A's belief.

Unfortunately, the final form of the 1989 Act has caused uncertainty about whether the doctrine of proprietary estoppel is available where an agreement fails to comply with section 2 because estoppel is not one of the exceptions listed in section 2(5) of the Act. For example, in an *obiter* comment in *Cobbe* v *Yeoman's Row Management Ltd* [2008] 1 WLR 1752 (HL), at 29, Lord Scott expressed his view that:

> proprietary estoppel cannot be prayed in aid in order to render enforceable an agreement that statute has declared to be void. The proposition that an owner of land can be estopped from asserting that an agreement is void for want of compliance with the requirements of section 2 is, in my opinion, unacceptable. The assertion is no more than the statute provides. Equity can surely not contradict the statute … statute provides an express exception for constructive trusts.

In *Yaxley* v *Gotts* (also considered at Section 18.3), Mr Yaxley, a builder, orally agreed with a friend (Mr Gotts senior) that he would take the ground floor of a house that Mr Gotts was about to buy, in return for renovating and rebuilding the house as a number of flats. In fact, Mr Gotts' son (Mr Gotts junior) bought the house, but Mr Yaxley carried out the work as he had promised. A few years later, Mr Yaxley fell out with the father and son, and they barred him from the premises and denied that he had any right to the ground floor of the house. At first instance, Mr Yaxley, having relied on the father's oral promise (which had apparently been adopted by the son), successfully claimed an interest in the house by virtue of proprietary estoppel and was awarded a 99-year lease of the ground floor. On appeal, Robert Walker LJ was reluctant to find an estoppel in Mr Yaxley's favour because of the wording of section 2(5) of the Act. Although he was not prepared to rule out the possibility of estoppel ever being appropriate in circumstances to which section 2 applied, he preferred to impose a common intention **constructive trust** on Mr Gotts. Significantly, section 2(5) expressly provides that the creation or operation of a constructive trust is not affected by section 2. Typically, this type of constructive trust arises where the parties have agreed that A shall have a proprietary interest in property, and A has acted to their detriment in reliance on that agreement: it is considered in detail in its original context in Section 17.3.1). Beldam and Clarke LJJ, while agreeing with the imposition of a constructive trust, also supported the first instance judge's finding of proprietary estoppel. They were prepared to give much more weight to the views of the Law Commission when interpreting section 2, since the 1989 Act was the consequence of the Commission's report. According to Beldam LJ, the underlying policy behind section 2 was not to prohibit informal agreements relating to land, but to make them void for the purposes of contract law if they did not satisfy the formalities contained in the statute.

At least two judges in the High Court have been willing to recognise the possibility that proprietary estoppel survives section 2(5), albeit probably only in exceptional circumstances: see, for example, Bean J in *Whittaker* v *Kinnear* [2011] EWHC 1479 (QB) and HH Judge Behrens in *Ghazaani* v *Rowshan* [2015] EWHC 1922 (Ch). However, the Court of Appeal has taken the narrower approach summarised by Arden LJ in *Kinane* v *Mackie-Conteh* [2005] EWCA Civ 45(CA), [26]:

> In *Yaxley* v *Gotts* this court recognised that the doctrine of estoppel may not be invoked to render valid a transaction which the legislature has, on the grounds of general public policy, enacted is to be invalid. However, it held that that principle was not violated where the circumstances giving rise to proprietary estoppel also gave rise to a constructive trust as the legislature has specifically made a saving for constructive trusts in section 2(5) of the 1989 Act.

According to Neuberger LJ (also in *Kinane*, at [51]), to give rise to a constructive trust, the proprietary estoppel must be based on:

> the element of agreement, or at least expression of common understanding, exchanged between the parties, as to the existence, or intended existence, of a proprietary interest.

The necessary elements of such an agreement were considered in *Cobbe* v *Yeoman's Row Management Ltd*. Mr Cobbe, an experienced property developer, had orally agreed to purchase a property comprising a number of flats from Yeoman's Row Management Ltd for £12 million. On the basis of this arrangement, he then spent 18 months and a considerable amount of money obtaining planning permission for the proposed development. Immediately after the grant of planning permission, the company demanded £20 million for the flats. The House of Lords held that Mr Cobbe's claim failed, because, as Lord Neuberger explained, in the subsequent case of *Thorner* v *Major* [2009] 1 WLR 776 (HL), at [92]:

> [Mr Cobbe] was effectively seeking to invoke proprietary estoppel to give effect to a contract which the parties had intentionally and consciously not entered into, and because he was simply seeking a remedy for the unconscionable behaviour of Yeoman's Row.

Herbert v *Doyle* [2010] EWCA Civ 1095 concerned an oral agreement to exchange some parking spaces. The question arose as to whether there was sufficient agreement upon which to found a constructive trust. Arden LJ considered *Cobbe* at length and concluded (at [57]) that:

> there is a common thread running through the speeches of Lord Scott and Lord Walker [in *Cobbe*] ... [1] if the parties intend to make a formal agreement setting out the terms on which one or more of the parties is to acquire an interest in property, or, [2] if further terms for that acquisition remain to be agreed between them so that the interest in property is not clearly identified, or [3] if the parties did not expect their agreement to be immediately binding, neither party can rely on constructive trust as a means of enforcing their original agreement.

In *Dowding* v *Matchmove Ltd* [2017] 1 WLR 749 (CA), both parties knew of the need for a written contract, but regarded this as a mere technicality. On the face of it, this would seem to fall foul of the first of the criteria identified by Arden LJ in *Herbert* v *Doyle*. However, according to Sir Terence Etherton MR, 'Arden LJ was not intending to describe three different situations in which section 2(5) would not apply, but rather to describe the Cobbe case ... in three different ways' ([32]); that is, all three factors combined meant that Mr Cobbe did not expect any interest in land to pass by virtue of his arrangement with Yeoman's Row Management Ltd. On the facts of *Dowding*, however, the parties had reached an agreement which they expected to be binding; the fact that they expected it to be formalised did not in itself mean that there was insufficient agreement upon which to found a constructive trust.

Dowding v *Matchmove Ltd* is the latest in a series of cases in which the Court of Appeal has avoided reaching a decision on whether proprietary estoppel survives section 2(5) by choosing to focus on whether or not there is a constructive trust. As many commentators have pointed out, however, this route is not without its own difficulties (see, for example, McFarlane, 2005; Boncey and Ng, 2017; and Dixon, 2017). Not only is the scope of what constitutes an agreement becoming dangerously stretched, but, on occasions, the Court of Appeal has been willing to start with a proprietary estoppel, which must be a constructive trust to escape section 2(5), but which can still give rise to a remedy that seems inconsistent with a trust. For example, in the foundational case of *Yaxley* v *Gotts*, the court held that Mr Yaxley had a long lease of the ground floor of the house. There is little doubt that such relief falls within the range of remedies available to the court to satisfy a proprietary estoppel (see Section 18.5). However, the imposition of a constructive trust would require Mr Gotts to be deemed to have granted a lease to himself which he then held on trust for Mr Yaxley, despite the long-established rule that one cannot grant a lease to oneself.

15.5   The creation and transfer of legal interests

15.5.1   The deed

As mentioned already, a deed is normally necessary to transfer a legal **estate** or interest. When the land is **registered**, the deed is a Land Transfer form from the Land Registry.

Section 52(1) of the LPA 1925 states:

> All conveyances of land or of any interest therein are void for the purpose of conveying or creating a legal estate unless made by deed.

Before 31st July 1990, a deed was a document that was 'signed, sealed and delivered'. Now, the ancient requirement for a seal is dispensed with. The requirements for a deed are now set out in section 1 of the Law of Property (Miscellaneous Provisions) Act 1989.

A deed is a document which:

- makes clear on its face that it is a deed;
- is validly executed; and
- is delivered.

15.5.1(a) Execution

An individual 'executes' the deed (that is, makes the document their deed) by signing it in the presence of one witness who also signs. Alternatively, the deed can be signed 'at [their] direction and in [their] presence' by another person, and in this case there must be two witnesses present who also sign the deed. Different rules apply to corporations, including limited companies.

15.5.1(b) Delivery

A deed is 'delivered' when the grantor (the person executing the deed) does or says something to 'adopt the deed as [their] own'. In practice, solicitors usually treat a deed as delivered at the moment they add a date to a document which has already been signed and witnessed; this is said to show that they adopt it.

15.5.1(c) Where a deed is not needed

There are a number of circumstances where a legal estate or legal interest can be obtained without a deed.

1. *Short leases* (defined in LPA 1925, s 54(2)): by section 52(2)(d), a lease is legal without any formality (even writing) if it does not exceed three years, the **tenant** is entitled to occupy the premises from the date of the lease and it is at the best rent reasonably obtainable. There is no need for any special formality, or even writing, for this kind of short lease, because there is little risk that a buyer of the property will be caught unawares: the tenant will be present on the property and paying rent. In addition, the expense and delay in conforming to the formality requirements of sections 1 and 2 of the 1989 Act would be bound to inhibit the creation of these commonly found leases or would lead to non-compliance. However, somewhat illogically, a deed is still needed to *assign* any lease (to transfer the whole of the legal interest to another person, as opposed to creating a **sublease**), as shown in *Crago* v *Julian* [1992] 1 WLR 372 (CA).

2. *Long use*: in unregistered land, using someone else's land for a minimum of 12 years can ensure that the user cannot be defeated by anyone; effectively, they become a legal owner. This is known as **adverse possession**. It is also possible to obtain **title** to registered land by adverse possession, although the rules are somewhat different. Adverse possession is considered in detail in Chapter 16. Long use of an easement or profit (for example, a right of way or a right to fish) can create a legal right by '**prescription**' (see Section 10.7.6).

3. *Personal representatives' assent* (Administration of Estates Act 1925, s 36(1)): if a landowner dies, their land automatically goes to ('vests in') their legal representatives. When they have completed their administration of the estate, they transfer the land to the heir(s). Writing, but not a deed, is necessary to do this; it is called an 'assent'.

4. *Trustee in bankruptcy's disclaimer*: where a landowner becomes bankrupt, the land automatically vests in their **trustee in bankruptcy**. If the land is more trouble than it is worth (for example, a lease with a high rent), the trustee can disclaim it in writing; a deed is not necessary.

5. *Court order*: a court can order land to be transferred.

15.5.1(d) The effect of a deed

The deed transfers not only the interest but also any advantages which belong to the land, unless the parties show that they intend otherwise. Section 62 of the LPA 1925 provides what a conveyance of land includes, in the absence of any statement to the contrary. Thus, a buyer of land may get, as an easement, the right to park their car in their neighbour's drive, enjoyed by their predecessor as a contractual licence (see Section 10.7.5). Sections 78 and 79 of the LPA 1925, respectively, ensure that they will automatically have the right to enforce, and will be bound by, any valid **restrictive covenant** over the land (see Sections 12.5.2(a) and 12.5.1(c)).

15.5.1(e) Where the formalities have not been complied with

The formalities described above are necessary for the valid execution of a deed. However, in the case of *Shah* v *Shah* [2002] QB 35 (CA), a person was induced to rely on what appeared on the face of it to be a deed. A later representation by the executor of the deed, that it was invalid since it had not been properly witnessed, was unsuccessful, and the executor was estopped from relying on their strict legal rights.

15.5.2 Registration

Almost every sale, transfer, lease or first legal **mortgage** of land in England and Wales must now be registered at the Land Registry (considered in detail in Chapter 4). The main exception relates to leases with less than seven years to run, although it is anticipated that this period will eventually be reduced to three years. The consequences of failing to register the disposition will depend upon whether the land was already registered at the time of the transfer.

15.5.2(a) 'Not yet registered' land

Section 4(1) of the LRA 2002 requires all transfers of freehold and the grant and transfer of leases for a term exceeding seven years to be registered. The grant of a first mortgage will also trigger compulsory first registration. In these circumstances, the legal title to the land is transferred to the buyer on the date set out in the deed of transfer. The buyer has two months within which to apply for registration (s 6); otherwise the legal title will revert to the seller, who will then hold the land on trust for the buyer (s 7). It is the responsibility of the buyer to ensure that the legal title is re-transferred to them and properly registered (s 8). In the meanwhile, the buyer will only have title to the land in equity, and they will not enjoy all the protection afforded to a legal owner.

15.5.2(b) Registered land

Different rules apply to the transfer of legal title to land that is already registered at the date of the transfer. In this case, there is no two-month window. Section 27 of the LRA 2002 provides that the transfer of registered estates (and the creation of several types of interest over them) will not operate at law until the registration requirements are met. In the gap between completing the transfer deed and completion of its registration (the so-called registration gap) the buyer will have only an **equitable** interest in the land.

15.6 Conclusion

The transfer of land is financially and socially so important that it is bound to be the subject of some ritual and, therefore, of technical rules. The present rules are only the latest in a long line of such requirements which have focused on the use of paper, but which are being adapted to a world in which transactions of all kinds are increasingly electronic. Whatever the future of e-conveyancing, the major issues that must be addressed will not change merely because of the availability or otherwise of a new technology. In particular, a compromise must be found between the need for clear rules and the need to make sure that people do not unfairly take advantage of one another. The requirements of the 1989 Act have a more ruthless simplicity than their predecessors, and cases on section 2 suggest that it does not successfully address all of the tensions between certainty and justice inherent in any system of formalities. The extent to which the formalism of section 2 is reflected in the decisions of the courts may change according to the state of the property market, and according to the attitude adopted by the courts towards **proprietary estoppel** and **constructive trusts**. That said, the present rules successfully facilitate many hundreds of thousands of transfers of land each year.

The rules relating to the buying and selling of interests in land are (and will probably remain) formalistic and detailed, but, in an area where the law is seeking to achieve a simple and certain resolution of complicated and dynamic human relationships, this is hardly surprising. Different legal systems tackle the problem in different ways (compare, for example, the system in Scotland), but none seems to be free from criticism. In any event, most non-lawyers are less concerned about the technicality of the rules than they are with their financial situation and the state of the property market. Rules that do not obviously hinder the market are unlikely to attract much attention or criticism.

Summary

15.1 In England and Wales, dealings with interests in land are typically divided into two main stages. The first stage ends when there is a legally binding contract between the parties. The second stage concludes with the transfer of title to the interest.

15.2 The buying and selling of interests in land usually requires certain formalities (writing, deeds or electronic) to be complied with. The rules are found in statute, supplemented by equity.

15.3 As soon as there is a contract for the sale of an interest in land, the buyer effectively becomes the equitable owner of the land, provided the discretionary remedy of specific performance is available.

15.4 In order for there to be a contract for the sale of an interest in land, normally the agreement must satisfy the terms of section 2 of the Law of Property (Miscellaneous Provisions) Act 1989. In particular, all the terms must be in writing and signed by both sides. If there is no contract, equity may nevertheless enforce the 'agreement' by finding a constructive trust, or under the doctrine of proprietary estoppel. A diagrammatic representation of the relevant rules can be found at Figure 15.1.

15.5 A deed, signed, witnessed and delivered, is normally necessary to create or transfer a legal interest in land. It also transfers benefits attached to the land. Most deeds must be registered at the Land Registry for the interest concerned to operate at (or be transferred at) law.

Exercises

 15.1 Complete the online quiz on the topics covered in this chapter on the companion website.

15.2 Critically consider the justifications for and the disadvantages of requiring dispositions of land and contracts for the dispositions of land to comply with the formalities contained in the Law of Property Act 1925 (as amended), the Law of Property (Miscellaneous Provisions) Act 1989 and the Land Registration Act 2002.

15.3 William owned the freehold of a rather dilapidated house. He agreed to sell it to Ajay for £150,000, and, once contracts were exchanged, Ajay began work on the repairs. Due to a change in his circumstances, William has decided he no longer wishes to sell the house to Ajay. William's solicitor has told him that, since no deed has yet been executed, William can withdraw from the arrangement. It also turns out that Ajay never signed his copy of the contract.

Advise Ajay.

 You can find suggested answer plans to exercises 15.2 and 15.3 on the companion website.

Further reading

Boncey and Ng, '"Common Intention" Constructive Trusts Arising from Informal Agreements to Dispose of Land' (2017) 81 Conv 146

Critchley, 'Taking Formalities Seriously' in Bright and Dewar (eds), *Land Law Themes and Perspectives* (Oxford University Press 1998) 507

Dixon, 'More Moves in Constructive Trusts and Estoppel' (2017) 81 Conv 89

Fouzder, 'E-conveyancing First as Digital Signature Used to Exchange Contracts' (2017), www.lawgazette.co.uk/practice/e-conveyancing-first-as-digital-signature-used-to-exchange-contracts/5060677.article. Accessed 1st September 2018.

McFarlane, 'Proprietary Estoppel and Failed Contractual Negotiations' (2005) 69 Conv 501

Law Society Company Law Committee and City of London Law Society Company Law and Financial Law Committees, 'Note on the Execution of a Document Using an Electronic Signature' (2016), www.citysolicitors.org.uk/attachments/article/121/LSEW%20%20CLLS%20Joint%20Working%20Party%20-%20Note%20on%20the%20Execution%20of%20a%20Document%20Using%20an%20Electronic%20Signature.pdf. Accessed 1st September 2018.

Owen and Rees, 'Section 2(5) of the Law of Property (Miscellaneous Provisions) Act 1989: A Misconceived Approach?' (2011) 75 Conv 495

Thompson, 'Oral Agreements for the Sale of Land' [2000] Conv 245

Chapter 16

Adverse possession

Key concepts

▶ **Adverse possession** – the acquisition of title to land by dispossessing the original owner for the requisite period.
▶ **Animus possidendi** – the requisite intention to possess the land being claimed.
▶ **Factual possession** – exclusive physical control of the land being claimed; the degree of control required depends upon the characteristics of the land concerned.

16.1 Town and country

16.1.1 The case of the common drive

Numbers 31 and 33 Rosedale Road are neighbouring houses in the suburbs of Epsom in Surrey. When they were built in 1934, the two houses shared a common drive. The owner of each house had **title** to the half of the drive running alongside their house with an **easement** to use the half of the drive owned by their neighbour. For convenience, the fence between the houses was built close to Number 33, which gave the impression that the drive belonged to Number 31. As it happened, the owner of Number 33 did not use the drive and, from 1952, did not even have access to it. In 1962, the new owners of Number 31 paved the drive and used it for parking their cars. When the Williams family moved into Number 33 in 1977 they decided to pursue their apparent legal right, as the 'paper owners', to their half of the drive.

▶ The argument in favour of the Williams family was that they were the legal owners of the strip of land (the original title **deeds** stated it clearly) and they ought therefore to be entitled to legal protection against trespassers. From their point of view, any rule that prevented them from recovering their half of the drive was a 'cheat's charter' (McCormick, 1986).
▶ However, the earlier owners of their house had 'slept on their rights', even later acknowledging that they did not think they owned the strip of land, whereas the owners of Number 31 had used it and repaved it 'at some expense, which went beyond any normal maintenance requirements'.

Should the Williams family be allowed to resurrect so stale a claim?

16.1.2 The case of the Berkshire fields

In 1982, John Graham and his wife purchased Manor Farm at Henwick Manor in West Berkshire, together with some 67 hectares of surrounding land. Mr Graham farmed the land with his son Michael. Four of the fields next to Manor Farm belonged to JA Pye (Oxford) Ltd. Pye hoped to be able to develop its land at some point in the future, but for several years it allowed the occupants of Manor Farm to use the fields as grazing land under the terms of various agreements. The Grahams entered into such an agreement with Pye in February 1983. Pye refused to grant a new grazing agreement for 1984 as it wanted to keep the land free, ready for its application for planning permission to develop the land. However, the Grahams continued to use the land, and in August 1984 they took a cut of hay from the fields in return for a payment to Pye. From September 1984 onwards, the Grahams used all four fields all year round for farming. They made a number of attempts to contact Pye with a view to regularising the arrangement and would have been happy to pay for the use of the fields had payment been demanded. Pye, however, did not answer their various requests.

In 1997, after farming the four fields for over 12 years without any interference from Pye, Michael Graham took the first steps towards protecting the 'squatter's title' that he believed he had acquired over them. Pye objected, but despite some negotiations, no progress had been made towards resolving the dispute when Michael Graham was killed in a shooting accident in February 1998. His widow felt duty bound to continue the claim, and at the beginning of 1999 Pye issued court proceedings in an attempt to reclaim its land. The value of the four fields, assuming planning permission was granted, was thought to be in the region of £10 million.

Who should be entitled to the land?

▶ There was no doubt that Pye had simply stood by while the Grahams farmed its land for a considerable period of time, and the Grahams had done nothing to hide what they were doing. But is the loss of ownership a proportionate response to Pye's indifference?

▶ The Grahams had put considerable work into the land over the years. However, they were aware that Pye owned the land and were willing to take the risk that they would lose the benefit of their work. As it was, they had reaped the profits of the land rent-free for over 12 years, and the land was worth far more than the Grahams had ever spent on it.

▶ How could Mrs Graham's claim be consistent with Article 1 of the First Protocol of the European Convention on Human Rights, 'No one shall be deprived of [their] possessions except in the public interest and subject to the conditions provided for by law and by the general principles of international law'?

16.2 The underlying issues

This chapter investigates the issues which arise when an owner's **title** is challenged because someone else has been in possession of their land for many years. Such a dispute might concern squatters claiming ownership of a house in a fashionable area or a large area of land with valuable potential for development, and may be worth pursuing to the highest courts. The dispute between Mrs Graham and Pye went to both the House of Lords (*JA Pye (Oxford) Ltd v Graham* [2003] 1 AC 419 (HL)) and the European Court of Justice (*JA Pye (Oxford) Ltd v UK* (2008) 46 EHRR 45). Other claims (perhaps the majority) concern a relatively small area of land, frequently land lying on the boundary between two titles. Such disputes are pursued with no less thoroughness. The Williams took their case as far as the Court of Appeal (*Williams v Usherwood* (1983) 45 P & CR 235 (CA)).

Historically, adverse possession is part of the general law of limitation of actions, now contained in the Limitation Act 1980. The basic principle is straightforward: after a certain length of time, a person using land may have a better title to it than anyone else, including the real or 'paper' owner, simply because the law will not permit anyone to remove them.

Many of the justifications offered for the doctrine of adverse possession arise out of the limitations of traditional, unregistered conveyancing, where there may be considerable uncertainty about who owns a particular parcel of land. The interests of certainty and the market in land require a rule that actions to recover possession may not be brought after a certain length of time has passed. They become 'time barred'; otherwise 'stale claims' will haunt landowners and their purchasers indefinitely. In addition, **deeds** can get lost, and people can forget what they own, but the land itself remains. If the law did not provide for cases where there is no formal proof of title, areas of land would be 'outside the law' and unmarketable. Adverse possession thus provides a way of curing defective titles in **unregistered land**, since the paper owner cannot evict the squatter after the required period of possession has passed.

In **registered land**, title is not based on possession, as it is in the unregistered system, but on the fact that ownership has been recorded at the Land Registry (see Chapter 4). Although the LRA 1925 incorporated the rules that applied to unregistered land with little significant amendment, it is now generally recognised that adverse possession has a much more limited role within the registered title scheme. Nevertheless, there are compelling reasons for retaining rules on adverse possession. In its consultation prior to the LRA 2002 (Law Com No 254, 1998, para 10.98) the Law Commission stated that:

> the title that registration confers should be capable of being overridden by adverse possession only where it is essential to ensure the marketability of land or to prevent unfairness ... namely –
> (1) where the registered proprietor cannot be traced;
> (2) where there have been dealings 'off the register';
> (3) in some cases where the register is not conclusive; and
> (4) where an adverse possessor has entered into possession under a reasonable mistake as to their rights.

This reasoning is reflected in the new set of rules introduced to govern claims to adverse possession of registered land in the LRA 2002. These rules (examined in Section 16.5.2) offer the registered proprietor considerable protection against a claim by 'squatters', as they will be given notice of any claim and have the right to object in all but a few circumstances.

Essentially, the argument justifying adverse possession is that if it were not for this doctrine, many pieces of land would be waste, forgotten and unutilised by the paper owner. However, the law of adverse possession inevitably causes problems for people who think that legal title to land, private property, for which the owner has probably 'paid good money', ought to be protected by the law, come what may. The idea that people can be deprived of their land in such a way certainly raises issues under the Human Rights Act 1998, which are considered in more detail in Section 16.7. In real life, few unregistered titles are perfect, and innumerable difficulties arise when a title needs to be traced to its origin. In most cases, however, it is normally sufficient to prove a good title (the 'root of title') going back only 15 years to satisfy a purchaser of land that has not yet been registered (Law of Property Act 1969, s 23).

In addition to these practical justifications for adverse possession, there are various ethical issues to be considered. The doctrine of adverse possession does not sit comfortably alongside the policy of State protection of private owners realised, for example, by the criminalisation of trespassing in a residential building (see Section 16.3). However, it may be equally argued that the public interest lies in supporting industrious and careful squatters who make better use of the land than neglectful paper owners as this encourages the efficient use of land resources (see *Hounslow LBC v Minchinton* (1997) 74 P & CR 221 (CA)).

The detailed questions that need to be addressed when considering a claim for adverse possession of land are considered in Sections 16.3–16.5. Figure 16.1 illustrates how to apply the relevant rules to a claim for adverse possession of **freehold** land.

16.3 When is possession adverse possession?

The most difficult issues in this area of law arise when the courts have to consider what the squatter must do if they are to show that they actually were in adverse possession of another person's land. In *JA Pye (Oxford) Ltd v Graham* [2003] 1 AC 419 (HL), the House of Lords reviewed the law of adverse possession and identified two fundamental elements.

The requirements of adverse possession

1. The possession must be real (or 'factual'): the squatter must act as owner, showing an 'appropriate degree of physical control'.
2. The trespasser must have an intention to possess the land (*animus possidendi*).

16.3.1 Factual possession

The case of *Buckinghamshire CC v Moran* [1990] Ch 623 (CA) illustrates the sort of behaviour required from the trespasser if they are to be able successfully to claim adverse possession. From 1971, Mr Moran had used as an extension to his garden a patch of land owned by the council which they intended to use for a future bypass. His predecessor had probably done the same since 1967. Mr Moran built a new fence, enclosing the land, and added a new gate and a lock. The council finally noticed him in 1985 and sued for possession. In its analysis of the sort of acts required to constitute factual possession, the Court of Appeal quoted with approval from the first instance judgment by Slade J in *Powell v McFarlane* (1979) 38 P & CR 452 (Ch), 470–1:

> Factual possession signifies an appropriate degree of physical control. ... The question of what acts constitute a sufficient degree of exclusive physical control must depend on the circumstances, in particular the nature of the land and the manner in which land of that nature is commonly used or enjoyed.

Physical control can be shown if the squatter encloses the land or improves it in some way, but trivial acts performed on the land will generally be insufficient to establish factual possession. In *Pye v Graham*, the facts of which are set out in Section 16.1.2, the Grahams kept animals on the land all year round, maintaining and improving it and excluding everyone from it. An occupying owner could not have done more,

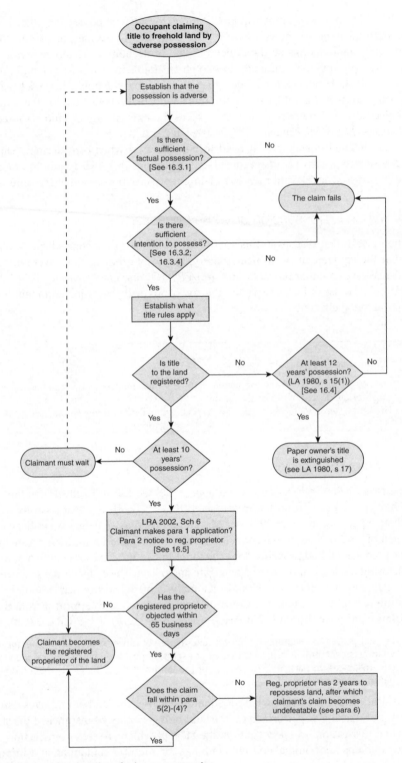

Figure 16.1 Applying the rules of adverse possession

and the House of Lords found that Mr Graham had clearly been in factual possession of the land.

What acts are required to show 'an appropriate degree of physical control' of residential property such as a house or flat? In *Simpson* v *Fergus* (2000) 79 P & CR 398 (CA), Robert Walker LJ reflected at [401] that:

> Possession of a flat with a front door which can be locked is obviously different from possession of part of an unfenced moor or hillside. But in either case there must be exclusive possession, in the sense of occupying and controlling the land in question to the exclusion of others.

In *Lambeth LBC* v *Copercini*, unreported, 1 March 2000, a housing co-operative had squatted in a council-owned property for many years. The judge found clear evidence of factual possession, since the co-operative had decided who should live there, arranged lettings, funded repairs and maintenance, and treated the property as their own. In *Ofulue* v *Bossert* [2009] Ch 1 (CA), Mr Bossert and his daughter were let into a flat by a former **tenant** in 1981 and took up residence. At that time, the flat was in so bad a state of repair that the local authority had condemned it as uninhabitable. Mr Bossert spent a considerable amount of time and money repairing the flat and by 1989 estimated its value to be between £150,000 and £200,000. Unsurprisingly, the Court of Appeal found that Bossert's acts were sufficient to amount to factual possession. The Ofulues' appeal to the House of Lords ([2009] 1 AC 990 (HL)) concerned a different issue (see Section 16.3.2).

16.3.2   Intention to possess (*animus possidendi*)

Exactly what constitutes the necessary intention to possess the land has been a contentious issue until relatively recently. It might be thought that a trespasser must show that they intend to become the owner of the land, but, although this may have been the case in the past, it clearly no longer is. The leading case is now *Pye* v *Graham*, in which Lord Browne-Wilkinson expressly approved the attempts of two earlier judges to explain *animus possidendi*. At first instance in *Buckinghamshire CC* v *Moran* (1988) 56 P & CR 372 (Ch), Hoffmann J observed, at [378], that what is required is:

> not an intention to own or even an intention to acquire ownership but an intention to possess.

and in *Powell* v *McFarlane*, Slade J explained at 471–2:

> *animus possidendi* involves the intention, in one's own name and on= one's own behalf, to exclude the world at large, including the owner with the paper title … so far as is reasonably practicable and so far as the process of the law will allow.

It is rare that the court will have direct evidence of an intention to possess the land and exclude the world, but the intention can be inferred from the acts of the trespasser, such as the enclosure of the land by the squatter in *Buckinghamshire CC* v *Moran* or through otherwise controlling access. Lord Browne-Wilkinson, who gave the leading speech in *Pye* v *Graham*, stated at [40] that:

> intention may be, and frequently is, deduced from the physical acts themselves.

Depending on the facts, a person may be deemed to have sufficient intention to possess the land even if they were prepared to accept a **licence** or a **lease** from the paper owner, so their claim to adverse possession could still succeed if the licence were not in the end forthcoming. In *Pye* v *Graham*, Mr Graham admitted that he would have accepted a licence from the paper owners if one had been offered. This was an admission that Lord Diplock thought 'any candid squatter hoping in due course to acquire a possessory title would be almost bound to make' (*Ocean Estates Ltd* v *Pinder* [1969] 2 AC 19 (PC) at 24) and that did not prevent them from being in possession.

There is a clear difference, though, between a squatter's willingness to recognise the title of the paper owner if asked to do so 'without prejudice' as part of court pleadings (see *Ofulue*) and the written acknowledgement of the paper owner's title. A squatter might make such an acknowledgement by, for example, writing to ask for a lease or a licence to use the land. In claims concerning **unregistered land**, such an acknowledgement of title is enough to stop time running in the squatter's favour under sections 29–31 of the Limitation Act 1980 (see Section 16.4.4). Sections 29–31 do not apply to cases concerning registered title, so in cases decided under the LRA 2002 the court will still have to decide whether any acknowledgement (written or otherwise) precludes *animus possidendi* on the part of the squatter.

16.3.3   Must the possession be adverse to the paper owner?

Possession cannot be adverse if it is enjoyed with the paper owner's permission. In the words of Romer LJ in *Moses* v *Lovegrove* [1952] 2 QB 533 (CA), 544:

> if one looks to the position of the occupier and finds that his occupation, his right to occupation, is derived from the owner in the form of permission or agreement or grant, it is not adverse.

This means, however, that a **mortgagor** is in adverse possession as against the **mortgagee** because their possession is not primarily derived from the **mortgage**. This will not normally cause any difficulty to the lender because the relevant limitation period will start afresh each time the borrower makes a payment towards the mortgage. However, in *Ashe* v *National Westminster Bank plc* [2008] 1 WLR 710 (CA), the bank had taken no action since a final payment some 13 years earlier. Consequently, Mr and Mrs Ashe were able to claim the title to the house.

A difficulty has arisen in cases where the paper owner intends to use the land in the future for some particular purpose, but has no present use for it. The uncertainty can be traced back to the judgment of Bramwell LJ in *Leigh* v *Jack* (1879–80) 5 Ex D 264 (CA), where he said at 273:

> in order to defeat a title by dispossessing the former owner, acts must be done which are inconsistent with his enjoyment of the soil for the purposes for which he intended to use it.

Subsequently, the courts developed the doctrine of the implied **licence** to show that the possession is not adverse. In *Wallis's Cayton Holiday Camp Ltd* v *Shell-Mex & BP Ltd* [1975] QB 94 (CA), a petrol company bought a garage by a proposed new road with the intention of extending the garage if the new road were to be built. Wallis's farmed this land and then used it to enlarge their holiday camp business. Their use of the land totalled just over the necessary 12 years, and they claimed adverse possession of it. They lost by a majority decision in the Court of Appeal. Lord Denning stated, at [103]:

> When the true owner of land intends to use it for a particular purpose in the future, but has no immediate use for it, and so leaves it unoccupied, he does not lose his title to it simply because some other person enters on it and uses it for some temporary purpose … his user is to be ascribed to the licence or permission of the true owner.

This 'heresy', had it been allowed to stand, could have spelled the end of adverse possession in cases where the paper owner had in mind a future use for the land, or at least severely limited its effect. The doctrine of the implied licence was expressly abolished by para 8(4) of Sch 1 of the Limitation Act 1980. In *Pye* v *Graham*, Lord Browne-Wilkinson made it clear that the heresy had not survived the 1980 Act (at [45]):

> The suggestion that the sufficiency of the possession can depend on the intention not of the squatter but of the true owner is heretical and wrong. ... The highest it can be put is that, if the squatter is aware of a special purpose for which the paper owner uses or intends to use the land and the use made by the squatter does not conflict with that use, that may provide some support for a finding as a question of fact that the squatter had no intention to possess the land in the ordinary sense but only an intention to occupy it until needed by the paper owner.

The spectre of the *Leigh* v *Jack* heresy briefly returned in *Beaulane Properties Ltd* v *Palmer* [2006] Ch 79 (Ch), when Nicholas Strauss QC held that the only way in which the law of adverse possession (under LRA 1925, s 75) could be consistent with the European Convention on Human Rights was to require the squatter's use of the land to be inconsistent with the use of the paper owner. This judgment was rejected by the Court of Appeal in *Ofulue* v *Bossert* [2009] Ch 1 (CA) as inconsistent with the subsequent decision of the European Court of Human Rights in *JA Pye (Oxford) Ltd* v *UK* (2008) 46 EHRR 45.

BP Properties Ltd v *Buckler* (1988) 55 P & CR 337 (CA) concerned not an implied licence, but one unilaterally granted by the paper owner. BP began possession proceedings against Mrs Buckler in 1974, but terminated them shortly after sending two letters to her giving her permission to remain on the land for the rest of her life. The Court of Appeal held that because Mrs Buckler had not expressly repudiated the terms of the two letters, she was in possession as licensee on those terms. Consequently, Mrs Buckler's son could not rely upon his mother's occupancy of the land as part of his claim of adverse possession. The case has been subject to some criticism (see Wallace, 1994), and is difficult to reconcile with the decision of a differently constituted Court of Appeal less than a year later that sending a letter demanding possession of the premises did not terminate adverse possession (*Mount Carmel Investments Ltd* v *Peter Thurlow Ltd* [1988] 1 WLR 1078 (CA)). The decision in *Buckler* was, however, accepted without criticism by the Board of the Privy Council in *Smith* v *Molyneaux* [2017] 1 P & CR 7 (PC) to help distinguish the heresy of the implied licence from unilateral permission to occupy the land given 'orally or in writing and by words or conduct' ([24]).

Parshall v *Hackney* [2013] Ch 568 (CA) and *Rashid* v *Nasrullah* [2018] EWCA Civ 2685 are somewhat unusual in that in both cases the claimants were, or had previously been, registered as the proprietor of the relevant land. In *Parshall* v *Hackney*, the Land Registry had, in 1980, incorrectly included a small triangle of land within two **Registers of Title**: that to No 29 Milner Street (correctly) and that to No 31 Milner Street (in error). The Parshalls, the registered proprietors of No 29, applied for **rectification** of the Register (see Section 4.9) in their favour. The registered proprietor of No 31 argued that she had acquired title to the land by adverse possession through the occupation of the land by herself and her predecessors for more than 12 years. The Court of Appeal held, however, that while the land was registered under two separate titles, neither registered owner could dispossess the other. The registered proprietors of No 31 occupied the disputed land by virtue of their **registered title**, not because they had dispossessed the true owner. However, this reasoning has now been rejected in *Rashid* v *Nasrullah* (the judgment being handed down at the last possible moment for inclusion in this edition). In this case the claimant occupier had acquired registered title to the land in 1990, following its fraudulent transfer to his father a year earlier. The original owner sought to recover the property, relying on the principle applied in *Parshall* v *Hackney*. A differently constituted Court of Appeal concluded that the basis of the decision in *Parshall* v *Hackney* (Mummery LJ gave the only substantive judgment) was ill-founded. Lewison LJ, explains at [47] of *Rashid*:

> As Lord Browne-Wilkinson demonstrated in *Pye* a 'dispossession' simply means that one person has taken possession from another without that other's consent. Mummery LJ appears to me to have re-introduced the concept of non-adverse possession, which Lord Browne-Wilkinson was at pains to abolish.

He went on to conclude that the Court of Appeal is bound by the decision in *Pye* and that on the facts of *Rashid* the test for dispossession in *Pye* was satisfied. The court did not reach this conclusion with much enthusiasm, as King and Peter Jackson LLJ explained at [82]:

> it is impossible not to feel sympathy for the victim of a brazen fraud of this kind and to wish to deprive a scoundrel such as this appellant of the benefit. However, correctly analysed, the outcome in this case is not the result of the fraud but of the true owner's subsequent failure to take effective action to challenge it.

16.3.4　Criminal trespass

On 1st September 2012, it became a criminal offence for a person to live (or intend to live) in a residential building as a trespasser if they enter those premises as a trespasser and know or ought to know that they are a trespasser (Legal Aid, Sentencing and Punishment of Offenders Act (LASPOA) 2012, s 144). It was not long before the relationship between this new offence and the ancient doctrine of adverse possession had to be considered by the courts. In *Best* v *Chief Land Registrar* [2016] QB 23 (CA), the court analysed the intention of Parliament behind both the adverse possession provisions in the LRA 2002 and section 144 of the LPSAO 2012 before concluding that the commission of an offence under section 144 did not operate as a bar to registration of adverse possession.

16.4　Establishing title to unregistered land

16.4.1　The limitation period

Section 15(1) of the Limitation Act 1980 provides:

> No action shall be brought by any person to recover any land after the expiration of twelve years from the date on which the right of action accrued to him or, if it first accrued to some other person through whom he claims, to that person.

The section states clearly that the paper owner cannot bring an action if 12 years have passed since the right to do so arose; that is, since the squatter (by definition, a trespasser) moved onto the land with the necessary intention to occupy it (see Section 16.3.2). The statute does not operate to transfer the paper owner's **title** to the adverse possessor, but, by refusing any remedy, merely ensures that no one can remove them.

Not only can the paper owner not bring an action to recover possession after 12 years, but their title to the land is extinguished after that period (Limitation Act 1980, s 17). It is important to remember that, as the squatter themself is not a 'purchaser' of land, they are, like someone who simply inherits land, bound by all earlier interests in the land, whether they are legal or **equitable**, and whether or not they were protected by registration or had **notice** of them (see Chapter 5).

By section 38 of the Limitation Act 1980, 'land' means more than just the legal **freehold**; it includes, for example, equitable freeholds and legal and equitable **leases**. Consequently, it is possible to obtain title to a long lease by adverse possession as well as title to freehold land (see Section 16.6). There are special rules for adversely possessing Crown land (the limitation period is 30 years) and for special classes, such as between **trustees** and their beneficiaries.

16.4.2   Dispossession of the paper owner

In order for time to start running in the squatter's favour, the paper owner must either have been dispossessed of the land or have discontinued possession (Limitation Act 1980, Sch 1, para 1). It is now clear, following the leading case of *JA Pye (Oxford) Ltd* v *Graham* [2003] 1 AC 419 (HL), that all that is required is for the squatter to take possession of the land without the permission of the owner.

If a **tenancy** is an oral **periodic tenancy** (see Section 7.4.2), time can begin to run in favour of the **tenant** from the time they stop paying **rent**, since the tenancy is then deemed to have ended (Limitation Act 1980, Sch 1, para 5(2)). In *Hayward* v *Chaloner* [1968] 1 QB 107 (CA), a quarter of an acre of land was let as a garden on such a tenancy to whoever was the rector of a small village. For some 25 years from 1942, no rent was paid, and there was no acknowledgement of the paper owners' title. The then rector decided to sell the land as his own, and the paper owners decided to fight him; they had failed to collect the rent, not because they forgot, but because of 'their loyalty and generosity to the church'. The rector won by a majority decision in the Court of Appeal, although all the judges regretted it. As Russell LJ explained at 123–4:

> The generous indulgence of the plaintiffs and their predecessors in title, loyal churchmen all, having resulted in a free accretion at their expense to the lands of their church, their reward may be in the next world. But in this jurisdiction we can only qualify them for that reward by allowing the [rector's] appeal.

16.4.3   Continuous possession

The squatter must prove that they have been in continuous possession throughout the required period. Any interruption to their possession means that the period must begin again. However, the adverse possession need not have been by one squatter. In *Williams* v *Usherwood* (1983) 45 P & CR 235 (CA) (see Section 16.1.1), there were several different owners of Number 31 who, in succession, adversely possessed the land continuously for the necessary period.

16.4.4   Stopping the time running

A paper owner can bring an action for possession within the limitation period. Of itself, this does not stop time running, but simply means that the paper owner is not time barred. They must, therefore, pursue the action and bring it to a successful conclusion (*Markfield Investments Ltd* v *Evans* [2001] 1 WLR 1321 (CA)).

The Limitation Act 1980 provides that the period of adverse possession will stop running if the squatter acknowledges in writing the **title** of the paper owner (ss 29–31). Whether a document amounts to such an acknowledgement depends on the true construction of that document in the context of all the surrounding circumstances (*Allen* v *Matthews* [2007] 2 P & CR 21 (CA)). In *Edginton* v *Clark* [1964] 1 QB 367 (CA), the claimant had occupied bombed land in the East End of London for about seven years and then offered to buy it from the owner. No sale followed and, after a further ten years, he claimed adverse possession. It was held that the offer to buy was an acknowledgement of the owner's title and that therefore the squatter's possession was interrupted.

Under section 32 of the Limitation Act, the adverse possessor must prove that they did not deliberately conceal their activities or keep their possession through fraud. If there is any deception, time starts to run from the date when the paper owner 'could with reasonable diligence have discovered it'. In *Beaulane Properties Ltd* v *Palmer* [2006] Ch 79 (Ch), Mr Palmer had originally occupied the disputed land under the terms of a **licence** granted by Beaulane's predecessor in title, but continued in occupation when this was terminated in 1986. In 1991, Mr Palmer told a representative of the then paper owner of the land that he had an arrangement to use the land without making it clear that it had been terminated in 1986. Nicholas Strauss QC, sitting as a deputy judge in the Chancery Division, held that this informal and unexpected conversation was sufficient to amount to concealment, and that the period of adverse possession only started to run in 1991.

16.5 Establishing title to registered land

Until the relevant provisions of the LRA 2002 came into force on 13th October 2003, the rules applying to claims of adverse possession over **registered land** were very similar to those that applied to **unregistered land**. In its 1998 Consultation Paper, the Law Commission recognised that many of the traditional justifications for adverse possession (see Section 16.2) hold no relevance in a regime where **title** to land is registered. The Commission went on to propose the fundamental changes to the operation of the principles of adverse possession which were enacted in the LRA 2002 (see Law Com No 254, 1998, Part X). Consequently, although the kind of conduct that will amount to adverse possession is the same whether title to the land is registered or unregistered (LRA 2002, Sch 6, para 11(1)), the rules that determine the consequences of such possession are very different.

16.5.1 The old rules: the LRA 1925

Prior to 13th October 2003, where the title to the land was registered, the rules prevented the registered owner from bringing an action to evict the squatter after 12 years. Unlike the position in unregistered land, however, their title was not extinguished; instead, they held it on **trust** for the squatter (LRA 1925, s 75(1)).

The squatter could also, if they wished, apply to the Land Registry to become the registered proprietor after 12 years (LRA 1925, s 75(2)).

16.5.2   The new rules: the LRA 2002

The rules in the LRA 2002 mean that since 13th October 2003 it has been much more difficult for a squatter to obtain **title**. The most significant changes are that:

▶ the rules set out in the Limitation Act 1980 do not apply to registered land after this date (LRA 2002, s 96): registered proprietors are no longer statute barred from pursuing claims against trespassers; and

▶ an adverse possessor must now claim the land by applying to the Registrar to be registered as the proprietor of the land, following the procedure set out in Schedule 6 to the LRA 2002.

An outline of the Schedule 6 process

Para 1   In most cases, a squatter may apply to the Land Registry to be registered as owner of the land after *ten* years' adverse possession (60 years in the case of the foreshore owned by the Crown: see para 13).

Para 2   The Registrar informs the following of the squatter's claim: the registered proprietor, the owner of any registered charge on the land (such as a mortgage lender) and, if the land is **leasehold**, the registered proprietor of the **freehold**.

Para 4   If the Registrar has received no response within 65 business days (LRR 2003, r 189), the adverse possessor becomes the new registered proprietor.

Para 5   If there is an objection within the three-month period, the squatter's application will automatically be rejected unless:

Para 5(2)   *(a) The paper owner has acted unconscionably and is estopped from denying title.* This would not include a situation where the applicant is on the land with the permission of the owner, since such occupation could not amount to adverse possession (see Section 16.3.3). However, it could arise where a person has developed land thinking it belonged to them, and the paper owner, aware of the true position, has allowed this to happen. It could also occur where a buyer of land has paid the purchase price but there has been no valid contract and thus no transfer of the **equitable** title.

Para 5(3)   *(b) The adverse possessor is entitled to be registered as the owner for some reason other than their adverse possession of the land.* This might arise, for example, where the possessor is entitled to a **conveyance** of the land under the terms of a will. It might also occur when, despite having purchased and paid for the land, the registered title has not yet been transferred to the buyer (see Section 12.5), although in this case it might be simpler for the possessor to seek specific performance of the contract.

Para 5(4)   *(c) The disputed land is next to land already owned by the adverse possessor, the boundary between the two plots is unclear and they have occupied the land for ten years, reasonably believing that it belonged to them.*

Para 6   If the squatter's application is rejected and none of the conditions in para 5 applies, they may make a further application to have title to the land transferred into their name after two years, provided that the registered proprietor has not taken steps through the courts to evict them. Following this second application, the registered proprietor cannot prevent the claimant being registered as the new proprietor of the land with the same class of title as that of the paper owner they have dispossessed.

These reforms in respect of registered land mean that the paper owner does not automatically lose their right to evict a trespasser after 12 years' adverse possession, as formerly, but will be warned by the Registry that a squatter is attempting to gain title to their land. However, if they do nothing to regain possession of the land, they will lose it unless it subsequently becomes apparent that the squatter had not been in adverse possession (as defined at Section 16.3) for the relevant period at the date of the application to the Registrar (as was the case in *Baxter* v *Mannion* [2011] 1 WLR 1594 (CA); see Section 4.9.1).

Other important differences between the new rules and those that apply to **unregistered land** include:

▶ Neither written acknowledgement of title nor concealment nor fraud by the squatter has any specific consequences under Schedule 6 (compare ss 29–31 and 32 of the Limitation Act 1980; see Section 16.4.4). In many cases, however, such factors will be sufficient to demonstrate that the squatter did not meet the requirements for being in adverse possession (see Section 16.3.2). They are only likely to be relevant if the registered proprietor fails to object in time to the squatter's application to be registered as proprietor of the land.

▶ Paragraph 11 of Schedule 6 limits the circumstances in which occupation by a previous squatter can count towards the ten-year period to:
  – where the applicant is the successor in title of the first squatter, having bought the land from them or having inherited it, and then moved into possession; or
  – where the applicant was the original squatter, was dispossessed by another squatter but then was able to regain possession.

16.6 Leases and adverse possession

The rules about **leases** and adverse possession can be complex and, again, the results may differ depending on whether **title** to the land is **registered** or **unregistered**.

If a squatter takes possession of land subject to a lease, the possession is adverse to the **tenant**; that is, it is the tenant who is liable to lose their interest in the land, not the **lessor**. This is because it is the tenant who is entitled to possession; the lessor is entitled only to the rent. The lessor has no right to possession until the lease ends, and it is also at that time that the squatter's period of adverse possession against the lessor begins.

An interesting situation arises if the tenant of a long lease, against whom a squatter has been in adverse possession for 12 years, surrenders their lease to their lessor (see Section 7.7). There is little point in the tenant continuing with the lease, since they now have no cause of action against the squatter. Following the tenant's surrender of the lease, the lessor can bring an action for possession against the squatter (*Fairweather* v *St Marylebone Property Co Ltd* [1963] AC 510 (HL)). Having evicted the squatter, there is then nothing to prevent the lessor from granting a new lease to their former tenant.

Under the LRA 1925 rules for registered land, the position was different. In *Central London Commercial Estates Ltd* v *Kato Kagaku Ltd* [1998] 4 All ER 948 (Ch), a squatter had adversely possessed registered land against the tenant for more than 12 years. However, the squatter failed to make an application under section 75(2) of the LRA 1925 to be registered as proprietor (see Section 16.5) before the tenant surrendered the lease to the **landlord**. Applying section 75(1) of the LRA 1925, Sedley J held that the tenant was **trustee** for the squatter, who was now entitled to remain on the land for the remaining term of the lease. This decision effectively prevented a tenant of registered land from surrendering their lease once the 12-year period of adverse possession had been completed.

It is unlikely that this situation will arise under the new rules contained in Schedule 6 of the LRA 2002, as adverse possession now gives rise to a right to apply to become the registered proprietor of the **estate**, rather than to a **trust**. The tenant will have no need to surrender the lease to the landlord, since either they will object to the squatter's application and subsequently gain possession, or the squatter will succeed in their application, with the result that the squatter's name will be registered at the Land Registry with the title of the former tenant (see Section 16.5). This means that they will now be subject to the covenants in the lease, and failure to comply with them may result in **forfeiture** of the lease by the lessor (see Section 8.5).

16.7 Adverse possession and human rights

In *JA Pye (Oxford) Ltd* v *Graham* [2003] 1 AC 419 (HL) the question was raised as to whether the use of the Limitation Act to deny a landowner the right to bring an action to recover their land amounted to a breach of Article 1, Protocol 1 of the European Convention on Human Rights (depriving a person of their property without compensation). Although the action was between private individuals, the deprivation of the property resulted from statutory authority (LRA 1925, s 75), thus allowing the Convention to be invoked. By the time the case had reached the House of Lords, it had become clear that the Human Rights Act 1998 had no retrospective effect and so did not apply in *Pye* v *Graham*. However, Pye was able to refer the matter to the European Court of Human Rights at Strasbourg. The period between the decisions of the House of Lords and the Court of Human Rights provides the context for the first instance judgment in *Beaulane Properties Ltd* v *Palmer* [2006] Ch 79 (Ch) (see Sections 16.3.3 and 16.4.4). Like *Pye* v *Graham*, this case concerned section 75 of the LRA 1925, but unlike *Pye* v *Graham* the Human Rights Act 1998 applied. The judge held that section 75 of the LRA 1925 could only be interpreted as being consistent with the Human Rights Act 1998 if the doctrine of adverse possession were limited to those cases where the squatter's use was inconsistent with the paper owner's purpose for the land. He went on to hold that for that reason, he was not bound by the House of Lords' decision to the contrary in *Pye* v *Graham*.

The Grand Chamber of the European Court of Human Rights finally settled the *Pye* case in 2007 (see *JA Pye (Oxford) Ltd* v *UK* (2008) 46 EHRR 45). A majority of the court concluded that the pre-LRA 2002 law of adverse possession was compatible with the principles of the European Convention on Human Rights, since:

- it was already accepted that periods of limitation were compatible with the Convention;
- the period required in this case was not excessively short;
- the paper owner should have been aware of the limitation period; and
- relatively limited action was required by the paper owner to stop the period from running.

The decision in *Pye* v *UK* means that section 75 of the LRA 1925 is generally compliant with the Convention and that compliance does not need to be determined on a case-by-case basis (*Ofulue* v *Bossert* [2009] Ch 1 (CA), applying *Harrow LBC* v *Qazi* [2004] 1 AC 983 (HL)). It also means that the decision in *Beaulane Properties Ltd* (see Section 16.4.4) is wrong.

There is little doubt that the provisions in Schedule 6 to the LRA 2002 are compliant with the Human Rights Act; indeed, this was expressly recognised by the dissenting minority of the Grand Chamber in *Pye* v *UK*.

16.8 Adverse possession in the twenty-first century

The traditional justifications for retaining adverse possession in a private system of **unregistered title** to land remain as convincing as ever. In unregistered land, titles to land are relative and an English court will assist the party with the better claim to possession, even if the final outcome in a particular case seems disproportionate or unjust. In a public system of **registered land**, where most titles are absolute and guaranteed by the State, some of the traditional justifications are not so persuasive. However, adverse possession is retained within the LRA 2002 scheme as it helps to ensure that land remains marketable and can prevent injustice.

It is evident that the LRA 2002 scheme in **registered land** will make it much more difficult for a squatter to gain title to the land. Indeed, this is a deliberate policy which the framers of the Act (and the Land Registry) hope will provide a strong incentive for the owners of unregistered titles to apply for voluntary registration. Much of the land that remains unregistered is made up of large estates, and the owners of such land (often public authorities or large corporations) must remain vigilant in order to protect themselves from being dispossessed by a squatter.

The first decade of the twenty-first century saw a number of significant cases concerning adverse possession, including those that explored the interface between land law and human rights. It seems likely that the doctrine will attract less attention from the courts as the rules of the LRA 2002 become increasingly dominant. However, while the role of the doctrine in high-value cases, such as *JA Pye (Oxford) Ltd* v *Graham* and *Ofulue* v *Bossert*, may be on the wane, it seems that it will continue to be highly significant to neighbours who find themselves in dispute, as the Williamses and the Usherwoods did. Disputes relating to adverse possession now form a significant part of the business of the Land Registration Division of the Property Chamber of the First-tier Tribunal (and its predecessor, the Adjudicator to Her Majesty's Land Registry. More details can be found by following the links on the Tribunal's website at www.justice.gov.uk/tribunals/land-registration).

Summary

16.1 The doctrine of adverse possession allows a person who has been in possession of land for a significant period of time to claim title to (that is, ownership of) that land.

16.2 The main justifications for recognising title by adverse possession are based on the weaknesses of a deeds-based conveyancing system. The LRA 2002 significantly restricts the doctrine in so far as it applies to registered titles.

16.3 To be in adverse possession, a person must:

- act as owner of the land, showing an appropriate degree of physical control; and
- have sufficient intention to possess the land (known as *animus possidendi*).

16.4 The Limitation Act 1980 is central to the operation of adverse possession in *unregistered land*. Twelve years' unconcealed adverse possession, without interruptions, prevents the paper owner repossessing the land.

16.5 A person claiming title of registered land can now apply to be registered as proprietor after ten years' adverse possession. The registered proprietor is given warning of the threat to their land and, except in a number of specific circumstances, can prevent the squatter being registered as proprietor. However, if the registered proprietor then fails to evict the squatter within two years of the initial application, the squatter will automatically be entitled to be registered as proprietor of the title.

16.6 Care must be taken when dealing with adverse possession claims where the land is subject to a lease, especially if the land is unregistered or the rules of the LRA 1925 apply.

16.7 After some controversy, it is now accepted by the courts that the various rules relating to adverse possession are generally compliant with the European Convention on Human Rights.

Exercises

 16.1 Complete the online quiz on the topics covered in this chapter on the companion website.

16.2 Consider the ways in which the nature of the land and the title claimed are relevant to a claim for adverse possession.

16.3 Olwen owns a 300-year lease in Animal Farm, the freehold owner of which is a pension company called Trusties. Neither the leasehold nor the freehold titles are registered. At one corner of the farm lies a small triangle of woodland of about one-third of an acre. Here Kate, an eccentric old woman, lives in a barrel with her tame goat, Peter, who finds his food in the wood. She moved into the barrel two years ago, just after the death of her friend Mumtaz, who had lived in the barrel, so he had claimed, since well before 1970. Mumtaz had originally been a weekly tenant but had never paid rent after the first week.

Olwen has just been offered an excellent price for her lease, if she can deliver vacant possession. She wishes to sell, but Kate refuses to leave. Olwen claims that, although she never gave permission for anyone to live there, she did not really mind as it was so

Exercises (continued)

far from the house. She had no particular use for the woodland, although, if she could have got a grant, she would have cut down the trees and erected battery hen units. Kate says that it is her woodland now and points out that her boundary was marked out by large boulders and electric cable (hung between the trees) by Mumtaz. She claims that Olwen has not been allowed in the woodland for years and years.

Advise the parties. How would your answer differ if Olwen's leasehold title were registered?

 You can find suggested answer plans to exercises 16.2 and 16.3 on the companion website.

Further reading

Davis, 'Informal Acquisition and Loss of Rights in Land: What Justifies the Doctrines?' (2000) 20 LS 198

Dixon, 'Adverse Possession and the Land Registration Act 2002' (2009) 73 Conv 169

Dixon, 'Human Rights and Adverse Possession: The Final Word' (2008) 72 Conv 160

Dockray, 'Why Do We Need Adverse Possession?' [1985] Conv 272

Hickey, 'The effect of supervening permission on adverse possession' (2017) 81 Conv 223

McCormick, 'Adverse Possession and Future Enjoyment' [1986] Conv 434

Tee, 'A Harsh Twilight' [2003] CLJ 36

Wallace, 'Limitation, Prescription and Unsolicited Permission' [1994] Conv 196

Chapter 17

Implied trusts of family-owned land

Key concepts

▶ **Common intention constructive trust** – a trust arising out of an express or implied agreement to share the ownership of property.
▶ **Implied trust** – a trust created by operation of law rather than by express words or statutory provision.
▶ **Resulting trust** – a trust arising by operation of law in which the beneficial interest is vested in the person who financed the acquisition of that property or in the person who transferred the property to the legal owner without transferring the entire beneficial interest in the property.

17.1 A cautionary tale

This is a cautionary tale, which all unmarried couples who are contemplating the purchase of residential property as their home, and all solicitors who advise them, should study. The facts are not in dispute and are unusual only in the sense that a great deal of time has elapsed since the parties separated.

Thus begins the judgment of Wall LJ in *Jones* v *Kernott* [2010] 1 WLR 2401 (CA). The relationship between the parties had lasted from 1984 to 1993. They never married, but they had two children and in 1984 they purchased a house in joint names. Ms Jones conceded that had the house been sold when the relationship first broke down, she and Mr Kernott would have been entitled to equal shares in the proceeds. However, this was not what happened. Instead, Ms Jones continued to live in the house with the children, paying the **mortgage** and all the other outgoings. She did not ask for, and did not receive, any financial assistance from Mr Kernott, who purchased another house in his sole name in 1996. It was not until ten years later that Mr Kernott sought to recover his share in the family home. The question was whether he was still entitled to half of the value of the house or whether the proportion of his share had changed after he left the house and ceased to contribute to the mortgage. The Supreme Court gave its judgment in the case in November 2011. How it finally answered the question is considered in Section 17.3.2.

When a marriage or civil partnership comes to an end, the courts have considerable powers to make the best provision in the circumstances under the Matrimonial Causes Act 1973 and the Civil Partnership Act 2004. However, these powers are not available in other circumstances. Consequently, disputes between partners who are neither married nor civil partners, between siblings, and between friends who have bought a house together fall to be decided under the general principles of property law. These principles were developed in the context of the nineteenth and early twentieth centuries, when property law was concerned more with enabling people to realise their investment than with sharing a home. Despite a broad consensus that some relationships need to be given special treatment, there seems to be insufficient political will to provide a statutory solution. For example, a new statutory scheme to apply to cohabitants proposed by the Law Commission in *Cohabitation: The Financial Consequences of Relationship Breakdown* (Law Com No 307, 2007) was broadly welcomed, but the legislation proposed has yet to be implemented by Parliament.

Of course, in an ideal world, people intending to share property would do at least three things (see Clarke, 1992); they:

▶ would agree what they intended to do;
▶ would then record their intentions; and they
▶ would take legal advice to ensure that what they wanted had been achieved in a manner which the law recognises.

In fact, this is often what is done in the case of a business venture. It is relatively rare for commercial cases concerning **implied trusts** in land to come before the courts. Unfortunately, the situation tends to be very different when the land concerned is a family home. However sensible it might be for two people to sort out their property and financial arrangements before they buy a house (or before a person moves in to live with someone who already owns a house), even to suggest opening these kinds of negotiations might be thought to be somewhat calculating and risk undermining the relationship. Equally, such thoughts might never have crossed the parties' minds at such an emotional stage in their relationship. Alternatively, there may have been some informal, but unexpressed, understanding between the parties. However, even if this was the case, the circumstances may subsequently change beyond what was originally envisaged: for example, the relationship may break down, or a mortgage lender might seek possession of the land because of mortgage arrears.

The simplest form of solution in such circumstances is to assume that a person's **beneficial interest** in the property is directly proportional to the financial contribution they made to the purchase price. For many years, this 'resulting trust' analysis (considered in Section 17.2) was used by the courts in domestic as well as commercial cases concerning the beneficial ownership of land. For example, the important cases of *Bull* v *Bull* [1955] 1 QB 234 (CA) (see Section 2.2.3(a)) and *Williams & Glyn's Bank Ltd* v *Boland* [1981] AC 487 (HL) (see Chapter 2 and Section 4.6.2) both refer to the claimant's interests being acquired by way of a resulting trust. However, by the end of the twentieth century the courts considered the resulting trust too blunt and inflexible a tool for use within the context of complex family relationships. In most cases concerning family land the court will now seek to discern what the parties intended from the wider circumstances of the case (hence the term 'common intention' constructive trust). These trusts are considered in Section 17.3. If a claimant is unable to establish either a resulting trust or a common intention constructive trust, then their alternative is to seek to establish rights to the land through the doctrine of **proprietary estoppel**, considered in Chapter 18.

17.2 Resulting trusts

A resulting trust can arise when a person contributes towards the purchase price of land, but the legal **title** is transferred into the name of someone else. In such circumstances, the *presumption* is that the parties intended that the legal owner hold the land on **trust** for the benefit of the people who contributed to the purchase price in proportion to their contributions. When determining the terms of the trust and the extent of the various beneficial shares, 'a resulting trust "crystallises" on the date that the property is acquired' (per Peter Gibson LJ *Curley* v *Parkes* [2004] EWCA Civ 1515 (CA) at [18]). When the land that is subject to a resulting trust is sold, the proceeds of sale are divided between the co-owners in direct proportion to their contributions to the purchase price. Since nowadays people tend to depend on **mortgage** loans to finance the purchase of their homes, it is common for people who do not hold legal title to attempt to establish a **beneficial interest** in the land through their contributions to the mortgage repayments. Accepting liability for a mortgage at the time the property is purchased may be enough to give rise to a resulting trust, as in the case of *Cowcher* v *Cowcher* [1972] 1 WLR 425 (Fam). However, merely contributing to the repayments of a mortgage granted by the legal owner is not sufficient (see *Curley* v *Parkes*).

The direct link between the contribution to the purchase price and the proportion of the beneficial share in a resulting trust means that the court cannot take any other circumstances into account in determining the beneficial shares in the land. This is the main reason why, in *Stack* v *Dowden* [2007] 2 AC 432 (HL), the House of Lords decided that the flexibility offered by a constructive trust (see Section 17.3.2) was more appropriate where properties were acquired jointly by a cohabiting couple. In the words of Baroness Hale and Lord Walker in the later case of *Jones* v *Kernott* [2012] 1 AC 776 (SC) at [75]):

> in the case of the purchase of a house or flat in joint names for joint occupation by a married or unmarried couple, where both are responsible for any mortgage, there is no presumption of a resulting trust arising from their having contributed to the deposit (or indeed the rest of the purchase) in unequal shares.

The traditional resulting trust analysis is, therefore, reserved for commercial arrangements. However, the division between 'domestic' and 'commercial' is not always clear. In *Laskar* v *Laskar* [2008] 1 WLR 2695 (CA), for example, a mother and daughter joined together to purchase the mother's council house, with the purpose of renting it out to **tenants** (what is referred to as a 'buy-to-let'). Neuberger LJ, as he then was, held that despite the familial appearance of the case, it gave rise to a resulting trust, saying (at [17]):

> the primary purpose of the purchase of the property was as an investment, not as a home. … To my mind it would not be right to apply the reasoning in *Stack* v *Dowden* to such a case as this, where the parties primarily purchased the property as an investment for rental income and capital appreciation, even where their relationship is a familial one.

In *Erlam* v *Rahman* [2016] EWHC 111 (Ch), Chief Master Marsh sought to apply the reasoning in *Laskar* to another 'buy-to-let', but in this case it had been purchased by a married couple. He concluded, at [41], that:

> To my mind, the principle which is applicable in this claim is clear and the *Stack* v *Dowden* approach *to the purchase of a domestic property as a home by married or co-habiting couples* will not apply if the joint intention at the date [of] purchase of [the house] was to acquire it for letting. (Emphasis added.)

However, in *Marr* v *Collie* [2017] 3 WLR 1507 (PC) the Privy Council rejected this focus on the purpose of the transaction in favour of seeking to establish the common intention of the parties as to how the property was to be held. As Lord Kerr explains, at [49]:

> The Board does not consider, therefore, that *Laskar's* case is authority for the proposition that the principle in *Stack* v *Dowden* … applies only in 'the domestic consumer context'.

> Where a property is bought in the joint names of a cohabiting couple, even if that is as an investment, it does not follow inexorably that the 'resulting trust' solution must provide the inevitable answer as to how its beneficial ownership is to be determined.

On this reasoning, it would seem that it is the nature of the relationship between the parties that is usually determinative of which approach is appropriate, rather than whether the particular transaction is for personal accommodation or investment purposes. While *Marr v Collie* is not binding precedent, it can be seen as a good indication of the present thinking of the judges of the Supreme Court on this issue (and note that Lord Neuberger, who gave the lead judgment in *Laskar*, was also a member of the Board in *Marr*).

There are a number of circumstances in which a contribution to the purchase price will not give rise to a resulting trust (or, indeed, a constructive trust), including:

▶ where the nature of the transaction is inconsistent with a trust: for example, the contribution was intended to be a gift or a loan (see, for example, *Fowkes v Pascoe* (1874–75) 10 Ch App 343 (CACh));
▶ the trust is defeated by the 'presumption of advancement'.

The doctrine of 'presumption of advancement' is an old rule under which it is assumed that money given by a husband to his wife, or by a father to his child, for the purchase of land was a gift, and that it was not intended that the parent should acquire any interest in the land. In *McGrath v Wallis* [1995] 2 FLR 114 (CA) the Court of Appeal followed the modern line that this presumption is now a 'judicial instrument of the last resort' and is rebuttable by even the slightest evidence. Here, where a father had provided money to help his son buy a house for them to live in together, there was evidence (from an incomplete **deed**) of an intention that the land was to be held on trust for them both as tenants in common. Therefore, the presumption of advancement did not operate, and when the father died intestate the son's sister was entitled on the intestacy to a share in her father's interest in the land. The presumption of advancement has been considered archaic and sexist for some time, and provision was made for its abolition in section 199 of the Equality Act 2010. It seems, however, that there are no plans to bring this section into force.

17.3 Common intention constructive trusts

Constructive trusts are potentially much wider than **resulting trusts**. There are a number of types of constructive trust. This section focuses on constructive trusts that arise out of the *common intention* of the parties in the context of a family relationship, and brief reference is made to *remedial* constructive trusts in Section 17.4. Other types of constructive trust tend to be covered as part of courses on equity and trusts rather than land law, and detailed accounts of them can be found in most of the standard textbooks on the law of equity and trusts.

There are two main questions that need to be addressed in common intention constructive trust cases.

▶ *Acquisition:* Is the claimant entitled to a **beneficial interest** in the land?
▶ *Quantification:* If so, what is the extent of that interest?

Where legal **title** to the land is vested in all the parties to the dispute, the beneficial interests will be acquired under the terms of any express trust or by virtue of a statutory trust imposed by sections 34–6 of the LPA 1925 (see Section 14.2). According to Baroness Hale in *Stack* v *Dowden* [2007] 2 AC 432 (HL), at [54] (see also *Jones* v *Kernott* [2012] 1 AC 776 (SC), at [75]), unless there is clear evidence of intention to the contrary:

> it should be assumed that equity follows the law and that the beneficial interests reflect the legal interests in the property.

Consequently, if legal title to the family home is vested in both partners, the court will normally move directly to the question of quantification. For example, the main issue before the court in *Jones* v *Kernott* was Ms Jones' argument that Mr Kernott's entitlement to the land had been reduced by the change of circumstances after their relationship broke down. However, in cases where there is no express or statutory trust (because, for example, the legal title is vested in only one partner, rather than in both partners), the court must determine whether a beneficial interest exists at all before it can consider the proportions of any beneficial entitlement (for a judicial summary of this statement, see Sachs LJ, *Capehorn* v *Harris* [2016] HLR 1 (CA) at [16]).

17.3.1 Acquisition: establishing a beneficial interest

In *Lloyds Bank plc* v *Rosset* [1991] 1 AC 107 (HL), Mr and Mrs Rosset wished to buy a semi-derelict farmhouse using money from a Swiss trust fund, but the **trustees** of the fund insisted that legal **title** was transferred to Mr Rosset alone. For six months, Mrs Rosset supervised the renovation and decoration of the house. Mr Rosset subsequently mortgaged the house to the bank without his wife's knowledge. When the bank brought possession proceedings, she claimed that she had an **equitable** interest under an informal trust. This, she argued, would enable her to claim an **overriding interest** under section 70(1)(g) of the LRA 1925 (see Section 4.6.2) and thus defeat the **mortgage**. The House of Lords held that she had not shown that she had gained an interest, and therefore the bank was able to defeat her claim.

The land was held in the sole name of Mr Rosset, and because there had been no express declaration of trust, Lord Bridge said that an equitable interest would only arise if Mrs Rosset could demonstrate that there had been a *common intention* that she should own a share in the land. Lord Bridge said that this could only be shown by either:

1. an *express agreement* that the land should be co-owned, together with some act by the claimant to her detriment or some significant alteration of her position in reliance on the agreement; or
2. in the absence of an express agreement, *an act by the claimant from which the court may infer a common intention*, giving rise to an interest under a constructive trust. Lord Bridge thought that the only act which would be sufficient to justify inferring an agreement would be the direct contribution of money (including the payment of mortgage instalments) towards the purchase of the property.

Mrs Rosset failed under the first category because there had been no express agreement that she should have a **beneficial interest**. She failed under the second category because her work on the house did not amount to a sufficient act from which to infer such an agreement.

17.3.1(a) Express common intention

In *Rosset*, Lord Bridge approved the earlier Court of Appeal decision in *Grant* v *Edwards* [1986] Ch 638 (CA) in which a man and a woman lived together for about ten years and had two children. He had told her that her name should not go on the legal title of the house that they shared because this might prejudice her divorce proceedings. Although clearly he never intended that she should have a beneficial share in the house, the Court of Appeal was prepared to find that his excuse for not putting her name on the title amounted to evidence of a common intention, since otherwise no excuse would have been needed. In addition, the couple had shared equally some money left over from an insurance claim when the house had partly burnt down. The woman had acted to her detriment in reliance on the common intention by paying all the household bills. Lord Justice Nourse explained, at 646:

> In a case such as the present, where there has been no written declaration or agreement, nor any direct provision by the plaintiff of part of the purchase price so as to give rise to a resulting trust in her favour, she must establish a common intention between her and the defendant, acted on by her, that she should have a beneficial interest in the property.

He went on to state (at 648) that to be sufficient, her actions must be:

> conduct on which the woman could not reasonably be expected to embark unless she was to have an interest in the house. If she was not to have such an interest, she could reasonably be expected to go and live with her lover, but not, for example, to wield a 14-lb. sledge hammer in the front garden. In adopting the latter kind of conduct she is seen to act to her detriment on the faith of the common intention.

As the claimant had established that there had been a common intention that the house should be co-owned and that she had relied on this to her detriment, the Court imposed a constructive trust on the man and awarded her a share of the beneficial interest.

In *Hammond* v *Mitchell* [1991] 1 WLR 1127 (Fam), a man and woman lived together for 12 years in a bungalow registered in his name. He had promised her that she was equally the owner of the property but said that he could not put her name on the Register for tax reasons. There were also several businesses and a house in Spain, and she claimed a half-share in all of these. Waite J, in some despair at the detailed and conflicting evidence and the 19 days of the trial, finally awarded her a half-share in the bungalow. The full flavour of the dispute can only be gained from reading the report. There was evidence of a promise that the land was half hers, of her involvement in the businesses and their sharing of whatever money they had, and of her agreement to risk any interest she might have in the bungalow as security for a bank loan for business purposes. All these taken together showed a common agreement plus an act to her detriment. She therefore satisfied what is now known as the first *Rosset* category. However, the judge commented (at 1139):

> The primary emphasis accorded by the law in cases of this kind to express discussions between the parties … means that the tenderest exchanges of a common law courtship may assume an unforeseen significance many years later when they are brought under equity's microscope and subjected to an analysis under which many thousands of pounds of value may be liable to turn on fine questions as to whether the relevant words were spoken in earnest or in dalliance and with or without representational intent.

To establish a common intention constructive trust under this heading, the claimant must establish an express agreement relating to the ownership of the land and detrimental reliance on that agreement. The claimant does not, however, have to show that the acts of reliance formed part of the bargain, or that they were specifically envisaged by the defendant. As Rimer LJ explained in *Parris* v *Williams* [2009] 1 P & CR 9 (CA) (at [42]):

> once a finding of an express arrangement or agreement has been made, all that the claimant to a beneficial share under a constructive trust needs to show is that he or she has 'acted to his or her detriment or significantly altered his or her position in reliance on the agreement'.

An express agreement that falls short of granting **co-ownership** (such as a loan between the parties) is not a sufficient foundation for a trust under this heading. Neither can the claimant rely upon an agreement that is unenforceable. For example, in *Smith* v *Cooper* [2010] EWCA Civ 722 the claimant was ultimately unable to establish a constructive trust because he had used undue influence to obtain his agreement with the defendant.

17.3.1(b) Inferred common intention

Under this second category, the claimant must establish that there are sufficient grounds to enable the court to infer the presence of an agreement to share ownership of the land. This is not the same as saying that the court can impose a trust or impute an agreement wherever it would be fair to do so (see Section 17.4). For example, in *Barnes* v *Phillips* [2016] HLR 3 (CA) the question arose as to whether the trial judge sufficiently distinguished between the decision to change the terms of a trust and the revised beneficial entitlements after that change. Following *Jones* v *Kernott*, it is possible for the court to determine what the shares of the parties should be, if there is no evidence of what, if anything, the parties actually agreed. However, this does not mean that the court can impose a change in the terms of the trust where there is no evidence that the parties intended any change at all (see *Barnes* v *Phillips* at [26]).

In *Rosset*, Lord Bridge indicated that he considered that nothing short of a monetary contribution to the purchase would be sufficient to justify inferring such an agreement. There is support for this view from the earlier case of *Burns* v *Burns* [1984] Ch 317 (CA), where an unmarried couple lived together for 19 years in a house, legal title to which was held by the man. The woman brought up their children, kept house and, when the children were older, took a job which allowed her to contribute to the housekeeping and buy various household items such as a washing machine. She also decorated inside the house. When their relationship ended, her claim to a beneficial interest failed because, according to Fox LJ at 328 and 331:

> What is needed, I think, is evidence of a payment or payments by the plaintiff which it can be inferred was referable to the acquisition of the house ... the mere fact that the parties live together and do the ordinary domestic tasks is, in my view, no indication at all that they thereby intended to alter the existing property rights of either of them.

The level of the hurdle set by Lord Bridge for establishing inferred intention is lower than what is required for a resulting trust. The payment of **mortgage** instalments and a discount given to a sitting **tenant** by the **landlord** selling a flat are sufficient to found an inferred common intention, but not a resulting trust (see *Curley* v *Parkes* [2004] EWCA Civ 1515 at [16]). However, as Lord Walker opined in *Stack* v *Dowden* (at [26]):

> Lord Bridge's extreme doubt 'whether anything less will do' was certainly consistent with many first-instance and Court of Appeal decisions, but I respectfully doubt whether it

took full account of the views (conflicting though they were) expressed in *Gissing* v *Gissing* [1971] AC 886 … It has attracted some trenchant criticism from scholars as potentially productive of injustice … Whether or not Lord Bridge's observation was justified in 1990, in my opinion the law has moved on, and your Lordships should move it a little more in the same direction.

Even before *Stack* v *Dowden*, there was some evidence that the strict approach taken by Lord Bridge in *Rosset* was being relaxed. Indeed, as Lord Walker observed, the House of Lords itself had pointed towards a more liberal approach in case of *Gissing* v *Gissing* [1971] AC 886 (HL), some 20 years before *Rosset*. In *Gissing*, Lord Diplock believed that indirect financial contributions to the household expenses might be sufficient to enable a claimant to gain a beneficial interest, but only if they enabled the legal owner to make the mortgage repayments. Ten years after *Rosset*, Nicholas Mostyn QC, sitting as a deputy judge in the Family Division, reflected on the arbitrary level of the hurdle when giving judgment in *Le Foe* v *Le Foe* [2001] 2 FLR 970 (Fam) (at [10]), a case in which a **mortgagee** was seeking possession:

I have no doubt that the family economy depended for its function on [the wife's] earnings. It was an arbitrary allocation of responsibility that [the husband] paid the mortgage … whereas [the wife] paid for day-to-day domestic expenditure.

More recently, the hurdle set by Lord Bridge has been criticised by the House of Lords in *Stack* v *Dowden* and by the Privy Council in *Abbott* v *Abbott* [2008] 1 FLR 1451 (PC). In *Stack* v *Dowden*, Baroness Hale (at [63]) questioned whether it was binding on lower courts:

There is undoubtedly an argument for saying, as did the Law Commission in *Sharing Homes, A Discussion Paper* [Law Com No 278, 2002], para. 4.23 that the observations, which were strictly obiter dicta, of Lord Bridge of Harwich in *Lloyds Bank Plc* v *Rosset* [1991] 1 AC 107 have set that hurdle rather too high in certain respects.

At [69], she went on to explain that the court should look at the whole of the parties' relationship in order to discern the nature of their agreement (see, also, Section 17.3.2):

Many more factors than financial contributions may be relevant to divining the parties' true intentions.

Baroness Hale's comments on *Rosset* are themselves *obiter*: the only issue in *Stack* v *Dowden* was quantifying the beneficial interests of the two parties. *Abbott* is an acquisition case, but as it is an opinion of the Privy Council it is not binding on the English courts. However, in *Hapeshi* v *Allnatt* [2010] EWHC 392 (Ch), Judge Hodge QC, sitting as a judge of the High Court, felt able to apply what he referred to as 'the holistic approach commended by the Law Commission and accepted in both *Stack* and *Abbott*' to the question of the acquisition of a beneficial interest as well as its quantification. It has yet to be seen whether the Court of Appeal feels able to accept this approach without clearer authority from the Supreme Court that the law has 'moved on' from *Rosset*.

17.3.2 Quantification: what share of the beneficial interest?

Once a court has found that there is a trust, it must then go on to quantify the share of the equity to which the successful claimant is entitled. This is unlikely to be a problem where the parties have expressly agreed the size of their respective shares. As Baroness Hale explained in *Stack* v *Dowden* (at [49]):

> No one now doubts that such an express declaration of trust is conclusive unless varied by subsequent agreement or affected by proprietary estoppel.

The law has been much less clear about how to quantify the **beneficial interest** where there is no express agreement. Two approaches can be identified. In the first, based on resulting trust principles, the parties are entitled to a share of the beneficial interest in proportion to their contribution to the purchase price. This approach, however, now seems to have been superseded by the second approach, described by the Law Commission in *Sharing Homes, A Discussion Paper* (Law Com No 278, 2002), para 4.27:

> a 'holistic approach' to quantification, undertaking a survey of the whole course of dealing between the parties and taking account of all conduct which throws light on the question what shares were intended.

In *Oxley* v *Hiscock* [2005] Fam 211 (CA), Mrs Oxley and Mr Hiscock had both contributed to the purchase of the house that they shared. Despite being advised to the contrary by her solicitor, Mrs Oxley agreed that the house be registered in the sole name of Mr Hiscock. Since the purchase of the house in 1991, both parties had contributed towards the maintenance and improvement of the property from pooled resources. When the relationship between the parties broke down, the court was asked to determine their beneficial shares in the proceeds of sale. The trial judge divided the proceeds of sale in equal shares. After a monumental review of the law, Chadwick LJ reached the following conclusion, at [69]:

> in a case where there is no evidence of any discussion between them as to the amount of the share which each was to have – and even in a case where the evidence is that there was no discussion on that point ... [it] must now be accepted that (at least in this court and below) the answer is that each is entitled to that share which the court considers fair having regard to the whole course of dealing between them in relation to the property. And, in that context, 'the whole course of dealing between them in relation to the property' includes the arrangements which they make from time to time in order to meet the outgoings.

After considering the history of the parties' relationship, and their respective contributions, the Court of Appeal concluded that a fair division of the proceeds of sale of the property would be 60 per cent to Mr Hiscock and 40 per cent to Mrs Oxley.

In the earlier case of *Midland Bank plc* v *Cooke* [1995] 4 All ER 562 (CA) a wife contributed £550 (her share of a wedding present) to the original purchase of the matrimonial home. The trial judge applied a resulting trust analysis and held that she was entitled to some 7 per cent of the value of the house. However, the Court of Appeal rejected this analysis. In the words of Waite LJ (at 574), once there was evidence of the common intention to share the property, then the judge has to:

> undertake a survey of the whole course of dealing between the parties relevant to their ownership and occupation of the property and their sharing of its burdens and advantages. That scrutiny will take into consideration all conduct which throws light on the question what shares were intended. Only if that search proves inconclusive does the court fall back on the maxim that 'equality is equity'.

Here, the Court felt that it was very clear from the wife's involvement in the couple's complex financial arrangements that they had intended to share the property equally. The wife was therefore awarded a beneficial half-share.

In *Stack* v *Dowden*, both Mr Stack and Ms Dowden were registered proprietors of the land concerned (and, therefore, joint tenants at law). Unfortunately, when they completed the Land Registry transfer form, they failed to indicate (by ticking the relevant box on the form) whether they held the beneficial interest as joint tenants or tenants in common. Normally in these circumstances, it is presumed that the parties hold the beneficial interest as joint tenants, since 'equity follows the law'. However, a majority of the House of Lords accepted that there were exceptional cases where the unexpressed intentions of the parties could displace this assumption: the court should use the same approach as in single legal owner cases (see *Oxley* v *Hiscock* and *Midland Bank plc* v *Cooke*, above). Baroness Hale provided a substantial list of the factors that might be relevant, at paragraph [69] of her speech. Unfortunately, *Stack* v *Dowden* fails to give any guidance as to when the circumstances would be sufficiently exceptional to allow the presumption of **joint tenancy** to be rebutted.

Of more serious concern to both academics and the Court of Appeal was the question of whether the reasoning used in *Stack* v *Dowden* allowed the court to impose the result it considered fair, or whether the court was limited to inferring some actual intention of the parties. *Jones* v *Kernott* [2012] 1 AC 776 (SC) offered the Supreme Court 'an opportunity for some clarification' of the principles in *Stack* v *Dowden*. In their joint judgment, Lord Walker and Baroness Hale summarise the principles that apply where a family home is bought in the joint names of a cohabiting couple, where both are responsible for the **mortgage**, but without any express declaration as to their beneficial interests. They explain (at [51]), (subject to minor reformatting):

1. The starting point is that equity follows the law and they are joint tenants both in law and in equity.
2. That presumption can be displaced by showing
   (a) that the parties had a different common intention at the time when they acquired the home, or
   (b) that they later formed the common intention that their respective shares would change.
3. Their common intention is to be deduced objectively from their conduct …
4. In those cases where it is clear either
   (a) that the parties did not intend joint tenancy at the outset, or
   (b) had changed their original intention,
   but it is not possible to ascertain by direct evidence or by inference what their actual intention was as to the shares in which they would own the property, 'the answer is that each is entitled to that share which the court considers fair having regard to the whole course of dealing between them in relation to the property': Chadwick LJ in *Oxley* v *Hiscock* …
5. Each case will turn on its own facts. Financial contributions are relevant but there are many other factors which may enable the court to decide what shares were either intended (as in case (3)) or fair (as in case (4)).

Case 4 as propounded by Lord Walker and Baroness Hale is significant because it recognises that there are circumstances in which the court can *impute* intentions to the parties where it is not possible to *infer* their actual intentions from the facts.

On the facts in *Jones* v *Kernott*, all five members of the court agreed that there was sufficient evidence from which to infer that the parties had changed their intentions as to the ownership of the property after the relationship broke down (case 2(b) of [51]). However, they did not agree whether case 4(b) had been engaged; that is, whether it was possible to infer in what proportions the property was to be shared between Mr Kernott and Ms Jones. Lord Walker and Baroness Hale, with whom Lord Collins agreed, felt that the proportions in which the property was to be owned could be objectively deduced as 90:10 (case 3). Lord Wilson and Lord Kerr disagreed, but felt able to impute a 90:10 ratio as reasonable in all the circumstances. As all five judges reached the same conclusion (despite their different lines of reasoning), the decision of the Court of Appeal (that the property was held in equal shares) was reversed, and the order of the trial judge (that Ms Jones held a 90% share in the property) was restored. Samples of three different academic perspectives on *Jones* v *Kernott* can be found in the series of case notes in [2012] Conv 149–80.

How holistic is the 'holistic approach'?
In *Graham-York* v *York* [2015] HLR 26 (CA), Miss Graham-York claimed a beneficial interest in the house in which she had lived with Mr York for the latter 24 years of their 33-year relationship. In determining the proportion of Miss Graham-York's beneficial share, the Court of Appeal distinguished the case from joint ownership cases such as *Stack* v *Dowden* and *Jones* v *Kernott*. In this case the legal title was solely owned by Mr York; consequently, there was no presumption that the beneficial interest was shared equally. Instead, the court needed to determine the size of Mr York and Miss Graham-York's shares by reference to the 'whole course of dealing between them in relation to the property'. This now familiar phrase was used by Chadwick LJ in *Oxley* v *Hiscock* (at [73], see also [69] and [70]) and adopted with approval by the House of Lords in *Stack* v *Dowden* and *Jones* v *Kernott*. However, as Sarah Greer and Mark Pawlowski note in their casenote at (2015) 79 Conv 512, it is far from clear that the Court of Appeal interpreted the phrase in the way intended in *Stack* v *Dowden*. In *York*, Tomlinson LJ stressed at [23] (original emphasis) that Miss Graham-York was:

> entitled to that share which the court considers fair having regard to the whole course of dealing between them *in relation to the property*.

So far as the court was concerned, factors that related to the property were confined to the financial contributions, most of which had come from Mr York. The court ignored, therefore, the length of the parties' period of cohabitation, and the fact that Mr York seems to have controlled almost every aspect of his partner's life, including her earnings. Indeed, the latter actually undermined Miss Graham-York's case because it indicated that it was unlikely that Mr York intended to share anything. However, although 'in deciding in such a case what shares are fair, the court is not concerned with some form of redistributive justice' ([22]), it is suggested that neither does fairness turn exclusively, or even mainly, on the financial contributions made by the parties. As Baroness Hale said at [69] in *Stack* v *Dowden*, relevant factors include all of the following:

> any advice or discussions at the time of the transfer which cast light upon their intentions then; the reasons why the home was acquired in their joint names ...; the purpose for which the home was acquired; the nature of the parties' relationship; whether they had children for whom they both had responsibility to provide a home; how the purchase was financed, both initially and subsequently; how the parties arranged their finances, whether separately or together or a bit of both; how they discharged the outgoings on the property and their other household expenses.

17.4 Alternative approaches to family property

This chapter began with Wall LJ's description of *Jones* v *Kernott* [2010] 1 WLR 2401 (CA) as 'a cautionary tale' for all unmarried couples. The same might be, and has been, said of many of the other judgments referred to in this chapter. Unfortunately, the only couples likely to be aware of this are those which include a lawyer or a law student. Even where justice is thought to be done, the rules are, to adopt the words of the Law Commission in its 2002 discussion paper *Sharing Homes* (Law Com No 278), 'unfair, uncertain and illogical'. One of the reasons for this is that principles that belong to (and work relatively well within) the commercial context are being used to resolve disputes where the relationship between the parties is based on commitment and trust rather than contract and property. For example, the common intention constructive trust is based on discerning the terms of a fictitious agreement between the parties. The evidential difficulties in establishing either an express or an implied agreement (see Section 17.3.1) are hardly surprising, given that neither party may have given any thought to their common intention until the non-legal owner found their possession threatened, either by a **mortgagee** or by the end of their relationship with the legal owner.

It seems that the circumstances in which common intention can be inferred are now somewhat broader than envisaged by Lord Bridge in *Lloyds Bank plc* v *Rosset* [1991] 1 AC 107 (HL) (see Section 17.3.1(b)). This may temper the indirect discrimination against claimants (most commonly female cohabitees) who, because of social expectations or personal circumstances, are not able to make a financial contribution towards the purchase of the home. However, it fails to address the fundamental problem: family disputes need to be addressed using principles that respect the character of the family relationship.

One alternative solution would be to use a different type of constructive trust, familiar to many other common law jurisdictions: the remedial constructive trust. Remedial constructive trusts are based on unconscionability and allow the court to impose a trust on a defendant who knowingly retains property of which the claimant has been unjustly deprived. Since the remedy can be tailored to the circumstances of the particular case, innocent third parties are not prejudiced, and restitutionary defences, such as change of position, are available (see Lord Browne-Wilkinson's comments in *Westdeutsche Landesbank Girozentrale* v *Islington LBC* [1996] AC 669 (HL) at 716). For example, the Australian case of *Rasmanis* v *Jurewitsch* (1969) 70 SR (NSW) 407 concerned three legal and beneficial joint tenants (A, B and C). A killed B, and the question arose as to how the beneficial entitlement was now shared. If the beneficial **joint tenancy** was automatically severed by the homicide (see Section 13.5.5), then A and C would hold the legal **title** on trust for themselves and B's estate in equal shares as tenants in common. The Court of Appeal of New South Wales felt that this would mean that A profited by their crime, and instead imposed a constructive trust with the **beneficial interest** being divided one-third to C and the remaining two-thirds to A and C as joint tenants. In England and Wales, during the late 1960s and 1970s, Lord Denning MR used remedial trusts as a means of achieving a fair solution to family disputes over land. However, this approach was firmly rejected by the House of Lords in the two seminal cases of *Pettitt* v *Pettitt* [1970] AC 777 (HL) and *Gissing* v *Gissing* [1971] AC 886 (HL). Despite some significant judicial support for the remedial constructive trust in subsequent years (see, for example, Lord Browne-Wilkinson in *Westdeutsche Landesbank Girozentrale* and Lord Scott in *Thorner* v *Major* [2009] 1 WLR 776 (HL) (at [20])), they have yet to be accepted as part of English law.

A second alternative is for Parliament to provide a 'fairer' solution through legislation, as it has already done for those cases where a marriage or civil partnership is dissolved (see the Matrimonial Causes Act 1973 and the Civil Partnership Act 2004). It seems that a majority of people do not appreciate that English law does not extend similar protection to common law spouses (see Appendix A of Law Commission, *Cohabitation: The Financial Consequences of Relationship Breakdown* (Law Com No 307, 2007)). After a wide consultation, in 2007 the Law Commission suggested a statutory scheme that would apply specifically to eligible cohabiting couples who separate. However, as Baroness Hale observed in *Stack* v *Dowden* [2007] 2 AC 432 (HL) (at [47]), a few months before the report was published:

> unlike most Law Commission reports, this one will not contain a draft Bill. Implementation will therefore depend, not only upon whether its proposals find favour with Government, but also on whether the resources can be found to translate them into workable legislative form.

It seems that Baroness Hale's concerns were justified. Neither the political nor legislative will has been found to put the recommendations into statutory form.

Summary

17.1 There are three main ways in which a person may informally acquire a beneficial interest in land: resulting trusts, common intention constructive trusts and the doctrine of proprietary estoppel.

17.2 A resulting trust requires a direct contribution to the initial purchase price of the property or to the mortgage. The beneficiary will gain a share in the property proportionate to their contribution to the purchase price.

17.3 A common intention constructive trust will be imposed on the legal owner when there has been an agreement that the claimant should have a beneficial share in the property, and the claimant has detrimentally altered their position in reliance upon that agreement. The agreement can be demonstrated by evidence of an express agreement between the parties, or it may be inferred where there are sufficient grounds for the court to do so. The courts now tend to adopt a 'broad brush' approach to the quantification of the beneficiary's interest, seeking, through an examination of their whole relationship, to establish how the parties intended the property to be shared.

17.4 The recognition of an informal trust or an interest by way of proprietary estoppel is a property-based remedy. It is not primarily concerned with achieving the fairest distribution of the property in the light of all the circumstances of the parties.

Exercises

 17.1 Complete the online quiz on the topics covered in this chapter on the companion website.

17.2 To what extent have the decisions in *Lloyds Bank plc* v *Rosset* [1991] 1 AC 107 (HL), *Stack* v *Dowden* [2007] 2 AC 432 (HL) and *Jones* v *Kernott* [2012] 1 AC 776 (SC) produced a coherent approach to the law of equitable ownership of the family home?

17.3 Jerome, who used to be a prosperous businessman, was the sole registered proprietor of a house which he bought 12 years ago for £200,000, paying for it with £20,000 from his savings and the rest by means of a mortgage. Two years later, he asked his student girlfriend, Lena, to move in with him, telling her that she would always have a home there. Lena looked after the house and garden and carried out any maintenance on the property. Seven years ago, Jerome's business failed and he took paid employment, but did not earn enough to cover all the outgoings. Lena, therefore, gave up her studies and took a job, and her contributions to the household budget enabled Jerome to pay the mortgage. Last month, Jerome was killed in a road accident. In his will, he left everything to his mother, who has told Lena to leave the house, now worth £400,000, since she wants to sell it.

Advise Lena.

 You can find suggested answer plans to exercises 17.2 and 17.3 on the companion website.

Further reading

Clarke, 'The Family Home: Intention and Agreement' (1992) 22 Fam Law 72

Davis, Hughes and Jacklin, '"Come Live with Me My Love": A Consideration of the 2007 Law Commission Proposals on Cohabitation Breakdown' (2008) 72 Conv 197

Gardner, 'Family Property Today' (2008) 124 LQR 422

Greer and Pawlowski, 'Imputation, Fairness and the Family Home' (2015) 79 Conv 512

Hopkins, 'Regulating Trusts of the Home: Private Law and Social Policy' (2009) 125 LQR 310

Law Commission, *Cohabitation: The Financial Consequences of Relationship Breakdown* (Law Com No 307, 2007)

Sparkes, 'Non-Declarations of Beneficial Co-Ownership' (2012) 76 Conv 207

Thompson, 'Constructive Trusts, Estoppel and the Family Home' (2004) 68 Conv 496

Chapter 18

Proprietary estoppel

Key concepts

▶ **Proprietary estoppel** – a right in equity arising out of the claimant's detrimental reliance on representations or assurances given by the defendant as to the claimant's interest in certain property.

18.1 The case of the taciturn farmers

Cheddar is a large village in the county of Somerset, in the south-west of England, famous for its cheese, its caves, and the largest gorge in the United Kingdom. Steart Farm lies to the south of the village and was farmed by Peter Thorner until his death in 2005. Peter had inherited the farm from his first wife, Sarah, in 1976, at which time it comprised some 350 acres. Peter was a man of few words, especially after the death of Sarah. This may not be untypical of farmers in the area around Cheddar, whose conversation can seem somewhat indirect to those who are not part of the local community. Land was bought, and land was sold over the years, and when Peter died, Steart Farm comprised between 460 and 560 acres in total, together with the farmhouse. David Thorner was the son of Peter's first cousin and began helping Peter at Steart Farm soon after Sarah's death in the late 1970s. By 1985, David was working 18 hours a day, seven days per week, split between his father's farm and Peter's farm, with the work on Peter's farm taking up more than half of his total time. Gradually, David came to hope, and then to expect, that he would inherit Peter's farm. Nothing was ever said directly, although in 1990 Peter did give David the bonus notice on two assurance policies on his own life and said, 'That's for my death duties.' David interpreted this as Peter's way of saying that he would inherit Steart Farm on Peter's death. Indeed, Peter's remark in 1990 was a major factor in David's decision not to pursue other opportunities that became available to him. However, when Peter died in 2005, he did not leave a valid will, and the farm, worth in the region of £2.4 million, passed to Peter's sisters and nieces under the intestacy rules.

David claimed the farm by relying upon the doctrine of proprietary estoppel, one of several forms of **equitable** estoppel that can arise when it would be unfair (the legal term is 'unconscionable') to allow a person to go back on an assurance they have given to another. In the words of Lord Denning MR in *Crabb* v *Arun District Council* [1976] Ch 179, 187–8:

> it will prevent a person from insisting on his strict legal rights – whether arising under a contract, or on his title deeds, or by statute – when it would be inequitable for him to do so having regard to the dealings which have taken place between the parties.

David argued that Peter was prevented from leaving the farm to anyone else because David had relied, to his considerable detriment, upon Peter's assurance that the farm would be his. In October 2007, Mr John Randall QC, sitting as a deputy judge of the Chancery Division, ordered that David should receive the land and other assets of the farm, but his decision was reversed by the Court of Appeal in July of the following year. David appealed to the House of Lords. Its decision in his case (reported at *Thorner v Major* [2009] 1 WLR 776 (HL)) is now the leading case on the doctrine of proprietary estoppel.

18.2 Introducing proprietary estoppel

Estoppels arise in a variety of contexts. Students of contract law, for example, should be familiar with the doctrine of *promissory* estoppel, which can be used as a defence to a claim (as a 'shield'), but not a cause of action (that is, as a 'sword'). It is important for such students to realise at the outset that there are important differences between estoppel in contract law cases and the doctrine of *proprietary* estoppel considered in this chapter, as Lord Walker, in his leading opinion in *Thorner v Major* [2009] 1 WLR 776 (HL), [61], explains:

> [Promissory estoppel] must be based on an existing legal *relationship* (usually a contract, but not necessarily a contract relating to land). [Proprietary estoppel] need not be based on an existing legal relationship, but it must relate to *identified property* (usually land) owned (or, perhaps, about to be owned) by the defendant. It is the relation to identified land of the defendant that has enabled proprietary estoppel to develop as a sword, and not merely a shield ... (Original emphasis.)

In the nineteenth century, the availability of proprietary estoppel was based on meeting a fairly strict set of requirements (summarised in the so-called five *probanda* (criteria) of *Willmott v Barber* (1880) LR 15 Ch D 96 (Ch); (1881) LR 17 Ch D 772 (CA)). During the next hundred years, however, it developed into a broader and more flexible approach, which, according to Oliver J in *Taylors Fashions Ltd v Liverpool Victoria Trustees Co Ltd* [1982] 1 QB 133n (Ch), 151–2:

> is directed rather at ascertaining whether, in particular individual circumstances, it would be unconscionable for a party to be permitted to deny that which, knowingly, or unknowingly, he has allowed or encouraged another to assume to his detriment.

In *Thorner v Major*, Lord Walker (at [29]) acknowledged that while there is no single comprehensive definition of proprietary estoppel:

> most scholars agree that the doctrine is based on three main elements ... a representation or assurance made to the claimant; reliance on it by the claimant; and detriment to the claimant in consequence of his (reasonable) reliance.

In his more cautious opinion in the same case, Lord Scott accepted this threefold classification, adding, at [15]:

> These [three] elements would, I think, always be necessary but might, in a particular case, not be sufficient. Thus, for example, the representation or assurance would need to have been sufficiently clear and unequivocal; the reliance by the claimant would need to have been reasonable in all the circumstances; and the detriment would need to have been sufficiently substantial to justify the intervention of equity.

In what follows, it is convenient to address reliance and detriment under a single heading. In fact, as Robert Walker LJ warned in *Gillett v Holt* [2001] Ch 210 (CA) at 225:

> it is important to note at the outset that the doctrine of proprietary estoppel cannot be treated as subdivided into three or four watertight compartments. [It is] apparent that the quality of the relevant assurances may influence the issue of reliance, that reliance and

detriment are often intertwined ... Moreover the fundamental principle that equity is concerned to prevent unconscionable conduct permeates all the elements of the doctrine. In the end the court must look at the matter in the round.

In some ways, the doctrine of proprietary estoppel is similar to that of the common intention **constructive trust** (see Section 17.2). For example, in *Lloyds Bank plc* v *Rosset* [1991] 1 AC 107 (HL), Lord Bridge discussed rights acquired 'under a constructive trust or proprietary estoppel'. However, it is best to treat constructive trusts and proprietary estoppel as separate, although not unrelated, doctrines. **Common intention constructive trusts** provide a successful claimant with a **beneficial interest** in the land under a trust. Proprietary estoppel is a much more flexible creature, offering the courts considerable discretion as to the remedy that will 'satisfy the equity'. These remedies are considered in Section 18.5, and the distinctions between the two doctrines are considered in more detail in Section 18.6.

The main elements of proprietary estoppel

- representation or assurance;
- reliance;
- detriment; and
- relief.

18.3 Raising the expectation

The expectation in the claimant can be raised either by an express representation as to their present or future rights in the land or by 'wilful silence' (that is, acquiescence). In the latter case, an estoppel may be established if a landowner, knowing the true position, stands by while the claimant does something on the landowner's land in the mistaken belief that they own the land. As Lord Wensleydale stated in *Ramsden* v *Dyson* (1866) LR 1 HL 129 (HL) at 168:

> If a stranger build upon my land, supposing it to be his own, and I knowing it to be mine, do not interfere but leave him to go on, equity considers it to be dishonest in me to remain passive and afterwards to interfere and take profit.

The courts have given a great deal of attention to the characteristics required of a representation or assurance for it to be a sufficient foundation for establishing an estoppel. In many cases, the character of the representation will be relatively clear. For example, in *Yaxley* v *Gotts* [2000] Ch 162 (CA), the facts of which are set out in Section 15.4.5, Mr Gotts had promised Mr Yaxley the use of the ground floor of a house in return for Mr Yaxley converting the house into separate flats. Mr Gotts' son (who actually purchased the building) was estopped from denying Mr Yaxley use of the ground floor (and the estoppel gave rise to a constructive trust; see Section 15.4.5). It is now accepted that a promise that a person will inherit under another's will can be the basis of an estoppel claim, even though a will can be revoked at any time up to the death of the person who made it. In *Gillett* v *Holt*, Mr Gillett had worked for a farmer for some 40 years, giving up opportunities to develop his career. During this time, the farmer gave him and Mr Gillett's family repeated express assurances that Mr Gillett would inherit the farm and the farm business. Eventually, however, the farmer transferred his attentions to someone else, dismissed Mr Gillett from his employment and excluded him from his will. The Court of Appeal found that the express promises that Mr Gillett would inherit the farm under the farmer's will were sufficiently certain to establish an estoppel in his favour. Detrimental reliance on the promise of inheriting under the will made the promise binding.

However, detrimental reliance cannot operate upon a representation that neither party expected to be binding on them. Consequently, an agreement labelled 'subject to contract' (see Section 15.4.2(a)) will not ordinarily be capable of giving rise to a proprietary estoppel (*Haq* v *Island Homes Housing Association* [2011] 2 P & CR 17 (CA)). In *Cobbe* v *Yeoman's Row Management Ltd* [2008] 1 WLR 1752 (HL), Mr Cobbe, an experienced property developer, informally agreed to purchase a property comprising a number of flats from Yeoman's Row Management Ltd for £12 million. The sale was to take effect once planning permission had been obtained for the development of the flats. Mr Cobbe put a great deal of time and money into obtaining the necessary planning consents, only for the directors of Yeoman's Row Management Ltd to demand a higher price for the flats.

The House of Lords held that Mr Cobbe's claim failed, because, as Lord Walker explained at [91]:

> as persons experienced in the property world, both parties knew that there was no legally binding contract, and that either was therefore free to discontinue the negotiations without legal liability – that is, liability in equity as well as at law … Mr Cobbe was therefore running a risk … Whatever his reasons for doing so, the fact is that he ran a commercial risk, with his eyes open, and the outcome has proved unfortunate for him.

Lord Scott, who gave the main opinion in *Cobbe*, made a strong defence of the need for sufficient certainty in the representation or assurance, saying (at [28]):

> Proprietary estoppel requires, in my opinion, clarity as to what it is that the object of the estoppel is to be estopped from denying, or asserting, and clarity as to the interest in the property in question that that denial, or assertion, would otherwise defeat. If these requirements are not recognised, proprietary estoppel will lose contact with its roots and risk becoming unprincipled and therefore unpredictable, if it has not already become so.

Lord Scott also emphasised the need for the representation to be clear and unequivocal, suggesting that a claimant needed to prove that the landowner intended or expected the representation or assurance to be relied upon in precisely the way that the claimant subsequently did for an estoppel to arise. Several judicial and academic commentators were very alarmed by the decision in *Cobbe* and suggested that it 'severely curtailed, or even virtually extinguished, the doctrine of proprietary estoppel', as Lord Walker observed in *Thorner* v *Major* [2009] 1 WLR 776 (HL) (at [31]). Fortunately, *Thorner* v *Major* gave the House of Lords the opportunity to set the record straight.

The facts of *Thorner* v *Major* are set out in Section 18.1. In the Court of Appeal the estoppel claim failed because the court decided that the implicit representations upon which David Thorner claimed to rely were not sufficiently clear and unequivocal that David could reasonably have been intended to rely upon them. The House of Lords unanimously reversed the decision of the Court of Appeal and awarded the farm to David. The majority line of reasoning in *Thorner* makes it clear that what is required for an estoppel is that the representation or assurance *conveys an understanding that it is to be treated seriously*. This, and the closely related question of whether it was reasonable for the claimant to rely on the representation, are questions of fact dependent upon the wider circumstances of the case. In *Thorner* v *Major* (at [56]), Lord Walker quoted the words of Hoffmann LJ in the unreported case of *Walton* v *Walton* [1994] CA Transcript No 479:

> The promise must be unambiguous and must appear to have been intended to be taken seriously. Taken in its context, it must have been a promise which one might reasonably expect to be relied upon by the person to whom it was made.

Consequently, much greater clarity of expression will be required in a business context (such as *Cobbe*) than in a case in which both parties are unusually 'taciturn and undemonstrative' (as in *Thorner* v *Major*).

In *Thorner* v *Major*, the House of Lords also had to consider the related question of whether David could know with sufficient certainty what he was expecting to inherit. The boundaries of farms tend to change from time to time, and Steart Farm had been no exception during the years that David worked there. It was decided that this did not cause a problem on the facts. Both David and Peter had known that the extent of the farm was likely to vary from time to time, and it was sufficiently clear that the assurances given by Peter related to Steart Farm as it would exist at the time of Peter's death.

18.4 Reliance and detriment

Once the claimant has shown that they were encouraged to act in a certain way, the courts will presume that their actions were in reliance on that encouragement, unless the legal owner is able to rebut this presumption (*Greasley* v *Cooke* [1980] 1 WLR 1306 (CA)). The question is whether the claimant would have acted to their detriment in any case as part of the relationship between the parties, or whether their actions were undertaken in reliance on the promise.

The Privy Council surveyed the leading authorities concerning the relationship between detriment and reliance in the case of *Henry* v *Henry* [2010] 1 All ER 988 (PC). Sir Jonathan Parker concluded that (at [55]):

> just as the inquiry as to reliance falls to be made in the context of the nature and quality of the particular assurances which are said to form the basis of the estoppel, so the inquiry as to detriment falls to be made in the context of the nature and quality of the particular conduct or course of conduct adopted by the claimant in reliance on those assurances. Thus, notwithstanding that reliance and detriment may, in the abstract, be regarded as different concepts, in applying the principles of proprietary estoppel they are often intertwined.

Consequently, one of the tasks of the court is to determine the correct balance between any disadvantages suffered by the claimant due to their reliance and any advantages they received because of that reliance. On the facts of *Henry* v *Henry*, Mr Henry had opted for a hard life, in which he had to struggle to make ends meet and to provide for his family, because of the promises made to him, despite more attractive prospects elsewhere. The Privy Council found that this detriment was not outweighed by the fact that Mr Henry had dwelt rent-free on a plot of land, living off its produce and the sale of any surplus.

The expenditure of money is usually sufficiently clear an act to show reliance on a promise. For example, in *Pascoe* v *Turner* [1979] 1 WLR 431 (CA), a woman who had been promised that the house in which she was living 'was hers' spent 'a quarter of her modest capital' (a few hundred pounds) on maintaining and improving the property. The true owner, her former partner, was estopped from denying her interest in the house. However, as Sir Jonathan Parker explained in *Henry v Henry* (at [38]):

> The detriment need not consist of the expenditure of money or other quantifiable financial detriment, so long as it is something substantial. The requirement must be approached as part of a broad inquiry as to whether repudiation of an assurance is or is not unconscionable in all the circumstances.

In *Greasley v Cooke*, a young woman went to work as a maid in a household. After some time, she formed a relationship with one of the sons and lived with him as if she were his wife. Although she was no longer paid for her work, she continued to look after the family, including a daughter who was ill, and was assured that she could live in the house for the rest of her life. Her partner, who had inherited the house, died, and the heirs attempted to evict her. Lord Denning MR held that her unpaid work in caring for the family, especially the daughter, amounted to acts in reliance on the assurances that had been made to her. Mr Henry, Mr Gillett and David Thorner clearly fall within this latter category: they would hardly have acted as they did had it not been for assurances they had received.

18.5 Satisfying the equity

A successful estoppel claim has the effect of raising an equity in the property. The courts must then find a means of 'satisfying the equity', and they have considerable discretion, within **equitable** principles, as to what remedy (often referred to as *relief* in estoppel cases) to award to the claimant.

It might be thought that the obvious relief would be to require the defendant to fulfil the promise. However, an 'expectation-based' approach potentially impinges on the law of contract and the doctrine of consideration, as well as on the rules of formality in land law. There are also practical problems with such an approach. Not only does it assume that the claimant's expectations are clearly focused upon a specific interest in the land, but it could lead to injustice where the consequences of honouring the expectation are disproportionate to the detriment the claimant will suffer if the promise is not kept. As Robert Walker LJ observed in *Jennings v Rice* [2003] 1 P & CR 8 (CA), at [56]:

> The essence of the doctrine of proprietary estoppel is to do what is necessary to avoid an unconscionable result, and a disproportionate remedy cannot be the right way of going about that.

Sir Jonathan Parker, delivering the opinion of the Privy Council in *Henry v Henry* [2010] 1 All ER 988 (PC), explains, at [65]:

> Proportionality lies at the heart of the doctrine of proprietary estoppel and permeates its every application.

However, this does not mean, in the words of Robert Walker LJ (*Jennings v Rice* at [51]), that:

> the court should … abandon expectations completely, and look to the detriment suffered by the claimant as defining the appropriate measure of relief.

Instead, as he explained in *Gillett v Holt* [2001] Ch 210 (CA) (at [237]):

> The court's aim is … to form a view as to what is the minimum required to satisfy [the equity] and do justice between the parties. The court must look at all the circumstances, including the need to achieve a 'clean break' so far as possible and avoid or minimise future friction.

How to appropriately balance the expectation of the claimant with the detriment actually suffered in order to reach an appropriate remedy was considered in detail by Lewison LJ in the only substantive judgment in *Davies* v *Davies* [2016] 2 P & CR 10 (CA). He concluded (at [41]) that the upper range of the claimant's expectations may make a suitable starting point in establishing the appropriate remedy. However, the weight to be given to them will depend upon the clarity of the expectation, the degree of the detriment, and the period of time during which the expectation was reasonably held.

The minimum necessary to satisfy the equity of estoppel will vary according to the circumstances of each individual case. In *Pascoe* v *Turner* [1979] 1 WLR 431 (CA), the court ordered the legal owner of a house to convey the fee simple to the claimant, who had spent a few hundred pounds on maintaining and improving it. Without more, this appears to be a windfall for the claimant and unjust on her former partner. In fact, the man was prosperous and, according to Cumming-Bruce LJ, at [438]:

> determined to pursue his purpose of evicting her from the house by any legal means at his disposal with a ruthless disregard of the obligations binding on conscience.

The court felt that the woman could only be protected from the man's harassing behaviour by requiring him to perfect his gift and convey the land to her. The award of some lesser right in the land, such as a **licence** to remain there during her lifetime, would not have been enough to achieve this. Similarly, in *Re Basham (decd)* [1986] 1 WLR 1498 (Ch), a stepdaughter was awarded the house that had been promised to her; and in *Thorner* v *Major* the claimant received the land, buildings, live and dead stock and other assets of the farm on which he had laboured for so many years.

In *Campbell* v *Griffin* [2001] EWCA Civ 990, Mr Campbell had initially been a lodger in a house owned by a retired couple. He gradually took on responsibilities as their carer, and they came to rely on him completely and treated him as their son. They assured him that he had a home for life, and the husband changed his will in order to leave Mr Campbell a life interest in the house. The husband died before the wife, who took the property by right of survivorship as the sole surviving joint tenant. She, however, was unable to make a will in the man's favour because she was suffering from senile dementia. Mr Campbell established that he had an equity in the property through estoppel. However, the Court of Appeal felt unable to give effect to the promise of a life interest, since this would have been disproportionate to the detriment Mr Campbell had suffered, and unfair on others who were to benefit from the estate. Mr Campbell was awarded £35,000, charged on the property.

Similarly, in *Gillett* v *Holt*, the court did not require the farmer to fulfil all his promises to Mr Gillett, who instead was awarded the **freehold** of the farmhouse and some land, along with £100,000 to compensate him for his exclusion from the farm business. In *Jennings* v *Rice*, an old woman's part-time gardener became, over the course of a number of years, her unpaid full-time carer, even sleeping on the sofa in her sitting room during the last three years of her life. Despite promising him that the house would be his one day, the woman never made a will. After her death, the man made a claim on her estate for the house. Although his argument of estoppel was successful, the Court again emphasised the need for proportionality between the expectation and the detriment. Instead of fulfilling his expectation by ordering the transfer of the house, the Court awarded him £200,000, less than half its value.

On occasion, this approach, essentially based on restitution, may result in no award at all being made, even though the claimant is successful in their estoppel claim. In *Sledmore* v *Dalby* (1996) 72 P & CR 196 (CA), Mrs Sledmore sought possession of a house she owned against Mr Dalby, her son-in-law, who had lived there for many years. Mr Dalby had undertaken some work on the property initially in reliance on an assurance that his wife would be left the property after her parents' death, and subsequently (his wife having died) on the assumption that he would be able to live there for the rest of his life. However, Mrs Sledmore had little money, was in danger of losing her home and had a greater need for the house than her son-in-law. He could afford to pay for his own accommodation and was actually only spending a few nights each week at the house. The Court of Appeal granted possession to Mrs Sledmore, and nothing to Mr Dalby, on the basis that this was, in the words of Roch LJ at 205:

> the minimum equity to do justice to the respondent on the facts of this case.

As Hobhouse LJ went on to explain, at [209]:

> The effect of any equity ... has long since been exhausted and no injustice has been done to the defendant.

18.6 Constructive trusts and proprietary estoppel compared

There is a considerable degree of overlap between **constructive trusts** and proprietary estoppel, as Robert Walker LJ noted in *Yaxley* v *Gotts* [2001] Ch 162 (CA), at 176:

> At a high level of generality, there is much common ground between the doctrines of proprietary estoppel and the constructive trust ... all are concerned with equity's intervention to provide relief against unconscionable conduct, whether as between neighbouring landowners, or vendor and purchaser, or relatives who make informal arrangements for sharing a home, or a fiduciary and the beneficiary or client to whom he owes a fiduciary obligation.

In *Jennings* v *Rice* [2003] 1 P & CR 8 (CA), he was of the view, at 45, that:

> Sometimes the assurances, and the claimant's reliance on them, have a consensual character falling not far short of an enforceable contract ... [and] the proprietary estoppel may become indistinguishable from a constructive trust.

In both constructive trusts and proprietary estoppel there is detrimental reliance on an understanding that the claimant will gain an interest in the land. However, whereas a constructive trust is based on an agreement between the parties, an estoppel does not necessarily require there to be a meeting of minds (see, for example, the distinction between an estoppel that also gives rise to a constructive trust and one which does not: *Kinane* v *Mackie-Conteh* [2005] EWCA Civ 45, [51], considered at Section 15.4.5). An estoppel arises because the courts will not permit a legal owner to stand back while the claimant acts in reliance on a mistaken belief as to their rights.

A further difference arises when considering the nature of the remedy a successful claimant might obtain. Under a constructive trust, they will have a **beneficial interest** in the land which is deemed to have arisen at the time of the acts of detrimental reliance. The only question will be the extent of the share to be awarded by the court. In proprietary estoppel, however, the nature of the right is not known until the court gives its decision. As discussed above, the relief granted to give effect to an estoppel can range from the award of the fee simple (as in *Pascoe* v *Turner*) to nothing at all (as in *Sledmore* v *Dalby*).

It is also necessary to consider whether rights arising under a constructive trust or a proprietary estoppel are binding on third parties, such as later **mortgage** lenders or purchasers of the land. The rules on the circumstances in which a beneficial interest under a trust is binding are now well established (see Sections 4.6.2 and 14.6.1). Case law previously indicated that an equity arising from proprietary estoppel could bind a purchaser of **registered land** (see *Lloyd* v *Dugdale* [2002] 2 P & CR 13 (CA)), and this is now confirmed by section 116 of the LRA 2002. It seems that such an equity can now be protected by the entry of a **notice** on the Register, although this is unlikely to happen, since the person in whose favour the equity has arisen will probably not know that it should be formally protected. However, when coupled with actual occupation, the equity will be an interest **overriding** subsequent **dispositions** (see Section 4.6.2). A major difficulty remains, however: the precise nature of the right will not be known until the court has granted relief.

Summary

18.1 Proprietary estoppel is one example of equity's use of estoppel to prevent a person profiting by going back on an assurance or representation.

18.2 The main elements of a proprietary estoppel are:

- establishing the representation or assurance;
- demonstrating that the claimant detrimentally relied on the representation or assurance; and
- determining what relief, if any, is appropriate to satisfy the equity.

18.3 To form the basis of a proprietary estoppel, a representation or assurance must:

- be unambiguous;
- appear to have been intended to be taken seriously; and
- relate to property that is sufficiently identifiable.

18.4 Once the claimant has shown that they were encouraged to act in a certain way, the courts will presume that they relied on that encouragement, unless the legal owner is able to rebut this presumption. What amounts to sufficient reliance will depend on the facts and context of each individual case.

18.5 In order to satisfy the equity raised by a successful estoppel claim, the courts aim to achieve proportionality between the remedy and the detriment suffered and will award the minimum remedy necessary.

18.6 The precise relationship between common intention constructive trusts and proprietary estoppel is unclear. They are best treated as separate doctrines.

Exercises

 18.1 Complete the online quiz on the topics covered in this chapter on the companion website.

18.2 'Proportionality lies at the heart of the doctrine of proprietary estoppel and permeates its every application.' Sir Jonathan Parker, *Henry* v *Henry* [2010] 1 All ER 988 (PC), [65].

Critically discuss this statement.

 You can find a suggested answer plan to exercise 18.2 on the companion website.

Further reading

Dixon, 'Confining and Defining Proprietary Estoppel: The Role of Unconscionability' (2010) 30 LS 408

Etherton, 'Constructive Trusts and Proprietary Estoppel: The Search for Clarity and Principle' (2009) 73 Conv 104

McFarlane and Robertson, 'Apocalypse Averted: Proprietary Estoppel in the House of Lords' (2009) 125 LQR 535

Piška, 'Hopes, Expectations and Revocable Promises in Proprietary Estoppel' (2009) 72 MLR 998

Thompson, 'Constructive Trusts, Estoppel and the Family Home' (2004) 68 Conv 496

Index

Page numbers in italics refer to a table or a figure on that page. Text in bold refers to a diagram or flow-chart illustrating how to apply the relevant rules to a problem question.